T0350543

We've Been Here All Along

WE'VE BEEN HERE ALL ALONG

Wisconsin's Early Gay History

R. RICHARD WAGNER

WISCONSIN HISTORICAL SOCIETY PRESS

Published by the Wisconsin Historical Society Press
Publishers since 1855

The Wisconsin Historical Society helps people connect to the past by collecting,
preserving, and sharing stories. Founded in 1846, the Society is one of the nation's finest
historical institutions.
Join the Wisconsin Historical Society: wisconsinhistory.org/membership

© 2019 by the State Historical Society of Wisconsin

For permission to reuse material from *We've Been Here All Along: Wisconsin's Early
Gay History* (ISBN 978-0-87020-912-3; e-book ISBN 978-0-87020-913-0), please
access www.copyright.com or contact the Copyright Clearance Center, Inc. (CCC),
222 Rosewood Drive, Danvers, MA 01923, 978-750-8400. CCC is a not-for-profit
organization that provides licenses and registration for a variety of users.

Front cover images, clockwise from top left: Maxine Bennett, University of Wisconsin–
Madison Archives 2017S00548; Miriam Frink and Charlotte Partridge, University of
Wisconsin–Milwaukee Archives; Ted Pierce, WHI IMAGE ID 71483; Bob Neal and Edgar
Hellum, Mineral Point Public Library

All images from the collection of R. Richard Wagner, unless otherwise credited.

Printed in Canada
Cover design by Percolator Graphic Design
Typesetting by Wendy Holdman Design

23 22 21 20 19   1 2 3 4 5

Library of Congress Cataloging-in-Publication Data
Names: Wagner, R. Richard (Sociologist), author.
Title: We've been here all along : Wisconsin's early gay history / R. Richard Wagner.
Description: Madison : Wisconsin Historical Society Press, 2019. | Includes bibliographical
    references and index. |
Identifiers: LCCN 2018049233 (print) | LCCN 2019002466 (ebook) |
    ISBN 9780870209130 (ebook) | ISBN 9780870209123 (hardback)
Subjects: LCSH: Gays—Wisconsin—History. | BISAC: SOCIAL SCIENCE / Gay Studies. |
    HISTORY / United States / State & Local / Midwest (IA, IL, IN, KS, MI, MN, MO, ND,
    NE, OH, SD, WI). | HISTORY / Social History.
Classification: LCC HQ76.3.U58 (ebook) | LCC HQ76.3.U58 W34 2019 (print) | DDC
    306.76/609775—dc23
LC record available at https://lccn.loc.gov/2018049233

♾ The paper used in this publication meets the minimum requirements of the American
National Standard for Information Sciences—Permanence of Paper for Printed Library
Materials, ANSI Z39.48-1992.

For Merle, Patrick, Doris, and Mark

The 602 Club in Madison, ca. 1965. The club welcomed gays during the 1960s and was listed in national gay guides. PHOTO BY JOHN RIGGS

*Publication of this book was made possible
in part through generous gifts from:*

Mr. Charles Bauer and Mr. Charles Beckwith
David Bedri and Jon Sorenson
Sue Riseling and Joanne Berg
Paula Bonner and Ann Schaffer
Frances Breit and Julie A'cci
Gary Brown and Paul Hayes
Barbara Constans and Deb Rohde
Paul Gibler and Thomas DeChant
Bob Dowd and Marge Schmidt
Julie Eckenwalder and Constance Anderson
William and Lynne Eich
Renee Herber and Tamara Packard
Joanne Holland and Margie Rosenberg
Kim Karcher
Scott and Mary Kolar
Donald Lamb
Phil Levy
Hank Lufler and Mike Gerdes
Katharine Lyall
Scott and Megin McDonell
Eileen Mershart and Sarah Hole
Mike and Sally Miley
Anne Monks
Richard Petran
Purple Moon Foundation, Inc. – Dale Leibowitz
Timothy Radelet
Mary Lou Roberts
Susan Schaffer and Joan Hinckley
Robert Stipicevich and Scott Short
Mary Strickland and Marie Barroquillo
Howard Sweet
Mike Verveer
William Wartmann
Mark Webster and Ryan Brown
Susan Zaeske
Jaime Zimmerman

CONTENTS

We've Been Here All Along

Introduction

I n *Angels in America*, Tony Kushner's stirring and searing drama about the AIDS crisis that opened on Broadway in 1993, the playwright calls for no more hidden deaths. More importantly, he has the character Prior Walter, the prophet, proclaim that gay folks will henceforth emerge from the shadows to be citizens of America.

The idea of claiming citizenship was familiar to me from my first full-time job as director of the Wisconsin American Revolution Bicentennial Commission. At the revolution's one hundredth anniversary celebration in Philadelphia in 1876, Susan B. Anthony had posed the question of whether women were indeed citizens. One hundred years later, in the Wisconsin Commission newsletter and in my speeches, I featured her statement as one that captured the unfolding dream of equality, enunciated though not realized in 1776.

As a semi-closeted gay man in the early 1970s, I faced the same question that Anthony addressed: What kind of citizen was I? Today most LGBT historians date the beginning of American gay liberation to the Stonewall riots of June 1969. In New York City, patrons of an LGBT bar, the Stonewall Inn, located in Greenwich Village, reacted to a police raid by fighting back against the oppression they had passively accepted for years. As David Carter wrote in *Stonewall: The Riots That Sparked the Gay Revolution*, "These riots are widely credited with being the motivating force in the transformation of the gay political movement."[1] Drag queens, street youths, and lesbians were all part of the persecuted group that pushed back on the streets of the Village for the several nights of the riots. This event led directly to the founding of the city's Gay Liberation Front and, not long afterward, like-minded activist organizations around the country, including here in Wisconsin. For all those who have been part of the post-Stonewall gay generation that has claimed the American dream of full and equal citizenship, it is important to know how that happened, and in particular how it happened here in Wisconsin.

It is too often presumed that most gay history in the United States took place on the East and West Coasts. But strong traditions and evidence prove that societal reform also happened elsewhere, on what in my days of campus activism was called the Third Coast—that is, the states bordering the Great Lakes. The very first gay organization in the United States was founded in the 1920s in Chicago. The state of Illinois, by adopting a model law reform code, was the first to decriminalize homosexual acts in 1961.

Before the 1969 Stonewall riots, Wisconsin had the first public call—in 1966, by a political body, the state's Young Democrats—for abolition of strictures against homosexuals so they could have "freedom of action." Before Harvey Milk was elected to the San Francisco Board of Supervisors in 1977, Madison, Ann Arbor, and Minneapolis all had out gay elected officials.

So there are stories to tell of the development of gay communities in places like the Upper Midwest, including Wisconsin. Some of them are quite intriguing, like the rural-urban "fairy network" of southern Wisconsin in the 1930s. Milwaukee has a long-running LGBT community. The North Woods had a vibrant same-sex tradition in the mid-twentieth century. Madison's LGBT community has been activist based, with links to the great university. Both Madison and Milwaukee began organizing for gay liberation within months of Stonewall. And Wisconsin was on the national circuit for early out speakers like Ginny Apuzzo and others who traveled to all three coasts. Stevens Point was a central place to which some of these speakers brought their messages of a new future for LGBT people.

There is another reason to write a Wisconsin gay history. Most of the gay histories to date that are geographically based are city focused. Yet a building block of polity in these constitutionally federal United States is the state entity. It is one of the bases for our constitutional and fundamental laws, as all the fights involving state marriage amendments demonstrated. States also enact criminal laws that all too often have touched homosexual lives in deleterious ways. In more modern modes, states have at times led in civil rights law and health policy. So showing how a state, through its legal structures, interacts with its gay community is another important story that needs to be told.

A state's political structures define its legal culture and to a degree reflect its social ideas. As LGBT people have sought to right past oppressions and avoid new ones, challenges have arisen. In the early twentieth century, safe enclaves of gay culture in Wisconsin may have provided a sufficient means of survival, but in modern times the gay community has had to vigorously enter the public square. What grounds do LGBT folks and their supporters choose for the battle? How are issues positioned? Where can allies can be found?

Wisconsin in 1982 became the first state to enact a gay rights law prohibiting discrimination in employment, housing, and public accommodations on the basis of sexual orientation. Wisconsin was also the first state to elect three openly gay/lesbian persons to Congress: Steve Gunderson, Tammy Baldwin, and Mark Pocan. How do such victories occur—not just in the isolated sense of a particular legislative maneuver or electoral campaign, but in the context of a political culture and community efforts?

The story of gay history in Wisconsin is the interaction of gay people with the power structures of the state. How that straight-dominated polity and social structure reacted to the impetus—that yearning for full citizenship on the part of Wisconsin gay people—is not too dissimilar from what happened elsewhere around the country in some instances, but in others it was influenced by our own unique Wisconsin circumstances.

I wish that this work could encompass all Wisconsin gay history. As a gay man, I feel most comfortable and competent in dealing with issues of male homosexuality, yet I have tried to be inclusive of lesbian, bisexual, and transgender issues where the record exists. I am sure a different feminist perspective would reveal many other things. Prior to the twenty-first century, the LGBT community was known variously as the gay community, or the gay and lesbian community. At times I use the term *gay* to be inclusive of non-normative individuals without regard to gender. The significant inclusion of bisexuals and transgender individuals occurred only in the last decade of the twentieth century. Thus, I have chosen to use the acronym LGBT to refer to the community described in this book, and I have avoided the more contemporary addition of letters such as Q, I, and A, in the acronym. After Stonewall, many gay men and lesbians worked together in the liberation struggles. There are, of course, many additional stories to tell about aspects of Wisconsin's LGBT past, and my wish is that other historians will take on the research and writing of those aspects, as a few already have.

Particularly worth reading are Will Fellows's works *Farm Boys: Lives of Gay Men from the Rural Midwest* and *A Passion to Preserve: Gay Men as Keepers of Culture*, and Michail Takach's *LGBT Milwaukee*. Visiting the website on Wisconsin LGBT history created by Don Schwamb, www .mkelgbthist.org, is instructive, especially for its depth of reporting on the Milwaukee community. The writer and historian Jamakaya also has written many interesting look-back items over the decades, especially with regard to the women's community in several LGBT publications. Schwamb and Jamakaya have had important roles in both creating and recording our history.[2]

We've Been Here All Along, covering the pre-Stonewall period before 1969, shows the dominant negative narrative about homosexuality in Wisconsin maintained by legislators, courts, and the culture in general. Yet during those days, Wisconsin's gay people began to develop and present their own sense of identity. For their own self-affirmation, they successfully sought others who were like-minded. They developed a sense of community that permitted many to reject the label of "sickness" applied to them. By participating in Wisconsin academic studies about homosexuality and other means, they began to enact positive counternarratives about their own lives. In discovering their hidden stories, I hope to balance out a regional history that has largely left them, or at least their identities, out of the narrative. As the title suggests, we have been here all along, even if not positively acknowledged. Another trend in LGBT history is to recognize that liberation did not spring full blown from the Stonewall event. The post-Stonewall activists, though they may have not believed it, stood on the shoulders of elders. Though the claiming of rights seems a post-liberation strategy, before 1969 many LGBT people were citizens even with their identities in the shadows. Post-Stonewall, these attitudes fueled a whole new generation of Wisconsin activists, as I will establish in volume two, *Coming Out, Moving Forward: Wisconsin's Recent Gay History*.

1

WISCONSIN GONE WILDE

The nature of the evidence and the whole circumstances of the case prove to be such of a character that we can not report it. The English public is at the present moment involved in one of those orgies of indecency permitted by the operations of open law courts and an enterprising press.

　　　　　　　　　　　—SUPERIOR EVENING TELEGRAM, APRIL 4, 1895[1]

Oscar Wilde Not Yet a Suicide

　　　　　　　　　　　—WISCONSIN STATE JOURNAL, APRIL 8, 1895[2]

A lthough clear evidence that same-sex activity has existed in America since colonial times is exhibited in the laws and trials of individuals for male sodomy and for women who changed their "natural use" into that which was "against nature," there is not much awareness of homosexuality as an identity until the very last part of the nineteenth century.[3] In the short arc of gay history in modern Western civilization, things opened with a bang with the sensational trial of Oscar Wilde in London in 1895. The coverage of the Oscar Wilde trials in the Wisconsin press allows one to examine attitudes toward homosexuality in late-nineteenth-century Wisconsin. The Wilde phenomenon stole center light on the public stage then, and resonates even now. Well before the trials, Oscar Wilde was a media star. In the 1880s and 1890s he published a novel, *The Picture of Dorian Gray*, as well as plays including *The Importance of Being Earnest*, stories, and fables, acquiring a reputation for creating cutting-edge modern literature. The press loved to quote his frequent witticisms.[4]

Oscar Wilde
photographed
by Napoleon
Sarony, ca. 1882.
LIBRARY OF CON-
GRESS #98519699

Wilde had appeared in America in 1882 on a lecture tour in part designed to promote the Gilbert and Sullivan opera *Patience; or, Bunthorne's
Bride.* The opera's main character represented an aesthete—perhaps modeled on Wilde or the poet Algernon Charles Swinburne—who posed with
a giant sunflower while spouting his opinions on the latest cultural trends.
Wilde adopted this outlandish pose using either sunflowers or white lilies

while lecturing on the English Renaissance or other literary topics during the tour. Upon arriving in America, he was asked whether he had anything to declare and responded, "Only my genius." The lecture tour brought him to Wisconsin, where he spoke in Racine and, as a *Chicago Tribune* reporter remarked, to "the Philistines of Milwaukee." He also crossed the Mississippi River to speak in Dubuque, Iowa.[5]

The timing of Wilde's trials in the late spring of 1895 is fortuitous for the modern reader's purpose of gauging attitudes toward homosexuality. Mid-nineteenth-century comments about and images of romantic male friendships are often ambiguous or only suggestive of sexual content. It's challenging for modern readers to deduce anything from these examples with evidentiary certainty. However, by the last part of the nineteenth century, concepts of same-sex identity were becoming more established owing to published scientific writings on same-sex attraction.

Karl Heinrich Ulrichs, a native of the Kingdom of Hanover (now the German state of Lower Saxony), started publishing pamphlets in 1864 describing a third sex, which he called an "Urning." Later, some English writers used *Urning*, which alludes to Plato's term for heavenly love, before *homosexual* became more popular. Karl Maria Kertbeny, a German Hungarian, was the first to use the word *homosexuality* in 1869. He campaigned against the Prussian law that criminalized sexual relations between men. In 1870, Karl Westphal invented the phrase *contrary sexual feeling* in prose detailing the history of a young lesbian. University of Vienna professor Richard von Krafft-Ebing's 1886 *Psychopathia Sexualis* popularized concepts of degeneracy, including his term *antipathic sexual instinct*. In 1896, the early British sexologist Havelock Ellis published his book *Sexual Inversion* in Germany, a choice reflecting the assumption that the title would be too controversial for English publishers. The concept of homosexuality was at least entering the vision of the educated classes. By presenting same-sex activity on the world stage, the coverage of the Wilde trials turned many of these concepts into realities for Wisconsin readers. How the state's newspapers chose to cover Wilde's trials, or whether they covered them at all, reveals differing regional attitudes toward homosexuality at that time.[6]

Wire services provided good access to news about the events in London to the Wisconsin newspapers and magazines that chose to publish items about the trials. It is important to remember that London in the 1890s was the world capital of the dominant imperial power of the age. The media in the British capital, consisting of numerous newspapers and wire services, served as a megaphone to distribute stories about what happened there to English-speaking countries worldwide. Thus, Americans were quite aware of London's dominance in the political and cultural milieus. In the 1890s, a number of Wisconsin daily papers regularly included news items from the British Isles, and some even ran a weekly "Letter from London" that featured fashion and culture. The London press covered the Wilde trials in a banner fashion, generating stories that reached far into the American republic.

The Wisconsin that was about to be exposed to the concept of homosexuality around the turn of twentieth century had a population of two million, according to the 1900 census, one-quarter of whom were foreign born. The two largest cities were Milwaukee and Superior. The average family size was 4.7, and literacy for those over ten years of age was 95 percent. Forty-two percent of the male workforce was in agriculture, with another 23 percent in manufacturing; 16 percent were employed in domestic occupations, and the remainder worked in other professions or were unemployed. The University of Wisconsin in Madison had 2,422 students. State data shows that 56 percent of males between the ages of twenty and forty-five were married, leaving a large group of single males comprising the remaining 44 percent of this age cohort.[7]

Many Wisconsin papers printed slightly different versions of the same stories as the wire services from London. A local editor might choose which stories to run and edit those stories to fit the paper's available space, which was at a premium. Many daily papers outside Milwaukee and Superior—the state's two biggest cities—had only four pages, and at least one of those consisted of advertising. For these papers, out-of-state stories had to be short. Headlines, and often there were three or four of them, were written locally and revealed how editors wished to portray events. Editorial comments by the male-only editors further indicated the views of the Wisconsin press. Some editors questioned whether their papers would or should cover the Wilde trials at all, and some wrote editorials about the dilemma. Ultimately, tens of thousands of words about Wilde were written and published in Wisconsin during this time, providing clear evidence of early views toward homosexuality in the state.[8]

The trials in London began on April 3, 1895, with a civil suit filed by

Oscar Wilde for libel against the Marquis of Queensberry, father of Wilde's younger friend and lover, Lord Alfred Douglas. The libel action was dismissed but was immediately followed by an indictment hearing against Wilde, and then two criminal trials. The first trial resulted in a hung jury, but the second trial found Wilde guilty.[9]

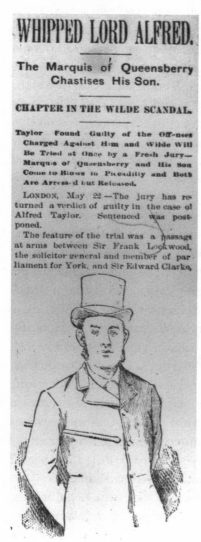

WHIPPED LORD ALFRED.

The Marquis of Queensberry Chastises His Son.

CHAPTER IN THE WILDE SCANDAL.

Taylor Found Guilty of the Offenses Charged Against Him and Wilde Will Be Tried at Once by a Fresh Jury—Marquis of Queensberry and His Son Come to Blows in Piccadilly and Both Are Arrested but Released.

LONDON, May 22—The jury has returned a verdict of guilty in the case of Alfred Taylor. Sentenced was postponed.

The feature of the trial was a passage at arms between Sir Frank Lockwood, the solicitor general and member of parliament for York, and Sir Edward Clarke.

A sketch of the Marquis of Queensberry. *APPLETON POST*, MAY 23, 1895

The legal battle had begun when Wilde sued John Scholto Douglas, the marquis, for having left a card with a porter at Wilde's club claiming that Wilde was "posing as a sodomite." The libel trial defense of Queensberry tried to portray Wilde's writings in a bad light, as favorable to homosexuality. More importantly, Queensberry provided evidence that Wilde lived in a European demimonde, or sexual underworld, consorting with young men of very questionable morals. The defense set out to prove that Wilde was a sodomite, and the Wisconsin press was left to decide how they would deal with this sensitive topic.[10]

TO PRINT OR NOT TO PRINT

The scandalous nature of the case led many Wisconsin newspapers to debate whether to publish articles about the Wilde trials at all and how to handle the topic of homosexuality. The *Racine Times* editorialized on April 5, 1895: "The Oscar Wilde libel suit has already developed such a degree of nastiness that some of the London papers refuse to publish the testimony. It is about what might be expected of men of the Wilde school, who are neither men or women." Although the Racine paper did publish some articles on the trial, its coverage of the event was overtly negative. Because Wilde had drawn a small crowd when he lectured in Racine during his 1882 tour, the editors may have felt he had few local admirers.[11]

The journalistic question of how to handle the trial was shared by the *Green Bay Gazette*, which opined on the subject on April 9 as more revelations were coming out. "The London newspapers almost without exception published verbatim reports of the testimony in the Oscar Wilde case," stated an editorial, which continued, "The St. James Gazette had the decency and courage to refuse to print the stuff." The *Green Bay Gazette* preferred that the world of vice not be given prominence in good society. Despite similar hand-wringing by a few editors over whether to print any details about the sodomy charge, most of the Wisconsin press covered the trials. The Racine paper ran nine stories and the Green Bay paper ran thirteen stories on the trials from early April to the end of May 1895.[12]

The *Superior Evening Telegram* on April 4, in a story headed "Wilde's Disgrace," actually quoted the English source, the *St. James Gazette*: "The nature of the evidence and the whole circumstances of the case prove to be such of a character that we can not report it. The English public is at the present moment involved in one of those orgies of indecency permitted by the operations of open law courts and an enterprising press."[13]

Some of the German-language papers in Wisconsin were also squeamish about reporting details of the trials, with the popular *Milwaukee Herold* reporting that the *St. James Gazette* had urged that the case be tried in closed session. When the *Milwaukee Herold* reported on Wilde taking the witness stand, the paper carried a notice: "The witness was confused several times, contradicted himself, and lost his temper at the questions of attorney Carson, which cannot be reproduced in print here." Even the Milwaukee-based German-language *Wisconsin Vorvärts*, the socialist paper that carried extensive coverage, noted that the trial concerned "unnatural, here not reproducible, crimes against young men." Significantly, the German-language press in Milwaukee had twice the circulation of the English-language press at the time.[14]

Ultimately, most Wisconsin papers carried some news about the trials, and quite a few published editorial comments. The two major English-language dailies in Milwaukee, one paper in Green Bay, and one in Madison each ran a dozen or more stories during April and May. The Milwaukee papers ran lengthy pieces with much of the trial in detail. They were all outdone by Milwaukee's *Abendpost* and *Sonntags-Post*, the *Superior Evening Telegram*, and the *Oshkosh Daily Northwestern*, which each carried more than thirty stories or short notices on the Wilde matter. This number of stories approached the number published in New York dailies like the *Sun* and the *World*. Wisconsin editors did monitor these big-city papers, as evidenced by other editorial comments. However, the New York papers had more space for in-depth coverage.[15]

As the trials became an international sensation, most reports left little doubt that non-normative male sexual activity was the most important part of the story. The word *homosexuality* was not used explicitly at this time, but the word *sodomy*, a criminal offense, was sometimes used, as were other suggestive phrases.

For example, the *Abendpost* carried a story headlined, "The Wilde Scandal in London." It noted that Mr. Carson, attorney for the Marquis of Queensberry, found it "his embarrassing duty to have to call people to the witness stand who would speak openly about the nature of their relationship with Oscar Wilde. Mostly these were between the ages of 18 and 23 and did not belong to Wilde's class. They were servants and so forth and were not in the slightest versed in literature or art. He further said a vast amount of evidence for the abominable immorality of this Wilde existed." The *Abendpost* used the term "unnatural crimes," but the *Wisconsin State Journal* got right to the heart of the matter in its first story on April 3 with the charge that "Wilde had for some time been in the habit of soliciting male persons to commit indecent offenses with him." It noted that Queensberry's counselor read from Wilde's book *The Picture of Dorian Gray* "to show the author upheld sodomy."[16]

In dealing with the homosexual content of the trials, the Wisconsin press struggled with how graphically to present the issues. The *Superior Evening Telegram* on April 3 printed more of the trial's early cross-examination than any other Wisconsin paper and included the passage in which the attorney asked Wilde, "Did you ever 'adore madly,' a person younger than yourself, 'and of the male sex?'" The *Milwaukee Daily News* on April 4 ran fairly detailed testimony from the trial that included the mention of specific acts. It noted that during cross-examination Wilde was asked if he had kissed a young male servant named Grainger. It also referred to Queensberry's action as one "to save his son from the influence of Wilde, who according to his own admissions, was a friend of a person who was known to be a procurer of boys for vicious purposes." The *Milwaukee Sentinel* reported details of a letter penned by Wilde that featured in the trial. Written to Lord Alfred Douglas, the letter described the younger man's "red rose lips" and "slim gilt soul" that walked between poetry and passion. Wilde was asked if the letter was decent. His reply: "Decency does not come into the question." Though the *Milwaukee Journal* ran a story on April 4 calling the questions in the cross-examination of the libel suit "unprintable," the story also noted that Wilde was asked about taking a newsboy of eighteen to a hotel in Brighton. Further, he was asked about "relations with various boys and men."[17]

As Queensberry's defense in the libel trial piled up evidence of Wilde's activities with young men, the Wisconsin press had more grist for the mill. The successful defense of the justification of the sodomite charge resulted in an expectation that Wilde would be arrested. On April 6, the *Milwaukee Journal*, under a lead headline of "Wilde in Court," carried a subheadline of "The Hearing of His Case Today Brings Out Sensational Evidence." It noted that Wilde was to be prosecuted "on a series of charges of inciting boys to terrible crimes and of actually committing acts of gross indecency." Wilde was described as "a man who gave much money to youths and men." One witness, Charles Parker, age nineteen, who had been invited by the playwright to dinner in a private room and then to London's Savoy Hotel, apparently gave "the most minute details of his intimacy with Wilde." The same paper on April 11 reported the testimony of Edward Shelby, a young clerk who "told how Wilde gave him copies of his works with tender inscriptions, took him to theaters, to the Prince of Wales club and to other resorts. The witness also testified in detail as to Wilde's criminal behavior to him." The first criminal trial in April resulted in a hung jury, so the crown prosecuted a second time and secured a conviction. At the end of the trials on May 25, the Oshkosh *Northwestern* reported on the final judge's comments in terms more explicit than most, naming one of Wilde's associates as "the keeper of a male brothel" and quoted the British jurist's distress that Wilde, "a man of reputed culture, should be such a perverter of young men."[18]

Thus, though the Wisconsin press might yet not dare speak the word *homosexuality*, the news stories that editors chose to run did frankly address sodomy and the culture of a male sexual underworld in London. The acknowledgment of this culture presumed the existence of a homosexual identity; that is, it did not simply describe Wilde's behavior as crimes of individual passion. Ultimately, in their roles as shapers of reality through the printed word and as community leaders, the Wisconsin editors presented a broad consensus that male homosexuality was evil.

CRIMINAL TREATMENT

After the collapse of the libel action on April 5, the Wisconsin press took up the new criminal matter of Oscar Wilde's sexual proclivities. Participants included both media sources that had extensively followed the libel matter and those that had not covered the libel. The new coverage began with Wilde's arrest on April 6. The *Milwaukee Sentinel* wanted to make sure everyone knew that the consequences of homosexual behavior could involve jail time, headlining two early stories "Oscar Wilde in a Cell" and "Oscar Wilde in His Cell." The Oshkosh *Northwestern* reported, "Wilde is Arrested, The Tables Have Been Turned, The Apostle of Aestheticism Charged With a Heinous Crime While Marquis of Queensbury Goes Free— The Great Scandal Growing." As the indictment hearing began, the *Superior Evening Telegram* made its judgment in an editorial comment on April 9: "The conviction of Oscar Wilde is almost a certainty and . . . the minimum punishment is ten years in prison, though the heinousness of his offense against society justifies a longer, if not life term."[19]

Other papers reported Wilde's arrest by publishing headlines that highlighted his loss of freedom and control. On April 19 the *Green Bay Gazette* ran a story with the headline, "Held Without Bail." The paper's headline when the first trial resulted in no verdict was, "Wilde Escapes the Stripes, No Convict Clothes for the English Author." In Eau Claire, the *Daily Leader* expressed its views with the April 27 headline "Says 'Not Guilty': Such Are the Idle Words Used by Wilde and His Disreputable Companions." The Racine *Times* reported the end of the second trial with the headline "Wilde is Convicted."[20]

On May 25, when Wilde was convicted of lesser charges than those originally made—indecent acts rather than the statute on sodomy, or the crime against nature, passed in the reign of Henry VIII—his sentence of two years at hard labor became one of the most frequent stories published by the press. The Milwaukee *Sonntags-Post* of May 26 reported the aftermath of the conviction as follows: "The Apostle of Aestheticism was hauled off to his cell posthaste, as a criminal." The *Appleton Post* on May 30 described British justice as swift and certain: "It is less than two months since Oscar Wilde was arraigned before the court for gross immoralities, and yet within this period he had had two trials and on Saturday the prison doors closed behind him."[21]

IS NOW A CONVICT.

The Jury This Afternoon Found Oscar Wilde Guilty as Indicted.

SENTENCE SPEEDILY GIVEN.

The Fallen Aesthetic Apostle is Given Two Years at Hard Labor.

London, May 25—The jury in the Oscar Wilde case returned a verdict of guilty at 5:30 this afternoon and the prisoner was sentenced to two years imprisonment at hard labor.

Alfred Taylor, Wilde's accomplice was also given a similar sentence.

SUPERIOR EVENING TELEGRAM, MAY 25, 1895

The *Milwaukee Daily News*, which saw itself as a pro-labor paper, must have delighted in the headline it ran on April 25 about the presumed English aristocrat: "Wilde Must Work Now." Perhaps for them prison hard labor was real work and writing was not. The *Wisconsin State Journal* seemed to agree, with its headline of the same day: "The Corrupt Aesthete Must Toil." The Oshkosh *Northwestern* put a different twist on its story with its headline: "The Poetry of Work, Oscar Wilde Gets Two Years, London Jury Finds the Dainty Esthete Guilty as Charged and He Is Quickly Sentenced—Crowd Goes Wild and Cheers the Verdict."[22]

The *Madison Democrat*, in what today seems like a foretaste of 1960s criminal justice in the capital city, reported on May 28, "The sending of Oscar Wilde to prison has had a good result thus early in the clipping of the great crop of hair which made the aesthete look even softer than he really was." Some sixty years later, Madison's antiwar radicals had their long locks shorn by the police after their arrests.[23]

Wisconsin's press coverage of Wilde's arrest gave unanimous approval to the criminal justice system's attacks on Wilde's homosexuality by emphasizing his loss of freedom and control, and his prison sentence. In fact, some editors called for even harsher penalties, such as the *Superior Evening Telegram* writing that a life sentence would be appropriate.[24]

SHAME AND DISGRACE

Wisconsin's press coverage of Wilde's character as a homosexual and the sentiment expressed toward him during the trials was also marked by negativity. The *Wisconsin State Journal* began its coverage on April 3 with its first and largest headline on the libel trial: "Shame for Oscar." The second day's headline was: "Beastley Wilde's Case." The third day's headlines included "Wilde in Disgrace," the fourth day's included "Charles Parker, a Valet Out of Work Tells a Revolting Tale," and the fifth day produced "England's Shame." Before the criminal trial even began, the paper had piled on the opprobrium.[25]

The subheads chosen by the *Milwaukee Daily News* for the April 4 libel trial story read "Unsavory Trial" and "Oscar Wilde Accused of Things That Are Horrible." The article noted that two men of Wilde's acquaintance were arrested in women's clothes. On April 5, during the collapse of the libel action, the *Superior Evening Telegram* wrote, "Oscar Wilde's ignominious defeat should be sufficient to drive him out of England, but it is hoped that it will not send him to America." Milwaukee's *Germania* on April 9 carried a story on "Oskar Wilde," who was characterized as "the celebrated fool." In reporting his sentence, the same paper uses the word *abominable* as a character description.[26]

The *Sonntags-Post* of April 21 reported that Lord Alfred Douglas had "written a letter to the Star in which he protests against the spectators condemning Wilde prematurely, who is now being handed over to be judged by a wild and common mob." Many of the stories noted the large and boisterous crowds at the trial. The *Wisconsin State Journal* on April 24 noted, "Wilde's home was sold out by the sheriff today in the presence of great crowds of curiosity mongers."[27]

In a story published on May 3, the *Milwaukee Herald* noted, "A demonstration against the accused did not happen despite the large crowd of people gathered in front of Old Bailey." This was because the accused was held back for a delayed departure. The *Herold* did note, however, that as Wilde was being sentenced, people in the courtroom shouted, "Be ashamed of yourself, be ashamed of yourself."[28]

The *Superior Evening Telegram* was probably projecting its own views when on April 11 it published the headline "Wilde Is Much Subdued and Feels His Disgrace Very Keenly." (Wilde's statement at the end of the trial, quoted later in this chapter in the section entitled "Oscar's Antidote," would contradict such misreporting.) In a subsequent comment, the *Superior Evening Telegram* of May 22 noted, "It is believed that Oscar Wilde cannot now be convicted. It is a strange thing how sentiment changes. A few weeks ago his life was in danger from the angry crowds that wanted to drive him from England. He'll probably be a bigger man than the Prince of Wales in another month. And yet he is not less guilty than he was when his disgrace first became public."[29]

HOMOSEXUALITY AND ILLNESS

Even though Wisconsin's editors chose both to emphasize the large demonstrative crowds that were hostile to Wilde's homosexuality and to use pejorative words in describing Wilde and his character, they also described him as physically weak, mentally ill, and even suicidal. The *Milwaukee Sentinel* on April 8 featured the headline "Unable to Eat or Sleep He May Commit Suicide." The *Wisconsin State Journal* on the same day outdid the *Sentinel*, headlining: "Oscar Wilde Not Yet a Suicide." For the Madison paper's editor, it must have seemed only a matter of time before Wilde would choose to take his own life. The headline could not have been based on the paper's story, which began "London, April 8—There is not the slightest ground for the report that Oscar Wilde has suicided."[30]

The *Milwaukee Herold* had it correct with its headline "Wilde Not Suicidal," and its story noted, "It is not even true that last night a rumor to that effect circulated here." The Oshkosh *Northwestern* was more straightforward, with the headline "Oscar Cannot Sleep." The *Superior Evening Telegram* of April 19 proclaimed, "Wilde Is Limp," and the *Abendpost* on the same day declared that Wilde looked "very drawn and ill. His hair was disheveled and he made a very bedraggled impression." On May 10,

> ## ENGLAND'S SHAME.
>
> ### Oscar Wilde Not Yet a Suicide—Bigger Reputations Involved.
>
> LONDON, April 8.—There is not the slightest ground for the report that Oscar Wilde has suicided. Further startling revelations are hinted at. It is said Alfred Taylor is determined to drag down with him all he can if he is prosecuted. This will involve the most prominent men of whose names have been freely whispered about in connection with this scandal.

WISCONSIN STATE JOURNAL, APRIL 8, 1895

Der Sebote headlined a story "Oscar Wilde Ill," which reported that he suffered from frayed nerves.[31]

After reading this coverage, one might draw the conclusion that editors viewed homosexuality as an infection or sickness. Though the later twentieth-century medicalization of homosexuality defined it as an actual psychiatric "illness," these earlier perceptions reflected the view of homosexuality not as an illness but as a symptom of the ill effects of immorality.

FINANCIAL IMPOVERISHMENT

The Wisconsin press took notice of the financial consequences of Wilde's exposure as a homosexual. The *Superior Evening Telegram* of April 6 carried a story noting that Wilde's recent success was not likely to continue. "Wilde has been making large sums of money lately out of his plays and books. His plays are now running at two London theaters and many companies are playing them in the provinces. Of course, in the future no one will accept his plays." On the same day, the *Milwaukee Daily News* reported that the bookings for Wilde's plays *The Ideal Husband* and *The Importance of Being Earnest* had steadily declined since the police court proceedings against him: "[T]he London public will never tolerate the performance of any more of Wilde's plays. Thus, his principal means of livelihood is gone, he has saved nothing from the large income he has had for years." The paper editorialized, "He seems to now have received a complete knock-out, but it is not at all certain that he will make up for it, in part at least by a successful tour on the American stage." Perhaps they recollected his successful Milwaukee appearance in 1882 at the city's Grand Opera House.[32]

The *Abendpost* of April 23 noted that "Oscar Wilde's valuable collection of printings, Moorish pottery, bric-a-brac etc., will be auctioned off tomorrow. [Thomas Carlyle's] desk is among them." The next day, it further reported that the sale was a sign that "his resources are depleted." The *Milwaukee Journal* on April 25 reported that the sheriff had sold Wilde's house. On May 3 both the *Journal* and the *Madison Democrat* reported, "A receiving order in bankruptcy was issued against Oscar Wilde." The

Nunnenmacher's Grand Opera House in Milwaukee, where Wilde spoke during his 1882 tour of America. WHI IMAGE ID 54284

Green Bay Gazette emphasized the matter with the headline "Oscar Wilde Is Bankrupt." The loss of his livelihood, personal effects, and house, and finally his bankruptcy, are presented in the coverage as natural consequences of Wilde's lifestyle.[33]

CULTURAL SUPPRESSION OF HOMOSEXUALITY

The imminent death of Wilde's career and the disappearance of works by a prominent homosexual were other common themes among the headlines. The *Green Bay Gazette* headlined its April 5 story on the libel suit: "Oscar Wilde's Sun Has Set; Famous Advocate of Estheticism Relegated to Oblivion." And just for good measure, the subheading was "Wilde's Career at an End."[34]

The Wisconsin press reported that Wilde's books and plays were under attack. The *Milwaukee Sentinel* in particular made it an issue. On April 9, shortly after Wilde's arrest, the paper's editor expressed frustration with the lack of action taken against Wilde's work: "They have taken his name from the advertisements and playbills. This action costs nothing. They have not withdrawn his plays. That would be too expensive a virtue." Following up on April 12, the paper wrote, "Nothing shows the strength of feeling against Oscar Wilde in England better than the action of the British Museum, which has withdrawn his books from circulation. Why they should be more pernicious now than when they were published is not clear but clear reasoning is not essential to an emphatic expression of disgust." Other papers reported the same British Museum story. Yet, the *Abendpost* followed with a small notice: "The main librarian of the British Museum denies the news that Oscar Wilde's books and publications had been pulled from the library of the institute."[35]

The Racine *Times* of April 13 carried an extremely long editorial on "Banishing Wilde's Books." It noted that his books had been removed not only in England but also in "public libraries" of America's eastern cities. The paper did not wish to stop there in "purifying libraries": "Nor are the works of Wilde the only ones that are the instructors of those vices that reigned supreme in the days of Rome's rottenness and in the palaces of the rich in the far east. Swineburne [sic] and the 'lurid school of Milwaukee poets,' as they have been termed by [Charles] Dana, are examples, and there are scores of lesser ones in the same category whose works cannot be read without contamination, so filled are they with suggestions that are revolting to decency." The Racine editor believed Wilde's teachings, which led to "such nameless crimes," needed to be rooted out: "Wilde's exposure . . . may be the means of destroying them in the fierce flame of public contempt that will envelope those who still seek to maintain and propagate them." This suggestion of the "flame of public contempt" would later be taken to its extreme by the Nazis as they actually burned gay books in Germany.[36]

The Oshkosh *Northwestern* joined the fray in a general way with an article borrowed from the *St. Louis Republic*, which it headlined, "An Evil Tendency, Trend of Modern Books and Drama." The *Superior Evening Telegram* carried the same piece with a similar headline. The *Northwestern* was even willing to use Wilde's name as an indicator of infamy. On April 22, it carried a story from Neenah about a public school janitor who "took liberties" with young girls, headlined, "Second Oscar Wilde." The *Appleton Post* on May 30 editorialized on the eclipse of the literary Wilde: "We don't think the sunflower will bloom very luxuriantly in the English bastile [*sic*]

A sketch of Oscar Wilde, published during the trials. *SUPERIOR EVENING TELEGRAM*, APRIL 22, 1895

at Pentonville, whither Oscar Wilde has been taken to serve out his two-years sentence at hard labor."[37]

As a result of the publicity occasioned by Wilde's trials and conviction, much of the public was denied access to his writings because of his homosexuality. Through the articles and editorials they chose to publish, many Wisconsin editors contributed to the effort to have Wilde's works suppressed. This might also be characterized as the effort to have the love that dare not speak its name disappear once more into what would later be termed the cultural closet.

FOREIGN OTHERNESS

The Wisconsin editors thought Wilde's presentation of his affectations and his homosexuality should not dupe democratic-minded American citizens. The *Madison Democrat* editorialized early on April 6, "Oscar Wilde would probably not be lionized if he should now visit the United States . . . he has lost estate with American anglomaniacs." And the *Wisconsin State Journal* joined in on April 8: "The Americans who made so much of Oscar Wilde on his tour—and he was a guest of honor at many a seat of learning and in homes of prominence—no doubt feel ashamed of themselves. He was asinine then but has since become vicious, as his plays indicated to healthy minds. The critics however, maintained they had 'a great moral purpose.'"[38]

In Oshkosh, the *Northwestern* on April 9 commented, "The ethics of the English aristocracy is getting another airing. It is almost fatal to scratch the upper crust in England." And later, on May 27, the paper added, "The affected aristocracy in this country which was so carried away by Oscar Wilde's sunflower aestheticism will now address all communications to their chief and idol in care of the warden, and enclose a stamp for reply."[39]

The *Northwestern* did note that "Oscar's only defense on this side of the water seems to come from Mrs. Frank Leslie." Mrs. Leslie was the publisher of *Frank Leslie's Illustrated Weekly*, founded by her first husband. At the collapse of the libel action, the Beloit *Free Press* headlined that Mrs. Leslie "Does Not Believe the Aesthete Guilty." She praised him as "a dignified high-minded gentleman, a perfect son, a kind considerate husband, and a doting, affectionate parent." The *Northwestern* later editorialized that Mrs. Leslie's devotion in going to England to comfort Lady Wilde, her mother-in-law since her second marriage to Wilde's brother, was "not conspicuously usual in this age."[40]

The Racine *Times* in its long editorial of April 13 noted an effect of the trial: "The exposure may also teach Englishmen and Americans that they can never adopt [the teachings of Wilde's books] without sinking into a cess pool of moral nastiness and physical degradation, the very thought of which is revolting." And on April 22, the same paper took to task the snobbery of "mental dudes of Boston" for their "slavish subservience to nasty European ideas and methods."[41]

Thus, many Wisconsin editors promoted the belief that good, moral Americans would have nothing to do with the likes of the homosexual Wilde and his upper-class supporters. The English aristocracy was the nominal target of this argument, but it was also a chauvinistic attack aimed at American cultural snobs.

A DEBATE ON THE LEFT

A unique perspective was brought to the discussion by the socialist press represented by the German-language paper *Wisconsin Vorvärts*. Although many of the same news stories ran in this paper as in others about Wilde's arrest, trials, and illness, *Vorvärts's* editorial notes had an extra dimension. On May 26, after the sentence of two years had been pronounced, the paper expressed its opinion that such a trial fully documented "the squalidness of certain high aristocrats and wealthy men." Thus, for Wisconsin's leading socialist paper, homosexuality was linked to the corrupt nature of the economic upper classes and could be blamed for class oppression and the exploitation of working-class youths.[42]

Vorvärts engaged in further editorial comment. Though it disagreed with *Der arme Teufel*, a prominent German-language literary journal from Detroit with a radical or anarchist bent, *Vorvärts* ran a large excerpt from the Detroit paper of a pro-Wilde defense of "Platonic love." This excerpt argued, "It would be of little help to direct the attention of these judges of morality, who notably do all the talking in the newspapers as well, to the fact that the 'crime' consisted in a kind of love, which most people regard

In London hat der zweite Unfittlich=
teits=Prozeß gegen den berühmten hoch=
vornehmen Novellenschreiber und Dra=
matiker, Oskar Wilde, damit geendet
daß derselbe zu zwei Jahren Kerker, bei
schwerer Arbeit, verutheilt wurde. Es
handelte sich in dem Prozesse um unna=
türliche, hier nicht wiederzugebende,
Verbrechen gegen junge Männer. Die
Verkommenheit gewisser Hochadeligen
und Reichen wird durch solche Prozesse
vollauf documentirt.

A paragraph about Wilde in *Vorvärts*, Milwaukee's socialist German-language newspaper. WISCONSIN VORVÄRTS, MAY 26, 1895

as absurd and unaesthetic, and to ask the question: What makes us judges of the tastes of others?"[43]

Next, *Der arme Teufel* gave a history lesson: "That so-called most noble love, which does not even have need for sensual exertion, one customarily calls Platonic love, and our highly moral fathers and mothers, who are however little acquainted with the practices of antiquity, would absolutely entrust a Plato with the education of their sons and daughters. Yet what did Plato celebrate in the immortal dialogues of his 'Symposium' and his 'Phaedrus' which treats the subject of love? Well love of boys, pederasty, the crime of Oskar Wilde."[44]

Also included in the issue of *Vorvärts* was a section from *Der arme Teufel* on literary suppression: "As is generally known, narrow-minded zealots appeared, which wanted to have the works of Wilde banned from libraries, they didn't know that with this the works of a Pindar, Sophocles, Anacreon, Virgil, Theocrites would also have to vanish. They didn't know, that they also insulted a Epaminondas, a Zeno, Alexander, Hadrian, a Socrates with the foul-mouthed swear words that they poured out over the unfortunate Englishman, that one would have to indict the noble German poet Graf Platen-Hallermunde as well."[45]

Though *Vorvärts* reprinted a large section of the anarchist paper's arguments, it dismissed these views with the comment, "Truly! There is no accounting for taste." What *Vorwärts* did not choose to run from the same *Der arme Teufel* piece was a concluding section that claims a jury of women would not have convicted Wilde: "I am confident that woman would enlarge the great axiom to forgive love everything to encompass perverse love as well." But as noted, *Vorwärts* did not buy the general pro-homosexuality argument nor agree that this was not a criminal matter.[46]

OSCAR'S ANTIDOTE

There were very few hints of positive perceptions about homosexuals or homosexuality during the Wilde trials as reported in the Wisconsin press. On April 30, in contrast to its other articles about the trials, the *Abendpost* carried a story that Wilde "spoke so brilliantly that he received applause." This observation also ran in a few other Wisconsin papers. The ovation, as reported in the *Milwaukee Journal* of the same day, occurred in response to Wilde's line spoken in his own defense, "I am that love; but dare not speak its name." The *Milwaukee Journal* carried Wilde's response: "It is a love not understood in this country. It is the love of David for Jonathan—a deep, spiritual affection, as pure as it is perfect. It is something this age does not understand. It mocks at it and sometimes puts one into the pillory."[47]

With the exception of the brief references above, the reporting in the Wisconsin press contained primarily negative perceptions of homosexuality, as well as Wilde's actions and writings. Yet even in 1895, one might have found a glimmer of hope in the coverage of these trials. When he was finally convicted at the end of the second trial, Oscar Wilde wrote a brief statement. Several Wisconsin papers, including the *Milwaukee Journal*, *Milwaukee Sentinel*, *Milwaukee Herold*, Oshkosh *Northwestern*, Superior *Sunday Telegram*, and *Wisconsin State Journal*, printed it in its entirety. It read:

> The charges against me are utterly untrue. Youth in every form
> always fascinated me because youth has naturally that temperament
> to which artists try to attain. All works of art are produced in the
> moment of youth. I have no sense at all of social class.
>
> I love society and the rich and well born on account of their lux
> ury, culture, the grace of their lives, the external accidents of life.
> But anyone, plough-boy, fisherman or street arab has an interest

for me; mere humanity is so wonderful. I do not ask of the young
what they do. I don't care who they are. Their ignorance has its
mode of wisdom; their lack of culture leaves them open to fresh and
vivid impressions.[48]

One could call this Oscar's antidote, and he offered it to those who may
not have been completely taken in by the reporting on the trial. First, he
rejected the "wages of sin" angle of the stories, along with their focus on
his criminality, illness, and financial ruin. He did not even deign to discuss
what had been published about him. Second, he reaffirmed his belief in
the principle of beauty as embodied in youth and the art that glorifies it.
He made the love of beauty, not sex, the focus of his statement. The court
may have tried him for the sex, but Wilde wanted the world to know that
he still appreciated beauty and love. His statement that "mere humanity
is so wonderful" was one of hope. Wilde's message conveyed his hope that
the future could be different from the present as it was reported by the
Wisconsin press.

THE WELL OF LONELINESS

Although the Wilde case involved male homosexuality, it is doubtful that
any non-normative sexuality would have been viewed favorably by the
male Wisconsin editors of the 1890s. Indeed, though it took the national
spotlight several decades later without inspiring anything close to the
degree of commentary that the Wilde trials did, the lesbian novel *The Well
of Loneliness* elicited similar reactions in the Wisconsin press.

The author, Radclyffe Hall, "a self-identified 'invert' who wore 'man-
nish' clothes and liked to be called 'John,'" had told her editor in 1928,
"I have put my pen at the service of some of the most persecuted and
misunderstood people in the world." One scholar credits the book with
"reigniting the debate over lesbian representation" after a lesbian play, *The
Captive*, had been suppressed from the New York stage in 1927. Both in the
United Kingdom and in America, *The Well of Loneliness*, much like Wilde,
was subject to multiple trial proceedings. The English banned the book as
"prejudicial to the morals of the community," a sanction that lasted into
the late 1940s. However, attempts to censor the book failed in America,

and it sold a hundred thousand copies in its first year of publication, even though its price of ten dollars was double that of a typical book.[49]

The concept of a lesbian novel was scandalous. Even the New York lawyer who defended the book's publication in America claimed that he "could not see a way to defend lesbianism in a positive or celebratory fashion." Leslie Taylor, the preeminent scholar of its American publication, notes that even the generally neutral *Book Review Digest* wrote, "This serious novel on a forbidden theme has received a notoriety out of proportion to the significance of the book." Taylor observes, "The scandal swirling around *The Well* suggests that, in fact lesbian desire had become too visible." As with the Wilde trial, many people reacted negatively to themes of non-normative love daring to speak its name.[50]

The Wisconsin press generally agreed that *The Well of Loneliness* should be suppressed. Librarian Lutie Stearns, writing in the *Wisconsin Library Bulletin* of 1929, explained that "questionable fiction and other works whose circulation was restricted at the local library, causing no doubt a heavy run on book stores by the curious adolescents and the perverts, sunk in a 'Well of Loneliness.'" In a column covering the national theater beat, the *Capital Times* of Madison reported that the Provincetown Players in their second season had dropped a proposed play based on *The Well of Loneliness* because of the censors. In October 1932, the *Wisconsin Jewish Chronicle* reported that a lecture on *The Well of Loneliness* by a psychiatrist at the city's Jewish Center had the effect of placing the book's topic in the realm of sickness. The lecturer noted that "the book dealing with abnormal sex" had caused a sensation. Interestingly, the preceding issue of the *Chronicle* included a column titled "On Books Written by Women" that observed, "That women can write well has been known for a long time, from as far back as the time of when Sappho was a poetess in Greece." Sappho wrote about love between women and thus was a classical Greek touchstone for lesbians; gay men similarly reached back to Greek classical traditions about homosexuality.[51]

Multiple items relating to Radclyffe Hall appeared in the *Appleton Post-Crescent* during this period. In a national column, Seen and Heard in New York, the paper ran a 1932 story about a bookseller's "run-in with self-appointed censors." It told of "monitors of morality" going around the city and "'advising' booksellers that they had better take copies [of

The Well] out of their windows." This bookseller, who had sold out of his copies but was expecting another shipment, found an extra dust jacket of Hall's book that he put on a cookbook. When the intruder grabbed it from the window, he was nonplussed when it was unmasked as full of recipes.[52]

In 1931, when Hall's next book, *The Unlit Lamp*, appeared, Eleanor Evans Wing wrote a long review for the Appleton paper, noting the book's sale at the Century Bookstore in Appleton. She excoriated "the censor and the stuffed shirt moralist [who] have on a previous occasion condemned Radclyffe Hall." Wing argued that in attempting to determine the origin of perversity, Americans "attribute it to an older more degenerate, more sophisticated world, than our own youthful country." Yet even this reviewer who defended Hall seemed to accept the commonplace characterization of homosexuality in the comment, "We stick our heads in the sand and refuse to see abnormality even though it most certainly does exist." One wonders what evidence led Wing in Appleton to know that lesbianism "most certainly does exist."[53]

Radclyffe Hall in 1932 donning the men's clothing she preferred. © NATIONAL PORTRAIT GALLERY, LONDON

In writing about *The Unlit Lamp*, Wing digressed to make comments about Hall's earlier work. She observed that the characters in *The Unlit Lamp* are "more loveable" than those in *The Well of Loneliness*. In further comments on *The Well*, she noted that it "was marvelously written, tragic in the extreme, provided one knew where the tragedy lay, and difficult to understand." She also observed that the book "was not bizarre nor untrue, though these adjectives were constantly applied to it in this country." However, she did stipulate, "You feel that the author's experience—her reservoir of information—is far removed from your own." It is too bad that the Appleton paper did not include a comment on the ending line from *The Well of Loneliness*: "Give us also the right to our existence."[54]

EARLY FRAMING OF HOMOSEXUALITY

The Oscar Wilde trials were the first events to break the general silence about homosexuality in Wisconsin in a big way. The state's editors were in broad agreement as to how they would speak about it. All approved of the criminal treatment of the subject, with some editors urging even harsher sanctions. Negative emotions and consequences were associated with homosexuality, from shame to financial ruin to ill health, even to suicide, and were touted and even hyped in the Wisconsin headlines and editorials. As one Racine newspaper's headline put it, "The Moral of This Sensational Trial Is Plain to All." That lesbianism, too, should be associated with sickness, abnormality, and censorship also emerged as part of the early established narratives about homosexuality. Aside from the glimmers of hope in Wilde's trial press statement and Hall's plea for sympathy that emerged through the gloom, the condemnatory narrative front on homosexuality was solidly maintained in the Wisconsin of the late nineteenth and into the early twentieth century.[55]

2

VISIBLE VICE AND ITS PUNISHMENTS

He was known as a homosexual by the police in the city where he lived. The police refrained from prosecuting him because of his previous good standing in the community.
　　　—PRISON RESEARCHER'S NOTES, CASE FILE OF LEO M., 1930S[1]

The root of the offense lies deeper than the intellect, inasmuch as the sodomists include men of both low and high intelligence.
　　　　　—UNIVERSITY OF WISCONSIN SOCIOLOGIST
　　　　　JOHN L. GILLIN IN *THE WISCONSIN PRISONER*, 1946[2]

A t the end of the nineteenth century, in conjunction with the World's Columbian Exhibition in Chicago, Wisconsin's great historian Frederick Jackson Turner presented his thesis on the significance and disappearance of the frontier in America. Turner's 1893 theory focused on diminishing rural growth, but the flip side of the coin was that America was becoming an urban nation with many large metropolises. The spectacular growth of cities—especially those with large immigrant populations—was a challenge to an older America and the upholders of its social Victorian traditions, including the negative attitudes toward non-normative sexual activity. Several Wisconsin cities had enormous growth in the thirty years between 1890 and 1920. Milwaukee's population more than doubled, from 204,000 to 457,000; Superior's more than tripled, from 12,000 to 40,000; and Madison's almost tripled, from 13,000 to 38,000. Such explosive growth put a great deal of pressure on social institutions. Additionally, these three cities were experiencing new political shifts as the Social-Democratic Party of Wisconsin came to domi-nate in Milwaukee, electing both a mayor and a congressman in 1910, and the Progressive reform wing of the Republicans that dominated Dane County and the Lake Superior shore.[3]

Nationally, the problems of urban growth and social dislocation were reflected in the truly big cities, causing many reformers to take up the challenges. The visible problems, however, also caused concern among the denizens of more traditional rural areas and small towns. One urban phenomenon of the period became the vice or sin tour, also known as slumming, conducted by Christian ministers who wanted to clean up their cities by highlighting immoral conditions. This impulse was related to the social gospel embraced by many Protestant leaders whose churches claimed responsibilities outside their parochial walls. Some famous New York sin tours were led by Charles Parkhurst, a Presbyterian preacher, in 1892. He even formed his own organization, the Society for the Prevention of Crime, which hired private investigators to demonstrate the widespread existence of vice and the lax enforcement of morality laws. Years later, private investigators were again used as a foil for official law enforcement when Wisconsin state senator Howard Teasdale used investigators to un-cover vice in 1913, and when Senator Joseph McCarthy used investigators in Congress in the post–World War II red scare.[4]

In Chicago, things really kicked off with Englishman W. T. Stead's publication in 1894 of *If Christ Came to Chicago*. The son of a Congrega-tional minister, Stead had published a newspaper in London, the *Pall Mall Gazette*, which pioneered a new, more colorful journalism that began the move toward tabloid-style sensationalism. His Chicago book included a coded map to the brothels and saloons of the infamous Levee District on the near South Side. Wisconsin cities also had ministers who took up the challenge and led sin tours.[5]

According to a 1908 book titled *The Intersexes: A History of Simili-sexualism as a Problem in Social Life*, "A special factor in homosexual uses of vapor-bath establishments in larger cities is the fact that in America these are kept open, and much patronized during all night hours." The book claimed that "New York, Boston, Washington, Chicago, St. Louis, Milwau-kee, New Orleans, Philadelphia are 'homosexual capitals.'" In Chicago's First Ward, Alderman "Bathhouse John" Coughlin and his aide Michael

"Hinky Dink" Kenna hosted an outrageous event, the First Ward Ball, from 1896 to 1908. Coughlin started out as a "rubber," or masseur, in the Palmer House Turkish Bath and then opened his own bath establishment. All the brothels, gambling dens, bathhouses, and saloons in the Levee District bought blocks of tickets to the First Ward Ball as a payoff for protection. Coughlin led a grand march at the ball that, in addition to madams and prostitutes, included "female impersonators." When Walter T. Sumner, dean of the Chicago Episcopal Cathedral of Saints Peter and Paul, attended as an observer in 1908, he denounced the ball as "an everlasting disgrace to Chicago," and the event was shut down.[6]

One aspect of the broader anti-vice movement was the effort for "social purity." Historian David J. Pivar, in his book *Purity Crusade: Sexual Morality and Social Control 1868–1900*, noted, "Traditional Christianity was limited in its capacity to come to grips with the new conditions that arose from industrialization and urbanization." Pivar cited even earlier exposé efforts of the 1880s, including one aimed at the lumber camps of Michigan and Wisconsin. Wisconsin governor Jeremiah Rusk, however, thought the reports exaggerated the vice that could be found there. Investigations led by the Woman's Christian Temperance Union in the late 1880s showed sixty dens of prostitution in the North Woods area, with the Wisconsin city of Ashland (which had a population of 9,956 in 1890) providing medical inspections and health certificates for the prostitutes. One common theme among these purity efforts—that immigrant workers had imported the loose morals of Europe—underlined the perception that the flourishing immoral activities were somehow un-American. This view tied back to earlier perceptions that Wilde's homosexuality was a foreign-based phenomenon, even though homosexual activities were occurring in bathhouses across America, including in Milwaukee.[7]

While the focus of the purity efforts was generally on booze and female prostitution as vice, homosexuals would appear around the fringes of the reform movement. On one New York tour, investigators led the Reverend Parkhurst to a house of ill repute with small open-doored rooms, each of which held a "youth, whose face was painted, eyebrows blackened and whose airs were those of a young girl." When the investigator whispered that these youths speaking in "high falsetto voice" were men crossdressing, the clergyman rushed out, saying, "I wouldn't stay in that house for all the money in the world." A lurid book published in 1911, *Fighting the Traffic in Young Girls or War on the White Slave Trade*, was written by Ernest Bell, who was identified as secretary of the Illinois Vigilance Association and Superintendent of Midnight Missions. The title of the poem on the book's last page, "Ye Rulers of Sodom," draws on the biblical passages most commonly referenced in arguments against homosexual immorality and enshrined in law as the definition of illegal male-male sex: sodomy. In the poem, Bell attacks the "sworn officials" who were the "perjured protectors of the slaughter-house, where youths and maidens die a thousand deaths." Note the reference to both sexes.[8]

While these anti-vice crusades did appeal to traditional Christian moralists like ministers and the prominent Baptist layman John D. Rockefeller Jr., they also attracted reformers whose primary concern was social morality. In New York, anti-vice reformers were linked to those fighting Tammany Hall's corruption. The progressive Theodore Roosevelt was brought in as New York City's police commissioner in 1895. In *Island of Vice: Theodore Roosevelt's Doomed Quest to Clean Up Sin-Loving New York*, Richard Zacks described Roosevelt's own midnight rambles seeking to capture police shirking their duties.[9]

In Chicago, Jane Addams of Hull House was among those concerned about the daughters of the poor, especially because, in her words, "Never before in civilization have such numbers of young girls been suddenly released from the protection of the home and permitted to walk unattended upon the city streets and to work under alien roofs." Jane Addams did not refer to her own life partner, a well-brought-up woman who financially and emotionally supported her in the work of reform, traveled with her, and shared her domicile. Milwaukee's first Socialist mayor, Emil Seidel, elected in 1910 by a city swept up in reform, also tried to curb the brothels by ending the city's red-light district.[10]

In the 1890s, popular journals ran headlines suggesting that a wave of sex hysteria and sex discussion had invaded the country. In 1895, a Milwaukee paper described local "imitators of Dr. Parkhurst," the slumming New York City preacher, who worked to shine a light on gambling and prostitution. Scott Herring, in *Queering the Underworld: Slumming, Literature, and the Undoing of Lesbian and Gay History*, put his own take on the period:

The formula for many of these mysteries was deceptively simple: a narrator inspires curiosity in his middle-class audience, tells it a story of startling revelation about urban classification in cities such as Boston, New York City, Philadelphia, Baltimore, Louisville and New Orleans; and leaves said middle-class audience with what counts for knowledge about a criminal underworld. Like so many discursive inventions of the nineteenth century, slumming literatures were often designed to comprehend and codify social contact across borders segregating social classes, including classes based on ethnicity, race, capital, gender deviance, and, in due time, sexual identity.[11]

Herring believed that the slumming literature failed in its attempts to create a coherent story that correctly captured an emerging homosexual world in tumultuous cities. At that time, most persons having homosexual sex, in all its variety, were not seen or identified by the slumming tour conductors and their reports, and thus the anti-vice effort did not truly capture a new or emerging identity based on sexual orientation. This would also be the case in Wisconsin.

Jessica Pliley, in *Policing Sexuality: The Mann Act and the Making of the FBI*, observed: "Though a thriving gay prostitution scene existed in places like New York in the 1910s and 1920s, most conceptions of prostitution articulated it as a heterosexual script with gendered roles that were always cast the same: prostitute-female, customer-male." Her thesis was that while white slavery might have been first on the list for reformers of the era, other forms of immorality were on the list, too. She argued that the Mann Act of 1910, which made the transport of women across state lines for immoral purposes a federal crime, "was the product of the Progressive Era's faith that thorough investigation reform could lead to solutions for any social ill."[12]

Nevertheless, the investigations of vice and the efforts of more mainline official structures to suppress it do offer glimpses into some early gay life in America and give perspectives on how homosexuals and homosexual activity were viewed. The story is wrapped up in the law and its enforcement—or rather, in many cases, its nonenforcement, which permitted gay people to live in Wisconsin in the early twentieth century. To understand this examination of the underworld of vice in Wisconsin, we

THE DANGERS OF A LARGE CITY

OR

THE SYSTEM OF THE UNDERWORLD

EXPOSING THE
WHITE SLAVE
TRAFFIC

PRICE ONE DOLLAR

This pamphlet reflected the popular turn-of-the-twentieth-century view that large cities bred vice.

begin with the traditional guardians of society's structures: the statutes enacted by the legislature, the courts' comments as they interpreted legal issues, and the forces of law enforcement on the ground.

THE CRIME AGAINST NATURE

The first specific Wisconsin official action acknowledging homosexuality was the 1836 inclusion of a provision in the territorial Statutes of Wisconsin criminalizing its practitioners and imposing a harsh sentence on those convicted: "That every person who shall commit sodomy, or the crime against nature, either with mankind or any beast, shall be punished by imprisonment in the state prison, not more than five years nor less than one year."[13]

When Congress created the new Wisconsin Territory in 1836, it used the laws that were already in force on that land. The lands on both sides of Lake Michigan had been one political entity—the Michigan Territory— before Michigan's statehood. In 1836, that Michigan Territory was divided into two—the Wisconsin Territory and the land that would become the state of Michigan in 1837. The Michigan territorial law on sodomy had provided a penalty of up to three years in prison, and this law was carried over to the new Wisconsin Territory. The three-year Michigan sentences proved not enough for the new Wisconsinites.[14]

Alice Smith, in the first volume of *The History of Wisconsin: From Exploration to Statehood*, observed that most of these territorial laws "were abstracted from those of the state of New York." She also noted that most judicial proceedings in the frontier territory were conducted without a copy of the laws, since all books, including law books, were scarce outside urban centers. Thus, it's possible that the increased statutory sodomy provisions had little effect. The same sodomy provision appears in the "Revised Statutes of the State of Wisconsin," published at Southport (Kenosha) in 1849, a year after the advent of statehood. The territorial legislature originally had passed the wording as part of an "Act to provide for the punishment of offences against chastity, morality, and decency."[15]

The early Wisconsin law regarding sodomy, or "the crime against nature," was based on English law going back to Tudor times. Such hoary tradition was not challenged in the nineteenth century. But in the twenty-first

Wisconsin's territorial capitol building in Belmont. The territorial legislature increased the legal penalty for sodomy. WHI IMAGE ID 102181

century, it has been disputed and even overturned. The Wisconsin gay marriage case of 2014, like many filed across the country at that time, argued that outlawing same-sex marriage in Wisconsin was a form of discrimination not permitted under the modern understanding of US constitutional law. The case was appealed to the federal circuit court in Chicago, where the judge's decision to uphold the district court ruling that struck down Wisconsin's anti–gay marriage law referenced this outdated adherence to English law. The Wisconsin attorney general's argument pleaded the tradition behind heterosexual marriage, but in response, the judge cited famous jurist Oliver Wendell Holmes Jr., who in 1897 thought it "revolting to have no better reason for a rule of law than that so it was laid down in the time of Henry IV." The judge pointedly noted that Henry IV died in 1413.[16]

Nevertheless, the Wisconsin territorial language on sodomy was not updated until 1897, when language was added to the section: "or who shall indecently assault any minor, and take improper liberties with the privates of such minor, either by the use of the hand or mouth, or who shall voluntarily suffer such defilement of his own person by such minor in the same manner." The sponsor of the update was Wisconsin state senator J. Herbert Green, Republican of Milwaukee, whose district also included

Whitefish Bay. In the previous election, he had beaten both Fred Fass, the Democrat-Populist candidate, and Socialist Labor candidate, Jacob Four. The legislative journals do not record any votes against the bill, and Republican governor Edward Scofield signed it into law on April 13, 1887.[17]

The Wisconsin Statutes published in 1898, nearly a decade later, separated the "sodomy" and the "improper liberties" provisions. Yet, the crime of sodomy was still linked with the phrase "the crime against nature." Both crimes remained in Chapter 186 about "offenses against Chastity, Morality, and Decency." Not until 1955 was the old sodomy law replaced by a modern provision against sexual perversion.[18]

The Courts Keep Pace

In addition to statutory law, the courts helped shape the body of laws and law enforcement actions through their rulings. Since the Wisconsin Supreme Court's rulings were published and carried great legal weight, its actions as it struggled to deal with appeals from trial courts provided the most significant record to which prosecutors, defense lawyers, and local judges could refer. Until late in the twentieth century, Wisconsin did not have an appeals court structure, so cases could go straight from trial courts at the municipal and circuit level to the Supreme Court. Various court cases and opinions provide particulars about the sodomy law's operation and its effect on presumed homosexual persons, and they reflect overwhelmingly negative attitudes toward gay men and their activities. Without attempting to retry these matters or to suggest innocence, describing these cases allows us to discuss the attitudes and social structures that homosexuals faced at this time.

In 1905, the first sodomy case reached the Wisconsin Supreme Court on behalf of the plaintiff in error, Arthur L. Means of Milwaukee. While the defendant denied having performed fellatio on a young boy, the conviction rested on the boy's testimony of such an act. The appeal's claim held that while fellatio was still chargeable as an offense, for technical reasons this was outside the common rulings of past courts and the state statute on sodomy. The trial judge had noted "that the crime charged is one of a heinous character, well calculated to arouse the prejudice of mankind." In his reply to the appeal, Attorney General L. M. Sturdevant noted, "It is to be said to the honor of the people of the state of Wisconsin, that the records of this court, so far as we have been able to discover do not show to this date that a single case involving the commission of this vile, abominable crime, has ever been before it heretofore." Echoing the reporting on Wilde's characterization, the Sturdevant brief refers to "this unspeakable offense" and calls the act "nefarious" and "abominable." The attorney general argued that this carnal act was not described in specifics in the statute because it was "condemned by law, human and Divine, and so condemned by human beings that law writers refuse to describe it other than as the 'infamous crime,' and courts and legislatures strive to relieve their volumes of its degrading and disgusting details."[19]

The decision denying appeal in *Means v. State* said, "We are unwilling to soil the pages of our Reports with lengthened discussion of the loathsome subject." The matter was considered so repugnant that Justice Winslow wrote in the opinion, "There is sufficient authority to sustain a conviction in such a case, and, if there were none, we would feel no hesitancy in placing an authority upon the books." While the violation of a minor was indeed a sizable offense, the court's animus appeared larger. The court made a summary ruling, a general point of law in the state, that a "conviction of a criminal offense may be sustained on the uncorroborated testimony of an accomplice." Thus, one party to a homosexual contact, or the aforementioned accomplice, could convict the other. In essence, the court upheld that all homosexual acts including fellatio could be covered by the "crime against nature." And for two-party homosexual contacts, one party could claim innocence and charge criminal activity by the other with some assurance of getting away scot-free.[20]

In 1916, the Wisconsin Supreme Court heard another appeal of a sodomy conviction. W. C. Abaly, an eye, ear, and throat doctor from Madison who also had a part-time office in Richland Center, was charged in Richland County of having performed fellatio on Frank Kilby, a young man. The prosecuting district attorney of Richland County, J. F. Baker, promised not to prosecute Kilby as an accomplice to the deed if he stood by his charge against Abaly. The charge was that the deed occurred on a Saturday night, March 13, 1915, and that afterward Abaly allegedly asked Kilby "if that wasn't better than going out and getting a piece and running the chance of getting a dose of clap or knocking a girl up."[21]

During the trial, the prosecutor hinted that he had found others who had provided statements against Abaly "similar to the one they got from Kilby." The prosecutor then listed several other men and implied that Dr. Abaly offered to send one of them away to school "and pay their expenses to California." Abaly denied this. The defense attorneys objected that the questioning was impeaching the testimony of the defendant. The prosecutor then was permitted to ask if Abaly had improper relations with one of these men, even though that was not the charge of the trial. On appeal, it was alleged that this line of questioning was intended to gain approval from the "passions of the mob, instead of the orderly and civilized conduct of a Court of Justice." In another note seeking fairness, an appeal brief complained that the trial judge "was permitting the jury to ignore evidence bearing upon the commission of the crime, and permitting them to decide the case upon their own prejudices, or those of the salacious mob which crowded the Court Room."[22]

A telling detail in the appeal brief was the complaint that the prosecutor impeached Abaly's character witnesses. These witnesses included another doctor, W. W. Gill of Madison, who had known Abaly for forty years and said his reputation for morality in Madison was good. The Record Transcript shows the following exchange.

Q. How old are you?

A. I am 55 years old.

Q. You say that you are very intimate with this Doctor.

A. I have been for years.

Q. You are not a married man, are you?

A. I am not.

Mr. Baker: That is All.

Another character witness for Abaly was Harry Sauthoff, who happened to be the Dane County district attorney and was also a bachelor at the time. The Richland County prosecutor put the same questions to him. The appeal implied that the value of the character witnesses was undercut by the fact that they were bachelors and that perhaps they were homosexuals, too. The defense at trial had produced six witnesses who said that Dr. Abaly was at his sister's place in Keysville, in another part of Richland County, on March 13, the date of the alleged crime.[23]

In reply to the appeal, Attorney General W. C. Owen noted that in the trial Thomas Shaughnessy, the Madison chief of police, and his captain, Harry Davenport, when asked about Dr. Abaly's reputation for morality, said that it was "bad on this particular case" and "Well, it isn't very good," respectively. This was echoed by P. E. Stark of the Madison Stark Land Company, who, when asked, "What is the doctor's reputation for morality in the city of Madison?" replied, "Not very good on this point." The state's brief concluded, "Juries as a general rule, are reluctant to find a professional man guilty of a crime. They realize as much as any one that this means his ruination professionally, and for that reason we believe the defendant has nothing to complain of in the treatment he has received from the court and the jury."[24]

Reviewing these briefs raises both legal and social issues. Were Dr. Abaly and his character witnesses truly part of a large urban homosexual network operating in Madison, a network that was known to the Madison police at least by reputation? Or was this the case of a rural mob led by the Richland County district attorney out to avenge a violation of a supposed rural innocent by a wealthy urban professional?

In the matter of *Abaly v. State*, the Wisconsin Supreme Court believed the trial judge should not have refused the jury instruction requested by the defense that "the jury should use great caution in weighing the testimony of the complaining witness, that it is ordinarily unsafe to convict upon the uncorroborated testimony of an accomplice." The prosecutor's strategy of asking Abaly about improper relations with other persons at other times was not focused on the initial crime based in the complaint, but seemed meant to determine or prove his status as a homosexually active man. In the Supreme Court's judgment, "This was improper." A further complication was that the trial court admitted testimony from a local doctor as if it was corroborating evidence: "That the reputation of defendant was bad, basing his opinion of defendant's reputation upon stories and talk he had heard after the prosecution of this case had been commenced." Again, this was more a reflection of Abaly's possible homosexual character than evidence of the crime. The fact that the prosecutors were attempting to link several homosexual acts suggests that they intended to prove the existence of some kind of vice network.[25]

Thus, though the defendant possessed a strong alibi, the prosecution was essentially trying to convict Abaly on the basis of his known status as a homosexual. Justice Kerwin, writing for the court, stated, "This evidence was incompetent and should have been excluded." The court decided that "the defendant did not have a fair trial and we are unable to say that justice was done him." It was concluded that he should "have a new trial," which would permit the prosecution to avoid errors. Ultimately, technical procedural issues temporarily overturned a bad sodomy conviction in *Abaly v. State*. However, this case demonstrates that local law enforcement officials felt that proof of homosexual status would be tantamount to corroborating evidence for a sodomy conviction. The Wisconsin Supreme Court would not let them go quite so far astray.[26]

The next sodomy case presented to the Wisconsin Supreme Court was *Garrad v. State*, in 1927. The court still showed a great prudishness in dealing with the topic of homosexual sex, referring to the "revolting nature of the facts." Nevertheless, the judges tucked up their robes and addressed the issue, saying,

> We are at a loss to see what a defendant who has been fined but $100 and costs, an amount so trifling in comparison with the nastiness of the conduct shown by uncontradicted evidence, or what his counsel either can gain in making such shame a public and permanent record by this review. Having so elected, however, to pursue his constitutional right to bring it here, whatsoever be the motives, we have no election but to follow our constitutional duty and pass upon the questions presented.[27]

In this Milwaukee case, a man was accused of having requested that two girls over age twenty-one "permit him to suck their private parts." The judge noted, "Sodomy, the crime against nature, had from earliest times been considered as involving the use of the male organ of generation." The court observed that this understanding of the sodomy law as

Operating out of their downtown headquarters (the building at right), the Milwaukee police made multiple arrests for sodomy and other moral offenses each year during the early 1900s.

requiring penetration by the male member was supported by both common law usage and the statutory language in the state. It concluded, "We are therefore constrained to hold that under the evidence the defendant cannot be convicted of the offense charged in the information." Here, again, local law enforcement understood sodomy to include actions of sexual misconduct outside normative heterosexual intercourse, though in this case it still involved heterosexual activity. Who knows how broadly the members of the court might have wished to apply the sodomy law had they not felt constrained?[28]

The Roaring Twenties continued with a 1928 case, *Verhaalen v. State*, on appeal from a sodomy conviction in Waukesha County. As in the Means case of 1905, the claimed trial error was conviction upon only the uncorroborated evidence of the other party to the sodomy. Even the defense attorney on appeal, however, said that the offense was "scandalous" and "revolting." Despite the earlier testimony of friends and neighbors as to the good character of the defendant, the Wisconsin Supreme Court deferred to the trial court. Justice Crownhart wrote, "The crime itself is so repulsive and detestable that one is loath to believe in defendant's guilt, yet we must recognize the offense existed in ancient times, and recent legislation broadening the common-law definition indicates that modern culture has not succeeded in abolishing the crime. Prosecuting officers and criminal courts recognize it as too prevalent to be ignored." The writ of error was denied, and the man in *Verhaalen v. State* remained in prison. But the justices had recognized, in their use of the phrase "too prevalent," that homosexuality was apparently widespread in the state and law enforcement officials had to continue to grapple with the fact of its existence.[29]

The next sodomy case came to the Wisconsin Supreme Court in 1935, also from Waukesha County. William Gutenkunst was a successful forty-two-year-old Milwaukee industrialist. He was president of the Milwaukee Hay Tool Company and the Malleable and Grey Iron Company and served on the board of directors of a bank and on boards of other companies. He had never been married and was developing a lake resort on Pewaukee Lake at Oakton. The trial was held in the municipal court of the Western District of Waukesha County. Gutenkunst had been charged on five counts: sodomy with three individuals on separate occasions over several years, and two counts of showing obscene pictures to multiple young men and thereby contributing to the delinquency of minors. The pictures were supposedly of naked men, some of them of Gutenkunst's younger associates and some from physical culture (health and strength training) publications. The young men involved in the charges as victims were all in their very late teens or early twenties. District Attorney Scott Lowry grouped all the charges in the indictment and said they were "against the peace and dignity of the state of Wisconsin."[30]

Waukesha prosecutor Lowry seemed to have a clear strategy in combining the charges to show Gutenkunst was a homosexually active man—if the actual evidence was weak on one count of sodomy, it would be buttressed by the corroboration of other homosexual acts. The defense attorneys objected strenuously, pointing out that the indictment "involves separate crimes" performed on "separate parties" at "separate dates." Lowry's response was, "It involves a series of acts committed in the course of one type of conduct, and is all part together." He claimed, "All evidence may be considered by the jury in reference to these counts."[31]

These prosecution statements were only the beginning. In addressing the jury, the prosecution said that its true target was "this perverted mind, this degraded sense of righteousness, who took them in and forced

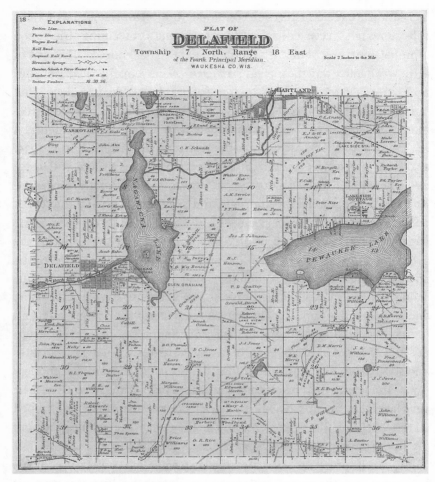

In a 1935 Wisconsin Supreme Court case, Waukesha's district attorney claimed there was a "school for sodomists" at Pewaukee Lake. WHI IMAGE ID 84424

it upon these boys" at what was termed Gutenkunst's "school of sodomists out there at Oakton." Multiple times the prosecutor referenced "this false academy . . . this training school, to prepare young men to satisfy his own unnatural perverted lust." Lowry claimed that Gutenkunst, "this man,— unmarried man, no other way to satisfy his perverted passions except a young boy,—showed him pictures to make him go down on him, or to commit the act of sodomy." Gutenkunst was convicted by a jury trial of only two counts, including one of sodomy, and sentenced to one to five years in Waupun Prison. The length of the sentence was unchanged from that penalty established during Wisconsin's territorial days almost one hundred years earlier.[32]

The plaintiff's brief in the Wisconsin Supreme Court appeal in *Gutenkunst v. State* contended that the grouping of the charges by the prosecution, and as permitted by the trial judge, was a reversible error and had the effect of attacking Gutenkunst's reputation by painting a picture of him as an active homosexual even if the evidence on each count might not be sufficient to convict. The appeal argued, "For the human mind to work so precisely as to consider five counts of the information involving three different witnesses, three different state of facts, and only consider the evidence that applied to each particular [statements] of facts is humanly impossible." The state's response brief said, "It is apparent from the testimony and the statement of facts as made in this brief that the defendant exercised a conscious plan of luring young men and boys to his country home at the Oakton Hotel in the town of Delafield." Here, again, the mere assertion of homosocial association impugned character.[33]

There were many technical legal issues for the court to sift through in this case, but the majority upheld the convictions, 4–3. Justice Fairchild wrote for the majority, "Although the offenses in the different counts were separate and distinct, they were not so different in character as to require separate treatment." And further, "The acts were of similar class involving similar characteristics." Thus, for the court majority the man's status as a homosexual also appeared to be a criminal matter. Fairchild added, "There was ample evidence of defendant's association with boys about eighteen years of age, and suggesting a disposition to indulge in the practice complained of." And since minors were involved, though they were below a statutory age of twenty-one and not prepubescent, Fairchild noted, "In cases of this nature involving young persons, more frequently perhaps than in any other class of crimes, the necessity for extreme caution will be present."[34]

A dissent by Justice Nelson, with two other judges concurring, stated that despite feeling that "abhorrent charges" were involved, "the defendant, in my opinion, was unquestionably embarrassed in his defense and therefore prejudiced." The dissent implies that the combining of the charges showed the man's inclinations or orientation rather than focusing on the specific criminal actions that were subject to prosecution. Overall, in this matter the divided opinion supported the local prosecutor and the trial judge in combining the multiple counts and supported the use of the phrase "school of sodomy" to paint the man as guilty of criminal acts of sodomy due to his presumed homosexual status. Perhaps the fact that a minority of justices rejected this approach represents a small shift in public opinion; however, the court still felt compelled to view homosexuality as "abhorrent."[35]

CHICAGO'S TEMPLATE

One of the ground-breaking reports on sexual vice, *The Social Evil in Chicago: A Study of Existing Conditions with Recommendations by the Vice Commission of Chicago*, was undertaken in Wisconsin's neighboring metropolis in 1910. Like Milwaukee in 1908, Chicago had been proclaimed one of the eight "homosexual capitals" of America. Many of these "capitals," including Milwaukee, had large German American populations. Though Milwaukee was then only one-sixth the size of Chicago, we can presume that it had some of the same features of a Midwestern gay sexual underworld found in Chicago. The Chicago study itself would have an impact on Wisconsin.[36]

The title page proclaimed the Vice Commission of Chicago referenced in its title to be "a municipal body appointed by the mayor and city council." The effort to conduct the study grew from a January 1910 meeting, at the Central YMCA, of clergy from six hundred congregations representing the Federated Protestant Churches. Mayor Fred A. Busse, while acknowledging that efforts had been made to localize vice in certain districts, called the issue a "most perplexing question" and suggested that "investigation will probably discover many other attempts at a solution of these questions." He hoped the commission would weigh the question, "What treatment of vice as a disease of society, is best for all concerned?" He appointed Walter T. Sumner, who had been instrumental in shutting down Chicago's First Ward Ball several years earlier, as chairman of the body. The group launched "a program of study and investigation" that resulted in a four-hundred-page report published in 1911 and citing ninety-eight conferences with philanthropic, civic, social and reform, and business organizations. The commission also interviewed police at several levels, and keepers and "inmates" of houses of prostitution.[37]

Though the commission formed with a focus on heterosexual prosti-

VICE IN WISCONSIN

Wisconsin's anti-vice effort was led by state senator Howard Teasdale, Republican of Sparta. After earning his law degree from the University of Wisconsin in 1882, he established a personal law practice and managed the family farm. In 1905, Governor Bob La Follette appointed Teasdale Monroe County district attorney. Teasdale continued to correspond with La Follette over the years, voting with the Progressive wing of the Republican Party on social legislation and favoring women's suffrage. One correspondent complained to Teasdale that the investigation he was conducting into female prostitution, then referred to as the white slave trade, was "one of the humbug ideas of what is called Progressive politics." A Methodist, Teasdale was described as "a lifelong enemy of Demon Rum." The senator had such a strong interest in the anti-vice committee, and as chairman was its most active member, that the press referred to the anti-vice group as the Teasdale Committee.[43]

The Chicago template and other urban studies were much on Teasdale's mind in 1913. In his introduction to *Report and Recommendations of the Wisconsin Vice Committee*, published in 1914, Teasdale noted, "Immediately upon its organization, the chairman and secretary of the committee went to Chicago to ascertain how other like commissions had pursued their tasks." Assistance for the committee's work was obtained from the American Vigilance Society. Encouragement was also received from B. S. Steadwell of La Crosse, who served as president of the

Senator Howard Teasdale made the Wisconsin anti-vice campaign of the early 1900s his personal crusade. His investigations turned up male homosexual prostitution in Milwaukee, which was named one of eight US "homosexual capitals" in 1908. WHI IMAGE ID 141104

World Purity Federation and published its official organ, *The Light*, from the same city. Steadwell had previously served on the Wisconsin State Central Committee for the Prohibition Party. Investigations from New York City and Philadelphia were also mentioned in the Wisconsin report, though it was believed that a statewide task was more difficult than one focused on a particular community. Jessica R. Pliley, in *Policing Sexuality*, listed some forty-three vice investigations across the country. The Philadelphia Vice Commission, which was quoted in the Wisconsin document at some points, also had uncovered sexual perversion in their investigations: "Numbers of boys with kneepants are commercializing themselves openly on our streets for the practice of perversion." A twenty-one-year-old told the Philly commission, "I notice that there are a lot of 'faries' (sexual perverts) hanging around the tenderloin. They usually go after the messenger [boys] first." The baths were likewise cited as places for homosexual perversion in the City of Brotherly Love.[44]

Other members of Wisconsin's six-man anti-vice committee were Teasdale's fellow Republicans Senator Robert W. Monk of Neillsville in Clark County, Senator Victor Linley of Superior, and Assemblyman George Bingham of Friendship, in Adams County. The lone Democrat was Assemblyman James Dolan of Platteville in Grant County. The Milwaukee socialist member was Assemblyman Carl Minkley of the Wisconsin Social-Democratic Party. Four of the members were from small towns: Sparta's population in 1910 was 3,973, Neillsville's 1,957, Friendship's 276, and Platteville's 4,452. Several legislators had faced Prohibition Party candidates in their last elections. The committee was named the Legislative Committee to Investigate the White Slave Traffic and Kindred Subjects. Some thirteen votes in the Assembly were cast against the bill creating the committee, mainly from the minority Democrats representing city districts near Lake Michigan. The committee's field investigations revealed what its vice efforts had uncovered about homosexuals. But in their published report and recommendations, they chose to remain silent about the discoveries and about general attitudes in the state toward enforcement of the public morals laws on homosexuals.[45]

As chairman of the committee, Teasdale used his judgment to focus its work on the investigations into female prostitution and saloon violations and the link between them. Under the heading of "kindred topics" in the legislation creating the committee was evidence about the sale of "French safes" (condoms), female investigators who tried to get doctors to provide abortions or to medically induce miscarriages, drug use by "hop fiends" (opium users), sales of "postals" (nude postcards of women and men), slot machines, race mixing in houses of prostitution, and even tango dancing. But Teasdale's focus on drink and female prostitution meant that not much on these kindred topics made it into the report he authored.[46]

The saloons and alcohol were particular targets for Teasdale, as reported by Paul Hass in his article "Sin in Wisconsin: The Teasdale Vice Committee of 1913": "The reports of the investigators indicate that in each city the most extensively used institution for the fostering of prostitution is the saloon." And in these houses of ill fame, Hass continues, "One madam examined by the committee acknowledged that when the sale of liquor was prohibited in her resort her custom fell off fully one-half. The physiological and psychological connection between intoxication and unnatural sexual impulses forms the groundwork for this conclusion." In another part of the report, the committee found that "the chief direct cause of the downfall of women and girls is the close connection between alcoholic drink and commercialized vice."[47]

One area of comment in the committee report was the "Ignorance of Sexual Phenomena," which was related to parenting. "Until very recently," the committee observed, "the majority of parents have felt that no definite information regarding sexual matters need be given to either boys or girls. . . . It was formerly believed that to say, 'Thou shalt not,' was sufficient, leaving the reasons and causes and results in the dark." The report stated that "best authorities" supported instruction and warning. Further to this point, the document stated:

> Undoubtedly the fact that a very large number of the men of every community have been so unfortunate as to develop an unnatural sexual desire is a great contributor to the maintenance and growth of prostitution. There are various ways in which this perverted sex impulse has been developed and accentuated. In most cases beginnings can probably be traced back to early training and various forms of parental neglect and ignorance of the sexual phenomena of children.

To counter early masturbation, the committee recommended "strenuous and exciting out-of-door sports." The report also deplored the double standard for men and women, resulting in their belief that "the present day demands chastity of men equal to that demanded of women."[48]

In conclusion, the 1914 *Report and Recommendations of Wisconsin Vice Committee* found "that there is no more demoralizing influence in the state of Wisconsin than prostitution with its attendant evils. . . . Investigation shows that in some cities of the state, many open and recognized houses of prostitution exist." In the past, some cities had segregated districts, La Crosse's area along the river being among the notorious. The report continued, "In addition to the above the committee's investigators found little difficulty in securing positive evidence of the existence of many other places where immoral practices were openly solicited and carried on, such as parlor houses, assignation houses, road houses, immoral hotels, rooming and lodging houses, cafes, chop suey restaurants, saloons with bedroom connections, and dance halls." This was quite a geography of vice in Wisconsin. The report provided a list of such places in seventeen selected cities; Milwaukee topped the list with 269 places, followed by La Crosse with 51 and Madison with 21. No other city had more than twenty. At the bottom of the list were Hartford, Waupaca, and Shawano, with two each.[49]

The Wisconsin document remained silent about homosexual perversion except to mention the statute on sodomy among the criminal laws. This is despite the fact that the Chicago vice report had demonstrated a way to talk about homosexuality, and police reports of the day showed arrests for sodomy in several Wisconsin cities. The committee's investigators did find some perversion, and in one of Teasdale's evidence-gathering forays to Milwaukee, a doctor discussing insanity from syphilis told him about a young male prostitute who had contracted a venereal disease from sodomy. The doctor reported that "some man gave [the prostitute] $1.00 to have connection with him, through the anus, and he was very seriously afflicted with the disease." In another instance, a committee investigator described a subject as a "pervert." Another male investigator approaching a different doctor for information on abortion practices wrote that the doctor described the woman in trouble as "monkeying" with boys, then, "He said: 'You are about thirty years old, and I bet you like boys too!' and a lot of other stuff that showed him to be a beast unfit to practice medicine, much less attend a young woman." Teasdale, again conducting his own investigations, was told by a private detective of a druggist and saloon keeper running a vice den in Eau Claire who was referred to as "a cocksucker." In his correspondence, Teasdale reported that his Milwaukee investigators looked into the issue of homosexual perversion, as the Philadelphia vice report had referenced. But, again, no evidence of homosexuality was presented to the public in Wisconsin. Though plenty of documentation exists to prove that the topic of homosexuality came up during the committee's investigations, the issue does not appear in the final report. This exclusion of homosexuality is an early example of cultural suppression.[50]

A particular focus for the Teasdale Committee in its effort against commercialized vice was the lax enforcement of the laws. It praised the work of private organizations like the Milwaukee Society for the Suppression of Commercialized Vice, which exposed vice that official law enforcement was ignoring. Milwaukee's use of private organizations to encourage sexual repression was a pattern that would be repeated in the city in the 1940s. To gauge levels of enforcement, the committee sent a questionnaire to the seventy-one district attorneys in the state, and sixty-three answered. The prosecutors reported knowledge of thirty-five houses of ill repute with eighty-six "inmates." Clearly, the prosecutors were missing something, because the committee had discovered 350 houses with more than a thousand "inmates." Those enforcing the law claimed to know about fewer than 10 percent of the visible sex workers discovered by the committee. Eight district attorneys flatly stated that public sentiment in their counties was opposed to enforcing the moral laws of the state, and eighteen thought the age of consent should remain at fourteen. Thirty-four reported that saloons, a favorite place for both the Irish and Germans after church services, were permitted to remain open on Sundays, and nine reported that saloons were permitted to remain open on election days. Twelve district attorneys said they required a written complaint before they would act to enforce any morality laws.[51]

District attorneys and police officers stated many reasons for their failure to enforce the morality laws with greater vigor. The district attorney of La Crosse was credited with the statement, "I do not consider that I am a sleuth as well as a prosecuting attorney." The sheriff of Sheboygan County stated, "I have had information that there were three houses of prostitution running in this city. There have been no complaints and [those enterprises] are not objectionable here." One of his concerns was the large number of single foreign men in the city. The sheriff of Marinette County felt that "there are certain things that I would not enforce here because the people of the community do not want them enforced." He knew the people of the town wanted the saloons open on Sunday. With regard to houses of prostitution, the mayor of Green Bay thought it "best for the morals of the people that they run, and I do not think it is violating my oath of office." Regarding the red-light district of Ashland, the mayor said, "It would take me and the chief of police fifteen minutes to close that district if I said so." But obviously he had not said so.[52]

To remedy lax enforcement, the committee called for morals courts and a state police force. Additionally, the committee considered a less than unanimous jury verdict of five-sixths sufficient to convict. It also called for local communities, cities, and towns to "organize private associations to assist officers in the enforcement of such laws." Today, we do not think of such vigilante justice as an instrument of the reforms of the Progressive Era.[53]

Socialist congressman Victor Berger's statement at the Milwaukee hearing of the Teasdale Committee included in the 1914 report focused on the economic aspects of prostitution. Berger traced the origins of prostitution in two ways, first to the ancient religious history of temple prostitution, and second to the days when men bought their wives. Never missing a chance to highlight class inequities, he observed, "Very few daughters of rich men are to be found in the house of prostitution." Declining to support open prostitution, he proclaimed, "It is a curse. I am in favor of doing all you can to wipe it out by making women economically independent, economically free. . . . You can't do it just by having the chief of police club the poor prostitutes." Berger's view was that under the capitalistic system, "We are more careful how we mate our horses, and dogs, and cattle, and even our swine, than we are in the mating of our boys and girls." His views reflected the Wisconsin Social-Democratic platform of 1912, which said, "We recognize that capitalism is the cause of white slavery and prostitution. The only complete remedy, therefore, is to abolish the capitalist system."[54]

This socialist economic argument underemphasized any impulse of sexual desire that might lead some to wish for a geography of places where either heterosexual or even homosexual "immoral" activities might be encouraged. Indeed, any assessment about the "sons of the poor" is totally absent from the reformers' comments. Certainly, it was assumed that men could find honest occupations, and therefore male sex workers must be perverted rather than driven to prostitution by economic forces as women were believed to be.

Teasdale, being a realist, did partially acknowledge that sexual impulse might play a part in what reformers saw as vice. He wrote to one correspondent, "The private acts, of course we can do little with. . . . It is more in the line of commercialized vice we have to work." In many of his committee's investigators' reports, women were asked whether they wanted to leave the life of prostitution. Frequently the investigators wrote down, "Has no desire to leave this life." Whether this was due to economics or sexuality, the investigators did not record.[55]

One of Teasdale's critics, the mayor of Algoma, wrote the senator about the investigation in 1913: "It is the 'stop thief' 'Holier than thou' order or manner of detracting [sic] the attention of fanatics and the press to something that cannot be prevented by investigation or law." An attorney from Wausau was also critical: "That vice exists in every community in the state is well known, and it does not need to be exploited by your committee." The attorney also thought recent arrivals to America were part of the cause, since "during the last twenty-five years, this immigration has come largely from southern Europe and the Slavic nations of Eastern Europe—largely superstitious and ignorant, largely uncivilized, and very largely immoral." One female critic from Milwaukee wrote to ask the committee to "investigate the part of both sexes." She asked, "Don't you think you have gone far enough in ascertaining why women are vicious?" Some in the press questioned whether hearsay evidence of the investigators was justified. An Eau Claire paper took aim at the "slippery and underhanded method of some sleuths in procuring evidence."[56]

Ultimately, the critics of the Wisconsin vice investigation saw the reformers as fanatics about something basic to human nature and believed their efforts to be one-sided in focusing on women rather than men. Some questioned the tactic of using private investigations altogether.

PROGRESSIVE SOCIOLOGY

Ten pages of the Wisconsin Vice Committee's report were devoted to the testimony of Professor E. A. Ross of the University of Wisconsin. Teasdale believed that Ross "so fully covers the entire problem with which we are directed to deal that we feel justified in publishing it in full." Ross had joined the Madison faculty in 1906 as the university's first full professor of sociology, with criminology as one of his subjects. He was part of the liberal faculty, and his 1906 book *Sin and Society* included an introductory letter of praise from President Theodore Roosevelt, a leader of the national progressive Republicans. Ross opened the book with a chapter on the "New Varieties of Sin," in which he castigated the purveyors of polluted water, the railroad corporations that annually injured one out of every twenty-six workers, and the owners of rotting tenement houses, and he stated flatly that factory labor of children was slavery. His presence on campus was a concern to the conservative regents, and things were not helped in 1910 when he escorted the radical Emma Goldman around Bascom Hill. Although he said he disagreed with anarchism, he defended her right to speak on campus. As an anarchist, Goldman had been one of the defenders of Oscar Wilde.[57]

Ross had what we might see as his own contradictions, supporting both Prohibition and, later, the recognition of the Union of Soviet Socialist Republics. A fan of the New Deal, he became national chairman of the American Civil Liberties Union in the 1940s. His biographer wrote, "No sociologist better articulated the hopes and fears of the Progressive generation." Ross's prominent testimony in the committee's report, based on a more secular social moralism, dovetailed nicely with Teasdale's own progressive view of anti-vice work.[58]

About Madison, Ross averred, "I have been here eight years, but I have not heard anything at all of there being any commercialized prostitution in this town." Clearly the committee's investigators and the Madison police, as discussed in the section that follows, were better on-the-ground observers than the social scientist. Ross pleased Teasdale by stating that, until four years previously, he had supported segregating vice districts, but no longer did so: "My present position is to hit the thing wherever you see it." In discussing the economics of prostitution, Ross believed married women should continue to work so they could get "a square deal

UW Sociology professor E. A. Ross, who
testified before the Teasdale Committee.
UNIVERSITY OF WISCONSIN—MADISON ARCHIVES
IMAGE S10904

in the matrimonial relations."
As a sociologist, he noted, "The
demand for the work of women
is increasing faster than the supply." He also agreed with Teasdale that women employed as
domestic workers had higher
rates of out-of-wedlock preg-
nancy (60 percent) than factory
workers (10 percent) because
"in domestic service, the girl
is meeting temptation single
handed." Thus Ross encouraged
domestics to join clubs and the
YWCA. Ross also believed in the
teaching of sex hygiene to both
boys and girls.[59]

Ross did not touch on homosexuality in his testimony, perhaps because Teasdale's focus
and questions did not raise the issue. However, it is likely that he was then
aware of homosexual activity as a component of vice. In the next decade, in
1922, he published *The Social Trend*, in which he reprised some of the vice
concepts he shared with Teasdale. Under a section titled "Folk Depletion
and Rural Decline," one of Ross's informants complained, "Only the 'sissy'
type of young man offered himself for social [i.e. public] service." Another
informant reported, "The moral conditions among our country boys and
girls are worse than in the lowest tenement-house in New York. . . . What
is more natural than that the boys should get together in the barn and
while away the long winter evenings talking obscenity, telling filthy stories, recounting sex exploits, encouraging one another in vileness, perhaps
indulging in unnatural practices."[60]

In this later period, Ross expressed his belief that homosexuality was
"unnatural," non-normative, and beyond the bounds of social morality. In
The Social Trend, he maintained many of these ideas, which aligned with
his earlier views presented to Teasdale. Ross's concept of the structure of

social morality, which he italicized in his book, included *"the presence of a certain small minority who set strict standards of private conduct . . . and persuade the majority that looser standards and practices are 'low.'"* This aptly described the general view of the anti-vice crusaders and regulators, who saw themselves as the small number of persons setting the strict standards of how to define normative sex behavior. For all of them, homosexuality in Wisconsin was clearly outside the norm.[61]

EARLY LAW ENFORCEMENT

In Wisconsin, as in most states, law enforcement was, and remains today, a job for local government. As keepers of public order, the Madison and Milwaukee police had been charged with enforcement of all the criminal laws, especially the vice laws. A review of annual reports filed by the Madison and Milwaukee chiefs of police for the early twentieth century reveals some facts about gay and lesbian life, though reports for all years in both cities were not available. The fact that sodomy crimes were frequently reported in Madison and Milwaukee police statistics shows that homosexual activity was present. Since it is unlikely that most acts were observed and reported, those that were must represent only a tiny fraction of ongoing gay life.[62]

The reports show that law enforcement was exercising vigilance, though both reporting and enforcement levels may be influenced by factors not in the reports. From a different source, to be discussed shortly, more particulars about Wisconsin law enforcement in the 1930s will be illuminated. These early police reports occasionally included some other items of interest in their narratives. By the mid-1930s, under pressure from the FBI to standardize crime reporting, most of the local character in the reports disappeared, and sodomy offenses were subsumed into published statistics on undifferentiated sex crimes.[63]

In the first ten years of the twentieth century Madison had two arrests for "an unnatural crime," presumably sodomy, and both perpetrators were sent to Waupun for between one and two years. One was described as a "colored" individual. The Madison police chief's reports often list sodomy outside the statistical section under the heading "important crimes." The "important crimes" included murder, major theft, and keeping a house of ill fame (prostitution), the crime that eluded Professor Ross. Such crimes were just part of the morality offenses of the day. In fact, heterosexuals were arrested for non-normative sexual behavior far more often than homosexuals during the purity efforts of this era. In the following year, police chief H. C. Baker listed in the report among his concerns the large conventions and frequent railroad construction crews that brought un-attached males to town in large numbers. In this decade, the leading oc-cupation among the individuals being arrested for all offenses was listed as laborer.[64]

The Milwaukee reports for the decade of the 1910s show more sod-omy arrests, as would be expected for a larger city and certainly for one of the "homosexual capitals" of America. The average number of arrests per year was eight, with the highest (seventeen) occurring in 1919 after the end of World War I. Starting in 1917, there was also a new category of

Homosexuals who ended up in Waupun, the Wis-consin State Penitentiary, were usually convicted at bench trials with no de-fense attorney and before only a judge.

sodomy attempts, with an average of three occurring over the next four years in addition to the actual sodomy charges. The three reports for the end of the 1920s show no sodomy arrests but many more arrests for lewd and lascivious behavior, which probably included but was not exclusive to homosexual acts.[65]

For this period, the Milwaukee arrests are overwhelmingly white, male, and native born. But a case in 1914 involved a cross-dressing woman who had passed as a man and was married to another woman. Somewhat sensationalized as the "Girl-Man," the person claiming to be Ralph Kerwineo had an African American father and a Potawatomi mother. After her arrest, it was discovered that her given name was Cora Anderson; she had a trial and was given a suspended sentence. Afterward, she remarked, "My heart and soul are more those of man than a woman." In general, the public's interest in the case seemed to be focused more on the masquerade than on any identity issues. Milwaukee's 1928 police report included a brief paragraph on vice but no mention of homosexuality. Thus, as in Wisconsin's capital city, law enforcement officials were aware of sodomy, but paid much more attention to heterosexual misbehavior.[66]

The 1921 Madison report lists two arrests for sodomy, and the list of important crimes shows that one perpetrator was sent to Waupun for three and a half years. In the same year, there were ten arrests for adultery, ten for fornication, and seven for keeping a house of ill fame; also arrested were four "inmates of disorderly houses." In this period, Thomas Shaughnessy served as Madison's police chief. In the preceding year, he had reported "938 arrests made of which 671 were taken to court and 267 released being harmless drunks, tramps and persons arrested for suspicion and who were ordered to leave the city at once." In 1924, three arrests for sodomy appear in the tables, none of which showed in the list of important crimes. By 1926, two more sodomy cases appear—one perpetrator was sentenced to six months in the county jail and the other to the Mendota Hospital for the Insane. The pattern repeats here: heterosexual misconduct predominates, but homosexuals are included in the moral dragnet.[67]

The 1930s saw a resurgence in sodomy charges in Milwaukee. Fifteen cases in 1930 included one female and two attempts by males. The next year, 1931, brought nineteen sodomy cases, followed by ten each for 1932 and 1933. By 1934 the cases were presumably included in the broader listing

Here's a Girl Who Lived Ten Years Dressed as a Boy

Cora Anderson was arrested in 1914 for dressing and presenting herself as a man.
MILWAUKEE SENTINEL, MAY 4, 1914

of sex offenses. One feature of Milwaukee's law enforcement was that in 1937 the policing of parks was placed under the jurisdiction of the police department, perhaps indicating that vice activity was known to occur in leafy bowers.[68]

Madison also adopted the catch-all category of sex offenses for its reports, though it still separately listed some major cases related to homosexuality. In 1934, the Madison report lists three sodomy cases, and two new cases are listed in the 1935 report. The perpetrators in the 1935 cases, though the crimes were listed under important cases, were fined $100 and costs or ninety days in jail. This appears to show some softening of attitudes. All of these sodomy cases, where detail was provided, involve males. In 1939, Chief William H. McCormick made reference to one case involving lesbians out of nearly 10,000 women's cases: "The Women's Bureau made a total of 9,927 contacts. . . . Some of the cases might be classed as unusual. A case involving two homosexuals was cleared by sending one to a sanatorium and the other to her home in another city in this state." This reflects a relatively mild disposition compared to the several women convicted of adultery in 1939: they were sentenced to one year at the Taycheedah Correctional Institution, a prison for women. What the sanatorium confinement meant is unclear, however.[69]

With the onset of World War II, new themes appeared in the police reports. For 1942, during the first full year of US participation in the war, Madison police chief McCormick noted in his introductory letter that the "influx of civilian and military personnel" meant that "we have had to detail plain clothes men to special duty in hotels, taverns, and around town in general in an attempt to keep down vice and immoral practices." The report showed that total sex offenses increased from twenty in 1941 to thirty-four in 1942. Thus, the work of keeping immoral practices in check had increased, and among these practices was likely homosexual activity. Information other than the police reports, as discussed later, shows that known homosexuals were associated with the military base at Truax Field.[70]

The Madison important cases listed two sodomy arrests in 1943 and one in 1944, each resulting in sentences between one and five years. In 1945, two more cases were on the list. One resulted in the individual (presumably a soldier) being referred to the Canadian authorities. The other individual was charged with sodomy and assault with intent to do great bodily harm, resulting in one to three years at the Green Bay Reformatory. Serious jail time was still being given in the important sodomy cases. A 1946 important sodomy case resulted in a "colored" individual being sent to Waupun for one to three years. Reported that same year were two other important cases of male individuals charged with taking indecent liberties with a minor boy. One resulted in a sentence of thirty days to six months in the county jail, and the other person was fined $100 and given the choice of paying the costs or serving thirty days in jail. Prior cases of indecent liberties had not specified gender, so the description of the minor boy was presumably needed for the unusual circumstance. After the war, in the 1950s, the Madison police began a summer parks patrol. In 1962 the reports noted, "We learned that the bulk of the situations that needed police attention involved those of immoral activity, unauthorized ball playing in the beach area, littering of parks and beaches, and beer drinking particularly by minors." In the summer of 1964, the budget-conscious council cut funds for parks patrol. As a result, the 1964 police report acts of immorality increased, but these conditions soon brought funds back and the parks patrol was reactivated in July 1964.[71]

Law enforcement in Milwaukee as shown from the reports during the war is different. The 1943 report observes, "Normally, a large number of crimes are committed by male adults between the ages of 18 and 26. Now, however, many in this age group are in the Armed Services and the balance are working long hours and earning good wages. To this we may attribute the decrease in criminal arrests in this age group."[72]

FROM CRIME TO SCIENCE

Professor John L. Gillin of the University of Wisconsin conducted one of the earliest academic studies in Wisconsin on homosexuals. When Gillin died in 1958, UW president Conrad Elvehjem characterized him as an "eminent criminologist." Born in 1871 in Hudson, Iowa, Gillin obtained bachelor's degrees from Upper Iowa University and Grinnell College. At Grinnell, he studied under E. A. Ross, who, after his own move to the University at Madison, would later help bring Gillin there as well.[73]

In 1904, while pursuing his graduate work, Gillin obtained a third bachelor's degree, in divinity, from Union Theological Seminary of New

York and was ordained a clergyman in the Church of the Brethren. Meanwhile, in 1897, he had married. Though attracted to Christian ministry, Gillin maintained his parallel interest in sociology, attaining a doctorate in 1906 from Columbia University. He taught sociology at Ashland College in Ohio and the University of Iowa before being called to the University of Wisconsin in 1912, where he would teach until his retirement in 1942. During World War I, he was on leave in Chicago and Washington, DC, working for the Red Cross in education. He served on the board of directors of the National Conference of Social Workers in the 1920s and was president of the American Sociological Society in 1926–1927. Gillin was a frequent contributor to the *Journal of the American Institute of Criminal Law and Criminology*. These accomplishments made him well known in his field.[74]

In the tradition of the Wisconsin Idea, which holds that the boundaries of the university are the boundaries of the state, Gillin's public service included stints on the Madison Police and Fire Commission, the Wisconsin Parole Board from 1935 to 1939 as an appointee of Governor Philip La Follette, and as a regional member on the National War Labor Board in 1943. He continued as an active emeritus professor until his death in 1958. A 1952 feature story from the University of Wisconsin News Service described him at age eighty-one as an "activegenerarian," working on his next book about theories of personal and social disorganization. Gillin had many ideas to improve criminal law and punishment in Wisconsin. He favored elastic parole and probation laws, argued for extending the prison forest camp system, and even supported lowering the legal age of consent for girls from eighteen back to sixteen because the law had been used as "an instrument of blackmail and revenge."[75]

Midway through his active academic career, Gillin conceived of a research project, which was touted as "A Pioneer Study of the Role of Inheritance and Environment in Producing Criminality." The University of Wisconsin Press published the book, titled *The Wisconsin Prisoner: Studies in Crimogenesis*, in 1946, though most of the research had been done in the 1930s. The publication may have been delayed by wartime shortages, as the rationing of wood pulp and paper cut the supplies available to publishers, forcing them to put off the release of many books during the war.[76]

In the book's introduction, Gillin notes his belief that criminology "had too long been descriptive rather than scientific." He noted favorably that

UW Sociology professor John Gillin studied incarcerated "sodomists" at Waupun in the 1930s. UNIVERSITY OF WISCONSIN–MADISON ARCHIVES IMAGE S04529

the fields of natural sciences "had made progress by applying the techniques of experiment, careful observation, and measurement." He believed in applying the statistical method to human problems. For his study, Gillin conceived of the idea of asking inmates of the state prison in Waupun to write "autobiographies that would supplement the information to be derived from interviews and the prison records." He successfully obtained funds for several years in the 1930s from the Research Committee of the University of Wisconsin to employ graduate students as research assistants. A unique part of the research included interviewing brothers of the prisoners who had been studied in Waupun, who were then viewed as a "control group with which to compare prison inmates." After acknowledging that other factors had not been studied, the book noted that there was no "attempt to answer the question whether their biological constitutions differed." Selected parts of the research were published as articles during the 1930s.[77]

As a careful scientist, Gillin noted that his own study was not one of the Wisconsin criminal but rather an examination of the prisoner in the state prison, or as might be said again, the one unlucky enough to be caught. The study encompassed 486 subjects, or slightly more than a fourth of the entire prison population of 1,700 inmates who were either in the prison at Waupun or sentenced to the Central State Hospital at Waupun for the criminally insane. The prisoners were classed primarily as murderers, sex offenders, or property offenders. All the sex offenders in the population who were sodomists were studied. The book presented the results in two parts, the statistical analysis and the case histories.[78]

The book, along with the research notes preserved at the Wisconsin

Historical Society, make important contributions to a modern understanding of gay history in Wisconsin. Notably, the book includes an academic essay authored by Gillin that surveys the literature on homosexuality and its causes, as well as Gillin's portraits of those convicted of sodomy. Most importantly, the research notes for the book offer an even more detailed picture of how the police and courts interacted with male homosexuals in Wisconsin over a period of years in the 1930s and how homosexuals lived their lives. The technique of asking prisoners who were literate to write their own histories was unique. Two lengthy handwritten essays from those who were "sodomists" are twenty-four and sixty-eight pages, respectively. They offer a treasure trove of insights.[79]

Gillin noted that the researchers were initially warned, likely by prison officials, that "these men could not be believed," so he devised field investigations to check their stories. The investigator would go to the inmate's home community and get in touch with relatives, employers, and social agencies. After some effort, however, Gillin determined that this system of checking was not worth the time and money it cost. He concluded that the "men were unexpectedly truthful about their early lives and about everything else except the circumstances of their crimes." Sex offenders were particularly more likely to exonerate themselves. He did note, however, that "the group included a few pathological liars, who could not have told the truth if they had wanted to, and these were the only ones for whom the field investigation was really worthwhile."[80]

In the book's seventh chapter, "The Making of the Sex Offender," Gillin explained his classification of individuals on a sociological basis (as homosexuals) rather than a legal basis (as sodomists). The legal definition of sodomy was still "the crime against nature." While there were two convictions of heterosexual sodomy and one of bestiality that met the definition, the overwhelming majority of the twenty-plus incarcerated "sodomists" studied were homosexual. One homosexual had been excluded from the study because he was unable to speak English, and another refused to cooperate. Unlike the overwhelming percentage of rapists who were in the Waupun prison, fully one-fourth of the "sodomists" were in the Central State Hospital for the criminally insane, thus suggesting that homosexuality was viewed as belonging in the medical sphere.[81]

CASE DETAILS

Gillin divided the published case histories of "sodomists" in the book into those with a "very low I.Q.," "others of very high intelligence," and "still others who are actually demented." He gave four examples of low intelligence and three examples of average or high in the case histories. About homosexuality, Gillin stated, "The root of the offense lies deeper than the intellect, inasmuch as the sodomists include men of both low and high intelligence."[82]

The "sodomists" were characterized as those "who distinctly preferred homosexual love relations, were fond of female pursuits, and had the physical characteristics of the female, and who felt closer ties of affection with the mother or considered themselves her favorite." Among the examples provided to the reader was one prisoner nicknamed "Lipstick Bill" and another who played with dolls. For Gillin, this "substantiated Freud's theory" as he understood it; he believed that Freud described homosexuality as a case in which "the sexual impulse may be fixed on a socially disapproved object, or may develop contrary to the socially approved course." As a sociologist, he presented the general negative attitude toward homosexuality as a social construct, not an eternal or revealed truth.[83]

Gillin's conclusions at the end of the selected case histories show that "numerous factors go to produce homosexuality." Among them, he listed "physical constitution," "early conditioning," and "proper stimulus." He believed some theories supported the contention "that everyone is potentially bi-sexual, the individual was capable of both heterosexual and homosexual relationships." Yet Gillin was not above judgmental statements, as when citing one man as "a case of pure perversion." Throughout the book, while Gillin did refer at times to homosexuals, he more frequently used the term "sodomists," which was hardly a value-neutral term at the time. Gillin noted as particularly important that some "sodomists" possessed "a weaker and smaller frame," which related to a sense of physical inferiority, and "an improper emotional development." All these comments can be seen as contributing to negative stereotypes.[84]

The selected homosexual case histories show two unskilled laborers, one skilled laborer, one schoolteacher, a defrocked priest, and a school administrator. The main religious denominations in Wisconsin were represented, as the prisoners were from Catholic, Lutheran, and Methodist families. Artistic pursuits such as painting and drawing, home decorating, and collecting antiques were associated with several of the sample "sodomists."[85]

The published narratives in *The Wisconsin Prisoner: Studies in Crimogenesis* provide glimpses into gay life in the state in the mid-twentieth century. One could be known or active in his community as homosexual without giving grounds for arrest. Arrest records show that two prisoners had several complaints of exhibitionism with boys. About another, a researcher mentioned, "In the community from which he was committed he has a long history of homosexuality but no record of previous arrests." Another prisoner admitted to several affairs with boys and had been living with a youth when arrested. Another said he "never had any long-standing love affair with a man but apparently had had many casual experiences." One was "a confirmed homosexual from the age of sixteen, he had no record of previous arrests and had not been recognized as a pervert in his home community until just before he was arrested on a charge of homosexual relations with a nineteen-year-old boy, to which he pleaded guilty." In some cases, older men were the ones who introduced the prisoners to homosexuality—one in the course of his education (at a teachers' college) and another by clergy. One man, recalling an early experience with his nephew and later with other men, stated at the time of the interview that he believed "homosexual love to be much finer than heterosexual." This same man was described by the researcher to be "as circumspect as possible and usually made contacts, as many as possible, at teachers' conventions." His arrest stemmed from "relations with a boy whom he treated as a mistress."[86]

Gillin's sociological analysis demonstrated that the members of the group of homosexual prisoners were not that different from the majority of the state's population in the diversity of their religions, occupations, and intelligence levels. And, like heterosexuals, they expressed a desire for love.

The research notes for the twenty case histories reveal much more than the published findings. The sample shows a variety of ethnic backgrounds, with several prisoners born abroad (Poland, Yugoslavia, Turkey, and supposedly the French Sudan). Others were born to first- and second-generation immigrants from Germany, Wales, Ireland, Denmark, Bohemia, and Italy. Their ages ranged from twenty-two to sixty-four. Most pleaded guilty at bench trials before judges and did not have attorneys. The average sentence was one to five years, according to Wisconsin statutes, and several had prior convictions for sodomy in addition to the conviction for which they were serving a sentence; thus prison had not been much of a cure. About one-third of the "sodomist" prisoners were from the Milwaukee area. In a couple instances, arrests had occurred in Milwaukee parks—Juneau and Kosciusko Parks in the city and Mitchell Woods in West Allis were mentioned. Another group of four, the researchers noted, were all arrested in Winnebago County (Oshkosh) and apparently knew each other. The investigator writing about one of the Oshkosh prisoners reported that the community "is reputed to have a large number of homosexuals." This represents evidence that homosexuals established early communication networks to find one another in the 1930s. This topic is discussed further in chapter 4, "Wisconsin Fairy Networking."[87]

Hearings for arrested homosexuals in Oshkosh were held in the Winnebago County Courthouse.

A Wisconsin table by county of residence shows the number of cases that Gillin studied.[88]

County	Cases
Milwaukee	7
Winnebago	3
Kenosha	1
Outagamie	1
Fond du Lac	1
Manitowoc	1
Sheboygan	1
Dodge	1
Marathon	1
Iron	1
La Crosse	1
Crawford	1

The prisoners' comments revealed many other realities about homosexual life in the state. About one prisoner it was noted, "He worked for many years with transient railway men among who[m] the incidence of sexual irregularity is high." This confirmed the fears the Madison police chief had about railroad crews. Indeed, the prisoners' employment histories showed that several had worked for the two major railroads in the state, the Milwaukee Road and the Chicago & North Western.[89]

The research notes also revealed that for many "sodomists," arrest was just one incident in a very active homosexual life. One stated that his experiences began in an orphanage at age seven. Another, who wrote that he "was brot up in that condition," was placed in a foster home where he "was forced to sleep with casual laborers who were hired by his foster father and these men taught him his first homosexual practices." Another prisoner said he began at age thirteen and yet another at age sixteen. One did not provide a specific age, but the investigator observed, "The sex life of this man seems to have been perverted from an early youth." Another was characterized as "definitely perverted in his sexual instincts for many years." And yet one more "had been practicing the diversion since adolescence." Many prisoners appeared to have been sexually active with other men for long periods before their arrests. The investigators made the following comments: "admits to similar feats in the past," "many homosexual contacts," "homosexual contact over a period of years," "promiscuous for some years previous to the commission of the crime," "innumerable occasions," and "a long history of homosexual relationships."[90]

If all this same-sex activity was going on, were the police just missing it, or were they overlooking it? What caused the arrests to come so belatedly? The research notes offered multiple views. In some cases, apparently, the homosexuals did pass as heterosexual. About one man it was noted, "He was never recognized as an invert in his home community." For another, "No one had ever suspected him of having homosexual tendencies." Clearly, several who were teachers or principals of schools must have appeared above suspicion until caught. But in other cases, the authorities were not so blind. One prisoner "was known as a homosexual by the police in the city where he lived. The police refrained from prosecuting him because of his previous good standing in the community." A second "was known to be a homosexual by the police in his local community." The police knew another who took "extreme care in dress" and whom the kids called "Powder Puff Joe" for his use of rouge. A fourth prisoner had been previously charged with exhibitionism but "was not prosecuted on these informations [because of] the high reputation of other members of the immediate family." Yet a fifth "was recognized as a homosexual in the town in which he lived. He was a fastidious dresser and always sought to associate with young boys." Indeed, it seems that fellatio sex with young boys and teens was most often the tripwire for arrest for many of these individuals. Under-age sexual assault was clearly beyond the boundaries of the blind eye of law enforcement. One prisoner admitted to paying boys fifty cents for the occasions.[91]

For some the sex was opportunistic pleasure, as shown by investigators' comments that "all of his contacts have been casual" or that one prisoner had "contact over a period of years with strangers whenever he went to large cities, or went away on conventions." Yet, there were recorded instances of "a strong mutual love" and a belief "that this is one of the strongest and purest of homosexual attachments." One man was recorded as having "had male lovers," and one "wanted to love boys rather than girls." For at least about half the case histories, love appeared as important as sex.[92]

LEARNING THE LESSON OF CHARITY

"Shows considerable insight into the genesis of the homosexual attitudes."
This was a note presumably made by the graduate assistant researcher on
the biographical essay of Waupun inmate Andrew Jastroch. His family,
from Prussian Poland, settled in Milwaukee and was devoutly Catholic.
In grade school he had an unreciprocated crush on the parish's young
curate. An uncle, a priest of the Order of the Holy Ghost, arranged for
Jastroch to attend a Catholic boarding school in Pennsylvania. While at this
preparatory school, he noticed "a lot of boys who had special friends, and
who paired off during recreation by themselves." At age sixteen, he met a
student from Villanova College who introduced him to homosexual acts in
the trunk room of a railway station. Jastroch subsequently enrolled in the
college. After graduating from Villanova, he returned to Milwaukee and
taught at a Catholic junior high. After a European tour, he landed in Boston
and described being kept by an older man for a while. Back in Milwaukee, a
drunken night of partying turned into sex with a bartender, but a sixteen-
year-old son of the bar owner was sharing the same room, so a complaint
was lodged and Jastroch got hauled before the judge. The research assistant
speculated that Jastroch's homosexuality might have been furthered by
his European experience when he was away from religious institutions.[93]

While he was in jail, Jastroch explained, "I didn't know whether I was
coming or going, all that I knew was, that I wanted to get away from there,
anywhere just so that I was away from Milwaukee." He refused to contact
his brother, an attorney, for his defense and pleaded guilty. While his com-
patriot who had a lawyer got a year's probation, Jastroch got two years
at Waupun from, as he said, "the Catholic Judge," who felt Jastroch had
thrown away the graces of God.[94]

Jastroch had a clear skepticism about the research project. "All the
learned professors on this point are merely beating around the bush," he
said, "no matter how or where they gained their knowledge, they have
never gotten the truth from the individuals questioned. Every prison inmate has learned from forceful experience, yes learned when he found
himself alone with the entire world against him to be mighty cautious of
each word he utters. . . . And only he, and he alone could tell you, but he
never does and never will."[95]

While admitting his own guilt, Jastroch nevertheless felt that those inside the walls and their crimes "are as nothing when compared with the crimes of some who are walking the streets today, the latter were never caught, that's the reason and not because they are better." His argument seems slightly similar to the one Ross made in *Sin and Society* about exploitive economic crimes, but Jastroch was not a fan of that science. "A student of Sociology," he wrote, "might say that the better grade of prisoners could do a lot of good by mingling more with the other class." But, he believed, "One has enough to do to watch his step, and mind his business." Upon release, Jastroch expected "to find hard knocks, but then every self-righteous critic, whose chief delight is to expose the faults of others, has himself a mind so unclean and so filled with malice that he is entirely incapable of even a generous thought. So why consider such a one?"[96]

He had little use for the anti-vice crusader, noting, "I have here learned the valuable and only lesson of charity, I have learned here to hate wrong of every shape and manner, and I have also learned never to condemn anybody because I could never qualify to throw the first stone, neither could any man on God's earth." Jastroch's story showed how exploring his sexual life led him on quite an odyssey before he landed in a Wisconsin prison. He had received little sympathy from the judicial system, but he retained some of his basic religious beliefs on the importance of practicing compassion even toward those on the sexual margins.[97]

"Happiness That I Hope Exists"

One of Gillin's subjects, who went by the name Ibn LoBagola, wrote his own sixty-eight-page autobiography. He stated in an acknowledgment that "it is so very difficult to find one who knows enough or who is honest enough to open up on this subject with, for my experience has been that when I sought to discuss the problem of sex inversion with anyone, be he student or artisan, he has, invariably, held me under the suspicion of wanting to do something to him, and instantly concluded that I was an immoral man, therefore dangerous." Gillin wrote multiple letters to at least three correspondents in New York trying to verify LoBagola's amazing tale. It remains unclear what Gillin thought about it in the end.[98]

LoBagola had recently visited Wisconsin when the front-page headline of the May 18, 1933, issue of the *Madison Mirror*, the newspaper of Madison's Central High School, reported on a student assembly: "African Bush Man Speaks to Students." The paper carried a picture of the speaker wearing a coat and tie and a fez, and identified him as Ibn LoBagola. Along with improbable tales of snakes and the thick vegetative growth of the African bush, LoBagola described his people as "intensely distrustful of any white people or even tribes living near them." Another quote, "Kindness among my people is a weakness and affection is unknown," also raised some questions. While purportedly describing tribal life in the African bush, LoBagola may have been repurposing stories of distrust and lack of affection from his secret life as a gay black man in the early twentieth century.[99]

For LoBagola, born in 1887, finding role models for a gay life had to have been a matter of creativity, doubly so in the racist culture of the day in the Western world. After lecturing throughout the East Coast on tribal customs, he came to the Midwest, speaking in Chicago as well as Ohio, Indiana, and Wisconsin. He addressed students at the Oshkosh State Teachers College and was set up to speak in Kenosha the day after his Madison Central High engagement. It was in Kenosha that his luck in the Midwest ran out.[100]

On May 19, the *Kenosha Evening Times* carried a front-page story, "Dramatic Tale Is Related by Ibn LoBagola." The talk, sponsored by the First Methodist Ladies Aid Group, was widely anticipated. Every available seat in the auditorium was filled, so extra rows of chairs were added. The paper reported that LoBagola was in a flowing robe and donned what the paper called a tarbush (more commonly called a fez), which "he candidly told the audience he wore for 'color.'"[101]

LoBagola's talk included tales of witch doctors, chiefs with councils of three hundred women, fetishism, Amazon woman warriors, and animal life. He claimed his people included a sect of black Jews headed by seven rabbis. This squares with Jewish history, which says the religious tradition came from Morocco across the Sahara Desert to French Sudan.[102]

The paper quoted LoBagola as saying, "I'm living out of place—a maladjustment. I have no friends, no companionship." He declared that his Western education had made him unfit for savage life, yet he could find no real place for himself in the "civilized" world. The paper had opened the article with the line, "A story so dramatic and fantastic as to be almost unbelievable." If they had only known the accuracy of that statement.[103]

On June 3, 1933, several weeks after his talk in Madison, the *Kenosha Evening Times* ran a review of his book, *LoBagola: An African Savage's Own Story*, published first as articles in *Scribner's Magazine* and then in book form by Alfred Knopf in 1930. The review referred to it as a best seller and literary sensation, and a later story would claim that the book had "been extremely popular in Kenosha." The paper also noted that LoBagola would be back in Kenosha for a return engagement on June 8, speaking first at a children's afternoon matinee at the First Methodist church banquet hall, and then in the evening at the YMCA gymnasium. The price was ten cents for the matinee and twenty-five cents for the evening lecture.[104]

On June 8, as LoBagola spoke to what the paper later called "an enthralled audience," he was quoted as saying, "It is no easy task to undergo complete ostracism. But I continue on the jump, always on the go, seeking that happiness that I hope exists for men somewhere in this western civilization."[105]

Then, on June 10, the *Kenosha Evening Times* had quite a different front-page headline: "Jail LoBagola on Boy's Story of Misconduct, African Bushman Lecturer Arrested after Disclosures Fri." On June 12, another story ran: "LoBagola Still in County Jail, Second Warrant Added to First against African Bushman Lecturer." On June 13, the story was headed "LoBagola Has a Long Record, Served 18 Months in Sing Sing on Immorality Charges."[106]

Apparently LoBagola's foray into America's heartland was an attempt to get away from his record on the East Coast, where he had been arrested for sexual immorality with men. The paper noted that Scotland Yard had also investigated the lecturer during a period in London. Two fifteen-year-old Kenosha boys had reported to YMCA counselors that LoBagola had performed oral sex on them, and the counselors referred the matter to police. Since the recently lionized speaker remained in jail unable to raise bail, his lectures and appointments in Sheboygan and Wauwatosa were canceled.[107]

At his preliminary hearing, LoBagola was ordered held for a trial by jury. The courtroom was crowded, with no standing room available, and had been packed long before the hour of the hearing. The sole witness to testify was one of the boys who said he had received oral sex from LoBagola. Here, as in other Wisconsin cases, the issue of uncorroborated testimony regarding the act in question surfaced in the courtroom.[108]

In the meantime, bail was set at $2,500. LoBagola's attorneys protested that it was too high and pointed to a similar case in the county court in which bond was $500. Evidently at least one other case of homosexual immorality was underway in the town. The defense in the trial also claimed that LoBagola was an American citizen by naturalization, though all the while he wore a robe and a fez, reportedly the attire of his homeland in French Sudan (now Mali).[109]

On June 16, the *Kenosha Evening Times* ran an editorial complaining about the "sensational" character of the hearing. Commending the court for excluding minors, the editorial called for a closed hearing, not one where the "merely curious" could come and gawk. To reinforce the argument, the editorial claimed that "even in crime ridden Chicago, according to reports, sensational cases of this kind are invariably held behind closed doors. Why should that not be the case here?" The paper, while seeking to avoid sensationalism regarding homosexuality, was also not trying to sweep it under the rug, since the matter had been on its front pages for the better part of a week.[110]

Bail was finally made, and LoBagola was released for a period. On April 9, 1934, however, the Kenosha paper headlined another front-page story: "LoBagola Gets Year in Prison, Goes at Once, Pleads Guilty to Charges of Immorality before Stewart Today." The forty-four-year-old lecturer was sentenced to a term of one to five years on each charge. In addition, a representative of the federal government was questioning LoBagola on his status as an American citizen.[111]

Though the tale was already quite interesting, there was another twist yet to come. The prices for LoBagola's lectures and the crowds he drew were indicative of a strong appetite in the Western world for information on Africa at this time. The Dark Continent, carved up by the European empires, inspired awe throughout the United States. The book *Africans on Stage: Studies in Ethnological Show Business*, edited by Bernth Lindfors, helps explain the phenomenon. American interest in Africa was especially sparked by the 1893 World's Columbian Exposition in Chicago, which featured a West African village complete with natives. The budding field of anthropology added a veneer of academic respectability to displays of African natives and their stories. The P. T. Barnum types realized there was money to be made, so promoters began booking Africans on the stage in vaudeville and other lecture venues.[112]

It turned out that LoBagola, who was earning his living portraying himself as a noble savage, was not from Africa after all. After US immigration officials threatened to deport him for his conviction, he confessed to having been born in 1887 as Joseph Howard Lee, the eleventh child of a black family in Baltimore, Maryland. Because LoBagola had been in violation of his parole for an earlier conviction in New York, he was returned to that state's prison system upon completing his term in Wisconsin. He died in Attica Prison in 1947. The cement headstone in the prison graveyard bears the name he gave himself, Ibn LoBagola.[113]

Joseph Howard Lee, a gay man from Baltimore, used his artistic talents to create the stage persona of Ibn LoBagola, a supposed native of the French Sudan. *LOBAGOLA: AN AFRICAN SAVAGE'S OWN STORY*, 1929

During his time in Waupun Prison, as the writer of a tale not yet unmasked as fiction, LoBagola poured out his heart to Gillin's research project, telling what he claimed was a true personal and sexual history. The public unmasking of his American origins is described in a biography included in the 1999 publication of *Africans on Stage*. As a gay man who had to hide his real identity, LoBagola had fabricated an entirely new public persona, and in that guise, he earned money on the lecture circuit. In his prison account, he blended his previously published "autobiography," *LoBagola: An African Savage's Own Story*, with a very active sexual history—one that had gotten him arrested on several occasions over the years.[114]

According to his new prison autobiography, LoBagola had volunteered for the US Army in World War I to go to war for America, but after his initial acceptance, he was discharged on the basis of the records of his arrest for perversion. In the published autobiography, he makes no mention of the perversion matter, and only says he "was not a fit person to be in the United States Army, as I was a very bad man." So he turned around and volunteered to fight with the manpower-starved British army, which was recruiting in America and did accept him. In the private autobiography written at Waupun, in which he was frank about his homosexual lifestyle, he noted, "Strange as it may seem, *the British Army was not demoralized by my having served in it*" (the italicization appeared as underlining in his handwritten version). LoBagola's experience with the British army foreshadowed later discussions about homosexuals serving in the military and provides an example of how, even before World War II, gay men did not accept the argument that they could not serve.[115]

In their chapter on LoBagola in *Africans on Stage*, David Killingray and Willie Henderson acknowledged their subject's creativity in inventing a stage persona and capitalizing on the popularity of the noble savage tale. They noted, however, that "his instability and sexual preferences destroyed him in the end."[116]

LoBagola's sexual life story written at Waupun makes it clear that, in his view, American society's antipathy toward homosexuals, and especially to a gay black man, in the first part of the twentieth century spelled his certain doom. It also shows that a gay man can reject normative sexual mores and the internalized guilt that society wants him to bear. Drawing on African masking traditions, LoBagola demonstrated how through creativity a homosexual can project a persona that society might find fantastic and engaging.[117]

"PERFECTLY HEALTHY, PHYSICALLY NORMAL"

For the chapter on sodomy, Gillin offered a unique feature: the essay "Existing Literature on Sex Crimes." Most of this seven-page essay is focused on a review of writings about homosexuality or sodomy. By calling his work "a pioneer study of the role of inheritance and environment in producing criminality," Gillin moved from the solely criminal context of sodomy toward views that would prevail after the war, which became known as the medicalization of homosexuality. He noted, "The psychoanalytic school of Freud, Adler, Jung, Rank, Stekel, and some of their colleagues and disciples has produced most of the writing on homosexuality." Gillin's footnotes cite an impressive array of scholarly publications by these authorities. For Wisconsin, with its Germanic heritage and respect for German universities, he included a number of publications in German published in both Berlin and Vienna.[118]

Gillin concluded, "In general earlier writers ascribe the homosexual tendency to inheritance, whereas later writers stress the importance of the individual's experiences after birth." He noted, however, with balanced academic caution, "There is some truth in each of these views." The most favorable citation was from Iwan Bloch, who had written *The Sexual Life of Our Times in its Relation to Modern Civilization*, published in 1914. Bloch is credited with conceding that while some homosexuals have a morbid constitution, "The largest section of original homosexuals, are perfectly healthy, physically normal persons." Gillin also cited several theorists who believed "disturbance in the endocrine function of the sex glands" to be a cause.[119]

Among the Germans cited are Magnus Hirschfeld, who in 1899 established the *Jahrbuch für sexuelle Zwischenstufen*, an annual scientific yearbook on the new study of sexology. Gillin wrote that Hirschfeld, as "the author of one of the most important books on the subject, considers that the tendency to homosexuality is inborn or at least hereditary." Hirschfeld wrote that at least 75 percent of the homosexuals he studied "were born of healthy parents and of happy and often prolific marriages, and that nervous or mental anomalies, alcoholism, blood relationship, and syphilis are no more frequent among ancestors of homosexuals than among the ancestors of those endowed with normal sexuality."[120]

Trying to include the most current theories, Gillin also cited Havelock Ellis's 1936 writings on "Sexual Inversion" in his *Studies in the Psychology of Sex*. Discussing Freud and Ellis on homosexuals' feelings toward their mothers as a possible cause, Gillin wrote, "A boy's love for his mother often involves feelings which later develop . . . his own feminine disposition, which prompts him to shun the amusements and society of his own sex." Gillin concluded that his own study did not find Freud's incestuous preference for the mother to exist among his subjects.[121]

The impact of Gillin's essay was to move the discussion of homosexuality almost entirely out of the field of criminal law. While his study subjects are "sodomites," his intellectual framing was not about criminal acts under the sixteenth-century Tudor law. Rather, it was about personality and identity. He believed modern science and knowledge could bring new contributions to the discussion of homosexuality.

On the origins of homosexuality, Gillin gave at least equal time to views that homosexuality was innate to individuals and that it was a choice. And overall, his views tended to position homosexuality in comparison to heterosexuality, as on almost parallel courses. Later in his life, a 1951 feature story quoted Professor Gillin as stating more clearly, "Poverty, crime, domestic disharmony, and sexual aberrations are as much a part of the social scene as wealth, orderly behavior, domestic felicity, and socially approved sexual behavior. All are social phenomena which sociology should seek to understand." In Wisconsin, Gillin is responsible for beginning the academic study of homosexuality outside the solely criminal view.[122]

THE STATE'S FIRST SEX PANIC

In his analysis of vice crusades mentioned earlier in this chapter, Scott Herring noted that the term *vice*, in a sexual context, was frequently used to mean all non-normative sex acts. Certainly, for traditional defenders of morality such as the Wisconsin legislature and the Wisconsin Supreme Court, "abhorrent" homosexuality fell in the vice category throughout the nineteenth and well into the twentieth century. Police reports showed that some sodomy crimes were consistently persecuted and, in the capital, were often viewed as "important crimes." The Teasdale Committee report of 1914 indicated that law enforcement officials on the ground, however, had very mixed views about enforcing morality laws. While the Teasdale investigators did occasionally stumble upon homosexuality during their examination of the geography of vice, such findings did not make the report. It is very likely that most homosexual acts and persons never appeared on the radar of morality enforcers, as the court cases indicate that police were quite well informed about its prevalence. Nevertheless, traditional moralists and politicians desired to enforce normative morality, including prohibitions on homosexual sex and on most visible vice acts, for the first part of the twentieth century.

The 1930s study by John Gillin showed that even when Wisconsin police knew that certain individuals were homosexuals, they often did not make arrests until something triggered action. Even once-convicted homosexuals continued to lead active sex lives over decades. Other homosexuals represented in the study appeared to refuse the guilt that society assumed criminals should have about a non-normative sex life. Although the Chicago vice report included the most explicit statements on Midwest homosexual social structures, it was clear that in Wisconsin, some communications networks were developing that enabled gay men to find one another.

Some of the individuals discussed in this chapter may have been transgendered, or people who present themselves as other than the sex they were assigned at birth, but the language did not then exist to place a person in such a context. Certainly Cora Anderson, who described her "heart and soul" as more those of a man, might have been such a person. "Lipstick Bill," rather than being a Freudian manifestation of homosexual inclination to the female, may also have been a transgendered person. At that time, all non-normative folks were considered part of the same category.

Ultimately, Gillin's essay in his book *The Wisconsin Prisoner* started to shift views about homosexuals, especially in university circles, away from criminality and into the academic and medical world. This helped create the basis for the view that a sexual identity could be based on a homosexual orientation rather than on penalized acts of behavior.

3

"Down on the Farm"

They keep looking at my cigarette-lighter, my gloves, my tight black cap, a Basque beret.
—From *Good-Bye Wisconsin* by Glenway Wescott, 1928[1]

Hordes of young fellows used to bathe in the hot summer evenings in a state of nature which was of course most shocking, but still at times very interesting.
—Will Gundry, 1933 letter on the London Serpentine[2]

Published in 1919, the popular song "How Ya Gonna Keep 'Em Down on the Farm?" expressed worries that the Great War and the European experience would undermine American values, perhaps including the purity efforts of vice suppression. An expressed concern in the lyrics was that folks would be "jazzin' around and paintin' the town" after they had seen "Paree." The chorus contained the line, "How ya gonna keep 'em away from harm, that's a mystery."[3]

In the preceding chapter on vice, we saw how Wisconsin's policing of sexuality in the early twentieth century worked to suppress homosexual vice, understood to comprise the genital acts of gay men and some lesbian relationships. These acts were criminalized through laws, policing, prisons, and courts. Now let's turn to how gay people in Wisconsin learned to develop their identities, and how they found a place and way to live in the state as if it were an alternative universe to the official normative world. Of course, the stories highlighted here are only a small part of the story of gay Wisconsin circa 1920. This is mainly because only a very partial written record has been preserved, but also because many gay people in that era never created any written record at all. Though the glimpses into these private lives may not be completely representative, and some lives were not always lived so privately, what the reports disclose can still be meaningful. They shine a light on those struggling and succeeding to build identity. The people in these stories would not be kept down on the farm.

SOME "PLACE" ELSE

Julian Mitchell's play *Another Country* premiered on the London stage in 1981. It described how gay men in the period after World War I, oppressed by their circumstances, could survive by refusing to internalize the homophobia of their society and envisioning a better place than their current reality. The modern campaign "It Gets Better" reflects the contemporary experience of inviting oppressed young non-normative folks in a similar manner to believe in a better alternative. [4]

Likewise, James Baldwin's 1962 novel *Another Country*, written partially in Paris, included a fictionalized account of his relationship with his French lover. The novel deals with themes of how race and homosexuality can internalize oppression and make finding love difficult. Such oppression can cause alienation from one's own identity. Perhaps a mythic other place can help, Baldwin concluded in the final chapter, "Toward Bethlehem." [5]

In 1895, Oscar Wilde had been urged by friends not to face trial in an English court, but to flee to another country, to literally go some "place" else. As discussed in chapter 1, Wilde did not flee and was convicted of gross indecency under English law. But after his release from Reading Gaol, he did go to France, where homosexuality had not been a crime since Napoleonic times. He died there and is buried in Père Lachaise Cemetery, Paris. Ideally, the "other country" is a place one goes not to die, but to live or learn to live.

Travel could be enlightening for homosexuals. Gay scholar Allan Bérubé has noted the "long tradition in which people have used other cultures to discover and explore their own homosexuality." For example, many Englishmen at the turn of the twentieth century would use the cultures of ancient Greece and Rome to depict homosexual activity. [6]

For many Americans following World War I, France was the place to go.

A great wave of artists, writers, and intellectuals flocked there. Gertrude Stein's charmed Paris salon captured many gay men in its embrace, and some of them had Wisconsin roots.

"Good-Bye to Wisconsin"

Glenway Wescott, born on a farm near Kewaskum in 1901, made his early reputation as a Wisconsin regional writer. His published short stories and his 1927 novel, *The Grandmothers*, drew on his Midwestern roots. Jerry Rosco's *Glenway Wescott Personally: A Biography* excellently chronicles how the writer's early sexual exploits with other males appeared in his fiction. Wescott attended West Bend High School, where another teenaged boy helped him discover his sexuality. This friend had dressed the teenaged Wescott as a girl for a masked dance. Much later, in his 1944 diary, Wescott would recall meeting this friend again "who had first kissed me in a bower of mock orange blossom twenty-eight years ago." Twenty-five or thirty years after that meeting, Wescott describes the friend as "a distinguished and amiable creature, and not undistinguished in the simple way of places like Milwaukee; unfortunately not at all attractive physically." The writer also recorded an incident when another boy gave him a kiss. Later Wescott recalled his own "series of love letters in the style of Walt Whitman," though addressed to a girl. Whitman is now considered one of the nineteenth century's most prominent American gay writers. According to Rosco, another episode in Wescott's early fiction had the narrator "discovering a circle of schoolboys in a woodshed, obviously masturbating—which Wescott also had witnessed during high school."[7]

A scholarship to the University of Chicago first took Wescott away from Wisconsin. While there, he wrote Imagist poetry and joined the poetry club, where another club member who carried around Oscar Wilde poems "fell in love" with him. In January 1919, Wescott met Chicagoan Monroe Wheeler, who was destined to become his life companion, though as Rosco shows, both would maintain many other relationships throughout their long years together.[8]

A 1920 sojourn in Santa Fe brought Wescott into contact with two British gentlemen who "admitted to Wescott that they had been intimate with

Oscar Wilde in their late teens when Wilde in his late twenties visited New Mexico, during his American tour of 1881–82." Back in Chicago, Wescott lived with Monroe Wheeler's family, and Wheeler published a chapbook of a dozen poems by Wescott. In 1921, the pair left the Midwest. Trips to New York and London followed, with a return to New York in 1922. Wescott did make occasional visits to his family back in Wisconsin. On a trip to Paris in 1923, Wescott called on writer Gertrude Stein and her partner, Alice B. Toklas. Returning again to New York, he and Wheeler settled on Christopher Street in Greenwich Village.[9]

Wescott's first novel, *The Apple of the Eye*, published by New York's Dial Press in 1924, features reflections on the rural Wisconsin of his childhood. One chapter deals with latent homosexuality. Back in Europe, Paris was too expensive for Wescott and Wheeler, so they went to Villefranche-sur-Mer in the south, near Nice. The town was home to the well-known French writer Jean Cocteau, who was gay. Both Wescott and Wheeler maintained a correspondence with Cocteau and shared friends. Later, they became friends with writer William (or "Willie," as they called him) Somerset Maugham, who was divorcing his wife and had established himself in Villefranche with his American partner, whom he had met during the Great War. Wescott and Maugham did not have a great rapport on first meeting, but would later become friends. In Villefranche in 1928, Wescott and Wheeler encountered writer Thornton Wilder, another gay Wisconsin native, whose early years had been spent in Madison.[10]

The Grandmothers, published in 1927 and written in part while Wescott was living abroad, established his reputation as a major writer among American expatriates. Set in the Wisconsin of his youth, the novel chronicles an American family. Great acclaim and some financial reward followed. Wescott's next book, published the following year, was a collection of short stories titled *Good-Bye Wisconsin*, which is also the title of the first story in the book.[11]

In the story "Good-Bye Wisconsin," the narrator resembles Wescott in many ways. He is homeward bound, and in the beginning of the story seemingly advises his readers to never live in Paris or New York. He makes many comments about a flight to another country that resemble Wescott's similar flight. Initially in the story, Wisconsin has a strong pull on the

Glenway Wescott in the French village of Villefranche-sur-Mer in 1927. COURTESY OF THE ESTATE OF GLENWAY WESCOTT

narrator: "The state with a beautiful name—glaciers once having made of it their pastures—is an anthology, a collection of all kinds of landscape, perfect examples side by side. Ranges of hills strung from the great lake to the Mississippi in long lustrous necklaces, one above another from the northern throat of the state until well below its waist."[12]

But the narrator's reservations about the state came quickly. "One would think of Wisconsin as the ideal state to live in, a paragon of civic success but for the fact that the young people dream only of getting away." Knowing that not all young people do get away, the narrator comments, "The others who have not yet taken flight, even those who never will, speculate a great deal in their own interest. They envy our apparent moral emancipation . . . suspect abnormalities which may have abetted us."[13]

Though still possessing affection for his native state, the narrator does eventually leave again. The triggering incident involves his self-presentation. On a train from Milwaukee, two workmen "keep looking at my cigarette-lighter, my gloves, my tight black cap, a Basque *beret*." Even his brother asks him "not to wear it in the street." Thus, he knows that all he has learned abroad, including acceptance of his homosexuality, will not fit in Wisconsin, because "the same law applies to manners and morals." "Wisconsin farmers," he observed, "are no longer rustics; they have become provincials."[14]

But it is not only the beret that suggests the narrator's homosexuality. The story is full of textual references. For example, Wescott cites the gay French writer André Gide, whose little book defending homosexuality, *Corydon*, came out in 1924. The narrator also speaks of "heavy hearted Ganymedes," a reference to the male love interest of the Greek god Zeus, which classically educated readers would have understood.[15]

Near the story's end, the narrator speaks: "It comes time to return to New York, which is halfway back to the South of France." Finally, he says, "How much sweeter to come and go than to stay; that by way of judgment upon Wisconsin." He does acknowledge, however, "Indeed it is melancholy leaving this land in which democracy is coming to a climax." Knowing the state's official policy toward homosexuality, Wescott could not view permanent return as a possibility, especially given his involvement with gay culture and the international literary scene. Wescott's friend and fellow writer Katherine Anne Porter commented about him: "His view of life . . . is innately tragic—yet he has a genius for friendship."[16]

By 1934, Wescott and Wheeler were permanently in New York, on their way to becoming leading figures in gay America. Their partnership included a multiyear threesome with the photographer George Platt Lynes. Later in life, they assisted Alfred Kinsey in finding homosexual subjects for his research. Wheeler and Wescott brought the manuscript of *Maurice*, E. M. Forster's posthumously released gay novel, to America for publication.[17]

PERHAPS YOU CAN GO HOME AGAIN

Unlike Wescott, other Wisconsin gay men, sometimes even after expatriate experiences, would find ways to construct their lives in their native state.

From an early age, Edward Harris Heth of Milwaukee was on track for literary success. While still a student at the University of Wisconsin, Heth was published in the book *Wisconsin Writings—1931: An Anthology*. The editors sought to publish "future great writers of America" and felt that drawing on students from the university scene would uncover some. They chose the University of Wisconsin because it "is one of the most progressive" with a "yeast of radicalism" at work "with resultant original thinking and freshness of point of view."[18]

The editors noted among the "literary minded undergraduates at Wisconsin" that "Edward Harris Heth, it should be said in passing, has already been published in *The American Mercury*." Dr. S. I. Hayakawa of the Department of English (later a US senator from California) assisted the editors in collecting Wisconsin manuscripts. Interestingly, in an introductory essay, Professor Paul Fulcher noted that the college writers often tend to a fault to write in the fashion of the literary gods of the day, listing Oscar Wilde as one such god from the past.[19]

Heth's 1931 contribution was a story titled "A Party for Ginevra." It is set in the post–World War I expatriate scene in Paris. A friend of a friend takes the young male narrator in hand upon arrival. On the newcomer's first night in the city, the two men go to a nightclub where, the narrator says, another man "put his arm around me" and his "drunken fingers were toying with my ear." The narrator notes that the man "looked angry when I moved away, so I laughed and tried to look friendly." Among the many persons he meets at the club is Ginevra, age thirty, from Syracuse, a plain-looking woman who does needlepoint. He also meets Bennie, who is interested in architecture and, though he is twenty-one or twenty-two, looks "like a little boy."[20]

Later in the evening, our narrator learns that both he and Bennie are from Chicago. "Then I wanted to put my arms around him," the narrator says, "because I suddenly understood that he was lonely. Let me put my arms around you, Bennie, I thought, because I know." A little later in the evening, Bennie "put his face close to mine. It was so close that I could hazily see my reflection in his soft dull blue eyes. His eyelids were thin, delicate, and his lashes were very long, of a rich dark color." The narrator discusses rebuilding Chicago with Bennie and then invites him to tea the next day—having also invited Ginevra. Upon leaving, when a French girl tells the narrator she would go home with him, he flushes and seeks to order another lemonade.[21]

After the tea, Bennie and Ginevra begin a whirlwind courtship and become engaged. The dinner party, the centerpiece of the story, is supposed to be an engagement celebration for Bennie and Ginevra. As the evening progresses, however, it gets later and later, but Bennie does not show, and Ginevra is left alone at the party, almost a metaphor for being left at the altar. Finally, the narrator takes a cab to Bennie's room and finds his friend asleep in a sort of Morris chair, looking "like a deserted baby left on an orphanage step." The narrator, not wanting to awaken Bennie, returns to the party and says Bennie was not at home. He notes, "Ginevra was still looking as if she had expected this." And this is, essentially, where the story ends.[22]

The young writer from Wisconsin set his story in decadent Paris, which allowed him to describe intimacies between men that would seem out of place in America. Despite the women around, the narrator turns down offers of hetero sex, and the party for a planned marriage fizzles out. Certainly, this story offers glimpses of a young homosexual's feelings of loneliness and his experience of finding male companionship in a guarded way.

After graduating from Wisconsin, Heth went off to use his writing

A young Edward Harris Heth. His career as a writer would lead to movie adaptions of his books. SOME WE LOVED, 1935

skills in an advertising career in New York, though he continued to write fiction, publishing several novels in the late 1930s.[23]

In his semiautobiographical 1953 book, *My Life on Earth*, Edward Harris Heth reflected on his love for the time he spent in New York City, referring to his "full breathless New York years." He described parties, "though they were only that hurried apartment variety, with the host rushing out for a bottle of whiskey and a bag of pretzels." His remembrances of New York include Bleecker Street in the bohemian (and even then lavender-colored) Greenwich Village. Reminiscing about walking down Madison Avenue after his decision to return to Wisconsin in the 1940s, he recalled a bar: "It was only when the men inside kept looking at me that I knew I had tears in my eyes. But this was a mist of happiness." Does "only . . . men" indicate that this was a bar frequented by gays? When he returned to Wisconsin after World War II, Heth lived with his partner in the Welsh Hills of Waukesha County. The details of his later life are described in chapter 6.[24]

WISCONSIN'S PIONEERING "OUT" GAY MAN

The story of Ralph Lorenzo Warner shows how a gay man could find a place to live in Wisconsin in the earlier part of the twentieth century and be reasonably open about his lifestyle. Of course, Warner was not "out" in the modern sense of openly declaring his homosexuality, but he was a man fully aware of his identity. Indeed, he created a public persona based around non-normative gender behavior and presented this to the world without apology. Some of his successful patterns were later adopted by other gay Wisconsinites.

Born in Milwaukee on November 23, 1875, the son of a locomotive engineer, Warner grew up in the fast-growing city. He studied piano, including a stint in Chicago in the late 1890s, and later taught others to play. While living in Racine, Warner made the acquaintance of Susan Porter, a teacher at Racine High. She was a native of Cooksville, Wisconsin, an unincorporated place in the Town of Porter in northern Rock County. Will Fellows, in *A Passion to Preserve: Gay Men as Keepers of Culture*, shows how Warner's 1911 summer visit to Porter in her hometown changed his life. That same year, Warner bought the house next door to Porter's; it was a lovely two-story red brick home from the 1840s in the Federal style.

He launched into a project of historic renovation that would bring him a degree of fame regionally and even nationally. For obvious reasons, Warner called his new domicile the House Next Door. He filled it with good antiques, and it became known as a "pioneer paradise." Historian Will Fellows dubbed Warner one of "the gentleman keepers of Cooksville."[25]

Warner taught arts and crafts and piano during the school year in Racine but spent his summers in Cooksville. The little village had been formed by New Englanders (Daniel Webster was an early investor), with the village buildings surrounding its common. In 1910, the population of the whole township was less than a thousand.[26]

While some press stories claimed that Warner was a recluse, it seems more likely that Warner was actually a publicity hound, as he was featured repeatedly in the Wisconsin press and national periodicals, including *House and Garden* in May 1914, *House Beautiful* in January 1923, the *Wisconsin State Journal* in 1923, the *Wisconsin Magazine* in September 1925, the *Milwaukee Journal* in 1926, Madison journalist Betty Cass's column Madison Day by Day in the *Wisconsin State Journal*, and the *Ladies' Home Journal* of March 1933. While many of these stories repeated the canard about Warner being a recluse, he denied this in his own correspondence, as evidenced by a 1933 letter draft in which he states, "You see I'm not a recluse." The diaries he kept during a 1928–1929 trip to Europe show a very sociable man going to the theater and dinner parties and chatting up shopkeepers. The published stories also noted he made multiple trips abroad.[27]

Stories further claimed that Warner's "simple habits of life, love for birds and flowers and large collection of antique furniture and dishes have attracted wide attention." He was referred to as "one of the country's leading authorities on antiques," and it was said that "people from far away came to see the gardens." As Fellows notes, reporters also often hinted at Warner's "queerness." However, the claims that he was a recluse gave him an aura of privacy that allowed him to live as he chose without too much detailed scrutiny as someone other than normal or mainstream. Thus, at a time when gay men like him were being sent to prison in Wisconsin, Warner devised a strategy to preserve his own safety through a claim of nonsociability.[28]

At this remove, we cannot know whether Warner was homosexually active, but his desire for relations with men seems clear. During one of Warner's trips abroad, his travel diaries revealed many things about the men he encountered along the way, though almost nothing of women he met. For example, he described the ship's doctor on one trip to Europe as "a very young man with a delightful voice and youthful laugh." Others onboard ship included a "sad looking young Russian" and "a Major Wise who has a farm near Newfoundland and has one of the most pleasant personalities I've met in many a day." On another occasion, "a very interesting waiter" served him, who he found out was also a footman at Buckingham Palace.[29]

Warner visited a number of attractions any gay tourist today would have on his must-see list, such as Michelangelo's nude sculpture of David in Florence ("Beyond any idea I could have had of it," he said) and Hadrian's villa outside Rome. Hadrian was the Roman emperor who erected statues all over the empire of Antinous, his male favorite, or lover. Oscar Wilde used references to Antinous as expressions of same-sex love in his works. Of Warner's visit to Capri, a place also commonly visited by gay travelers, he noted that a family of natives performed songs and dances, and "two of the younger children were very good to look at and the boy especially interesting in the dance." Of the Italians, he reported, "I like the people, these guides are such gentle fellows and when they are possessed of blue eyes with long dark lashes they certainly move me. We had such a nice charmer yesterday." This is not the kind of diary entry a straight man would be likely to make.[30]

Warner's trip to Algeria resulted in an entry in which he wrote, "I found these Arabs quite good natured chaps almost like boys playing and joking, laughing." He also commented that the French staff in Algiers "interest me very much. They are anxious to learn English and I should like nothing better than to teach them. The waiter in the dining room is a splendid type and would make a wonderful servant."[31]

During his 1928–1929 trip in London, Warner engaged with two young men. One was Hamilton Beatty of Madison, whom Warner knew was in the English city and eventually discovered at the theater several rows in front of him one night. "Ham," Warner wrote, "certainly looked good to me and I had the warmest little feeling bout my heart all evening. He did make me feel he was glad to see me." He subsequently asked the Madison-ian to dinner for "a real visit." On another occasion, he recorded lunch with "Ham."[32]

At the Tower of London, Warner struck up a conversation with "a young southerner from Atlanta." They talked "quite awhile," visited churches, and came back to the hotel and rested. The southerner was leaving for Paris the next day, but the diary note reads, "I should like to have seen even more of him and hope he looks in" on his way back. Several days later, the two met after Warner found himself in Piccadilly in the evening. Matt Houlbrook in *Queer London: Perils and Pleasures in the Sexual Metropolis, 1918–1957* shows that this area was the stalking ground for West End "poofs," English slang for homosexuals. The term *Dilly Boys* was used for the young working-class men who frequented the area seeking companionship and sometimes robbing the better-off.[33]

Whether Warner and his friend were just acting as tourists and viewing the scenery or participating in the sexual underground remains unclear. The man from Atlanta told a sad story in which a fellow approached him, supposedly hoping to go to America, and asked him questions about the United States, then relieved him of all his cash. Such risks were often involved in gay cruising because thieves, like other criminals, knew that their homosexual victims were unlikely to go to the police. Warner, however, thought the Atlanta native had been "foolish."[34]

The first of the national periodical articles featuring Warner appeared in a 1914 issue of *House and Garden*. The piece fictionalized Warner's town and referred to him not by name but as "the Craftsman" and "the Musician." Warner was called "artistic," and this common code word used to describe homosexuals may have been used to distinguish him from other men in the area. According to the author, "The spell of the place possessed him." A closing poem noted, "No noisy neighbor enters here, nor intermeddling stranger near," implying the safety of Warner's refuge.[35]

In 1923, a Madison writer, Adelaide Evans Harris, writing about Warner for *House Beautiful*, described a visit through the persona of a stout lady who announces she has come to look at Warner's curios. Unabashedly, Warner speaks up, "Won't you look at me? I'm the most curious thing here." She goes on to write that Warner's was a remarkable story, but, "It wouldn't be so much of a story, or so interesting perhaps, if Ralph Warner were a woman." Like the previous writer, Harris called her subject an artist, noting that "people may smile or scoff or call him eccentric; he doesn't

argue the matter." This characterization in a magazine demonstrates Warner's pride in the non-normative identity he presented.[36]

In her article, Harris noted that Warner fully displayed gender role
reversal. She described how "paying guests who come for the first time
to the house insist that there must be a wife or a housekeeper somewhere
concealed. If they accept the flawless housekeeping as Mr. Warner's own,
they challenge the delectable food. Confronted by proof, they are still
skeptical about the dishwashing." The visitor, who wondered if Mr. Warner "possessed a set of values different from most people," presented her
sense that he was different in several ways. Before meeting Warner, Harris
"had been certain that the owner of the house she was about to visit was an
ancient man with a flowing white beard and steel spectacles. And a man
in this district who didn't milk cows or plant corn must naturally be too
decrepit to travel without a cane." A big surprise, then, "was Mr. Warner
himself. Instead of being old he looked on the young side of middle age."
Clearly, he did not conform to the area's male standards.[37]

For the reader who needed further hints, Harris describes the place as "a
gay spontaneous little house" with "velvet pillows gorgeous cross stitched
with purple pansies perched on the sofa," and she mentions "bachelor but-
tons" among the garden flowers. George Chauncey, in *Gay New York*, has
shown how the term *gay* was beginning to get some currency as a word
for homosexuals in the 1920s. Randall Sell and Jonathan Katz, in the essay
"'Millions of Queers': A View from 1940" in the January–February 2015 issue
of *International Gay & Lesbian Review*, suggest that *gay* was indeed in use
during the period before World War II. Certainly, *pansies* and *fairies* were in
common usage. Bachelor culture carried its own connotations. Chauncey
has also discussed how bachelor subculture "had certain distinctive elements
that made it particularly amenable to the presence of fairies."[38]

In an article that appeared in *Wisconsin Magazine* in 1925, Warner
was called "the Gentle Guardian of the Land of Long Ago." Notably, the
question was raised: "Where is Mrs. Ralph?" Warner's unapologetic answer was, "I've never found one that fitted into my Land of Long Ago."
By filling his house with history and antiques based on Wisconsin's pioneer period, Warner had created his own version of "another country," a
world distinct from the one that then surrounded him in the farm fields
of southern Wisconsin.[39]

Ralph Warner at the gate of his House Next Door in Cooksville. His restoration of the building helped preserve early Yankee pioneer culture in the village. COOKSVILLE ARCHIVES AND COLLECTIONS

In a 1926 article, Warner's wish to avoid publicity was interpreted by the writer as part of "his desire to live alone, free to his own whims." The unnamed writer touches on common themes, noting that Warner seemed young, perhaps contributing to a subtext of boyishness, and therefore nonmanliness: "He appears to be in his 30s, but claims more than 50 years of age." The repeated code word *artistic* is used, and observations that Warner does his own cooking and mending suggest a gender role reversal. This story notes, "His dining room is artistic perfection."[40]

Madison newspaper columnist Betty Cass called him "a very pleasant romantic gentleman." She also called Cooksville "the adorable, sleepy, fairy-story village," without explicitly mentioning who was its chief fairy.[41]

In 1933, the journalist Eleanor Mercein began a *Ladies' Home Journal* story about Warner with a poem that has the opening line, "I like the Bohemian life." Like others, she referred to Warner as an artist, a person she defined as having "the unique capability of turning nothing into something and selling it—more or less—for cash." This statement echoes the sentiment of a Longfellow quote Warner had clipped for his scrapbook: "Art is the power of man's soul working outward." Warner's soul was that of a gay man, and his environment was his art.[42]

In the article, Mercein counted interior decorating as a form of artistry along with other more frequently recognized genres, like sculpting and painting. She praised tea rooms in general and described one in Concord, Massachusetts, as "a little establishment which might well grace the left bank of the Seine, where two quite American young men dispense at quite American prices, excellent French food and equally interesting French antiques." Clearly this is a setup about gay men running a special type of tourist business.[43]

The part on Warner carried the subheading "Wisconsin Witchery," the usually female term *witch* hinting at a gender role reversal. About Warner, Mercein wrote, "His hard-working farmer neighbors regard him, of course, as a harmless curiosity, this artist who paints no pictures, writes no books, sings no songs, but who makes life his medium. Indeed, they are not quite sure of his harmlessness."[44]

She noted that Warner "grows herbs and simples for strange medicaments, such as would once have assured his burning at the stake in the colony from which his forbears emigrated." Of course, homosexuals were also burned in the past, but most readers of *Ladies' Home Journal* probably did not know this.[45]

Finally, she wrote, "He performs in person what housekeeping is needful, does his own gardening, and cooking, and dishwashing. . . . And because a young man of this sort may well find himself a little lonely sometimes, lost in the middle of the Wisconsin wheat fields, he welcomes strangers not too reluctantly, and even feeds them—if he happens to feel that day like cooking."[46] Despite embracing some traditional feminine gender roles, Warner did not wish to be thought of as feminine. His travel journals record a London incident in which a hotel maid "insisted on calling me Madam" upon hearing his high voice over the phone. When Warner tried to explain, "But I'm not a madam," the woman replied, "Well you have a voice like a madam." Warner's diary notes, "That damned voice has always gotten me in bad."[47]

If Warner had been afraid of being widely known, he could have refused the repeated visits of journalists. A nonattributed scrapbook statement in his own hand attests, "Art consists in being completely one's self." Warner's ideas about his own self-presentation were bold for his day. His experience demonstrates that even in times of oppression, one can take steps to let one's true self be known.[48]

The articles on Ralph Warner draw attention to his otherness and portray him as an "artistic" type. One from 1933 categorized him in a larger group of like-minded males, or as the author put it "a secret fraternity." Yet another used the term "a young man of this sort," suggesting that a non-normative man was not a rare figure. The articles noted the absence of a woman in Warner's household and consistently denoted the gender role reversal in functions Warner performed himself. Anyone reading for clues about gay identity could find quite a lot in the pages of these publications.[49]

Warner kept a poetry/clipping scrapbook, in addition to his diaries. My research has shown that a remarkable number of the archives of homosexual men have a scrapbook-type document in their collections. I believe this was a way for them to create a mirror, reflecting other identities that lay outside the norm. In earlier times, these archives were often coded, even as private papers. But the need to express oneself is strong. Ralph Warner's diaries were an expression of his desire for relations with men. Some scrapbook items achieved the same effect. His handwritten statement that "art consists in being completely one's self" reflects his lived experience insofar as he could express it in those times.[50]

Warner's scrapbook includes the poem "Fairy Gifts" by A. H. Perkins of Waukesha. One stanza includes the lines,

> My mother had said I was born at the hour
> Twixt daylight and dark when fairies have power.

Another stanza:

> Still I doubt if more I was blest or banned
> By waving wand in a fairy hand
> For, though the world sneers at my notions unwise,
> I look lightly on life through fairy touched eyes.

Since *fairy* was then one of the most common terms for homosexuals, it's clear why this poem resonated with Ralph Warner.[51]

Another curious element of his scrapbook was a saved clipping titled "Is It Manly to Eat Salad?" While the initial thrust of the article was about a salad being considered a female meal choice, the article then described a "feminine man," observed by the narrator and some companions "at a table in a restaurant, one hot day in July, several years ago." Lest there be any uncertainty as to the characterization of this man, it is noted that he "wore several rings on the fingers of both hands, that the hands bore evidence of being innocent of toil, that the lines of his face were impressively effeminate. He was what would be called in curb-stone vernacular, a Willie boy. There was no doubt about that." When he was served a salad and a "half-dozen 'lady fingers'" the narrator continued, "[our] astonishment gradually changed to indignation, and we made up our mind that a large section of lead-pipe would be the proper remedy for a gastronomic freak of this kind." The article's happier conclusion was that men were progressing and that it was not a sign of "moral degeneracy for a man to eat salad." Certainly, however, it was a cautionary tale for any Willie boy to read or save.[52]

Despite his concern, apparently Warner was not shunned for his otherness in Cooksville. One article described him as "the most cherished and beloved citizen," winning his neighbors' "highest praise" and proud claims of personal friendship. Another author noted that young men called out to Warner from the gateway to his yard, seeking a companion for the old swimming hole. Later, when Warner was in ill health, newspaper accounts praised his work to save the artifacts of the pioneer period and noted, "The people of Wisconsin owe [him] a great debt." Debilitated by a stroke in 1933, Warner spent his final years with a sister in Florida. His creation of a safe place to live as a non-normative man was one of the great successes of his not-so-private life.[53]

Beyond his own unflinching self-portrayal, Warner made other contributions to gay men in Wisconsin. His beloved House Next Door would eventually become a home for several generations of gay men. And in later years, other gay men and artistic types would make Cooksville their home. Edgar Hellum, from nearby Stoughton, who knew Warner well, would eventually collaborate with Bob Neal to create Pendarvis in Mineral Point. These Mineral Point partners combined the revival of the Cornish pioneer experience with antiques and food, much as Warner had done in his village. Both Cooksville and Mineral Point catered to the high tourist trade, with particular interest among ladies' groups, garden clubs, faculty wives, and society types. An examination of both Warner's and Pendarvis's guest books show these types were the predominant guests. But there is another group that appears in the guest books as well: bachelor gentlemen. Connections such as these, established by the work of Ralph Warner, helped to build an early Wisconsin communication network of gay men.[54]

WORLD TRAVELER FROM WISCONSIN

Another Wisconsin gay man for whom London was a major influence was Will Gundry, a lifelong bachelor born in 1858 in Mineral Point, the early lead mining town. The family history noted that if "asked to describe himself with one word, Gundry would undoubtedly have called himself a 'pianist.'" After early schooling in Mineral Point, he enrolled at the University of Wisconsin in Madison to study classics. Participation in a college musical resulted in a review of Gundry as "the best artistic performance of the evening." Forced to leave the university early because of his participation in a prank, he was sent by his family to Paris for one year.[55]

Back in the United States, he was known to vacation with other young fellows. In 1879, in his twenties, he again went abroad, to London, where he worked and remained for three years. In his scrapbook he kept the ticket stubs for the many arts events he attended. Returning again to the States, Gundry worked in various businesses, some associated with family investments. The grounds of Orchard Hill, the family home in Mineral Point, were in his particular care. He offered a garden tour to the local newspaper reporter, who described him as "quite an expert in floriculture."[56]

Gundry's musical nature led him to study piano at the New England Conservatory of Music in Boston during the 1880s. Once back in Mineral Point he put on seven annual musical evenings, complete with printed programs, for a select audience at Orchard Hill. A local review noted, "Will Gundry is in every truth an artist of ability." He sponsored the career of a young pianist friend, John Clark Williams, "even to the extent of traveling with him, in 1892, to Berlin where John continued his musical education." The local news reported that Gundry and Williams "left last Monday for their annual outing," an eight-day trip by a team of horses through southern Wisconsin. Several of the yearly trips made the papers, as well as one the two men took in 1898 to visit the Trans-Mississippi Exposition at Omaha.[57]

Orchard Hill, the mansion in Mineral Point where Will Gundry was born and raised.

In the 1890s, Will became an active partner in Gundry and Gray, the main department store in Mineral Point. It was described as a progressive firm, up to date in every respect. A local report said the modern nature of the store spoke well for "the enterprise of the proprietors," and advances, such as lighting the entire building with electricity and using steam heat, were made by the junior members, Messrs. William P. Gundry and John L. Gray. Locals compared the brand favorably to Marshall Field and Company in Chicago. In fact, Will Gundry made many buying trips to Chicago. During his trips to the big city, he may have developed gay contacts—later correspondence shows mentions of names and news about male friends he had in common with Bob Neal, who worked in Chicago in the 1930s and participated in its gay circles. Later in life, Gundry managed Neal's inherited wealth and investments. He was one of the first people in Mineral Point to have an auto with a chauffeur. In his later years, he and his sister, with whom he sometimes lived, would travel the Wisconsin River to Frank Lloyd Wright's Taliesin to see foreign movies at the Fellowship.[58]

Gundry also kept a scrapbook of clippings and many other things, including news items about theaters and concert halls, poems by Walt

Will Gundry enjoyed traveling around the state with young men like the companion in this photo taken at Devil's Lake in 1891. MINERAL POINT LIBRARY ARCHIVES

Whitman and Algernon Charles Swinburne, and an unfavorable review of a novel by Henry James, *Washington Square*.[59]

The scrapbook contains a number of Oscar Wilde items from the Irish celebrity's 1882 tour of America. One item is a caricature drawing of Wilde used in an ad to sell clothes. Another is the story of Wilde's arrival in America, full of Wilde celebrating the "clean beauty of my strong limbs"; another quote Gundry clipped reads, "But I am here, in my creamy lustihood, to pipe of Passion's venturous Poesy, and reap the scorching harvest of self-love!" Wilde is reported to have said of poetry, "She is only to be compared to Salmacis, who is not boy or girl, but yet is both." Gundry's interest in Wilde can also be seen in a Gundry and Gray store card with the image of the aesthete in his velvet outfit, holding a sunflower. All the material, however, dated from before Wilde's disgrace.[60]

One of the young men whom Will Gundry mentored in interior design was Robert Neal of Mineral Point. Gundry referred Neal to the English decorator Syrie Maugham, the estranged wife of author W. Somerset Maugham, for employment in her Chicago shop. When Depression-Era economics forced her to close the Chicago shop, Neal went to work in her New York shop. When that too had to close, Neal was offered the opportunity to work for her in London, and he accepted. Thus began a correspondence between Neal and Gundry.[61]

In a 1933 letter to Neal, Gundry fondly remembered his own London days: "Just writing the names of the streets, well known corners and places of the West End gives me quite a thrill, and makes me even smell the well defined odors of the fascinating place." Among his bits of advice, having visited as recently as 1929, Gundry penned, "There are still occasions for adventure plenty of it of every kind in that Piccadilly Circus, Haymarket neighborhood." He mentions that "the loafers in the doorways and looking into shop windows were quite as curious, male and female, as they used to be."[62]

Gundry also recalled his own cautious and apparently chaste early days: "I often think of the many opportunities and hints I used to have but never dared to take advantage of." He mentions Hyde Park, another of queer London's haunts, where one could "look over the jaunty soldiers on perverted pleasure" who frequented that part of the park in the evening. Another memory he describes to Neal is walking past the Serpentine lake,

Will Gundry probably selected this image of Oscar Wilde for an advertisement in order to promote his department store as a place of taste. MINERAL POINT LIBRARY ARCHIVES

"where hordes of young fellows used to bathe in the hot summer evenings in a state of nature which was of course most shocking, but still at times very interesting." Gundry seems to have remembered the geography of gay London quite well.[63]

In the same note to Neal, Gundry implied that Neal's stints in Chicago and New York had opened the younger man to the gay world of those cities. Gundry wrote, "I differed in a way from you too in as much as I was ignorant of so much that your Chicago and New York experiences have cultivated in you, and which meant so much to you in the past five years and is bound to be such a tremendous item in your London life." Hoping to receive details in his return letters from Neal, Gundry was clear: "I shall be very circumspect as to what I divulge." Gundry was encouraging, telling young Neal, "I have great confidence in your being able to grasp the outstanding features of London life, especially those that appeal to your sense aesthetic and otherwise."[64]

Lastly, in an avuncular manner, he continued: "Your opinion in regard to gray flannel trousers coincides with mine, and I well remember when a similar rage for thin gray flannel reigned I was taking a bus at the junction of Fleet St. and Chancery Lane when I saw a slim young blond fellow in his gray flannel ascend a bus of those days to get on what they called the 'Knifeboard' on top. He made a bas relief that I have never forgotten and never expect to see eclipsed, the kind that entrances you in these advanced days."[65]

That the correspondence between the two men was intimate and frank is also made apparent when Gundry complained of the summer heat, penning, "I am wearing as little as I can, no unders at all." He asked Neal to let him know "what happens to you and 'Brad,'" an apparent New York friendship. That Gundry was fond of Neal shows in his expressions "I think of you oftener than often" and "wished you were nearer at hand."[66]

Neal's responses revealed his own exploration of gay London. He stated his intent in writing: "I do not, in any regard[, wish] to diminish our correspondence, for, probably, the things that I do and shall be doing, will be of interest to you, and for that reason, for one, I want to keep on as steadily as possible. The other reason, I have told you times before, and the potency and same regard is still very much alive, and will always be."[67]

On one of his first days in the city, Neal walked around Piccadilly Circus and came home through Hyde Park. In a later letter, he described watching his expenses and explained about not going to the theater, but, he said, "Hyde Park & the Marble Arch occupy my time, for no expense is entailed from them." Whether he was listening to an orator at Speakers' Corner or exploring this area of gay London at night remains unclear.[68]

In his early letters, Neal mentions meeting young men—one who looked like Ramon Novarro and another with whom he planned a picnic in Kew Gardens. Neal described meeting the rising star, gay stage designer Oliver Messel: "He is about 28, dark, and is a German Jew. Very wealthy, and very - - - -. After our little visit he extended his hand, which of course I shook. I only hope that I can see more of him, but he flies too high for me. But then." Presumably, the dashes imply Messel's homosexuality. Neal also socialized with young American concert pianist Clifford Herzer from Michigan and gave Gundry reviews of his concerts.[69]

About his New York entanglement, Neal told Gundry, "I think that I shall never hear from Brad or even expect him over here." He elaborated, "'Brad' is still among the unknown and I feel now that will continue to be so. I felt all along that it was only a flighty meeting and that it would soon pass (which it seems to have done) but I did enjoy it while it lasted. I have come to the conclusion 'Gather the rosebuds, while ye may' and in that perhaps have settled for a little while."[70]

Yet Neal followed with this: "It was strange, as you say and a museum piece, and strangely enough I have all too soon contracted another here, the intensity of which is insurpassable in my short life." Neal described connecting with Emmanuel Braune, a "lad of 22 from Rio de Janeiro." They went on a several-day Whitsun holiday walking tour of Lambourn and stayed in a private cottage. Neal spent a lot of time with Braune, going to Proms concerts and Hampton Court, though in the end, Neal wrote, "Emmanuel is almost out of the picture. . . . Such a break is bound to be noticeable, and yet while I miss his being around all the time—I feel much more free—not so tied down."[71]

In another letter, Neal included this interesting tidbit: "I finally mailed a letter of introduction to a Jimmie Watts (an impersonator of women, I understand) that I had given to me in N.Y. before I left." Neal's ability to obtain such a letter further indicates his participation in gay life in New York. In perhaps a coded reference he said, "I might casually remark that I did become the victim of my virtue (as might be expected)." While Neal's writing included plenty of hints about a shared interest in a gay world, his fondness for Gundry also compelled him to send lists of garden flowers from various visits, as he knew Gundry would enjoy them.[72]

During these early days in London, Neal appreciated his association with his employer, Syrie Maugham, who even took him on a quick five-hour visit to Paris. By September 1933, however, he was no longer fascinated with Maugham. Complicating matters was the fact that Neal's visa renewals required him to state that he was not employed in London. And his duties in the shop were limited when Maugham brought in another partner. Suddenly, Neal's income was not sufficient to enable him to do the things he wanted to do in London, such as buying handmade English suits from Savile Row. Neal had to scrimp on expenses and was eating cold baked beans in his flat for his evening meals. He wrote, "I should love to get out of this profession completely and have a decided change." He spoke of coming back to America, though he mentioned wanting to see Cornwall before returning, perhaps because his grandmother was Cornish or because of the Cornish lore in Mineral Point.[73]

Neal's return to America in 1934 after exploring the homosexual world of England shows how another country's liberating influences could reinforce an individual's gay identity upon return to the States. One insight into his return may lie in an undated clipping included in his archives titled "A Prodigal Returns: And Discovers His Native Land," written by someone identified only by the initials W. R. J., though details indicate the author is perhaps a native of Mineral Point.[74]

The writer W. R. J. clearly knew of the Glenway Wescott odyssey, for his article opened, "Saying 'Goodbye, Wisconsin' in somewhat the same mood perhaps as another Wisconsinite who had fled from what he called this 'abstract nowhere' and joined the ranks of the literary expatriates in southern France, I too, after three frustrated years of university, took flight from what then seemed the tedium of the middle west and landed, though a bit short of southern France, in a very satisfactory haven." This writer's refuge from Wisconsin was New York City, where he "settled down to the serious business of life in Greenwich Village." While W. R. J. made references to his ostensible heterosexuality, he clearly interacted with the artistic and gay communities in Greenwich Village and connected also with the members of the Provincetown Playhouse.[75]

According to the article, W. R. J. went "Home to Wisconsin" upon the death of his father and began a period of transition and readjustment. His new location is mentioned as scarcely more than a good day's walk from Taliesin. W. R. J. learns to rediscover "the illimitable beauties of our own Wisconsin." He recalls Will Gundry as "another loyal son who after wandering over the world is always happy to return." W. R. J. quoted Frank Lloyd Wright as saying, "Yes, Mr. Gundry, you and I have been faithful to Wisconsin." The article concludes, "Insufficient unto myself, beset by loneliness and a gnawing hunger for the stimulation of people and events, I have mushed on through the 'abstract nowhere' and come upon a fertile field of ever growing interests." Returning to Wisconsin would prove re-warding to many gay expats.[76]

A LIFE PARTNERSHIP

Bob Neal's return to Mineral Point in 1934 would spark his interests in historic preservation, pioneer Cornish culture, and his partner, Edgar Hellum of Stoughton. These were all wrapped up together in a package called Pendarvis.

The Pendarvis story followed the Cooksville model, and writer Will Fellows has shown the connections through Hellum's purchase of a house near Warner's and his helping Warner in the latter's work. Pendarvis began as an antiques shop and eventually became a restaurant with a Cornish flavor, where the initial meals of full tea were similar to those served at Cooksville. Neal and Hellum's restoration of nineteenth-century buildings with pioneer furnishings also followed Warner's model. Additionally, the early press accounts of Pendarvis noted the non-normative gender roles performed by Neal and Hellum, who did their own cooking, dishwashing, decorating, and gardening.[77]

One difference between Cooksville and Pendarvis was that Pendarvis consisted of a complex of buildings (three, initially, in the 1930s), and journalists could reference other nationally known historic restoration complexes as points of comparison, such as Colonial Williamsburg or New Salem in Illinois. Though this chapter focuses on the 1920s and 1930s, Pendarvis would go on to become nationally known after World War II through articles that appeared in the *Saturday Evening Post* and *Coronet* magazines. Duncan Hines even recommended its food in his famous restaurant guides.[78]

Most writers who covered Pendarvis during its early period, and even later on, stressed Bob Neal's time working abroad as a decorator with Syrie Maugham. Sometimes they noted the rooms and sets he and Maugham had worked on in England for Alfred Lunt and Lynn Fontanne, who per-formed on the London stage. Neal preserved the autographed celebrity photos the actors presented to him. Neal must have provided the press with these London details to boost his credentials as an artistic interior decorator. Recalling his life and experiences in London also would have

Edgar Hellum (left) and Bob Neal pose in front of the Pendarvis House, one of several buildings they restored in Mineral Point. MINERAL POINT LIBRARY ARCHIVES

reinforced his own sense of identity. In an interview conducted in 1982, despite what he wrote to Gundry, Neal would claim he had planned to go back to London up until the time he and Edgar Hellum bought the first stone house for what would become Pendarvis.[79]

In the first story about the place, written in 1935, *Wisconsin State Journal* columnist Betty Cass posed a question to Bob Neal, "'And who are you?' I asked. 'The Fairy Prince with the Magic Wand?'" Another writer called Pendarvis "a Magic Land" and made references to Avalon. Clearly Pendarvis was not viewed as a run-of-the-mill household.[80]

This unusualness of two men opening an English tea shop with Cornish accents provoked reactions. "Naturally people were curious," a *Milwaukee Journal* article stated. "What were these two young fellows doing that kept them so busy?" A Janesville story referred to the place as an "unorthodox hostelry" and observed, "Visitors to Pendarvis house, oddly enough are more often than not from quite a distance."[81]

Betty Cass was the most explicit about local reactions in a 1939 piece:

Betty Cass, a Madison journalist, was an early promoter of Pendarvis and made space in her columns to praise the exploits of other gay men in the 1930s.
WHI IMAGE ID 140724

"Not more than a dozen or so Mineral Point residents have taken the time or trouble to go down to Shakerag Street to see what is going on in their midst about which people and papers all over the country are beginning to talk." She noted that Neal and Hellum "were often referred to as being 'slightly pixilated,' a good Cornish term." "Piskies" are part of the fairy lore of Cornwall. In America's post-war period during the Army-McCarthy hearings (see chapter 7), the term *pixies* was understood as a code for homosexuals, and it may have been used even before the war.[82]

With tea offered at Pendarvis as a light repast costing fifty cents (about nine dollars in today's currency) when whole meals could be had for less, the local folks in Mineral Point understandably might have passed on the Pendarvis dining opportunity. Gundry's patronage to the local boys extended to his will, in which he left Neal a thousand dollars and Hellum five hundred (which today would represent at least $15,000 and $7,500).[83]

Betty Cass may have overestimated Neal and Hellum's isolation in the town. When the Gundry estate, Orchard Hill, was threatened with demolition in the late 1930s, Bob Neal was able to devise a strategy to save it by

A room in Pendarvis House in 1936. WHI IMAGE ID 103242

forming the Mineral Point Historical Society and renaming the property Orchard Lawn, thereby getting it off the tax rolls. Such a civic endeavor required engagement with other residents. Certainly it was a fitting tribute to Neal's mentor Mr. Gundry. Later, Bob Neal would serve on the city council, create Wisconsin's first historic district, and establish the local history room at the Mineral Point library. He lectured frequently on Cornish culture. Hellum, who was of Norwegian descent, would gain fame as a designated Cornish Bard (an old Celtic honor bestowed by a society in the United Kingdom charged with preserving Cornish language and culture). The couple's success and genuine involvement in their community was undeniable.[84]

If the press had been challenged in deciding how to portray Ralph Warner as a single non-normative man, their new challenge was how to portray the non-normative duo of Bob Neal and Edgar Hellum. More attention was paid to Bob Neal, the Mineral Point native. Betty Cass described him as "a charming young man with a great deal of wavy black hair, beautiful deep-set dark eyes, and grey flannels." Those fashionable English "grey" flannels were a lingering echo of London.[85]

Most of the pre–World War II accounts of Pendarvis in newspapers throughout southern Wisconsin used various expressions to describe the couple. The most common phrases were "two young men" or "the boys." Variations on this included "two young artisans," "two young fellows," "young men with the soul of an artist," "these versatile young men," and "two clever young men." This was when Neal and Hellum, both born in 1906, were in their early thirties. Given that life expectancy at this time was less than sixty years, they might more appropriately have been called middle-aged. The variations on "boys" or "youths" may have implied that they were not perceived as fully developed men. Then again, newspaper writers were not always the best estimators of age; in 1939, when Neal and Hellum were thirty-three, one writer guessed that they were "bachelors apparently both somewhat under 30 years of age." Both Neal and Hellum were rail thin, which also may have contributed to their youthful appearance. And as noted before about Warner, the word *artist* also was also used as a code for homosexuals at the time.[86]

The press accounts also used the terms "partners," "Cornish partnership," "Neal and his associate," and "the young man and his partner." One writer said of Neal that he had found "another young man with similar

Most reporters described Bob Neal (left) and Edgar Hellum as young men and partners who lived in the same building, rather than business partners.
MINERAL POINT LIBRARY ARCHIVES

ideas." Another wrote that a "Friendship developed." The stories made it quite clear that the two lived in the small stone cottage together, and journalists did not qualify the term *partner* with an adjective like *business*. The strategy of actually being business partners, however, afforded a plausible cover. After they sold the Pendarvis complex in the 1970s, Neal and Hellum lived separately. Whether this was a result of their growing apart or the need to obscure the nature of their relationship is not known for sure.[87]

Later in life, Hellum would recall that Neal's relatives had treated him "just like I was a member of the family." That their relationship remained strong and loving even after they sold Pendarvis was made apparent when Neal became sick and Hellum took him in: "We set up a bed and I took care of him for two years." Hellum remembered telling Neal, "You sure as hell don't want to go to a nursing home. I said if I have to crawl on my hands and knees [I'll] look after you as long as I'm able." Preserved among Neal's archives is the first Christmas card he received from Hellum.[88]

The choice to buy buildings on Shakerag Street, while admittedly all they could afford (at ten dollars for their first house), also put them on the economic margins of Mineral Point, where the working-class houses were being torn down. Those presumed social margins were probably safer for the couple as well. Will Gundry, his sister, and the other wealthier residents lived up on the hills of town. Gundry later admitted he was amazed to be having tea on Shakerag, the street where workingmen lived in cottages.[89]

Bob Neal collected Cornish lore and included in his scrapbook a clipping of the words to an old bachelor's song. This and other Cornish information was sought by the American Archives of Folk Song at the Library of Congress as part of an effort by the WPA, FDR's Works Progress Administration, to preserve cultural lore.

I have no wife to bother my life
No Children to cry for shoes
I never sit down in my chair upside down
I paddle my own canoe.[90]

Hellum would much later recall that as a youth he told his family, "I don't think I'm ever going to get married." Hellum's recollections also reveal how gay networks could support gay men in lieu of biological family.

Hellum's visits to Cooksville and his friendship with Ralph Warner eventually led to a connection between Neal and Warner. On a trip to Florida, Neal and Hellum stopped in to see Warner, who, toward the end of his life, was living there with his sister.[91]

Hellum, in the same late oral interview, remembered that he and Neal had agreed to work things out by talking about them: "That's the only reason we ever lived together that long. We definitely worked things out." Hellum portrayed himself as a "country boy" even though he had studied at the Art Institute of Chicago, while Neal portrayed himself as an art lover who liked ballet and the opera. In reality, however, Hellum's art was acknowledged in exhibits at the Wisconsin Historical Society Museum and at the Art Institute.[92]

When Neal died in 1983, some stories and obituaries noted that his partner survived him; others did not. When Hellum died in 2000, all notices stated that he had been predeceased by his partner. This reflects the media's growing comfort with talking about a gay couple.[93]

THE BACHELORS OF HISTORIC TOURISM

Chester Holway, a journalist and publicist, was the gay man who owned the House Next Door following Ralph Warner. Holway wrote about Mineral Point and Pendarvis in an article titled "Cornish Town Lies Serene in Wisconsin Hills," found in an undated newspaper clipping. Larry Reed, a Cooksville archivist who has written on Holway, tentatively dates this article in the late 1930s. In Holway's telling, "One day two bright young men came along, discovered that these houses were picturesque, and chose one to restore. . . . Almost before the citizens knew it their town was on the tourist route." In his own experience, Holway says, "My hopes for saffron cake and a dish of tea expire when I find a notice tacked to the Pendarvis door saying the houses are closed for the day." However, he notes, "Travelers will also want to visit the restored Gundry mansion."[94]

In 1949, Holway wrote *How to Profit from the Tourist Business*, noting that during his own career in advertising and tourist promotion he had "traveled thousands of miles through mid-western resort regions." The book's purpose was to help "the smaller community" that might benefit from tourism.[95]

Chester Holway at his
typewriter in the 1930s.
COOKSVILLE ARCHIVES AND
COLLECTIONS

In chapter 8, titled "How Can You Profit from Your Historic Past?," Holway warned that because "Williamsburg shines so brilliantly . . . there is danger we may overlook our lesser restorations." On his list of lesser restored areas to consider are sites related to mining, such as Mineral Point.[96]

Holway also probably knew about New Glarus and its tourist attraction, the Chalet of the Golden Fleece, a copy of a Swiss mountain residence built by Edwin Barlow, another lifelong bachelor. In the Bernese chalet, Barlow created a museum of old Swiss artifacts and other items acquired during his world travels. Though Barlow was born in Milwaukee in 1885, his mother was a native of New Glarus in Green County. Barlow spent his youth and school years in Monticello, Wisconsin. He served overseas with the Thirty-Second Division hospital unit during the Great War and then worked as a theatrical director and producer. By 1937, he was back in New Glarus, where he built the chalet and opened it to visitors who wanted to tour the building and see its collections.[97]

Barlow's obituary noted that he had made sixty-three Atlantic crossings in his lifetime. Before World War II, he lived for a while in Lausanne, Switzerland. Like Weimar Germany, the German-speaking part of Switzerland around Zurich had an active gay scene as early as the 1930s.

The Chalet of the Golden Fleece in New Glarus, Wisconsin.

Lausanne, being in the French-speaking canton of Vaud, followed the Napoleonic code of 1798, which decriminalized homosexual acts from that time forward. The Swiss magazine *Banner of Friendship* was founded in 1932 by the lesbian Anna Vock; Karl Meier joined her in the magazine's production in 1934. The magazine, which came to be known as *Der Kreis* (*The Circle*), would later help inspire America's *ONE* magazine in the 1950s. Magnus Hirschfeld was the leading voice for the unsuccessful effort to repeal Paragraph 175 of the German penal code, which criminalized homosexual acts. Echoing Hirschfeld's efforts, there was also a movement to decriminalize homosexuality across the entire federal Swiss republic in the early 1930s, and it would come to fruition in 1942. Unlike the Nazis, who suppressed Germany's open gay culture of the Weimar days, the neutral Swiss did not send gays to concentration camps or harshly suppress the country's gay movement. In fact, the active gay efforts helped to influence Switzerland's new penal code, adopted in 1942, which decriminalized homosexual acts across the republic, not just in the French cantons.[98]

A good friend of Barlow's was another New Glarus native, Herbert Kubly, the world-famous travel writer, who also returned to Wisconsin after living for a couple of years in Italy in the early 1950s. In a 1960s interview with the *Milwaukee Journal*'s book editor, Kubly referenced Wescott's "Good-Bye Wisconsin." Barlow was also credited with the idea for New Glarus's Wilhelm Tell pageant and directed many of its early performances. According to local lore, Barlow liked to cross-dress at private parties.[99]

On his passing on September 21, 1957, the *Monroe Evening Times* commented that Barlow was "widely known for his efforts to perpetuate Swiss culture and art in this country." The paper reported, "The Chalet was a mecca for travelers from all parts of the country and from Switzerland." In an editorial on September 24, 1957, the preservationist was praised as "a scholar largely self taught through his travels." The editor called Barlow a "wonderful person" for turning over his museum and its treasured collection to the village of New Glarus.[100]

In addition to Neal and Hellum (and possibly Barlow), Chester Holway found many examples in Wisconsin of gay men or bachelors who had built historic tourist businesses by drawing on their creative and artistic skills. His book on historic tourism concluded: "It will heighten local pride in the past in the part your community played in the building of America, and it will provide pleasure and instruction to your own citizens as well as to your guests."[101]

OVER HERE

Clearly a number of Wisconsin gay men used their travel to Europe in the period around World War I to understand and experience a homosexual culture unknown to them in their state, with its official policies of sexual suppression. That many were able to follow this path suggests that Wisconsin in the Age of Normalcy was less insulating with respect to homosexual information than might be imagined. True, the Wisconsinites profiled here were generally well-educated men with some means and had more access to information than most; but how they used that education contributed to their understanding of themselves.

Glenway Wescott was both right and wrong in his thinking that it was better for homosexuals "to come and go than to stay" in Wisconsin in the

1920 and 1930s. For someone like Wescott, who would live an active gay life and even have the opportunity to participate in the gay rights movement before his death in 1987, saying good-bye to Wisconsin was probably wise. But other gay men resolved not to say good-bye and found ways to lead their lives in the state.

These men devised ways to present themselves outside of the masculine norms and roles common in Wisconsin. In this sense, they truly were the artistic individuals they were so often labeled as. They had the strength of will to create identities that marked them as different, and they took pride in their unorthodox lifestyles.

Their personal archives prove that these men were interested in relations between men. While small in number, their scrapbooks, diaries, letters, and even published stories demonstrate the men's desire to inform others about how they discovered the culture and geography of European gay life. The record probably preserves just a fraction of what they shared with others while alive. As they told their tales, they spread their knowledge of an emerging gay world to others in the state and, by doing so, created part of Wisconsin's own gay subculture.

These men constructed safe places to live their gay lives, acts that were often acknowledged by those around them. Korinne Oberle, a curator at Pendarvis when it opened as a state historical site in 1971, would observe, "Edgar [Hellum] and Bob [Neal] built in Mineral Point a safe port in the storm for like-spirited creative folks who were looking to live the way they wanted to live."[102]

Will Fellows has discussed how gay men like Neal had a cultural intelligence, in that they often made unique contributions to their home areas of the state. Their communities recognized these contributions, though sometimes grudgingly. Men like Neal cleverly lived nonconventional lives under the guise of preserving the early pioneer cultural life of the state, whether New England for Cooksville or Cornwall for Pendarvis. By becoming custodians of history and tradition, they cloaked themselves as authentic Americans, despite their otherness. Chester Holway's book celebrated the profit to be made in these historic restorations—and what could be more American than that? These creative gay pioneers made their lives in Wisconsin both viable and productive.

4

WISCONSIN FAIRY NETWORKING

We were to meet as fixed in law; Divine—
Satanic—any law we might define;
It matters not! We've met, and not too late.
　　　　—FROM "SONNETS TO LEON" BY KEITH MCCUTCHEON, 1930S[1]

"Serenade" will give our ever-present blue noses just the chance they've
been waiting for to dust off their old stove-pipe lids and go around
waving umbrellas in people's faces.
　　　　—BOOK REVIEW, *THE DAILY CARDINAL*, DECEMBER 9, 1937[2]

Martin Duberman, in his 2017 book *Jews Queers Germans: A Novel/ History*, describes the work of the gay sexologist Magnus Hirschfeld and his Institute of Sexual Research in Berlin. In the interwar years of the 1920s and 1930s, the institute undertook counseling for homosexuals. As Duberman put it, "Hirschfeld understands far in advance of most specialists that counseling should include awakening the individual sufferer to the knowledge that he or she is not alone, that a potential community exists, and that becoming part of a social network can do wonders for depression and thoughts of suicide." In this chapter, we examine how Wisconsin homosexuals arrived at a similar understanding and worked to build networks and find community as non-normative individuals.[3]

These Wisconsin gay men and women would see their visibility as a way to present their identities, admittedly with circumspection, to a still largely hostile society. Their willingness to be forthright in their expressions of themselves allowed them to build a network that could eventually usher in a more favorable narrative about homosexuality in the state.

THE BACHELOR LIFE

Ralph Warner in Cooksville and Bob Neal in Mineral Point illustrated how gay men built communication networks in the period between the two world wars. They knew of each other's work through the common agency of Edgar Hellum, who worked with both Warner and Neal. Examining their guest books, we can see clear links to other single men and known bachelors. One such guest was Frank Riley from Madison, who visited the House Next Door in Cooksville every summer. Warner knew him well enough to mention, in his London diaries, that he had written Riley to help track down Ham Beatty of Madison. Riley also shows up in the Pendarvis guest books in Mineral Point.[4]

Frank Riley, born in 1875, studied architecture at Boston Tech, now the Massachusetts Institute of Technology, and lived abroad for four years prior to World War I. He then returned to Madison, where he practiced architectural design. Betty Cass, in her *Wisconsin State Journal* column Day by Day of January 4, 1949, took note of an article in *American Magazine* by a cousin of Riley's, Louise Welch, who wrote under the name Aiken Welch (at the time, female journalists still sometimes masked their identities). In the article, titled "The Happiest Man I Ever Knew," Welch writes about Riley: "Cousin Frank, who certainly led a gay, self-centered life, seemed happier than anyone I knew." He was presented as a bachelor who "lived by himself in a grand house surrounded by a handsome garden." Welch learned that he saw himself as an epicurean in the mold of the Greek philosophers and was "happy to be backed by the ancients." From early in the twentieth century, gay men reached back to classical Greece for a model of homosexuality. Welch also used coded language in her statement, "Nobody was very elegant—that is nobody but Cousin Frank." The caution had to be added, "Yet nobody regarded him as a sissy."[5]

Welch recalls a visit to Riley's house, during which she suspected he was his own housekeeper and noted that he took care of washing his own dishes. Riley cooked her "a truly Epicurean breakfast, simply but perfectly done." She suspected he might be lonely, because he minded his own business. But Welch discovered that Riley actually had many friends and had even put up others in his house when they needed shelter. Recipients of his hospitality included a medical student and a couple of wives of returned World War II veterans.[6]

Bob Neal followed Frank Riley's career and corresponded with him. In 1942, when Riley liked a poem that he heard read over WBBM, the CBS radio station in Chicago, he wrote the script department to obtain a copy and passed it along to Neal. "Little Woodland God" is written in the fairy tradition, opening with the lines:

> I think that surely there's a god
> > For little hunted things:
> A god whose eyes watch tenderly
> > The droop of dying wings.

It closes with:

> I think his pensive Pan-like face
> > Is often wet with tears
> And that his little back is bent
> > From all the weary years.

In Neal's papers, Riley ascribed to the poem a title different from the author's, calling it "The God of Hunted Things." This personal note seems to express the risk of being "found out" shared by the woodland creature and the "fairy" homosexual.[7]

Frank Riley's 1949 obituary noted that he "never married." His architecture projects, which included East High School, Yost's, a prominent Madison department store, and the Madison Club in Madison, were praised in the *Wisconsin State Journal*: "No period of architecture will find them ugly, and that should be one of the important tests of any building, regardless of its period." As might be expected, Riley was described in the article as an artist. Such persons, the paper noted, "are entitled to their eccentricities, and Frank Riley had his."[8]

Riley and other educated bachelors like Warner and Neal left records that demonstrate how Wisconsin homosexuals could build social networks among themselves. They visted one another and exchanged letters and information on topics of joint interest. And all three devoted themselves to curating singular houses and gardens, engaging in the stereotypically feminine aspects of domestic life. The connections among Riley, Warner, Neal, and likely others show that they built more than private lives in isolated enclaves. Their successful lives and the pride they felt in their identities served to reinforce each other.

A SHAKESPEARE OF THE SANDBARS

Keith McCutcheon was born in Arena, a Wisconsin River Valley town, in the early twentieth century. He was roughly the same age as Bob Neal and Edgar Hellum. While not invested in heritage tourism as deeply as the gay men in the preceding chapter, McCutcheon did write a historical pageant based on Old Helena, a now-lost river town. Viewing himself as a writer, he believed that with the pageant, a WPA project, he had taken a "definite step away from an old and overworked form."[9]

McCutcheon's River Valley connections had been evidenced earlier, however, for he spent the year 1930 working with Frank Lloyd Wright as a secretary at Taliesin. Wright's Hillside School would inspire McCutcheon to write poems, and one poem about Taliesin later appeared in McCutcheon's first book of published verse.

In describing Arena, McCutcheon wrote, "Oh, this is a small town— only a tiny place—yet here is home—where acquaintances are friends, and all society is equal—and one's affairs are common knowledge." McCutcheon did not stay in Arena, though his sonnets, his favorite poetic form, often drew themes from the river valley of the Wisconsin.[10]

Unlike the small-town historic renovators of the last chapter, McCutcheon moved permanently from his home community and spent most of his life in Madison. He was not concerned primarily with carving out a personal space, but he actively defined his own gay identity and moved in broader circles of gay men. Because a substantial number of sources related to his life and works are available from the 1930s and 1940s, one can use a review of McCutcheon's writings to show how his self-affirming sense of identity developed over successive stages in his life.

McCutcheon began his explorations of sexual identity while attending the University of Wisconsin in Madison. During his lifetime, as the *Alumni Magazine* later put it, he was a "poet, artist, and interior decorator." On campus, he lived in a fraternity through 1927, his senior year.[11]

Among McCutcheon's papers are many essays written for his English classes at the UW. Some of these describe the campus as a place of nine thousand students, many of whom went to the south side of town to get their illegal gin during Prohibition. One English instructor commented on the essays, "Your style is too highly colored for my taste." McCutcheon would retain this highly colored, romantic style throughout his life. The appeal of his work probably decreased when newer, sparer forms of writing were the vogue after World War I.[12]

Even in his 1920s writings, McCutcheon was beginning to write about same-sex love, though he used guarded language. Often, for example, the word *friend* meant something much more. A student essay, "A Letter Sent and a Letter Received," began: "I wrote a letter to my friend, a better friend than I can tell. It was filled with loving phrases, that thrilled as I penned them, and praises that sincerity alone could prompt. Would he be filled with equal fire, and filled with a desire to meet me, and then greet me once again." The friend responded that the two would be "known as friends that no ordinary thing could part." In the composition, McCutcheon takes the letter and puts it "away where common men cannot see, and ridicule me." In another instance, he wrote about the same man in the context of "real friends in the sacred sense of the word; he is a friend that I love."[13]

In yet another essay, McCutcheon's subject was a friendship's growth as "a universal experience—as charming and as sacred as the more subtle and more primitive form of sex attraction called love." McCutcheon likened friendship to "a tonic in the blood, vitalizing and invigorating the whole being." He also described a man "who loved his friend with the devotion of Jonathan." The biblical friendship between Jonathan and David has long resonated with homosexual men. As McCutcheon noted in the essay, "Jonathan and David made a covenant because he loved him as his own soul."[14]

An additional example of McCutcheon's writings about homosexuals is a manuscript for a one-act play featuring two young men, John and Rodney. John, while trying to explain poetry to his friend, says, "Poetry is like you Rodney. Like when you were under the shower this afternoon after track. Water streaming all over you. Your body glistened like marble in the rain. I thought how beautiful you were; and the lines of that poem we had the other day in class." In the play, John invites Rodney over to hear readings of poems by Shelley. Rodney, who now appreciates poetry, concludes, "Say anybody who can string words together like that would never be a sissy: it takes brains my friend, brains."[15]

The campus atmosphere of the 1920s was not receptive to outright expressions of same-sex love. For example, the April 2, 1924, issue of *The Proletarian*, which described itself as "Not an Official Student Publication," printed a Great War tale containing the following line: "No effeminate white livered weaklings ever partake in our fights." The effeminate weaklings, most likely homosexuals, were contrasted with "red-blooded he-Americans."[16]

The sandbars, swimming holes, and nude beaches of the lower Wisconsin River Valley inspired Keith McCutcheon's poetry.

The Proletarian notwithstanding, it's possible that McCutcheon later wrote in a coded way about nude beaches frequented by gay men. In his newspaper columns, McCutcheon described visiting the river: "It is the Wisconsin and not a very big and wide river at all at this point. But it has a peace and quiet beauty that is restful. My friend is sitting near me; smoking his pipe and watching the sky." In another column, he describes a scene of "gleaming muddy sloughs, and then along the silver water the golden stretches of the sandbars." One unpublished poem is titled "Twilight Songs from a Wisconsin River Sandbar."[17]

It's quite possible, as well, that he participated in the early days of the nude beach at Mazomanie. A series on "The Rivers of America," created by Constance Lindsay Skinner in 1935, covered at least thirty rivers and proves that the beach at Mazomanie was well established by the 1930s. The river and its famous beach were featured in a 1942 volume, *The Wisconsin: River of a Thousand Isles*, by the well-known regional writer August Derleth of Sauk City and illustrated by John Steuart Curry, the first artist in residence at UW–Madison. Derleth, according to his biographer, was bisexual.[18]

In *The Wisconsin*, Derleth, whom McCutcheon knew, wrote, "And the swimming holes! They are still in use, as they should be. Off Third Island east of Sauk City is Bare-Skin Beach, which is just what its name implies, of course; looking upstream at any time during the hot weather from April to October, it is possible to see the lithe bodies of the boys gleaming in the sun, white against the cobalt water and the massed trees behind." Certainly, this description implies an existing tradition.[19]

McCutcheon wrote several unpublished poems drawing on river swims, including "To One Swimming," which could have been set on the same-sex beach described by Derleth:

And others now will look upon your body
Sacred once to only me, and once pressed close to mine
And thrilled fingers of water will fondle you,
And sand will feel your press . . .
And you fling your garments down.
You splash in the swift running river:
Dive, roll . . . on your back . . .
And then you sprawl in the sand, ah, sand . . .

The most explicit poem is "Twilight Songs from a Wisconsin River Sand-bar." In one line, a breeze blows "swift riffles over the moon-silvered river: / futile caresses . . . like man-lovers." This work also includes references to "strange" or "sterile" love, which McCutcheon used in other poems to indicate same-sex attraction.[20]

Among McCutcheon's papers are many unpublished works that show how he grappled with his own sexual identity. An early hand-produced work titled *Lyrics of the Night and Other Verses* is a collection of his poems from the 1920s. He would later recycle this title for his first published work. That he made this and other hand-produced chapbooks seems to indicate that he planned to show and share them with others, even if they were not officially published. In *Lyrics*, he proclaimed, "And let me dream and dream of things that are not now—can never be!" One sonnet hinted at sexual exploration and another at hidden love.[21]

Keith McCutcheon's handmade poetry chapbook, *Lyrics of the Night and Other Verses,* included coded references to same-sex love.

26th Sonnet

lived my whole life through in a night,
And died in the dawn!
Died!
But, O! the fun of a Life!!

52nd Sonnet

Where silence acts as handmaid to a flame
That burns within the temple of my soul
Where none can see—But could I once the veil
Remove, its glowing coals might light the world![22]

The most revealing expression of McCutcheon's early struggles with sexual identity appears in *Twilight Verses*, a sixty-eight-page compendium dated 1932. The cover, drawn by McCutcheon, displayed an image of a man named Leon, the subject of the book's last sequence of poems. "Sonnets to Leon" describes McCutcheon's infatuation with another tuberculosis patient at Statesan, the State Tuberculosis Sanatorium in Wales, Waukesha County. McCutcheon dedicates the chapbook to those "destined to remain within the pale of Pagan groves," also called the "acolytes of sterile love." The poems contain references to "petulant masculine kisses," "sterile love," and "a world of infinite pleasure perverse."[23]

The last of the twenty-five "Sonnets to Leon" exposes the theme of internalized homophobia most transparently.

And men have worshipped me as I do you
But bitter chastity proved most unkind;
Strange fears half-filled,—repulsed me when I knew;
Yet still returned caresses loathed in mind.

With bold language, McCutcheon wrote of the wild joy in this bittersweet perversity: "Along the crimson stem of heart's red blood, again my love is in the blooming bud." While he used sexual imagery, McCutcheon made love his theme: "But one—inseparable as Love and Heart."[24]

McCutcheon explains the strength drawn from knowing other homo-sexuals in "Twilight Verses":

> One consolation is: I'm not alone:
> For many more are feeling what I feel,
> In passive mis'ry gambling on Fate's wheel,
> But eyes diverted seeing Beauty's own
> Sweet profile; and despite near danger zone
> We'll ever wise because a certain zeal
> Of passion makes their lives too keen and facile
> In the mold of beauty and the sweeter tome.[25]

Finally, in the sequence's last sonnet, "L'Envoi," the once-hinted-at be-comes clear:

> Rare Virtue—rarer Vice! Anomaly
> Of passion—homosexual—perverse!

The poet, while describing himself as homosexual, was also aware that such love could not be broadly proclaimed. "L'Envoi" also included a play on McCutcheon's name, which includes a variant of the word for the area of a knight's shield that displays symbols: "And would its scutcheon be an endless curse that from Society receives a terse cold shoulder, and a lost monopoly?" In all these early unpublished poems, the author shows a strong desire for homosexual love but also a very large internalized homo-phobia that he has not yet discarded.[26]

McCutcheon also ventured into the genre of gay pulp fiction with a twenty-nine-page unpublished short story called "Mountain Summer." The plot involves Dick, a "very good looking" twenty-three-year-old collegian, who is traveling from the East to a ranch in Wyoming that belongs to one of his father's fraternity brothers. The ranch has fifty head of cattle and some twenty-plus ranch hands, which appeals to Dick, who "felt it would be more fun to sleep in the bunk house with the hands." As the story develops, Dick is sent to upper mountain pas-tures and the foreman tells him that Ted, twenty-eight, the pasture's "real handsome" hand, is "good company," adding, "Yeh, you two'll get along swell."[27]

The night before going up the mountain, the easterner dreams of the "pardner." Upon arriving, Dick "looked directly into light blue eyes, down a straight nose, at a pleasantly smiling mouth, with full red lips, along a square, but not hard jaw and chin, to the strong supple man so free and easy in his saddle."[28]

After meeting on the mountain, Ted leads Dick to "a nice pool to bathe, with a waterfall that makes a natural shower." After swimming, "they crawled to the mossy bank and stretched out in the warm sun to dry. . . . In a sudden easy movement, Ted rolled close to Dick, raised his head, leaned over, and with a tenderness, with instinctive passion, kissed him on the mouth." That night in the cabin, Dick returns Ted's kiss. Thus, an early version of *Brokeback Mountain* was written by a gay Wisconsin man in the 1930s.[29]

Things end happily for the two lads in "Mountain Summer." Many people assume that before Stonewall, gay fiction always ended tragically, as it does in the more widely read published fiction about gay characters from that era. The sad ending of Sebastian Flyte, Evelyn Waugh's gay character in the 1945 novel *Brideshead Revisited*, is an example of this phenomenon. E. M. Forster's "Terminal Note," which describes what happens to the characters in his gay novel *Maurice*, makes the case that "the lovers get away unpunished." However, though he wrote "Terminal Note" in 1960, it was not made available to the public until 1971, when the novel was published posthumously because Forster had thought the ending would have to remain in manuscript form. Forster was insistent that for this story, "a happy ending was imperative." He had circulated the 1914 manuscript privately to "carefully picked" friends. In 2003, however, Michael Bronski exploded the myth of the homosexual character meeting an unhappy end in pre-Stonewall fiction. One chapter in his *Pulp Friction: Uncovering the Golden Age of Gay Male Pulps* is entitled "The New Gay Novel: Happier Homos and Happier Endings"; it examined four gay novels from the late 1940s into the 1950s as examples. Whether McCutcheon circulated his story is unknown, but in the following decades he was known to declaim his work at gatherings of gay men, further indicating his desire to share his literary arts.[30]

In 1931, McCutcheon published *Lyrics of the Night*, a forty-page book of poems that is quite different from the earlier handmade version. Yet, the poems still show him struggling to value his acknowledged sexual identity and search for love. He inscribed one copy as "poems written half in ink, half in tears." But for the knowing reader, this collection marks the beginning of McCutcheon's expression of his desire for gay love.[31]

One poem, "Night," contemplates what he calls "longings I cannot explain." It closes, "And throwing to the winds my veil of control / I submit myself to you, Night, / Lustful conqueror—enfold me in your dusky arms." Another is replete with images of the "Sistine slaves" and "David's graceful form," which in a person becomes "lustful fascination incarnate!" The following poem, "Symbolic," contains the line, "Even I rise not above the reddened bruises of soft mouths of lovers—mine a sweet perversity." "The 'Cupola'" notes, "That I suffer with men who are just like myself: And I like it—Yes, love it." The poem "A God," ends with, "Apollo's arms about my neck, a drunken god lay on my breast."[32]

In August 1933, McCutcheon began contributing a column in the weekly *Rio Journal*, published as In the Heart of Columbia County, pausing only when he contracted tuberculosis and entered Statesan (later the Ethan Allen School for Boys at Wales, a juvenile detention center). Rio, which is located just southeast of Portage, was a village of 641 in 1930. In the columns, McCutcheon reviewed works by Thornton Wilder, discussed W. Somerset Maugham's short stories, and recommended Thomas Mann. He praised Oscar Wilde as one of the great literary geniuses of the world and said, "We must not judge his folly." Writing about Wilde's *De Profundis*, McCutcheon said, "Love is a sacrament that should be taken kneeling."[33]

In May 1934, McCutcheon published "A Group of Love Songs" in *The Beacon*, which was known as "Wisconsin's Sanatorium Journal." The editor thought McCutcheon's sketches, or articles, approached those of *"Vanity Fair* and other national magazines in quality." McCutcheon then published two small books of poetry, each containing seven poems, one of which was written while at Statesan. In 1935 came *Seven Sonnets Sung Softly for the Soul* and in 1936 *Seven Love Poems from Old Nippon*. Also during the 1930s, McCutcheon published poems and stories in several issues of the *Daily Cardinal*, the UW student newspaper. Betty Cass wrote in the *Wisconsin State Journal* in 1935 that McCutcheon's "verse was like delicate cameos cut from virgin stone." Cass knew McCutcheon well enough, as "poet, musician and lover of truly beautiful things of life," to turn over one of her daily columns to him.[34]

In 1941, with the publication of *Two Pieces of Venetian Glass*, McCutcheon returned to the topic of gay love, for the book is dedicated to his life partner, Edward Joseph Koberstein, known as E. J. K. The *Capital Times* headlined an article about the book, "McCutcheon's Poetry, Warm, Artistic." No feminine pronouns were used in this material, which was full of romantic love. Herein McCutcheon spoke of love's strength built to endure. In the poem "Our Secret," he wrote, "I could shout it from the housetops, / But who's the world to hear, / How terribly much I love you." He described his love as "wild" and "mad."[35]

The title poem played on images that reflect McCutcheon's romantic and realistic sides. The Venetian goblets, used as a metaphor for him and his love, were described as "Two yet one, so like the two appear." The covert

Keith McCutcheon's references to same-sex love were more overt in his 1941 collection *Two Pieces of Venetian Glass* than in his previous publications.

TWO PIECES
OF
VENETIAN GLASS

By
Keith McCutcheon

nature of their relationship was hinted at in the line "And precious values are not named." The danger of gay love was acknowledged: "Two pieces of Venetian glass a breath could break if carelessness betrayed." Nevertheless, the poet assured readers, the goblets are strong: "To hold the wine-mad force of life and death through many years for toasts that love be long."[36]

In McCutcheon's last published book, there is no more talk of perversity or of sterile love. The internalized homophobic phrases from his earlier days have been discarded. While not foolhardy as to circumstances, he appears totally confident in his gay identity and love.

NETWORKING AMONG GAY CONTACTS

Because of the bout with tuberculosis, McCutcheon followed his stay at Statesan with a period of convalescence at Statesan's associated camp at Lake Tomahawk, in the fresh air of the North Woods. There he met Robert Monschein, a young man from Walworth County, and in 1934 they both wrote poems for the institution's magazine, *The Beacon*.[37]

In that same year Monschein, apparently back in the Walworth area, wrote in a letter to the editor that was published in the Elkhorn paper, "You might be interested to know about the guests which my friend Keith McCutcheon and I have had in the past few months." He reported that during the summer of 1934, the pair had had several visits from Alfred Lunt and Lynn Fontanne, who were once accompanied by gay playwright Noel Coward, a frequent visitor to Ten Chimneys, the Lunt-Fontanne summer home in Genesee Depot. The letter also talked about Coward's play *Design for Living*, which starred Lunt, Fontanne, and Coward, calling it "a gay sophisticated thing."[38]

In an October 1935 *Rio Journal* column, McCutcheon recalled an earlier episode in which the editor of *The Badger*, the UW yearbook, had invited him to the Loraine Hotel. There, among friends, "sitting carelessly with one leg over the arm of his chair, was Edward Harris Heth." He described Heth, then also an undergraduate, as an aspiring writer. He told his readers of Heth's literary career, which McCutcheon had obviously followed, and talked of anticipation about Heth's upcoming novel *Some We Loved*. Through all his networking, literary and otherwise, McCutcheon found other homosexuals and became a more self-affirming gay man who accepted his sexual identity. He was able to express, if sometimes in a coded manner, same-sex love in a positive manner before World War II.[39]

NAZI RUMORS REACH WISCONSIN

In his published writings, Keith McCutcheon showed antipathy to Hitler's Germany. In one *Rio Journal* column, probably from 1938 or 1939, he reported that the Nazis were eager to get helium gas and had sent an ambassador to America, which had a plentiful supply. McCutcheon wrote, "It would be as well to liberate our entire supply into the air rather than let a government of such rapine policies, racial intolerance, and professed ungodliness as Germany under the minute-Hitler to even have a sniff." In another column, he referred to "world dictators generally, and the small spoiled brat with the misplaced eyebrow, Hitler, specifically." He wrote, "By virtue of my love of freedom, to be intense in intelligence, I believe Hitler to be the most utterly detestable individual now coexisting with other mortals upon this tiny lost speck of stardust. His mistreatment of people, Jews and Christians, Catholics and protestants, Germans and all others, is not in keeping with sane behavior."[40]

A piece titled "Far and Near," which appeared in the *Rio Journal* (a version also was published in the *Daily Cardinal*), described a fictional incident in Salzburg in annexed Austria. The main character is a young Jewish writer named Franz whose usual café is one day "filled with a strange group of brown-uniformed men." Franz comes to realize "that he had been buried so deeply in the old history and tales of the old city, that something had happened of which he was not aware." After leaving the café, Franz stops by the statue of Mozart, "a sort of shrine to Beauty," where he is shot by the men in brown uniforms for being a "damned disobedient Jew" and not moving on. The piece reveals that McCutcheon was following events in Nazi Germany.[41]

McCutcheon's knowledge of German developments suggests that he knew of, and guardedly wrote about, the Nazi persecution of homosexuals. Presumably they were among the "others" mentioned in the list of Nazi victims in the column about Hitler cited previously.[42]

Also, in a late 1930s column from the *Rio Journal*, McCutcheon wrote of "Karl," a fictional young man, probably gay, in Hitler's Germany. Karl had been branded a "young socialist" by his professors, and McCutcheon hinted at his character's sexuality when he wrote that the German

> at last . . . should drift with others—men young like himself, from whom opportunity had been unjustly cut off by stupidity; had been strangled by political smallness. . . . They met together; had to meet in out-of-the-way places, to play music, to sing, to write and to talk about life, and love. . . . And to hear their voices laugh, and to drink bock, and weep on each others' shoulders.

This is perhaps a description of gay life from the earlier Weimar period, when gay bars had flourished. McCutcheon also described Karl as having a "handsome face; the blue eyes like the Danube river, and the hair blonde as the sunset gold." This physical description suggests that McCutcheon is describing a gay man, an ideal Teutonic specimen as well as a homosexual fantasy, and not a socialist.[43]

McCutcheon's story next described Karl being taken to a camp: "What he did there I cannot say. . . . I dare not say, for I have only horrible rumors of what they did to young men in the camp. But after three years he was freed." Note the focus on what they did to young men, not to political prisoners like socialists. McCutcheon's own politics aligned with the faction known as the Stalwart Republicans, so the socialist angle was probably not his real interest.[44]

After his time in the camp, "Karl . . . who had been youthful and gay, whose hair had been gold, and whose eyes had been blue . . . now was an old man. . . . He was a ruin of what beauty man has as his right. His kidneys crushed by beating; his body was welted. He was sore; he was lame . . . and life held no love." In the end, he was back with "those other crushed creatures that once were men."[45]

The German concentration camps were no secret before the war, though the full extent of the Holocaust was yet to be widely acknowledged. The Nazis characterized the early camps as centers for beneficial "reeducation."[46]

As UW–Madison professor Jim Steakley has shown in his pioneering work *The Homosexual Emancipation Movement in Germany*, the early Nazi regime in 1935 broadened the Paragraph 175 provisions of the German antisodomy law. The added "175a" made nine new acts illegal, such as mutual masturbation and homosexual kisses, embraces, and even fantasies. The numbers of gay men arrested and charged went from below one thousand in each of the final years of the Weimar Republic to near ten thousand annually under the Nazis. Steakley informs us that many more were sent to the camps, though they were never charged.[47]

Richard Plant in *The Pink Triangle* states that some of the first homosexuals jailed by the Nazis were directors of homosexual rights organizations, many of whom were Jewish and Socialist. Heinrich Himmler gave a public speech in 1936 calling homosexuality "a symptom of racial degeneracy destructive to our race." John Lauritsen and David Thorstad in *The Early Homosexual Rights Movement (1864–1935)* and Steakley show that some gay men were released from the camps, as was the fictional Karl. One fairly well-known real example was Kurt Hiller. In 1936, a pardon decree aimed at freeing some of the Nazis imprisoned by the Weimar regime also released some other early arrestees. McCutcheon seems to have been aware of examples such as this.[48]

McCutcheon explained that his knowledge came from "rumors" that had reached America about what happened to "youthful and gay" men in the camps. His story about Karl has only the briefest mention of a political cause, which is quickly dropped in favor of Karl's youthfulness and homosocial activities. This suggests that McCutcheon had access to informal but active gay communication networks. In Wisconsin, with its significant German heritage, there may have been added interest about German gays among gay American men. McCutcheon felt the "horrible rumors" he heard deserved to be told in the press. Unfortunately, his story, published in a Wisconsin weekly paper, never reached a mainstream audience.[49]

Several themes emerge clearly in the work of Keith McCutcheon. At the start of his writing career, he expressed a biological drive for same-sex activity and an emotional romantic drive, as he put it, for a true friend of Love with a capital L. Later, he accepted his homosexuality. However, he was thoroughly aware early on of the stigma and illegal nature of his identity, and he had plenty of internalized homophobia, as evidenced in his references to sin and perversity. Through knowing other homosexual men and networking with them, McCutcheon moved beyond his early self-doubting identity. He had a strong desire by the end of this period to share the positives of gay love.

A Graced African American Heritage

Born in Chicago in 1907, Theodore "Ted" Pierce moved to Madison at age three to live with his maternal uncle, Samuel Pierce, who raised him as his own son. The Pierce family on his father's side came from Louisiana, where his grandfather had been a member of the Reconstruction state legislature and a New Orleans judge. Ted Pierce would later claim that the family tradition of "graceful living" came from the New Orleans branch of the family, whom he called "suave and polished people." His paternal grandmother, Hettie, was born into slavery in Rochester, North Carolina, in 1829. A family Bible recorded the date. Her husband, John, had been born into slavery in Virginia. Both had been moved into the Cotton Kingdom lands of Louisiana; when the Civil War ended in 1865, they were living and working on a plantation. In her later years, Hettie lived with the Pierce family at 1436 Williamson Street on Madison's near east side and was often featured in the local press because of her age and her experiences under slavery. Wisconsin Republican governor Walter Kohler Sr. and his wife, Charlotte, visited Hettie Pierce with flowers on her 102nd birthday.[50]

Samuel Pierce had been a Pullman porter, a high-status job for African Americans, working the Northwestern Railroad's line between Milwaukee and Madison. He was noticed for his demeanor and "matinee-idol looks," and in 1925, progressive Republican governor John Blaine appointed him as his messenger in the executive office at the Capitol, a job he would keep through five governors—Blaine, Fred Zimmerman, Walter Kohler Sr., Albert Schmedeman, and Philip La Follette. Pierce was the third African American messenger to work for a Wisconsin governor; the first, William Miller, had been appointed by Governor Robert M. La Follette Sr. Miller family descendants recalled that since Miller was African American, even though he had a law degree, he could not be called an aide, so the title of messenger was used.[51]

The Pierce family also ran the Sam Pierce Loraine Tailor Shop in the Hotel Loraine, the most prestigious hostelry in Madison. Sam was an advocate in 1928 for "a Negro community house" to help new members of the African American community, since they had no public place for youth activities. When Samuel Pierce died in 1936, Governor Philip La Follette ordered capitol flags to fly at half-staff as a token of the community's esteem of the deceased. Pierce's portrait was painted and presented to the State Historical Society in 1958.[52]

Ted Pierce, named for Republican president Teddy Roosevelt, who was in office at the time of his birth, lived on Williamson Street in the family home until illness forced him into a care center in 1998. He recalled Williamson as "a most gracious, and always most interesting Street." The street's name memorialized Hugh Williamson of North Carolina, a signer of the Constitution. Perhaps Hettie Pierce knew of this home state connection.[53]

Ted Pierce attended the University of Wisconsin in 1924 and 1925, after which he managed the family tailor shop. Following the death of his uncle Sam in May 1936, Ted at age twenty-nine was appointed executive office messenger in his place and served under governors Philip La Follette, Julius Heil, and Walter Goodland. In 1926, the position paid $120 a month. Governor Oscar Rennebohm eliminated the position in the late 1940s, and Pierce was unemployed for several years. Later he worked in the acquisitions department of UW's Memorial Library until his retirement.[54]

At age ninety-one, Pierce was characterized as "a droll and fastidiously mannered boulevardier." He surely loved the French term. He often referred to group gatherings of cultured gay men as *salons* in the Parisian mode, and noted that they should be filled "with intrigue, charming malice." Pierce believed pre-Stonewall gays had created a Beau Monde in the Golden Triangle of Chicago, Milwaukee, and Madison. To Pierce, *Beau Monde*, a French term ascribed to the world of fashion and society at the end of the eighteenth century in England, meant a satisfactory world of taste and grace. He said, "Sometimes only French will do justice to certain circumstances. . . . The creation of this happy Beau Monde . . . was desperately needed by a large number of people who could not draw breath comfortably." Pierce claimed to be a devotee of Marcel Proust and said his digressions in conversations simply followed those of this French master. His death notice described him as "a great lover of art, literature and the theater."[55]

When Pierce was young, his mother, a cook by trade, labored for two weeks to make him a Little Lord Fauntleroy outfit. It had black velvet knee pants, patent leather pumps with black grosgrain bows, a white pique vest, a lace collar, a silk tie, and a black velvet jacket. The East High School year-book of 1924 dubbed Pierce "Our Fashion Plate." His high school activities included chorus, the technical club, and the Latin club. A photo of black high schoolers of the era including Pierce remains in his papers and bears the note "The Elite Club."[56]

Pierce recalled that during the period between the wars, the bellhops at the Loraine were part of Madison's gay sexual underground. Single male travelers—often salesmen, lobbyists, and others who came to do business at the Capitol—were likely targets for seduction. Perhaps the frequent presence of single men in Madison was why the Pegasus Bar of the Belmont Hotel on the other side of Capitol Square was also a gay hangout, a place recalled by Pierce as "a dream of beauty" on weekends. Again, later in life, he described his self-presentation as encompassing a "lifelong pursuit of fine, very attractive Company" and "my eternal pursuit of Beauty." Based on his archives and the materials about him that remain, Pierce apparently

As a student in Madison, a young Ted Pierce attended East High School and the UW.
WHI IMAGE ID 71483

showed no internalized homophobia but rather a graceful acceptance of his homosexuality.[57]

While working in the governor's office, Pierce observed how networks functioned. As the governor's aide, he met the iconic American actress Tallulah Bankhead when she came to the governor's mansion during Philip La Follette's tenure. Pierce observed that Bankhead and La Follette had known each other growing up in Washington, DC, because their respective fathers had been senators.[58]

Pierce's own networking included private encounters and correspondence. In a 1939 letter, a correspondent in Missouri wrote to Pierce about how it "was really wonderful, as you said in your letter, to meet in the night, only to have to say goodbye again in that same darkness of another night," and also refers to "our beloved Wisconsin."[59]

Among the gay men in Pierce's network was actor Don Pryse Jones, a native of Portage who sometimes stayed at the American Students' and Artists' Center in Paris. Jones once chattily wrote, "I will go by the Ecole Militaire and watch the handsome officers, and find a lovely one and send him in this letter to you."[60]

Pierce truly admired the physical form. He was a major fan of ballet and recalled bringing "the eternally young, truly beautiful people the performers of the Dance from the various Ballet companies" to his gay house parties. His fondness for ballet was driven by the beauty of the dancers, who, he said, "have to be young so they're good looking on stage and off stage." In his house, he kept a mural of a nude young man with a lyre and wreath crowning his head. Pierce's theory was that the gay world "could only protect itself with its Beauty" since it had to remain "beyond the power of ill-managed Authority."[61]

One dance enthusiast whom Pierce met was David Zellmer. While a student at the UW in the late 1930s, Zellmer performed in campus productions of the Haresfoot Club, the school's all-male, cross-dressing theatrical troupe, and also wrote a column on dance for the *Daily Cardinal*. After graduating, Zellmer headed east and joined Martha Graham's dance troupe, where he also met a fellow gay dancer, Merce Cunningham. An occasional letter from Cunningham, the future dance icon, to Pierce mentions Zellmer. Zellmer's own correspondence with Pierce after he left campus continued into the mid-1940s. After World War II, during which

Ted Pierce loved literature and the arts, especially ballet. WHI IMAGE ID 75562

Zellmer served as an officer aviator, he returned to the dance world of New York and married.[62]

In an early letter to Pierce, apparently written when Zellmer was first in New York with Graham, Zellmer tartly referenced his competition with Cunningham in those days. "Admit you never really dreamed I could be interested in glorifying Merce," he challenged Pierce. In the same letter, Zellmer deprecated the "chi-chi world" of an artist Pierce had written about and disparaged gay photographer George Platt Lynes. Comments like these, about how the gay men he observed in the art world networked and provided support for one another, portray Zellmer as a conflicted bisexual.[63]

In late 1945, Pierce wrote to Zellmer about the public's tolerance and acceptance of gay men in dance. Zellmer was annoyed by the communication. While admitting in his response that "one's homosexuality or bisexuality is an integral part of one's personality," Zellmer wrote, "I especially resent the presence of the half-men in dance. They alone have impeded the progress of male dancing in America by several decades; and Ted Shawn, to name but one, is a monument to the decadence and singular lack of taste brought into the theatre by them. Broadway today still reeks of their influence and presence." Zellmer told Pierce there were a surprising number of "powerful" and influential men of this kind in key positions who *were* approachable, and who in fact were constantly in search of protégés but, he said, "Such short-cuts do not tempt me." For Zellmer, navigating the dance world and conflicts over sexuality proved challenging. Perhaps by referencing bisexuality and his reluctance to provide favors as a method of advancement, he was expressing resentment about the more self-admitting homosexuals in the dance world—some who acted effeminately as a way of signaling their identity, and some who behaved in a predatory manner or acted opportunistically to advance their careers.[64]

Before arriving in Madison in the 1950s, world-famous travel writer Herb Kubly, a New Glarus native, sent a postcard to Pierce picturing the Chalet of the Golden Fleece and asked to be "put up at the Pierce Youth Hostel if reservations are still available." Before another visit, Kubly selected a postcard "especially for you" that showed Brigham Young's birth marker, which describes the Mormon leader as "A Man of Much Courage and Superb Equipment." Kubly's message noted Young's hundreds of progeny.[65]

Though Pierce was based in Madison, his networking had a far reach. Lee Hoiby wrote a letter to Pierce in the early 1950s describing sex in the Milwaukee parks—specifically, meeting someone at the Solomon Juneau statue. Hoiby, a classical pianist and, later, composer, hailed from Stoughton; he played at UW's Memorial Union on Sunday afternoons and was part of the gay circles in the capital city. Pierce once commented, "You could see that he was going to be someone, even while in college." Mutual friends in New York would mention Hoiby's comings and goings in other letters to Pierce. And once Pierce connected with his east side neighbor Keith McCutcheon, they discussed their many mutual acquaintances.[66]

Pierce's interest in young men brought him letters of solicitation for photos of the male physique in the mid-1950s. Several decades later, Olin Wood, a UW instructor in French, sent Pierce and other Madisonians photos of Richard Thomas, John-Boy from television's *The Waltons*, on the beach wearing only a posing strap.[67]

Pierce's gaydar seems to have been well tuned. He collected fan items of handsome stars long before they came out. Some of the oldest go back to 1943, when he collected extensive clippings about David Gaspar Bacon, an actor who was stabbed to death at age twenty-nine. Bacon had supposedly gone to swim at Venice Beach, but police reported that he had picked up a man in his sports car. One of Pierce's photos showed Bacon, who was married, wearing women's clothes and painting his nails for a 1936 Harvard theatrical. Among Pierce's scrapbook items were early notices of the "bachelor" actors Richard Chamberlain, Rock Hudson, and Tab Hunter, collected long before these men came out. Pierce had created a whole set of loose-leaf binders of scrapbooks, now lost, of attractive young men; there were clippings from the press and photos of his circle of gay friends.[68]

The black actor Canada Lee, who had gone from racetrack roustabout to prizefighter to Harlem jazz bandleader before his acting career took off, got to know Ted Pierce and would stay in his house when he came to Madison. Lee played such roles as Caliban in Shakespeare's *The Tempest*. In January 1942 Lee was onstage at Madison's Parkway Theater performing in Orson Welles's Mercury Theater production of Richard Wright's *Native Son*, a role he had performed on Broadway. That same month, the *Milwaukee Journal* carried a story about Lee arguing that black soldiers should have rights equal to those of their white counterparts since "there are no Jim Crow bullets."[69]

On one occasion in 1945, Lee stayed with Pierce when he was in town to be honored by the Madison chapter of the NAACP. On that trip Lee stated, "I will not play the stock Negro character since I feel it is a libel on the race." On Lee's death in 1952, Madison newspapers mentioned that he had been a guest of Pierce.[70]

Ted Pierce (standing, third from left), Keith McCutcheon (sitting at far right), and local African American leaders at a Madison reception for black actor Canada Lee (standing on right). WHI IMAGE ID 71481

Perhaps the longest-running gay correspondence in the Ted Pierce papers is the one between Pierce and Willard Motley, the African American writer who graduated from Englewood High School on Chicago's South Side, where he played football. Motley came to Madison hoping to go to the university. However, his dream could not be realized because his funds were too low, and at 135 pounds he did not make the football team. Yet he did meet Ted Pierce.[71]

Motley later recalled, "Time, perhaps May 1933. I am in Madison Wisconsin with a dog and no where to stay and no money but with the idea that I want to go to college and to write books. I met someone working in a tailor shop who was to become my friend, a true friend." Later again he would write Pierce, "I wonder if you remember the days when we used to sit around in the Loraine tailor shop or take long walks under the trees of the town, along the lake talking about writing." In 1938 he wrote, "I still rank Madison third among all the cities and towns I've visited," and in 1953, recalling the campus and the lake, he said, "A part of me lives there in Madison."[72]

For a while, Ted Pierce worked at his family's tailor shop in the Loraine Hotel, the fanciest hostelry in Madison. WHI IMAGE ID 3610

Over the years, Motley would visit Pierce in Madison and often went to UW football games on those weekends. In his letters to Pierce, he fondly recalled "my many trips to Madison and your hospitality there," and their "long friendship, so important to me." While living in Chicago during the 1940s, he wished Ted lived only a few blocks away, "so that I could run over . . . [and] ask your advice on some of the stuff I am writing." He also queried Ted about press contacts in Madison to publicize his work, mentioning Betty Cass among them.[73]

The Pierce–Motley correspondence is full of mentions of mutual friends and inquiries into how so-and-so is doing. The two discussed who they had met in each other's cities and the beautiful parties. Pierce, of course, mentioned dance and other arts events. Pierce reported that Chicago was growing on him, after making three visits in one year. Their correspondence ranged over twenty-seven years.[74]

Motley's 1947 novel *Knock on Any Door*, dealing with juvenile delinquency, was set in part on Chicago's skid row, where the hero, though supposedly not gay, makes money through sex with men. The protagonist does have one homosexual friend, however, who visits him in prison while he waits for the electric chair. The novel was well received, selling over 350,000 copies. Eleanor Roosevelt praised it in her daily newspaper column. It also became a movie in 1949 starring John Derek and Humphrey Bogart, but Motley did not like it, nor did the critics. Motley then moved to Mexico and wrote the novel *Let No Man Write My Epitaph*, which was also made into a movie in 1960, with music by Ella Fitzgerald.[75]

Though Motley was black, he wrote about white characters, seeming to avoid issues of race. He once said, "My race is the human race." Historians of gay literature give him mixed reviews. In his 1983 book *The Gay Novel: The Male Homosexual Image in America*, James Levin wrote about the main characters in *Knock on Any Door*. "Nick has a friend, Owen, who seems to be gay although it is never stated," Levin observed. "There are also some hints that Owen and Nick have some sort of a sexual relationship." Levin dismissed this as dealing with homosexuality in a "cursory manner." St. Sukie de la Croix, in *Chicago Whispers: A History of LGBT Chicago before Stonewall*, was more appreciative of the novel's "homosexual subtext." Michael Bronski, in his article "The Politics of Gay Pulp Fiction," said "the novel is infused with a gay sensibility—you can't beat Motley's lush, erotic descriptions of male beauty." Anthony Slide, in *Lost Gay Novels: A Reference Guide to Fifty Works from the First Half of the Twentieth Century*, praises Motley's "strong fascination for gay characters."[76]

Motley wished to explore homosexuality more explicitly in his work. In a 1960 letter to his agent, he said, "For three or four years I have been considering writing a homosexual book and have taken a lot of notes." Surely some of those notes could have been inspired by his many interactions with Wisconsin's gay community since 1933. Motley critiqued Gore Vidal's *The City and the Pillar* as a gay novel on the grounds that in the end the protagonist kills his friend "because the friend has called him a queer when the homo made a pass at him." Motley asked his agent, "Is there a publisher policy that such books as *Lolita* or a homo book must have an unhappy or tragic ending. If so I wouldn't write this book I have in mind." Motley died in 1965, and never wrote the book. Lost are the likely glimpses it might have provided of gay life in the Upper Midwest.[77]

A Union Scholarship Student

One UW student in the late 1930s offered another view into Wisconsin's gay scene during the interwar period. Milt Sherman grew up in New York City in a union-supporting Jewish family. A scholarship for gymnastics from the university and another small one from his mother's union enabled him to come to Madison. He graduated in 1940.[78]

Many decades later his stepdaughter, Elena Sherman, who was three when her parents married, would move to Madison to be with her lesbian partner. She believed her father was gay and may have belonged to a gay club at the university. The family story is that Milt went into the Army Air Corps at the start of World War II. He was under investigation for discharge toward the end of the war, but once he married, the discharge investigation went away.[79]

The newly constituted Sherman family resided in Chicago, where Elena's mother was a professional musician, a viola player with the Chicago Symphony. Elena can remember male couples from Milt's college days (several having been male cheerleaders) visiting the home and the family having gay friends who were sometimes her babysitters. These friends would take her to all-male parties dressed as a boy. In her teens, Elena frequented lesbian bars in Chicago. When she came out to her father, he said he knew her true orientation when she was a young child. Elena believed her mother to be bisexual, and could identify female lovers with whom she had torrid love affairs.[80]

After the war, Milt Sherman became a professional magician, and as a good red-diaper baby (someone whose parents were members of the US Communist Party or strong leftists), he was a member of the Chicago Stage Guild. He performed in drag for charity productions in the Windy City. Performing also meant traveling on the road to theaters across the country; he took his daughter along as a stage helper dressed as a boy, since a father and son traveling together would raise fewer questions.[81]

Family photos from Milt's high school and UW days reveal someone who pushed boundaries. Several show the young gymnast posing in only a jockstrap. Another series shows Sherman helping student Dave Zellmer get into women's clothes, perhaps for a campus Haresfoot production. Yet

The gymnast Milt Sherman poses in a jock-strap. FROM THE AUTHOR'S COLLECTION, COURTESY OF ELENA SHERMAN

the clothes in Sherman's photos do not match either of the performance costumes shown in *The Badger* yearbook or the *Daily Cardinal*. Using what he'd learned from his theater experience, as the photos show, Sherman also helped with the makeup for Zellmer's transformation. With Sherman in his suit and tie, they made a fetching couple. His grandmother referred to Zellmer as "the pretty boy," and Sherman identified him on the back of one photo as his "handsome friend."[82]

Haresfoot was a UW theatrical tradition going back to the 1890s. When the group started to tour, university officials did not want females traveling, so men played the women's roles and performed as chorines, or chorus girls. The group's slogan was "All our girls are men, yet everyone is a lady." Dave Zellmer was in Haresfoot productions for two years as part of the "female" chorus.[83]

While in Madison, Milt Sherman was deeply involved with the *Daily Cardinal* as a frequent contributor of editorial cartoons. Zellmer also worked for the paper. Sherman contributed prose, as well, such as book

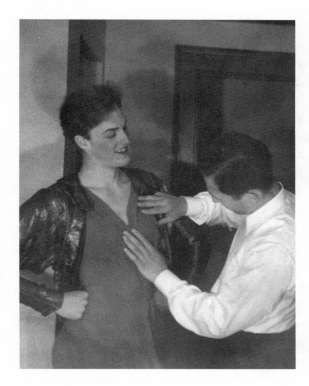

Milt Sherman (right) helps his friend, Dave Zellmer, who is cross-dressing. FROM THE AUTHOR'S COLLECTION, COURTESY OF ELENA SHERMAN

reviews and brief movie reviews of shows in town for a column titled At the Theater. He worked on the college paper at the same time as Edwin Newman, who later gained fame as a journalist. When most of the staff on the *Daily Cardinal* went on strike over campus politics, Sherman supported them and the strike paper they put out for several months.[84]

Sex was a taboo topic at the university in the 1930s, and President Glenn Frank tried to downplay issues of sex and morality on campus. In 1932, the *Daily Cardinal* published an anonymous letter titled "Virginity—a Woman's View." The piece, written by a junior, stated, "We who are not virgins can smile at the notion that we have lost self esteem" and expressed skepticism that "those who have engaged in premarital sex would suffer a loss of our self respect." Historians E. David Cronon and John Jenkins noted that this letter stirred one of the perennial claims about the bad moral status of the campus. There were calls to censor or suppress the campus paper, but President Frank headed off the efforts. The paper, however, appears to have taken the message to heart and become cautious about sex matters.[85]

During Milt Sherman's years on the paper (1937–1939), a time of general reticence on campus regarding sex issues, he appears to have been the only one to break the silence about what he termed "homosexualism." The overall lack of information and thirst for knowledge was exhibited when the *Daily Cardinal* reported in April 1938 that five hundred men filled Tripp Commons at the Memorial Union and more than three hundred milled around the entrance, attracted by a lecture titled "Anatomy and Physiology of Sex" by Dr. Elmer L. Severinghaus of the Wisconsin General Hospital (now UW Hospital). The lecture was part of an unusual series sponsored by the house presidents' council. Dr. Severinghaus noted, "Sex knowledge is difficult to obtain because of an accumulative taboo against it." The second lecturer in the series, Professor Howard Becker, advocated "sticking to the conventions," remarking that "taboos of society can be broken, but they can never be broken lightly. The closer you can stay to these conventions, the happier you will be."[86]

In December 1937, when Milt Sherman reviewed *Serenade* by James M. Cain, he did not yet have the benefit of Professor Becker's advice, but the campus atmosphere was likely still one of reticence. Sherman notes in his review that the novel's central character, an opera baritone, had his vocal qualities eradicated by "unnatural love." These are restored by the love of a "three-peso" Mexican prostitute, and the story then presents the possibility of the protagonist's backsliding into "homosexualism." But the opera singer's once and putative male lover is stabbed to death, ending the threat.[87]

Sherman characterized the book as a "swift kick in the pants of the aesthetically minded moralist." He concluded, "'Serenade' will give our ever-present blue noses just the chance they've been waiting for to dust off their old stove-pipe lids and go around waving umbrellas in people's faces. But if you like to read shady stories about shady people in shady corners, don't pay any attention to the blue-noses." Either Milt Sherman or his editors titled the review "Feelthy Book." The review is notable because Anthony Slide, in *Lost Gay Novels*, mentioned *Serenade* for its early depictions of homosexuality. Though not terribly sympathetic to the gay character, Cain included scenes of "young guys with lipstick on, and mascara eyelashes, dancing with each other." One review in a national publication, in commenting on the inclusion of drag performers in the novel, noted "the frou-frou of pixie petticoats." In finding published gay-themed literature and writing about it in a public newspaper, Sherman was ahead of many of his contemporaries.[88]

Sherman may have thought the "homosexualism" matter relevant because of an incident in the spring of 1937 when the Madison press reported that a twenty-year-old UW premed student had pleaded guilty to charges of taking liberties with teenaged boys. In a fall 1937 evaluation of this student and his participation in the practice of mutual masturbation, Dr. W. J. Bleckwenn, a professor of neuropsychiatry at Wisconsin General

Women, in addition to men, engaged in cross-dressing in the early twentieth century, as demonstrated by these two women from West Allis in sailor garb.

Hospital, deemed the behavior part of a continuation of adolescent sexual relations. An interesting twist in the record is that the student denied that he had homosexual tendencies and, the student discipline file said, "denies ever having had contact with homosexual individuals until after the newspaper notoriety when he was approached by telephone and letter by homosexualists on campus and in town." Although this student was permitted to continue to attend the university, the incident uncovered an active homosexual life on the campus and in Madison.[89]

Milt Sherman's networking included finding friends like Zellmer who participated in theater with reversed gender roles. Other members of the Haresfoot troupe from this period would later be found out for having engaged in homosexual acts. Sherman also found largely hidden gay literature and disseminated information about the existence of "homosexualism." His references to bluenoses and the tongue-in-cheek "feelthy" headline demonstrate a rejection of negative attitudes toward homosexuality. In many ways, Sherman's boldness was ahead of its time.

Partners in Art and Life

In Milwaukee, another hub of networking appeared in the interwar years at the Layton School of Art. In *Odd Girls and Twilight Lovers: A History of Lesbian Life in Twentieth-Century America*, Lillian Faderman points out that pre-Stonewall homo-affectional female couples were seldom termed lesbians before the late 1800s, when widespread information on Freudian types of sex identity became part of popular culture. At this time, female couples living together were described as being in "Boston marriages." Such female coupledom, as Faderman observed, might be nourished "more safely in all-women institutions such as summer camps, residence halls, or colleges and universities." Milwaukee-Downer College would be the incubator for the over-fifty-year friendship of Charlotte Partridge and Miriam Frink.[90]

Frink, a native of Elkhart, Indiana, attended Downer College in her freshman and sophomore years, then transferred to Smith College, graduating two years later. (Interestingly, a survey found that 57 percent of women in Smith's 1884 graduating class never married.) As a student, Frink wore her hair short and was described as strong and athletic. At

Downer, she played basketball and was an oarsman, rowing on the Milwaukee River. She hoped to play basketball at Smith, but there were many better players there. After graduation, she was offered a position teaching English at Downer and returned to the Midwest in 1915. She lived on campus, with a room as part of her compensation. The principal of the associated high school gave her D. H. Lawrence's *Sons and Lovers* to read, an example of the school's liberal sexual attitudes. In her teaching, she would cite the works of the bisexual Edna St. Vincent Millay and Emily Dickinson, who may have been a lesbian.[91]

Charlotte Partridge spent her childhood in Duluth. She attended Dana Hall, a college preparatory school in Massachusetts associated with Wellesley College, which, along with Smith, was one of the northeastern US women's colleges known as the Seven Sisters. She too returned to the Midwest and graduated from Northern Illinois Teachers College in DeKalb in 1905, after which she took various teaching jobs. Her interest in art led to studies at the progressive Chicago School of Applied and Normal Art (later named the Church School of Art, after founder Emma Church). While doing freelance commercial art, Partridge earned a certificate from the more traditional Art Institute of Chicago, and in 1914 she was hired as an art faculty member at Downer. Even in the early years of her tenure, she was credited with focusing the Downer art program away from the stiff academic style that was then dominant. A 1919 review on a Downer student art exhibit attributes the pupils' self-expression in their work to Partridge's "progressive spirit." She later became head of the school's fine arts department. Partridge also lived on campus and had her own art studio as part of her compensation; indeed, this arrangement had been offered as an incentive to come to Downer.[92]

Partridge found the Victorian ideas of Downer's president, Eleanor Sabin, constricting. Over one Christmas holiday, someone stole the fig leaf from the model of the David statue in the art department and Partridge was tasked by the shocked Sabin with getting a fig leaf back on. The school had never offered a life drawing class until she came, but Partridge introduced one with a nude model. She would later comment, "That was frowned upon, but the powers that be just pretended they didn't notice it." Later, at the Layton Art School, she used nude models for the school's coed life drawing classes—a notable innovation in conservative Milwaukee.

In writing about Partridge's life at college, her niece Susie Habernicht observed, "There she began her lifelong career as a liberated woman with progressive ideas." Faderman has said that women's colleges "not only 'masculinized' women but also made men dispensable to them and rendered women more attractive to one another."[93]

Mutual interests in art and music fostered a friendship between Partridge and Frink at Downer, and by 1921 they had taken up a domestic relationship and rented an apartment together off campus. They would live together for more than fifty years, until 1973, when one moved to an elder-care unit. In 1930, they built a studio summer cottage in Fox Point and in 1938 their lasting home in Mequon. Partridge designed both structures. Their cottage was featured in the press and was described as one twenty-by-thirty-foot room that served as "living room, bedroom, and studio in one." The two women put their initials in the wet cement of the cottage fireplace.[94]

Charlotte Partridge (left) and Miriam Frink of the Layton School of Art encouraged a number of gay artists in Milwaukee. UNIVERSITY OF WISCONSIN–MILWAUKEE ARCHIVES

When Emma Church, who had fallen into poor health, sought to have Partridge take over her Chicago art school, Partridge instead bought the equipment, moved it to Milwaukee, and in 1920 started her own art school in the basement of the Layton Art Gallery. The Layton trustees offered her the basement space rent free, so the new art school was named after the benefactor who had founded the gallery. Miriam Frink was the codirector. She looked after the business side of things and taught literature appreciation. Partridge taught art classes and supervised the faculty. She once said of her life's companion, "Miss Frink is the head and I am the feet of the school." A friend observed, "Charlotte was marvelous and Miriam was tremendous along with her. . . . Miriam was like a Great Dane—[she] protected, undergirded, and saw to it that things worked out for Charlotte." During the Depression, they opted to forgo their salaries to continue to run the school.[95]

Partridge was known as a "staunch supporter of modern art and design." Later, when she became curator of the Layton Galleries, she set aside the Victorian paintings in favor of works by contemporary local artists. She staged a show of Frank Lloyd Wright's work in 1930, which helped revive his career. She consulted in 1933 with New Deal administrators on the program to give work to unemployed artists, and from 1935 to 1939 she was director of the Wisconsin Federal Art Project. When Partridge took a leave of absence from that project, Frink was appointed its acting director, surrendering the position when Partridge returned. By 1951, the Layton School had 1,100 students and its own building. In 1954, the board of trustees "retired" both Partridge and Frink; the record is silent as to whether this occurred because the women were lesbians or simply as a result of the new director's ambitions. The school itself experienced financial difficulties and closed in 1974. Its successor was the Milwaukee Institute of Art and Design.[96]

In a 1925 essay in the *Smith Alumnae Quarterly*, Frink described the Layton School approach: "The old way in art academies of making a student put in a wearisome apprenticeship of drawing what he saw before he tried to originate anything himself undoubtedly had a stultifying effect on the imagination." Since Frink's own background was in English, the art school also had a literature class. "Frequently the class will be given the same subject for pictorial composition as they have for the literary composition," Frink explained. The Layton school founders believed they were following educational reformer John Dewey's ideas "to develop the instinctive, aesthetic creativity and feeling for design."[97]

That a progressive art school attracted other non-normative individuals was not a surprise. Frink later in life recalled that the early school had a male teacher who was a favorite with the middle-aged women who liked to paint. Frink asked one of school's trustees, a banker, if she should be concerned about a teacher and one of the women in the class whom he knew. The banker laughed and commented that he "didn't think [the teacher in question] was a masculine sort of person at all."[98]

The faculty of the Layton School included two artists who had strong gay connections: Richard Lippold and Karl Priebe. Lippold, a sculptor, was a Milwaukee native born in 1915. While later employed at another teaching position at Black Mountain College in North Carolina, he began a long affair with gay artist Ray Johnson, whom he would introduce to the New York art world. For a period, Johnson and Lippold lived with two other gay artists, dancer/choreographer Merce Cunningham and composer John Cage. The Leslie-Lohman Museum of Gay and Lesbian Art has a 1963 drawing titled *Penis* by Lippold. Karl Priebe, another Milwaukee native who had studied at Layton, returned to the school in 1947 as an instructor. A winner in 1941 of the Prix de Rome, he exhibited his work in New York galleries, which brought him into contact with bisexual Carl Van Vechten and gave him an appreciation of the Harlem arts scene. Priebe had a long relationship with Frank Harriot, an editor at *Ebony* magazine. Thus, the work of lifelong partners Partridge and Frink begun in the 1920s had expanding ripples in the broader gay art world through the decades.[99]

The two women conducted many efforts jointly and were often portrayed as a couple. They knew the daughters of Victor and Meta Berger, prominent Milwaukee Socialist leaders, and the letterhead of the Meta Berger Memorial Committee in the 1940s showed Partridge as a member of the event's executive committee and Frink as the corresponding secretary. In later life, Berger lived on a farm in Thiensville near the Partridge–Frink home. A 1965 feature article on the couple's retirement activities described their home as one "which the two friends share." The journalist also noted that the women could complete each other's thoughts. When the art school closed in 1974, the *Milwaukee Journal* published an article

The decades-long relationship between Charlotte Partridge (left) and Miriam Frink encompassed their professional, civic, and personal lives. UNIVERSITY OF WISCONSIN–MILWAUKEE ARCHIVES

about the school and its "two indomitable founders." To Susie Habernicht, author of an unpublished biography of the two women that presents their lives side-by-side and as a couple, her aunt, Charlotte Partridge, had found "a helpmate and lifelong friend and companion in Miriam." Habernicht also describes the couple's travels abroad to Europe and Mexico. On an early trip west, Frink was given a pistol, which she retained for the rest of her life. Lillian Faderman wrote that people frequently described such "proper-seeming maiden ladies" of these early decades of the twentieth century as "close friends and devoted companions" without attributing any sexuality to their relationship. "But in creating jobs for themselves through their skills," Faderman continued, "they achieved the economic freedom (such as their middle-class counterparts in the past never could) to live as what the later twentieth century would consider lesbians." In 2010, when the Museum of Wisconsin Art in West Bend honored the women together with a joint lifetime achievement award, the *Wisconsin Gazette* named them as lesbians.[100]

THE CHAPPLEISM WITCH HUNT

The growing boldness of Wisconsin's homosexuals in the 1930s was parallel to the bold actions of other Americans as they fought back against the Depression. Naturally, the guardians of traditional morality and traditional concepts of American nationality responded to these challenges to the established way of things. The Hearst newspapers, known nationally for "yellow journalism" since the Spanish–American War, stirred the pot of mini–red scares across the country in the 1930s. In Wisconsin, the *Wisconsin News* in Milwaukee was the chief Hearst organ, though William Hearst also owned the less-sensational *Milwaukee Sentinel*. In one issue during this period, the *Wisconsin News* carried the following banner on its editorial page: "WISCONSIN SCHOOLS AND COLLEGES Must Be Kept Free of Communism and All Other Forms of Subversive Radicalism." Radical scares popped up elsewhere. For example, in Illinois, drug magnate Charles Walgreen withdrew his niece from the University of Chicago in a public spat because "she was exposed to insidious radical propaganda" and communism. However, Wisconsin's experience was unique, owing to the state's four-party political system and its success in blunting attacks on radicals and non-normative morality.[101]

A big part of the Wisconsin red scare plot began at the Milwaukee Extension of the University of Wisconsin. Labor agitation was occurring as the Wisconsin Federation of Teachers tried to organize faculty on the campus and made some charges about how faculty were being treated. The Milwaukee dean, Chester Snell, in turn brought complaints against several teachers to the attention of UW president Glenn Frank. This instigated an inquiry by a Board of Regents committee, which resulted in a thousand-page report of carefully compiled testimony. The testimony examined charges of immorality on the UW's Milwaukee Extension campus and also aired some faculty grievances. Dean Snell would later charge that his request for an investigation had turned into an investigation of him. Frank and the regents proceeded to fire Snell, charging him with being dictatorial and lacking the ability to preserve harmony.[102]

Meanwhile, the state senate, controlled by conservative Democrats, had taken up charges of radicalism on the Madison campus. Wisconsin was unique in that it operated on a four-party system for most of the 1930s. The right-wing Stalwart Republicans had been fighting internally during most of the century, pitted against the progressives led by the La Follette family and others, like governors Francis McGovern and John Blaine. In 1934, the Republican Party was split when a new Progressive Party was formed. The Wisconsin Socialist Party had a strong base in German areas of Milwaukee and a few other spots. The Democrats held sway mainly in the Lake Michigan cities, though the midterm sweep had enhanced their power, making them the most numerous party in the state senate.[103]

One of the courses available to seniors at Madison that could have provoked legislators to investigate radicalism on campus was Capitalism and Socialism, taught by Professor Selig Perlman and colloquially called "Cap-Soc." In 1976, a book based on a student's painstaking notes outlined the Perlman lecture material for the course. In his foreword to the book, Professor Merle Curti said, "Professor Perlman's exposition of Marxist-Leninist theory reflects a deep understanding, resting on his own early commitment to it as a young man in Czarist Russia." Though also noting that Perlman had given up doctrinaire Marxism, Curti called the lectures "one of the most justly famous courses in the history of the University of Wisconsin." Perlman began with his certainty that the capitalist system "was just a historical phase," though the twentieth-century experience through the 1930s had raised his skepticism about the applicability of Marxist ideology to the class struggle.[104]

In addition to professors with radical views, UW students could join leftist organizations on campus such as the League for Industrial Democracy. A May Day episode in 1935 developed into a crisis as students staged a clenched-fist rally with red flags on the steps of the Memorial Union and sang the "Internationale," the left-wing anthem. The rally of two hundred students was addressed by Marvin Baxter, the Socialist mayor of West Allis, who advocated for the abolition of capitalism. On this same May Day, Milwaukeeans awoke to find red flags flying over the City Auditorium, North Division High School, and Juneau Park. In addition, Colonel Stephen A. Park, executive secretary of the Wisconsin Reserve Officers Association, referred to the Milwaukee State Teachers College as "spotted" with communistic influences. Madison's vocational school also was challenged to clamp down on the play *Waiting for Lefty*, by New York playwright Clifford Odets, described in Hearst's *Wisconsin News* as a "writer of proletarian plays" who used vulgar language.[105]

Even as the controversy surrounding Dean Snell was developing, the state senate committee was busy poking around. They had called famed sociology professor E. A. Ross to testify in mid-April to satisfy their interest in a student tour of Soviet Russia that Ross had led in 1934. A letter advertising the tour stated that the professor "stood well with soviet authorities." Committee chairman Senator E. F. Brunette (D-Green Bay, 1933–1937) asked Ross, "Have you ever advocated Communism for this country?" According to newspaper reports, Ross boomed back, "I have never advocated Communism for any country." He then produced friendly letters from Theodore Roosevelt, William Jennings Bryan, Woodrow Wilson, and Oliver Wendell Holmes Jr. Ross believed the inquiry "was commenced without evidence to warrant it" and asserted that to "dignify unsupported charges by setting up this committee is unfair to our 90-year-old institution." He believed letting students sing the "Internationale" "helped maintain our majestic tradition of freedom."[106]

Senator Brunette owned lumber and fuel businesses, served as town chair of Howard, and was a member of the Brown County Board of Supervisors. He was elected to the Assembly in 1928 and then to the state senate when Roosevelt swept Wisconsin in 1932. On April 23, 1935, the *Wisconsin News* reported the charge by Senator Morley Kelly (D-Fond du Lac) that "the regents do not appear to have taken official cognizance of the fact that communists are working tooth and nail to make the university communistic in its teachings and attitude and that they have been making considerable progress." Kelly quit the committee and subsequently faced accusations by a woman in a sex scandal during the same period.[107]

When the Brunette Committee called former UW dean Chester Snell to testify on April 25, the *Wisconsin News* stirred up readers before his appearance with the banner headline: "Ousted U.W. Professor Expected to Bare Scandals." Snell electrified the committee meeting on April 25 in front of an audience estimated at six hundred to a thousand. Snell claimed to have "fought against moral standards and love affairs he felt were amazingly unconventional for university educators." He also claimed to be "tangled in a mesh of intrigue laid by the politically powerful family of the late Victor Berger, nationally known socialist leader." Snell charged former university regent Meta Berger, Victor's widow, with seeking employment for her family members.[108]

The Berger connection as reported in the *Wisconsin News* also included "Mrs. Doris Berger Wells, daughter of the late Victor Berger and member of the extension staff, Milwaukee center, engaged in an unconventional love affair with Frank Hursley, an English professor, also married." Doris Berger Wells was married to Colin Wells, who as president of the Milwaukee Federation of Teachers was in the union fight with Snell.[109]

A *Wisconsin News* story about the adulterous couple, headlined "Link More Aides in 'Free Love Quiz,'" reported, "Assorted moral indiscretions of at least three more University of Wisconsin professors will be bared by the Brunette senate committee trailing communistic and 'free love' activities at the school, it was indicated by a member of the probe group." Thus, the attackers' refrain now cited both radicalism and immorality.[110]

On April 26, *The Milwaukee Leader*, the only daily socialist newspaper in Wisconsin and in the nation, carried the headline "Hunt for Reds Turns to Cries About Morals." It noted that the committee was "far removed from the alleged red propaganda hunt in state colleges, for which purpose it met originally." The paper carried a spirited defense by the other Berger daughter, Dr. Elsa Edelman.[111]

Among Dr. Snell's charges against Glenn Frank was that the university president did not want "lurid" moral issues aired. Specifically, it was reported that "Pres. Frank advised Snell not to tell the regent committee which investigated the extension division about Mrs. Wells and Prof. Hursley."[112]

Perhaps the president did not want the morals issues raised because even though there was mention of "screwing parties," there was more than just heterosexual misconduct that would have to be explained. Included in the testimony in the thousand-page regents' report was an incident

University of Wisconsin–
Madison president
Glenn Frank. UNIVERSITY
OF WISCONSIN–MADISON
ARCHIVES IMAGE S15417

concerning a young Milwaukee woman at UW, described as an "incipient homosexual," and recommendations for how she should be counseled. In addition, Professor W. H. Lighty made a note to the regents' committee about professors on the Madison campus "who are high queens, one an outstanding professor on the campus." A different reference stated, "This was told me by a high queen and chairman of a department, one of the finest scholars we have in the university."[113]

Even more fraught with danger was that Snell, posing as a morals martyr, portrayed Frank's attitude as very lax toward morals. The *Capital Times* story of April 26 printed Snell's charge:

> Frank then told me about a case of misconduct in the university which had been brought to his attention involving alleged indecent advances of a male staff member to male students. Frank said he thought he ought to transfer the offender to another department. This astounded me, but it gave me a clear indication that I would not be backed up on Milwaukee.[114]

On April 27, the Socialist *Milwaukee Leader* reported to its 48,000 readers on the Snell charges against Frank with the headline "Answers to Dean Snell Being Prepared." The *Leader* had also covered the improper male advances in its April 26 story. So on the next day, adding to the material on homosexuals, next to the column on responses being prepared by the university, the paper ran a front-page national story with the headline "Male Triangle Uncovered in Film Slaying." Paul Wharton, a dress designer to the stars in Hollywood, had been shot by his chauffeur after they had quarreled over a blond sailor from the USS *Pennsylvania*. The article included speculations about a romantic cruising party and information from Hollywood's "half world." Investigators reported that Wharton was a "habitué of questionable resorts frequented by neurotic men and masculine women." Over the next two days, the paper would carry two more follow-up stories on the murder and a crime scene photo of the dead designer.[115]

On April 27, 1936, John B. Chapple, seeing an opening created by the press stories involving scandal at the university, announced he would run for governor against the incumbent, Philip La Follette, with the ultimate goal of ousting UW president Glenn Frank. Born in 1899, Chapple had been an early enthusiast of the 1917 Russian Revolution, had written pro-Soviet articles between 1924 and 1927, and described himself as "pink as a lobster." By the 1930s, now an editor of the *Ashland Press*, he had reversed his stance and was a confirmed anticommunist.[116]

In the 1932 Republican primary for US Senator, Chapple had pulled off a stunning upset and defeated incumbent progressive Republican senator John Blaine, who was also a former governor. Chapple then went on to lose the general election to Democrat Michael Duffy in the Democratic sweep. In 1934, he was again the Republican senatorial candidate but ran third in the general election behind the successful Robert "Bob" La Follette Jr., who was seeking reelection, now on the new Progressive Party ticket. Philip La Follette, Bob's brother, won as governor also on the new party ticket, returning to the office he had lost in 1932.[117]

Under John Chapple's editorship, the Ashland paper sensationalized the matter, running stories like " 'Free Love' Charged" and reporting on Snell's "overnight visits to the regent's daughter's country home after her husband had left to take an apartment in the city." The paper further reported on Meta Berger's complaints about "old fashioned ideas of morality." Chapple called the Progressive Party "the La Follette racket." Other headlines from the *Ashland Press* included "Teachers' Morals Are to Be Investigated" and "Communistic Tie-Up Revealed."[118]

The paper also reprinted a *Milwaukee Journal* editorial: "If Dr. Frank did the things he is charged by Dean Snell with doing, if he did not act vigorously on questions of morality but instead took the position that the private life of an instructor was his own affair . . . then he is not the man to be president of the University of Wisconsin."[119]

While the Snell issue consumed the state Senate Committee, a different lavender incident emerged in the state's press on May 11. The Ashland paper headlined it "Improper Conduct of 'U' Faculty Member Charged." Myron Stevenson, a man imprisoned for various thefts in Madison, had made application to the State Pardon Board; as his sister told the board, "Criminal sexual practices on the part of university faculty members brought about an emotional instability to Myron which led to crime." He had come to the campus as a student in 1929. He claimed to have been "morose" as a result of sexual abuse by a male faculty member in the summer of 1930; he committed the thefts and was sentenced on January 19, 1931.[120]

In his race for governor, Chapple made the most of the charges regarding homosexuality at the university, some of which had been in the news thanks to press coverage. As a campaign document, he published in 1936 a large-sized, hardcover book, *La Follette Road to Communism: Must We Go Further along that Road?* His basic charge was that "LaFolletteism and Socialism stand openly together." Explaining in the text why Snell was fired, Chapple reprinted Snell's charge against Frank, whom he called "LaFolletteism's No. 1 Man," with added emphasis.[121]

> Frank then told me about a case of misconduct in the university which had been brought to his attention, INVOLVING ALLEGED INDECENT ADVANCES OF A MALE STAFF MEMBER TO MALE STUDENTS. Frank said he thought he ought to TRANSFER THE OFFENDER TO ANOTHER DEPARTMENT.

If the screaming capitals did not make the point, Chapple added,

> In other words, LaFolletteism's University president, Frank, face to face with the problem of a sex pervert on the University faculty who

John Chapple blamed Philip La Follette for radicalism and gay immorality on the UW campus in his book, *La Follette Road to Communism*.

was making indecent advances to male students, failed utterly to act with decision and could think of nothing better than to transfer the individual in question to another department where he might come in contact with and contaminate still other students.

And in one caption, he wrote, "Dean Snell testified further that Glenn Frank admitted to him that Frank DID NOT EVEN DISMISS A SEX PERVERT ON THE UNIVERSITY STAFF WHO WAS MAKING INDECENT AND ABNORMAL ADVANCES TO MALE STUDENTS and endangering the moral welfare and possibly the whole moral future of students."[122]

Thus, by repeatedly focusing on the homosexual matter, Chapple targeted both commies and queers as the extremes of radicalism and immorality— encouraged by Frank and all wrapped up in "LaFolletteism." Among the leaders of the movement to repel the attacks were the *Daily Cardinal*, *Capital Times*, and *Milwaukee Leader* newspapers and *The Progressive* magazine.

William T. Evjue, editor of the *Capital Times*, had already on April 26 written a column proclaiming, "For weeks hostile Chicago and Milwaukee

FIRED! WHY? Case No. 2

Dean Snell (University Extension Division) objected to what he felt to be serious "unconventional conduct" on the part of teachers. But President Glenn Frank of the University DID NOT EVEN WANT MATTERS INVOLVING MORALS OF TEACHERS REVEALED to the university board of regents, Snell testified.

Dean Snell testified further that Glenn Frank admitted to him that Frank DID NOT EVEN DISMISS A SEX PERVERT ON THE UNIVERSITY STAFF WHO WAS MAKING INDECENT AND ABNORMAL ADVANCES TO MALE STUDENTS and endangering the moral welfare and possibly the whole moral future of students.

SNELL WAS FIRED!

Yet 27 members of the faculty courageously risked their own jobs to testify that the charges which were worked up in order to "oust" Snell were UTTERLY FALSE!

126   PLATE 63

In *La Follette Road to Communism*, John Chapple recounted the testimony of Dean Chester Snell, who accused Glenn Frank of protecting homosexuals on the UW–Madison campus.

newspapers have been carrying lurid headlines seeking to place the stigma of 'free love' on the name of the University of Wisconsin. The story has been one of the big anchors on which to base justification for the legislative investigation into university affairs." Evjue claimed that Snell had started his innuendo-ridden morals campaign six months earlier when he visited

Evjue. Evjue noted that marriage and divorce actually were common on college campuses.[123]

The *Capital Times* gave prominence to Frank's comment that the attacks were "a carnival of demagogic claptrap." It carried a letter from a student who wrote, "No one considers the investigation anything but a farce." The student held the opinion that hundreds of farmers losing their farms and thousands depending on charity did more for communism than thirty Reds at the university. Another *Capital Times* headline referred to the "communist Bogey-Man." A notice about the third annual banquet of the University Progressive Club reported that the group heard Senator Harold Groves (P-Dane) refer to the Senate committee as "a fine exhibit for Adolf Hitler himself." At that time, Groves was also a professor of economics at the university. On May 9, another *Capital Times* editorial ran under the heading, "Time to Stop These Legislative Rackets." The paper reported that E. A. Ross, the well-respected sociologist, urged people to boycott Hearst newspapers in a speech to the Baptist Fellowship Club's annual dinner on campus.[124]

The *Daily Cardinal* also attacked "depraved newspapers," noting, "Banner headlines in the metropolitan press have proclaimed Wisconsin to be a center of immorality. . . . We, the students of the university, know that charges of immorality on campus are grossly exaggerated." The *Cardinal* extensively covered the formation of the Committee of Nineteen, "made up of leaders of various student activities" on campus to defend the university from the probers. Included was Caryl Morse, representing the campus Inter-Church Council. The *Capital Times* followed this story with another that showed the wide defense against the charges aimed at the university with the headline "Athletes Hit Slurs on U.W. in Red Probe." Members of the "W" Club went on record "refuting the groundless charges" and "backing completely the activities of the student committee." The Committee of Nineteen would claim morals at the UW were better than average.[125]

On May Day, the workers' holiday, the *Milwaukee Leader* editorialized, "The inability of the legislative investigating committee to find anything more important to investigate about the university than the marital affairs that are nobody's business shows the wisdom of those who opposed the appointment of an investigating committee." The paper had already attacked the "reactionary" Hearst press for fanning the flames of the red scare and reinforced that with a new attack. The paper wrote that the moral charges could, perhaps, "impress the sixteenth century minds of moron readers." The paper's headlines blasted "the hypocrisy of the investigation" and called it a "Red Herring."[126]

President Glenn Frank also strongly fought back. Addressing a campus convocation of fifteen hundred on May 17, Frank was clear: "This university is so much more authentically American than the head-hunting, witch burning kind of journalism that seeks to brand it as a center of radicalism, that it is incredible that the university should have to make any reply to such insane charges."[127]

By this point, the fight had become a major political battle, and political action would be the thing to take the winds out of its sails. The state senate investigating committee was piling up expenses and needed more money than the body's contingency fund could provide. So the state senate passed a bill for an appropriation of $2,000. However, the Assembly, with the combined strength of Progressive and Socialist members, refused to concur. Among the members of that body, Edward Kiefer (S-Milwaukee, 1931–1936) stated it was a "campaign of muckraking" and that the committee had "deviated to go into private homes, open closets, and take out skeletons." Member Clarence Olson (P-Ashland, 1933–1936) charged the Senate committee with trying to hamper free speech. When Vernon Thomson (R-Richland, 1938–1951) charged that the committee was after both Communism and free love, Olson asked, "How does the gentleman expect the committee to prevent free love?"[128]

The Assembly defeated the appropriation by killing the bill with a vote of 57 for denying funding and 34 for funding. Forty-three Progressives and three Socialists voted against appropriating the money and were joined by eight Republicans and two Democrats. Voting to give the probe more money were thirty Democrats and four Republicans. Several members did not vote.[129]

The next avenue Senator Brunette explored was to ask the state emergency board for funds. This board was chaired by Governor La Follette and included Brunette as Senate Finance Chair and C. A. Begg (P-Rice Lake) as chair of the Assembly Finance Committee.[130]

At this point, state labor joined the fight. Henry Ohl Jr. was president of the Wisconsin State Federation of Labor. He had worked to reconcile the

Progressive leaders and the Socialist-linked labor movement through the work of a Farmer–Labor Progressive Federation started in 1935 "for unified political action." In Ohl's 1936 annual report he noted the Milwaukee Newspaper Guild (a union) had gone on strike against the *Wisconsin News*, published by "the Hearst interests," and characterized it as an "autocratic employer, intoxicated with wealth." Ohl urged Governor La Follette not to approve the requested $2,000, calling the investigation a "travesty." Arnold Zander, executive secretary of the Wisconsin Federation of Teachers, seconded this plea.[131]

Ultimately, the state emergency board did not grant funds for a continued investigation. In September 1936, Chapple lost the Republican primary nomination to Alexander Wiley. Governor La Follette went on to an overwhelming victory in the general election of 1936, winning almost more votes than his Republican and Democratic opponents combined. Chapple, who campaigned again for statewide office by running in the 1938 Republican US Senate primary, lost again to Wiley, who went on to beat the incumbent Democrat, Michael Duffy. Chapple would later become a supporter of Joe McCarthy.[132]

The Senate committee had a milder response and filed a report that mattered little as the Democrats lost control of the body and Senator Brunette was not reelected in the fall of 1936. On June 23, the *Capital Times* ran an editorial that proclaimed: "Here at Wisconsin, the Hearst-inspired 'red' investigation has collapsed." It also noted similar failures at the University of Chicago and at an unnamed school in California.[133]

Doris Berger Wells divorced her husband and married English professor Frank Hursley. The couple started writing radio scripts during World War II and afterward moved to California, where they became successful writers of TV soap operas including *Search for Tomorrow* and *General Hospital*.[134]

Chapple's claim that university president Glenn Frank was "LaFollette-ism's No. 1 Man" turned out to be false. A faction of the Board of Regents linked to Philip La Follette fired the university president in January 1937. Frank then joined the Wisconsin Republican primary for US Senate in 1940 but died in a car crash during the campaign.[135]

Wisconsin had weathered an attack in 1936 that would be waged again after the war by Joe McCarthy. Looking back in his 1968 memoir, *A Fighting Editor*, William Evjue would correctly observe that the Chapple episode "featured all the techniques that were later to become the hall-mark of McCarthyism." Evjue reiterated that Chapple "charged 'commu-nism' against the Progressives and attacked the University as a hotbed of atheism, communism, and free love." He was proud that "the *Capital Times* fought 'Chappleism' as vigorously as it fought . . . McCarthyism in later years."[136]

One other aspect of the Chapple/Brunette fight would reemerge in the attacks of the McCarthy Era. On May 2, 1936, Senator Brunette was quoted in the *Ashland Press* responding to the state emergency board request. He said, "It is little interest to me whether the board does this or not because if we are forced to go outside we can get plenty of money." When asked if it was proper for the board to use outside money, he answered, "The com-mittee can pay its own expenses and where we get the money is nobody's business. I assume we would make public the names of donors and the amounts of donations." It does not appear that such money was used in 1936, but the idea of using outside money to support a government witch hunt would be employed by Wisconsin Republicans in the early days of the McCarthy attacks.[137]

Why did "Chappleism" with its lavender tinge fail in the 1930s and McCarthyism with its red and lavender scares succeed in the 1950s? For one thing, many Wisconsin journals fought back strenuously, as exempli-fied by the *Daily Cardinal*, *The Progressive*, *Capital Times*, and Milwaukee Socialist *Leader*. The university when attacked was not without allies. For another thing, Wisconsin's unique four-party political structure in the 1930s was able to combine the Progressive and Socialist votes in the As-sembly to defeat the requested witch-hunt funds, and in the 1936 general election this coalition reelected Philip La Follette.

After World War II, the separation and isolation of the progressives who supported presidential candidate Wallace from other Truman-supporting progressives in Wisconsin prevented such political flexibility. The worldwide threat of communism with the Soviet advance into the heart of Europe was much more present to McCarthy-era fearmongers than it was to prewar Wisconsinites. While Chapple could make charges based on some evidence of immorality, which then included homosexual acts, it did not appear that gay immorality was widespread. After the war,

Alfred Kinsey's famous report would change public views about the size of the threat posed by perceived widespread homosexuality.

SEIZING IDENTITY, BUILDING NETWORKS

In the 1930s, Wisconsin gay men, while needing to be discreet, could come to an acceptance of who they were. They created poetry affirming their love, and they circulated and even published such poetry. Though not officially "out," they operated publicly as gay members of society in various roles, including newspaper columnists, executive office staff, and respected UW professors. Books about homosexuals were reviewed in campus newspapers. Their willingness to be quietly known and their courage in spreading knowledge enabled them to create networks of association and communication that would endure for decades. Gay poets met gay novelists and gay playwrights in Wisconsin. They even developed informal systems to communicate about the persecution of homosexuals abroad.

Lesbians, too, could find support in places like the state's women's colleges and in the arts world. Charlotte Partridge and Miriam Frink lived their joined lives in a very public fashion and were tied into the state's progressive networks in many ways. The Regents' investigation of 1935 would also uncover a lesbian presence on the UW Extension campus in Milwaukee.

When a few homosexuals came under attack for being too visible, the state's political system, dominated by Progressives and Socialists, refused to become swept up in a hysteria about morals. Milt Sherman's bluenoses did not carry the day. The progressives had moved from Howard Teasdale's and E. A. Ross's stance on policing sexuality in the 1910s to seeing it as more of a private matter by the 1930s. By that time, Wisconsin's Socialist legislators seemed even more disinclined to police traditional morality. Perhaps they had been influenced by their German Socialist brethren in the Social Democratic Party, who had supported the efforts to decriminalize homosexuality in the years before the rise of the Nazis.

Nevertheless, John Chapple's proto-McCarthy attack on commies and queers came within six thousand votes of winning the Republican primary of 1936. This would prove to be a harbinger of difficulties to come for gay Wisconsinites in the state's postwar days.

5

Acting Jam in World War II

*My cousin joined the Army to fight and die, if necessary, for our Free
Country. But he's fighting more for freedom of the Middle-Sex than
anything else. His idea is that if we lose the war the middle-sex will
be lost too, along with everything else.*

— Wisconsinite Wally Jordan
in letter to Jim Kepner, June 12, 1943[1]

*They all expressed difficulty over their sexual excitation because of the
stimulation that resulted from their living closely with other soldiers.
In none of these cases was there a true neurotic type of conflict over
homosexuality as such.*

— From a 1945 study of homosexual
soldiers at Truax Air Field, Madison[2]

In America's mainstream memory, the young men who fought and won
World War II have become the Greatest Generation. Though the qualifiers are never stated, it is implied that the group is straight, white, and male.
Sometimes women are included, but since they did not generally serve in
combat, they are not venerated to the same degree. Only occasionally do
minorities like the Tuskegee Airmen or the Navajo code talkers receive
admiration for their wartime efforts.

Without taking away from the legend of this Greatest Generation, it's
clear that not all sailors, soldiers, and airmen have been treated equally
in recorded history. Gay soldiers and sailors did not typically appear in
World War II narratives—at least not in positive roles—for many decades

following the war. Yet gay people from Wisconsin did indeed participate in the war.

Nationally, the silence surrounding gay military service was broken in a big way by the 1990 publication of Allan Bérubé's *Coming Out under Fire: The History of Gay Men and Women in World War Two*. Bérubé based much of his research on oral interviews conducted with gay and lesbian veterans about their experiences. Notably, he uncovered some of the letters of Wally Jordan from Rhinelander (discussed in depth later in this chapter), though the letters are listed under the pseudonym of Jerry Watson in the book. Bérubé also traced the development of the government's official policy of refusing to induct gays into the military and expelling them if they were discovered. He showed that despite their conspicuous absence from history books, many gay Americans were indeed part of the Greatest Generation. Gay and lesbian historians John D'Emilio and Estelle B. Freedman, in the foreword to the twentieth-anniversary edition of Bérubé's book, acclaimed the work as "especially notable." The American gay men and lesbians who fought in World War II were patriotic citizens who wanted to help defeat fascism. The histories of some Wisconsinites who served also reveal the early stirrings of gay identification and liberation in this period.[3]

The war would change America in so many ways, and homosexual men and women experienced part of that change. Leaving the local social structures of their hometowns, entering a predominantly single-sex environment with men and women from diverse populations, and facing their own mortality made some homosexuals open to acting on their otherwise suppressed sexual desires. One gay soldier from Wisconsin said, "You're facing Eternity at every step." It's not surprising that some used this period to seek love by exploring same-sex experiences.

In both World War I and World War II, some worried about young, arguably innocent American men being taken from their families and home communities and being exposed to the wider world and all its presumed vices. During World War I, the army cooperated with police and other authorities to shut down the flourishing red-light districts where urban prostitution, presumably heterosexual, occurred near military bases—a fitting culmination of the social purity anti-vice crusades begun before the war. The same issue arose during World War II, but at that time authorities were required to overtly state a concern about homosexual vice.

A CAMP FANTASY

Even before the US officially entered World War II, American men were being mobilized at military camps around the country. These camps were often the first place where men met each other and developed relationships in the lead-up to the war. Madison poet and writer Keith McCutcheon used a military camp as the setting for a story that demonstrated what such an experience might have felt like for two young, potentially gay men in the early 1940s.

McCutcheon moved to California in 1939, before the war, to try to break into Hollywood's film industry, though by the early 1940s he was back in Madison. During the 1930s while still in Madison, he had done radio work, including writing scripts for *The Dramatic Hour of the Air*, sponsored by the UW on WHA, the university's radio station. Describing the Los Angeles movie industry as "Hollywood the Amazing," he wrote that the city possessed "but one industry—and that is the most intriguing of any industry in the world—except war." He noted the presence of "glamour boys and glamour girls," and described the "young men jerking sodas at every drug store—many would easily eclipse the most striking man on the screen." To support himself, McCutcheon began writing a travel column. In September 1939, Wisconsin's *Rio Journal* announced that his column would reappear in the paper after a bit of a hiatus. The publishers had "received many compliments" on his material.[4]

One of the results of the outbreak of war in Europe was that Americans began thinking seriously about issues of war and peace. Though he wrote, "I despise Hitler," McCutcheon was not a fan of Roosevelt's New Deal, nor did he side with those eager to rush into war. In his column for Christmas 1940, he urged readers to have "faith in this country." The poem he included gave thanks for a land "unpacked with ugly scars of war; unfilled with dead." He hoped that the power of the pen could "swerve toward Peace desires of mankind." But that was not to be.[5]

A peacetime draft instituted in 1940 to bolster America's preparedness resulted in millions of young men moving around the country on their way to and from military camps. McCutcheon, his imagination grasping this new social phenomenon, wrote a short series of columns for the Rio

Keith McCutcheon in his house on Jenifer Street in Madison. FROM THE AUTHOR'S COLLECTION, COURTESY OF TED PIERCE

paper describing Joe and John, two presumably fictional draftees caught in this upheaval.[6]

McCutcheon created a romantic atmosphere for the relationship between Joe, who is described as "young, handsome," and John, who is "so good looking." He writes, John's "life has been suddenly changed by this new order of things—this army business. In camp he met Joe—a friend that it seemed his whole life had been destined to meet." At one point, John tells Joe, "I'm awful lonesome now. If I hadn't found you well I don't know what I'd have done." When Joe gets ready to meet up with John, "He knotted his tie as meticulously as though it were his first formal." John is inspired by the friendship to write poetry and reads it to Joe in a voice "low and soft." One stanza reads:

Like a lovely lilting tune
With a subtle melody
Through the lovely afternoon
I press you close to me.

This same-sex courtship would be hard for even the casual reader to miss. One line reports, "Arm in arm they walked down the camp street."[7]

In one column, the couple walk "a little ways from the camp, out into the quiet evening, where the sounds of day are being hushed, and dusk is gathering slowly like dark smoke along the ground." Joe says, "We'll talk—you and me, and be near; and learn about each other, and discover what new things can be found. Ready?" The happier of the pair, Joe, describes a vision: "Where friends are—there is a good place, a lovely place." John, who had been lonely and now is not, asks, "But—where Joe? Where's this place that sounds like a dream? You talk as if you'd been there before." Perhaps Joe has experienced same-sex love before. After commenting on the wonderful evening, John "tossed his head in a quaint little way. 'You know, I believe I could almost love you.'"[8]

Did McCutcheon's fictional war buddies live happily ever after? We will never know. Joe ends up in the camp hospital with heart problems, and

In the lead-up to World War II, many young men were sent to military camps, including Camp McCoy in Wisconsin.

John risks "many camp dangers by getting to the hospital and tossing in the magnolia flower to his friend Joe." Later the author describes this act as "poetry in action: like sending up a prayer or tossing a magnolia flower covered in dew through an open window." The story ends with John praying to God for Joe's health while surrounded by air "filled with the sharp and heady scent of magnolia blossom."[9]

That the war would provide opportunities for young homosexuals to have new experiences was not just a fiction in Keith McCutcheon's mind. Steve Estes, in *Ask and Tell: Gay and Lesbian Veterans Speak Out*, published in 2007, spread his interviews over a wide time period that includes World War II. An essay titled "Tail Gunners Too" recounts the experience of gay Army Air Corps member Bill Taylor. Though born in Madison, Taylor had been living in Kentucky before the war. Taylor recalled gay people getting together during his war service with the Army Air Force in England. As he put it, "I had approaches. In those days, I was considered cute [*laughs*]. Tail gunners were small and cute." Further on in Estes's book, the section on out gays and lesbians fighting for their right to serve in latter periods features Wisconsinite Miriam Ben-Shalom, who fought her discharge in the 1970s. Ben-Shalom's experience is described in *Coming Out, Moving Forward: Wisconsin's Recent Gay History*.[10]

THINGS ARE COOKING AT TRUAX

In the early 1940s, Bob Neal and Edgar Hellum, the gay men who had undertaken pioneering historic preservation work in the Cornish settlement of Mineral Point, also contributed to the war effort at a military base. They wanted to help; however, both were rejected for military service for physical conditions. Another famous gay Wisconsinite, Wladziu Valentino Liberace, was also rejected for service because of "a childhood back injury." He spent the war years playing piano and entertaining in bars and clubs in New York and California. One biographer avers that Liberace enjoyed performing for servicemen, writing, "He also found compliant young men, both in and out of uniform, in search of an evening's pleasure."[11]

Neal and Hellum's patriotism was not to be deterred, and they wanted to do something "essential." So, in early 1942, they closed up Pendarvis House, where they had served Cornish cuisine, moved to the east side of

Madison, and got new jobs—Neal as a cook and Hellum as a stores manager at Truax Air Field.[12]

Madison's Truax Field was used during the war as a technical training base for both radio operators and radio mechanics of the Army Air Force. Radio was the backbone of air force communications at this time, and each of the war's large bombers had one operator and one mechanic in its crew complement. Area Boy Scouts collected used radios for trainees to disassemble and thereby learn to fix.[13]

In her *Wisconsin State Journal* column Day by Day of February 14, 1943, journalist Betty Cass described Neal and Hellum's transition from civilian life. They had been accustomed to serving guest parties of four to twelve. Now they were cooking "for a thousand to 1,500 people every day." Five hundred hungry soldiers and civilian workers at the base had to be fed three times a day. "We want to do something useful," Neal told Cass. She wrote that they learned about quantity cooking, which was not quite the same as the artistic dishes they had prepared with loving care for the last eight years. In one Truax booklet from the era, a large mess sign reads, "Eat all you want BUT you must eat all you take." This yearbook-type publication for the classes passing through the Truax base includes a section on "MESS." The booklet, which affirmed that "without a doubt one of the most important parts of any Army post is the 'good ole mess hall,'" also asserted that the US army's top-quality food and capable cooks made it the "best-fed army in the world." Neal did such a good job at Truax that after the war the army asked him to help set up a new cafeteria at a military base in Florida.[14]

Recreation at Truax was important. One published photo shows a man cross-dressed as a woman with a long cone covering his nose. The caption reads, "A soldier asks advice from 'the woman with the paper nose.' This character first made famous in 'Radio Post,' Truax's own newspaper, later went on the air." Allan Bérubé describes this sort of playful cross-dressing as a "skirt and wig" culture encouraged by the military. As a sign of the times, there is also a separate service club that offered dancing for black troops, or, as they are called in another part of the publication, the "Colored Detachment."[15]

The Truax booklet also described the city of Madison, which is referred to as the "capitol [*sic*] city that eats cheese three times a day." An aerial shot of downtown was captioned, "This is the area known as 'the square.' It is Madison's heart." The military maintained buses that ran directly from the base to downtown Madison. A study of Truax personnel conducted late in the war would later show that the Capitol Square was a gay cruising area, made convenient for military personnel by the bus system. Soldiers liked to let off steam by drinking and socializing in the city, and things occasionally became rowdy, as indicated by one group shot of twelve military police officers who, according to the booklet, reported to the Madison police for duty downtown to help with extra enforcement.[16]

Madison's Capitol Square was known as a gay cruising area, both before and after the war.

Bérubé notes that many bars around the country served as cruising grounds for gay military personnel during World War II; among such venues was Milwaukee's Royal Hotel at Fifth and Michigan Streets. The website History of Gay and Lesbian Life in Milwaukee indicates this was a popular place in the mid-1930s and throughout the war. In the 1960s, the former hotel bar was given new names, including The Stud, and even later, Club 546 and Michelle's. Its last day, as reported in Milwaukee's *GPU* [Gay Peoples Union] *News*, was September 23, 1973. As the building was being torn down, the *GPU News* notice commemorated its continued presence in the collective memory of the gay community.[17]

From the North Woods to Germany

The same-sex environment of the all-male logging camps in northern Wisconsin in the late nineteenth century provides an interesting parallel to the army camps of World War II. From the camps come tales of the same-sex "stag dance." One of the folk tunes from Wisconsin logging life was "Shanty Boy on the Big Eau Claire." While the song tells the story of a boy's doomed love for a maiden, the lyrics include the lines, "This shanty boy was handsome, / there were none so gay as he." While the term *gay* is used as a synonym for *happy* in the song, there may have been homosexual undercurrents to the male loggers singing about a handsome shanty boy.[18]

Memoirs and letters show that for soldiers from the North Woods of Wisconsin, gay life was vibrant during World War II. Among these resources is the 1995 memoir *For You, Lili Marlene: A Memoir of World War II*, by poet, scholar, and gay man Robert Peters of Eagle River, Wisconsin, in Vilas County. The University of Wisconsin Press has published several of Peters's memoirs. After the war, he attended the University of Wisconsin on the GI Bill and received a doctorate in Victorian literature from UW–Madison in 1952. Peters taught at several universities, principally the University of California at Irvine. He married in 1950 and had three children. But after his divorce in 1972, he met his life partner, fellow poet Paul Trachtenberg, with whom he had a thirty-six-year relationship. Peters received a distinguished alumni award from the UW–Madison Gay, Lesbian, Bisexual, and Transgender Alumni Council at the turn of the twenty-first century.[19]

In the memoir focusing on his youth, *Crunching Gravel: A Wisconsin Boyhood in the Thirties*, Peters recalls his aversion to gym class. Claiming modesty, he says, "I dreaded showing myself nude to strangers." He used the locker door to hide his body. Yet in nature he reveled in stripping down with his male friends and swimming in the lakes. About one friend, he muses, "Perhaps I had a crush on George, of the kind youths have on one another. I don't know. The more masculine—and crude—he was, the better I liked him."[20]

In *For You, Lili Marlene*, Peters describes leaving "the sheltered Wisconsin farm for the war" and reveals things about his gay life up north, including homosexual experiences with men before he entered the service—for example, a slightly older neighbor friend in whose "barn one summer I discovered sex." The friend died in the war, and when Peters visited the other man's mother, she said, "You two was friends, I know," but Peters was almost tongue-tied: "'We were close,' I said fumbling for words."[21]

In the same memoir, Peters writes, "The only homosexual I had earlier known well was Roy Kamen, a stocky senior at Wausau High School. . . . Craggily handsome, he wore his black hair swept up in a pompadour. He effused an outrageous humor. His general demeanor, while masculine, had a touch of the drag-queen." Kamen had even dressed in drag to crash the junior prom with Peters, where they did some dances together before watchful chaperones chased them out.[22]

Despite these prewar experiences, Peters could not admit to being homosexual in the army. Through his recollections, he portrayed himself as being in denial and trying to suppress his sexual identity during the war, claiming at one point that his sexual identity crisis and self-denial were a means to personal growth. Yet he recorded that in his boyhood a girl had asked him if he "preferred boys," and he admitted to himself his youthful attractions to boys. While *For You, Lili Marlene* described male sex being offered to Peters and occurring around him during the war, there is no record of his participation in such activities.[23]

In one section of the memoir, another soldier whose "tone is more educated than queer" attempted to bring Peters out. The soldier brushed Peters's hair from his face and teasingly said he was sending out a message of "Come take me." Peters blurted out, "I'm not queer." But the other man responded, "I know what jiggles your tits, Peters. I've been around. I've seen them straight off the farm smelling of cow shit. They're ready to play. In the right light they show true colors. So, don't hide from me, Mary. . . . It'll be our secret." *For You, Lili Marlene* does not describe an ensuing encounter with this soldier.[24]

Another notable aspect of Peters's experience in the military is that his military status was changed from infantryman to clerk typist by another clerk typist before his unit shipped out. According to Allan Bérubé, clerical positions often provided havens for gay soldiers and enabled them to do administrative favors for other gays. Peters also volunteered as a chaplain's assistant, another role Bérubé claims was commonly held by gay men in the service.[25]

For You, Lili Marlene includes a scene in which Peters accompanied a friend through the dark streets of London near the Eros Fountain, the infamous gay cruising area of Piccadilly Circus. There the friend received oral sex from a man in women's clothing whose hairy arms gave him away. The friend later stated that no woman performs "as well."[26]

Later, as a sergeant, Peters was attracted to a soldier named Danny Jackson, a lanky, "well-proportioned, sandy haired" man who dominated his fantasies. "I dreaded that the CO might order me to investigate Jackson as a 'queer' and 'undesirable,'" Peters recalled. "If that happened, my rational self would follow orders, even if it meant a dishonorable discharge [for Jackson]. What a hypocrite! While I hungered for Jackson, I felt self-hatred and vowed to God that I would never sin again." Peters worried about the consequences of shedding hypocrisy and admitting his homosexuality to himself. At one point, his superior, Major McKinney, told Peters, "This is confidential. . . . But there are rumors about Jackson. Keep your eye on him, and let me know if anything untoward is going on." Then, after a pause, he continued, "We've got to be on top. No perverts here."[27]

Despite the danger of discovery, Peters went along with Jackson to a lake near Heidelberg, Germany, where Jackson sunned and acquired a tan. Peters wrote, "There are times when I am gazing at him, when he suddenly looks up and catches me, opens his legs (if he is seated), and smiles." He wonders, "Had the CO asked Danny to find me out, as he had asked me to investigate Danny? My paranoia was a mouthful of bitter grapes."[28]

As they were demobilizing, Jackson introduced Peters to his special friend. When Peters said, "You could be brothers," Jackson replied, "Other guys have said that." He continued, "We plan to meet in Chicago.

Robert Peters in a studio in France in 1945. *FOR YOU, LILI MARLENE*

We'll go to the university there—if we can get in on the GI Bill. . . . It's a lifetime thing."[29]

The epilogue of *For You, Lili Marlene* describes the author's sexual restlessness back in Wisconsin on the family farm and his fantasies over the gay soldiers with whom he served: "Danny Jackson in Germany and Roland Stephan in England. . . . [When] I dreamed of love as tenderness, males were the object." Though he had the model of Jackson, who proclaimed lifelong love as an ideal, Peters did not come out as a gay man until many years after the war, a pattern that was not uncommon among gay veterans. A return to "normal" life after the war was the desire of many a soldier.[30]

HODAG BOY'S VIEWS

One of the most distinctive views of gays in World War II comes from the letters of Wally Jordan, from Rhinelander in Oneida County. Jordan served the military in an Arizona internment camp and then overseas in North Africa and Italy. He was an indiscreet letter writer to other homosexuals and described many gay activities taking place in the army. During the war he was rightly concerned about the privacy of his correspondence and papers. His forty-some letters to one of his wartime buddies, Jim Kepner, are preserved in the *ONE* National Gay and Lesbian Archives at the University of Southern California, along with carbons of Kepner's response letters. Kepner would go on to play key roles in the early homophile efforts on the West Coast, especially with the homosexual magazine *ONE* and later as a gay archivist.[31]

Jordan wrote his first letter to Kepner from his military assignment in Florence, Arizona, on February 28, 1943, based on a pen pal fan ad in the science fiction magazine *Weird Tales*. Even in this letter Jordan was sending signals, describing himself as "unmarried & would prefer single Correspondents" and mentioning that he once considered the priesthood. He described himself as having wavy hair and hazel eyes and weighing 148 pounds, as well as being a twenty-three-year-old bookworm, lover of music, writer of poetry, and practitioner of drawing and painting. He wrote: "Friendship is the sweetest fruit a soul can taste is my byword."[32]

James Kepner wrote back from San Francisco, "Our interests certainly run close to the same track." Kepner, who went by Jimmy, was nineteen and a Texan by birth and upbringing. For ten years, he had planned to enter the ministry but had become an agnostic. He mentioned reading a biography of Oscar Wilde, as well as Walt Whitman's *Leaves of Grass*. Whitman was then considered to be an advocate for strong male comradeship and bonding, so many gays used his writings as a marker for homosexuality. "I'm a rather gay fellow," Kepner wrote. "I am not married and have no prospects." He closed with the hope that "we should soon become close buddies."[33]

In his second letter Jordan picked up on the signals and sent more of his own, though hedging a bit, claiming "I am feeling pretty high, and my writing isn't very straight." He then asked if Kepner had read the life of Tchaikovsky, who was probably known to be gay at the time, and if he knew Powell Street—a street that borders Union Square in San Francisco and was known among gays in World War II as a popular homosexual cruising spot—and if it was "as corrupt as I have been made to believe." Jordan wrote, "In *Leaves of Grass*, Whitman has a number of poems which I shall call his 'special poetry.' If you can distinguish them from the maze of ideas you will discover some very delightful unusual things hidden there, almost out of sight to a good many people."[34]

Kepner's second letter signaled right back, claiming not to consider anything about *Leaves of Grass* the least bit vulgar but also expressing great surprise "that certain passages did not draw down the wrath of the puritans." Then he quoted from Whitman on singing "the song of companionship" and the "ideal of manly love." Becoming a bit bolder, Kepner wrote, "By the way, you said my choice of reading matter APPEARED to possess certain revealing characteristics. Hum—I wonder what that could mean. Course I could take a guess at it, but I'll wait awhile." He brought up the issue that Keith McCutcheon addressed in his column about the wartime buddies John and Joe: "I guess a lot of soldiers must get rather lonesome with so few girls around." Finally, Kepner signed off: "Hope you were able to get the point of this rambling letter." In these first two letters, both Jordan and Kepner dropped many hints but left themselves with outs, should either be wrong in supposing that their homosexual interests were mutual.[35]

By Jordan's third letter of March 19, 1943, a lengthy forty-one pages, all caution had disappeared: "I am slinging ink with almost no reservation whatsoever." He responded to Kepner's mention of soldiers' loneliness by explaining: "This situation, Naturally, forces many soldiers to resort to other means of obtaining their desires. In this camp the prevalence is a good percentage higher than usual, and It seems as tho this camp was Selected for persons of like inclinations and proclivities. The gay ones here seem to segregate, undoubtedly due to certain fears."[36]

Kepner in his next letter of March 22 wrote, "So at last it is out in the open. I wondered how long we would continue to beat around the bush. Of course, my last letter, while not right out in the open, was far from subtle. . . . You see, it is only within the last month that I have ever known any one else who was 'gay.' And you are my first correspondent along that line." He reveals he first heard the word *homosexual* less than a year earlier and had to look it up in the dictionary.[37]

That Kepner was relatively new to gay life and that his signaling could be rudimentary, especially for someone living in San Francisco, is demonstrated in another episode found in his early letters. With the intention of finding other gays, Kepner paraded around skid row, where he'd heard there were homosexuals, prominently carrying a copy of *The Well of Loneliness*. It didn't work, as he reported to Jordan: "No results." He knew the book was about homosexuality because his friend Bill, age fifteen, had been expelled from school after the librarian turned him in for reading it. Kepner later wrote of seeing Bette Davis in *Now, Voyager* and opined, "I'd love to see her in a properly directed version of *The Well of Loneliness*."[38]

Jordan, on the other hand, portrayed himself as quite an experienced gay man. He described a group of gays in his own area of the North Woods, including a fellow "who possessed none of the outward or noticeable traits of the pervert-convert-or what have you—which in most cases is a tendency toward effemination." Jordan wrote of having sex in a panel truck, on a secluded pile of logs, and in an abandoned warehouse. He also described other experiences in a warm lake, with a "handsome Italian," with a motorcyclist, and with dozens of others. He also attended several "drag parties" in his neck of the woods. In one letter from Arizona, he reported that members of his North Woods group "being yet aways from the induction notice, or even the actual registration are still carrying on." One of Jordan's friends from back home, after four years of denial, wrote him a wartime letter admitting his true sexual identity. Life in northern

Wisconsin had not been sexually limited for Wally Jordan in the years before the war.[39]

Jordan also remembered two weeks in the summer of 1939, when he was perhaps nineteen. In Montreal, Quebec, he met "horribly handsome" Ramon, who "possessed a figure like a young Greek god of love—Apollo." Jordan described sitting in a car's passenger seat while Ramon drove "along, one hand on the wheel, the other in my elevated lap." They went to a secluded spot in the woods known to "sex fiends." Then, the next night, Ramon took Jordan to a club with a back room where a three-act male-on-male sex show was presented. The last act was a five-way, with one individual that Jordan said he "wished that I could have taken . . . back to Rhinelander with me." This sort of idealization and romanticization of gay men would occur constantly in Jordan's letters to Kepner.[40]

In addition to describing his past experiences, Jordan told Kepner about real gay life in his military camp, noting he had met "Several Outstanding Queens here, but fate Seems to Split us Up." He mentioned a private in his company, Ray Shultz, "who is the Queen of Queens it seems. The drag parties she has gone to would stagger the imagination." Jordan counted "eight in our little group" in his Arizona camp and talks of necking in the tavern in town and on the bus on the way back. Kepner, in response to this letter, described his own experience in a movie theater observing two good-looking queens in the row in front of him, who only made a few cautious advances toward each other: "Others can love in public, but we must pretend there is no affection or emotion." He also told Jordan he met a Wisconsin boy at a gay bar who was staying at the Mark Hopkins, one of San Francisco's most distinguished hotels, and "had a very enjoyable night." Kepner's letters mention gays frequenting the hotel's bar, the well-known Top of the Mark.[41]

After describing his crush on a sergeant, Jordan wrote on June 22, 1943, "Oh to be a sargent's wife!!!" Before being shipped to another camp that would separate him from the sergeant, Jordan "discovered that our tastes ran so parallel that marriage would have been the best and only alternative, so we had an *informal* marriage. It was quite ridiculous in itself, for a pair of uniforms linked together isn't the most beautiful set-up at all." Acknowledging that "it is damn certain that we'll never meet again while we're in the Army," Jordan and the sergeant severed ties rather than spend the duration of the war waiting. As in this case, shifting assignments could also contribute to young soldiers' loneliness. [42]

Kepner was not Jordan's only gay pen pal. Nor was Jordan the only wartime gay pen pal that Kepner had. Jordan mentions a gay soldier, Fredrick Brugge, stationed at an internment camp in Ogden, Utah, and a nineteen-year-old gay cousin in the air force at Robertson, Missouri. According to Jordan, another soldier in the homosexual network "knew 'another of us' . . . in Fort Bliss, Texas who has been a member of his wild Milwaukee Clan." Yet another of Jordan's gay correspondents lived in Hondo, Texas, and had friends in San Francisco. Jordan also listed a gay friend in Australia, another three in the navy, and one in the Coast Guard. And Kepner was not the only man Jordan approached through ads in publications. In mid-1943 Jordan wrote, "Recently I got names from a magazine & have 'discovered' two new homo correspondents." [43]

Inspired by his various gay pen pals, Jordan told Kepner in 1943 that he was working on a book, a treatise on homosexuality perhaps to be titled *All Under God* or *Who Pleads Our Cause*. He expected to include topics such as homosexuality in the past, the impossibility of destroying the homosexual or his nature, the ignorance of society, "the fine characteristics and love of the homosexual, and a hundred other things." In part, material for the book was to be drawn "from angry torn letters of homosexuals which I have here at the present time, & a great deal more comes from the attitudes & standings in reference of other Q's here. I intend to publish some of those letters which are so torn by loneliness and despair because of the forces of Intolerance." By April 1943, Jordan reported he was up to fifty-four pages. When he was in a more despairing mood, he thought of retitling the book *The Legion of the Damned*. Jordan did not publish his postwar book, but in 1951 Donald Webster Cory's *The Homosexual in America: A Subjective Approach* realized Jordan's dream of a book about gays written by a gay person. [44]

On March 26, 1943, Jordan wrote to Kepner, "We are on alert for overseas duty." Knowing the army got rid of admitted homosexuals, he mused, "As far as that goes—the overseas business—If I decide that I will dislike going, I can always resort to that one and final *tack* to declare my homosexuality. Then they will put me out of the Army for good. Hmm, that doesn't seem so very nice tho." Jordan also reflected in his letters on the patriotism expressed by his unnamed gay cousin. "My cousin joined the

Army to fight and die, if necessary, for our Free Country. But he's fighting more for freedom of the Middle-Sex than anything else. His idea is that if we lose the war the middle-sex will be lost too, along with everything else." Perhaps Jordan's cousin had also heard rumors of the Nazi persecution of homosexuals. In 1943, Jordan shipped out of Arizona with his unit to North Africa, which the Allies had invaded in November 1942.[45]

In 1944, while stationed briefly in North Africa, Jordan came across Casablanca's large gay community. He described the gay society in the Moroccan port city as consisting of "250 gay people stationed in that area." At least one problematic situation developed. Jordan wrote, "There was an investigation by the 2-star general in command of the entire Atlantic Base section, and the gay crowd had to split up and act very jam for the next month, at which time it cooled off with no arrests and no comfort to the suspecting higher-ups." He added, "The crowd was composed of members of every unit in that area and the informers were countless, so the crowd was saved by the in-the-knowitiveness of some of its members." The gay slang expression "to act jam," used frequently in Jordan's wartime letters, meant to act straight. Donald Webster Cory in *The Homosexual in America* notes that "jam," while it might have been used on the East Coast, was particularly characteristic of San Francisco gay circles.[46]

Jordan had been shipped in an invasion force to Salerno, Italy, where the Allies first landed on the Italian mainland. He was sure that, despite the language barrier, he had found his mate in a local man and hoped to return to him after the war. About the later Anzio landings, in which he participated, Jordan explained, "all hell broke loose" as the German Panzer divisions opposed and counterattacked the Americans. "I have Seen Action," he wrote, "and Know well the comfort of a fox hole (even a wet one) when under fire or bombing." In February 1944, he was in the hospital. No longer free to maintain his gay life, he admitted to being "lonesome as hell," and even wrote a poem titled "Lonely." But, he said, "I have had my gay moments both here and in Africa, so the match is balanced."[47]

In June 1944, Jordan wrote Kepner from a North Carolina hospital describing his experience of having gone before two medical boards:

They both decided that I should get home as quickly as possible, and under a medical diagnosis—because my facts would only cause red

Wally Jordan was one of the many men landing in "ducks" for the battle of Anzio in Italy.
US ARMY PHOTO

> tape & possible inconvenience to my well-being if I was listed in the
> true diagnosis. In fact one of my doctors, a major, young, handsome,
> and mad as a hatter, covered up all traces for me before he sent me
> back here to the States.

The word *mad* was often used by Jordan and Kepner as a synonym for gay. Yet, Jordan was not sure the deal would stick, for he also writes, "of course If I get a Section VIII, then there might also be rising complications, and inconvenient contingencies to contend with—unavoidable, perhaps, but nonetheless existent." The Section 8 dishonorable discharge was used by the military for known homosexuals.[48]

Jordan also knew others facing the difficulties of the army discharge system. He writes later about his kid brother, who was also gay, "He may try the Queer way out of the Army, but I hope he gets the breaks I got so it won't be too tough on him during the last days of his military life, that is during the time his discharge is being prepared." Gay men trying to do their bit fighting in the war were in turn compelled to fight the homophobia of the army and the larger society, which considered them unmanly and therefore unfit.[49]

In Harm's Way

Another Wisconsin gay man who came into harm's way was Lieutenant Kenneth Palmer from Edgerton. A navigator with a B-24 Liberator bombardment group flying out of conquered parts of Italy in 1944, he had fifty missions under his belt. He describes a particular mission to bomb Munich: "About 20 minutes before reaching the target, heavy barrages of flak started to burst all around us. As we came up to the target, it really got bad. Just before 'Bombs away,' one big chunk came through the nose of the ship and tore into my arm." He survived, noting, "If they can come that close and not get me, I'm safe." In 1948, Palmer would be arrested as part of a homosexual ring in Madison; he entered a "no contest" plea to a disorderly conduct charge. The defense attorney said Palmer had admitted to "committing indiscretions." The charge was ultimately reduced from a more serious morals offense. UW records show that the combat veteran had been implicated in similar behaviors during 1941 before entering military service.[50]

Some straight soldiers from Wisconsin, in their oral history reminiscences, mention having an awareness of gay men fighting alongside them. James Zeasman, a Madison native who served in the Pacific theater with the Army of Occupation, describes two men in one unit: "They were both gay. Everybody knew that they were gay. . . . They were combat veterans, they'd been through Okinawa, they'd been through the Philippines, they'd been through a lot of heavy combat." Since they were "both heavily decorated," Zeasman said, nobody "cared. But, it was all unofficial." "I'm sure," he concluded, "the Company Commander was fully aware of it."[51]

Sigurd Sivertson, a La Crosse native, recalled, "Those who were gay kept it to themselves and never said anything. We weren't aware of a problem and they were good soldiers." Sivertson later served in Korea and recalls "a lot of lesbians" in the nursing corps.[52]

John Bach from Madison served in the Coast Guard, doing convoy duty in the submarine-infested North Atlantic. He talked about military life requiring adjustment for gay men: "Some homosexuals had quite severe problems. They couldn't—they weren't practicing, but they just couldn't—they just got totally depressed." Bach recalled that some gay soldiers did suffer consequences for making their sexuality known: "A couple of them were taken off because they were admitted homosexuals. I don't know what happened to them when they took them off the ship."[53]

Although the veterans just quoted seem sympathetic to their gay brethren, one Dodgeville Marine was less kind in referring to a fellow serviceman in the South Pacific. The gay man, whom he designated by the pejorative term *queer*, was a gunner with twenty-five or thirty years' service. The Dodgeville Marine's attitude became clear when he called the gunner's suggestive sexual approach to a younger marine an "oddball" experience. Nevertheless, this Wisconsinite observed, "That was not a normal thing that happened. But it did happen and I don't think I better tell you his name." The gay machine gunner was sent back to the States.[54]

Home Front Gay News

While Wisconsin soldier Wally Jordan was stationed in Arizona, he still had contacts in Wisconsin that kept him informed him of goings on in the state. In May 1943, he learned of a crackdown on Milwaukee's gay bars, with "seven different places raided, 4 or 5 others closed shop for the duration, and a number of others are saturated with undercover men." Milwaukee had a reputation for attracting sailors on leave from the large Great Lakes Naval Training Station just north of Chicago. No doubt some found their way to gay bars. One attractive aspect of Wisconsin was the post-Prohibition drinking age of eighteen for beer in Wisconsin in contrast to twenty-one in Illinois. (This disparity was corrected in 1957 when Wisconsin changed the minimum drinking age to twenty-one for residents of states bordering Wisconsin that had an age-twenty-one minimum.) The Wisconsin gay bar crackdown was part of a national effort chronicled by Allan Bérubé in *Coming Out Under Fire*, and James Kepner's letters also described raids occurring in California. Jordan's correspondent informed him that there were "a few places still open, still free of suspicion, but just how long will they last under the vulture-eye of the Intolerance Squads?"[55]

Civic leaders were concerned that gays had become visible in the Beer City. During the war, the Metropolitan Commission on Crime Prevention, a private body, conducted a study on Milwaukee's homosexuals and their local haunts. To their shock, they reported nearly a thousand homosexuals living in the Milwaukee area. Milwaukee's police chief, Joseph Kluchesky, told a legislative hearing that "the sodomists hang around the theaters and make advances to high school youths as well as finding people of their own kind." Statistics from a February 1945 report showed that 871 men had been convicted of sodomy in the city of Milwaukee since 1938. The annual conviction numbers had increased from 72 in 1938 to 198 in 1944. And this did not count the many who had not been caught in an overt act and thus were charged only with disorderly conduct.[56]

Also in 1945, before the end of the war, the Wisconsin Legislative Reference Library compiled an index to articles in legal periodicals for the period 1937 to 1945 pertaining to sexual psychopaths. This research was related to a bill introduced into the legislature that would permit the confinement of "confirmed sodomists." The bill had a hearing in February 1945. Milwaukee police chief Kluchesky, speaking in favor, noted, "We want to take these confirmed sodomists out of circulation and either cure them or isolate them." Also speaking in favor of the bill was Dane County district attorney Norris Maloney, who noted that in Madison the problem of homosexuals was that "they congregate in the capitol park." Mahoney said that "progress had been made in treating such persons, especially by the army, and if sodomists were institutionalized the state could follow through with the work started by the army."[57]

The Metropolitan Commission on Crime Prevention drafted the bill with assistance from Dr. William F. Lorenz, professor of neuropsychiatry at the University of Wisconsin, and C. Stanley Perry of the Milwaukee County Corporation Counsel. Additional supporters included the Wisconsin Chiefs of Police Association, the District Attorneys Association, the Milwaukee City Council, and the League of Women Voters of Milwaukee County. The only noted opposition was from citizen lobbyist Gladys Walsh. As a strong Roman Catholic, Walsh was not a homosexual advocate, but she was a strong supporter of constitutional rights. The 1945 bill did not pass, but the issue did not disappear, as will be apparent shortly in the section on the sexual psychopath bill of 1947.[58]

Bold Correspondence

Early in their correspondence, Jordan cautioned Kepner not to name any service personnel in their letters because of his belief that "sodomy is punishable by death in the Army—so *we* are very careful here." He also wrote, "Even in this man's army you got to watch your step, 2 men in a bed: 20 years; Two men satisfying a personal desire they both must forfeit 1/3 of their lives in prison. . . . Prison sentences here also."[59]

Once Jordan was back in the States but still in a military hospital awaiting discharge, Jim Kepner penned on June 19, 1944: "Wally, I hope that now you are using the regular mails again, our letters can get back to what they were before, when both of us were rather open. Such a feeling of restraint has been built up that I hardly feel natural any more in writing you. V MAIL was such an un-private affair." On July 6, Jordan added a postscript to his return letter: "You needn't worry about dishing, its OK."[60]

V-mail, or Victory Mail, was used in various military theaters to reduce the cost and weight of shipping actual letters. A soldier in the field would write on small letter sheets, measuring about seven by nine inches, which then went through military censors before being photocopied onto microfilm. According to the National Postal Museum, thirty-seven mailbags could be reduced to one mail sack, thus reducing space and weight in transport, which was critically needed for munitions and supplies. On arrival in the United States, the microfilm negatives were blown up and printed on paper, then sent out for delivery. This system also reduced espionage risks, as the photocopy precluded the use of invisible ink and microdots. However, since no envelopes were used in the field, sender privacy was nonexistent.[61]

In August 1944, after Jordan had at last been demobilized, he received a shocking letter from Kepner, who had moved to southern California, about an incident from mid-1943: "Shortly before I left San Francisco, a plainclothesman from the Army intelligence visited me, and demanded to see any correspondence I had with you. . . . The officer informed me that all of your mail was to be watched, and that I was not to mention the incident to you. I do hope you haven't had anything too confidential in your mail." That statement seems a bit tongue-in-cheek, since Kepner had received letters from Jordan explicitly describing, for instance, the three-act homosexual sex show he'd seen in Montreal in 1939. Even though the agent was sitting two feet from the file case where Kepner kept all his correspondence, Kepner told his visitor that he destroyed all his mail immediately after reading it. Apparently, Jordan's letters to another soldier whom he believed to be gay had gotten into the wrong hands. The agent showed Kepner portions of the purloined letter during the investigation interview, including a part of the letter naming Kepner.[62]

Jordan had tried to cover his tracks. Knowing his mail was being read by censors, he sent Kepner a letter that described the homosexual narrator of his writings as fictional. In December 1943, he wrote in a V-mail, "Several months ago a manuscript I had well on its way to completion was stolen. . . . It dealt with perverted sex—and to follow a suggestion of a now famous writer, I wrote in the personal point of view of the subject matter. Before I could arrive at the point where I was to complete the solution of the problem regarding the subject matter, and return the voice back to the third person singular," the manuscript was stolen. Several days later, he received a blackmail note. This development led him to write frankly, "The contents of that M.S. are extremely dangerous to my well-being, and unless I can retrieve it, without publicity or investigation, I will be in hot water." Jordan never saw the "manuscript" again. It's known that his letter was seen by the censors because there are two deletions, but the parts about the manuscript on perverted sex went through the military mails untouched and the letter was delivered to Kepner.[63]

Perhaps Jordan's letter was allowed through the mail by Lieutenant John Horne Burns, a gay man from Connecticut whose job in intelligence made him one of the wielders of the censor's X-Acto knife. Burns, like Jordan, served in both the North African and Italian theaters. Critics praised Burns's postwar novel *The Gallery* for depicting military rear echelon service personnel, and one noted that the novel depicted a homosexual hangout. Burns thus confirmed the existence of active homosexual networks during the war. Jordan, in trying to build a semiformal gay organization through his correspondence and drafting a book on homosexual lives and rights, was not just a gay soldier, but an early gay activist. Scholars now acknowledge that gay men have always served in the American military and that gay sex occurred among soldiers during wartime.[64]

STUDYING GAY SOLDIERS

Despite their patriotism, many gay Americans in the service remember the years of World War II and the following McCarthy era as particularly dangerous for homosexuals. Ted Pierce, the cultivated African American gay man who lived most of his life on Madison's Williamson Street, used to compare the period to "the Terror" that gripped France during the waning days of the French Revolution. In an oral history he recorded decades later, Pierce recalled: "There was a point in that period where you didn't have to have any evidence that you could definitely say anybody was gay. All you had to do was say you felt they were gay to the police, and the police would investigate you extensively right down to the point of asking if you had wet dreams who was it you were seeing in your wet dream."[65]

Pierce's boyfriend during the war, originally from St. Louis, worked at the military base at Truax Field. Within the military, there was a concern about the possible blackmail of gay folks as security risks regarding sensitive war equipment. Pierce remembered the army arresting people every day. Dishonorably discharged soldiers were denied all military benefits. Pierce remembered the uncertainty and the anxiety of the period, and that his friend would phone "to let me know he was still not taken in."[66]

Twenty-one gay men at Truax who were "taken in" during the first half of 1945 became guinea pigs in what would become a historic research project. The results of the research, published as "A Study of Homosexual Adult Males" in the journal *Psychosomatic Medicine*, showed homosexuals rejecting the suggestion that they were sick. It was noted that all "these men voluntarily brought their homosexuality to the attention of the Chaplin, Unit Commander or Medical Officer." Apparently not much weight was given to religious and medical confidentiality in the army in those days. "[The gay men] expressed a realistic anxiety that their homosexuality would lead to court martial," the report noted.[67]

Dr. Elmer L. Severinghaus of the UW and Major John Chornyak of the Truax Army Air Force Hospital led the research for the study. These two physicians evaluated the gay men under diagnostic observation in a psychiatric ward. They "were required to collect three 24-hour urine specimens for bioassay." Another control group of seven soldiers in the same ward, of whom the researchers had "no reason to suspect homosexual behavior," also provided samples, as did some university research assistants. The purpose of the research, which ultimately proved inconclusive, was to seek an endocrine-related explanation of homosexuality, since some suspected that an elevated level of the female hormone estrogen was present in homosexuals.[68]

The principal investigator, Dr. Severinghaus, a native of New Albany, Indiana, graduated from the Madison campus in 1916 with a bachelor's degree, which he then followed with a master's degree. He earned his medical degree from Harvard Medical School in June 1921. After Harvard, he returned to the UW where he became an associate professor of medicine in 1927. By 1938, he was a physician with the Wisconsin General Hospital on campus, the forerunner of the UW–Madison School of Medicine and Public Health. Severinghaus participated annually in the UW Union's lecture series on friendship and marriage. He was a member of Madison's First Congregational Church and the Rotary Club. Although he was a religious person, his approach to homosexuality was based in secular science rather than ideas of sin.[69]

Severinghaus was well respected in his field, as shown by his editorship in the 1930s of the endocrinology section of *Yearbook of Neurology, Psychiatry, and Endocrinology*. He authored *Endocrine Therapy in General Practice* and *Guide for Diabetic Patients*, and more than sixty journal articles. He also served as president of the American Association for the Study of Internal Secretions. After World War II, in 1945 he assisted in the attempt of the United Nations Relief and Rehabilitation Administration in Italy to control the spread of tuberculosis. The disease was being spread in part by tubercular returning refugees who had been workers in German war plants but had been repatriated by the Nazis because of their illness.[70]

The coinvestigator in the Wisconsin study with Severinghaus was Dr. John Chornyak, a major in the Medical Corps with the Army Air Force Regional Hospital at Truax Field in Madison.

Dr. E. L. Severinghaus in 1942 when he was a professor of physiological chemistry at UW–Madison.
UNIVERSITY OF WISCONSIN–MADISON ARCHIVES IMAGE S04383

Chornyak came to Wisconsin from Pennsylvania, where he had been active with the Philadelphia Psychiatric Society. He was a commentator in 1936 on a paper studying psychoses, which suggested (among other things) that larger testes appeared related to a higher incidence of homosexuality as shown through autopsies. One cannot be sure how many homosexuals were dissected for them to arrive at this strange thesis. Chornyak's comments on the 1936 paper had focused on the psychochemical aspects of the endocrine theory, and he based his insights on his own research and psychiatric practice.[71]

In the Wisconsin study, the joint authors developed their hypothesis on homosexuality from a review of the existing literature that led them to claim: "the data is nevertheless highly suggestive that there is some type of endocrine disturbance in these atypical adult males." They noted the medical community's "widespread opinion that homosexual behavior is related to an abnormality in sex hormones." Yet, they observed that few reports of investigation had been published on this point. They reported that most of the studies in this narrow field had found an endocrine pattern in male homosexuals with a relative increase in urinary estrogens (female) and decrease in androgens (male). Dr. Alfred Kinsey, who had published a scholarly article in which he challenged endocrine-based research, did not believe in this theory.[72]

The resulting chemical analysis of Severinghaus and Chornyak's study showed that ten of the homosexual subjects had no gonadotropic component in their urine samples, and the researchers concluded that this "failure to find the pituitary hormone is a distinct contrast with the results of the control group" and with the results from other adult men in the laboratory. But ten other homosexuals had levels comparable to those of the control group, and four even showed higher-than-usual levels. The study also examined "the neutral 17-ketosteroids"; but again, the results were mixed. And the two chemical indicators did not themselves offer a correlation. Thus, the doctors had not proved their hypothesis.[73]

They concluded that "any statistical treatment of such data is apt to be misleading." Nevertheless, the authors maintained, "We are inclined to suspect that there may be very real endocrine disturbances in these subjects but that we do not have available the most direct measure of these disturbances." The judgmental use of *disturbance* versus a more neutral word like *variation* to describe the difference between homosexuals and heterosexuals would not be acceptable in a scientific paper today.[74]

Yet, the doctors felt further efforts should continue. "Elusive as the field may be," they wrote, "it seems worthwhile to attempt to devise methods for studying this type of psychosomatic disorder rather than to assume that it is merely a perversion of mental or emotional status which is not amenable to the methods of chemical and physiological investigation." This statement challenged the common perception of homosexuality as a "perversion," as well as the Freudian theories of homosexuality as a psychological status.[75]

These researchers employed the common technique of asking their homosexual subjects "to write their own stories concerning their sexual habits." While case histories are cited in the earliest scientific writings about homosexuality, Severinghaus and Chornyak, like UW sociologist John Gillin before them, tried to use statistics to reach general theories about homosexuality, in addition to taking case histories. An analysis of the biographies in the Wisconsin study apparently showed that "all these cases were extreme types and had been aggressively homosexual both actively and passively since late childhood and early adolescence."[76]

Dr. E. L. Severinghaus conducted his endocrine exploration of the origins of homosexuality at the Wisconsin General Hospital.

An important truth that comes through strongly in the Severinghaus and Chornyak study is that the homosexual subjects rejected views of themselves as mentally sick. The authors noted that the subjects "had participated apparently without conflict in a wide variety of homosexual practices. These homosexual stories were remarkably similar. . . . The homosexual subjects would probably be termed overt homosexuals." The doctors accepted that "the cases would be considered extremely questionable from the standpoint of profiting from any therapy; in fact, therapy was not requested or desired by any of them." These gay men demonstrated that they had found and accepted their own identities. Like Gillin's subjects, they were also willing to share their stories.[77]

Another observation worth noting is that although these men rejected sickness as an explanation for their homosexuality, they were not unmindful of the military tensions of the day, the negative public attitudes about them, and the consequences they might face if their sexual preferences were to be discovered. "They all expressed difficulty over their sexual excitation because of the stimulation that resulted from their living closely with other soldiers," the report noted. "In none of these cases was there a true neurotic type of conflict over homosexuality as such." The authors wrote, as a sign of the subjects' true understanding that the society was sick, and not themselves, "They expressed a realistic anxiety that their homosexuality would lead to court martial." Perhaps the single most startling revelation was, "Our subjects were all definitely aggressive in their homosexual activities and in fact four of them were known to be members of an organized group." Here, presented casually as an aside, was the discovery that homosexuals were organizing in the mid-1940s in Wisconsin, thereby establishing a rudimentary sense of community. While the study was inconclusive in its science, it reveals fascinating details about homosexuals in the Midwest during the war.[78]

IMAGINING A NATIONAL GAY ORGANIZATION

Wally Jordan's views concerning the inborn nature of homosexuality inspired him to mobilize gay men, knowing that this tactic could motivate future gay activists. "We know we can't live as others, for we aren't born that way," he wrote to Kepner. "Our perversion is our destiny, our right.

And we'll fight for what we know to be our right." He viewed his own wartime "Correspondence Club" as a way to unite homosexuals, and he believed that from this burgeoning network of gay servicemen, "organization must and can be constituted and extended." The purpose of such an organization would be "to openly manifest our rights and succeed."[79]

Jordan discussed with Kepner what he termed the "Sons of Hamidy." He claimed the underground homosexual organization was founded in 1888 and reorganized in 1934. "After a long, tedious climb," he explained, "a few socially and politically prominent men joined themselves together in love and faith." The name derived from a young Greek soldier hero, Harmodius, who killed a relative of the tyrant Peisistratus, with his older lover and fellow Athenian, Aristogeiton. The killing was viewed as a key step in establishing Athenian democracy in Greece, and a celebrated public statue was erected to the pair of lovers. Jordan claimed the modern-day Sons of Hamidy group had operatives in major cities of the Middle West.[80]

For Jordan, finding new members was not a social but a political effort:

> I know that eventually we will hold a respected, possibly envied place
> in the world, but I want it to take place while I am still young and
> active enough to enjoy it. . . . Sometime in the near (I hope) future,
> when we have a strong enough force of us, we will hold a conference
> at some point in the country and there and then declare our rights.

That Jordan imagined his work as an activist effort to inspire the postwar generation showed in his words: "But we must get everything organized for that one day, that irregardless [sic] of our fears we shall pound society with accusation, anger, and vengeance." Jordan thought the names of homosexuals in the organization should be "stored away 'till after the war." He urged Kepner to print membership cards for the Sons of Hamidy with green ink, which was used by FDR's postmaster general, James Farley, a master of patronage and political organization. In his 1962 book *The Homosexual Revolution*, R. E. L. Masters thought there were likely no more than twelve persons in the Sons of Hamidy, and that "most of these, it is said, were located in Rhinelander, Wisconsin." Unfortunately, a large sophisticated cell of gay political thought did not exist in Wisconsin's North Woods in the 1940s, despite Jordan's own advanced thinking and dreaming. Nevertheless, Jordan's confidence that homosexuals would eventually gain their rights shows a Wisconsin-based progressive belief that American society could reform itself to include gays as citizens. Jordan's optimism would also contribute to later homophile activism, such as the efforts of his friend Kepner who helped to establish *ONE*, the 1950s homosexual magazine.[81]

Later, another correspondent would write Kepner, "All in all, I fear the Sons of Hamidy idea was only an idea. Somebody ran up a flag, nobody saluted." James Sears in *Behind the Mask: The Hal Call Chronicles and the Early Movement for Homosexual Emancipation* refers to the "myth of this club." Other gay histories treat it as a hoax. Perhaps a vision of a national organization for homosexuals in this period had to start with science fiction fans like Jordan and Kepner, who were adept at imagining a future very different from their present.[82]

RETURNING HOME

By late 1944, Jordan had returned to the North Woods, where he came out to his family. He traveled to Chicago for gay experiences but also found gay companions closer to home. In various letters, he mentions a Norwegian beauty, a sixteen-year-old intellectual, and "men swishing madly along the streets" of Hurley, Wisconsin, a notoriously wide-open town for sexuality. Jordan knew of other gays in the North Woods, including an Episcopal priest, the nephew of a brewery owner, an "auntie" who cruised the pool hall, and the district attorney. He wrote, though, that "almost all of the gay people who come out of around this region are ignorant of true gay society and the mammoth size and appearance of its assorted offspring, and so all they know is the desire, & in some cases the way and opportunity to satisfy it."[83]

Jordan's intimate gay friends had taken to calling him "Hodag Boy," after the Hodag, which he describes as "a legendary monster of fantastic appearance who roamed the woods near here." Friends also called him "the Apostle of Gaiety." He admitted, however, that in heterosexual society, "I stayed jam as possible, & experienced boredom." Many of his earlier liaisons grew up and married. One homosexual friend got caught and was sent to prison for five years. Now that wartime had ended, gay and lesbian

Wally Jordan was known for networking with gay men in the North Woods, and he earned the nickname "Hodag Boy" after the mythical North Woods creature.

service personnel were returning to hometown structures that enforced the prevailing norms. Jordan tried to revive the local Sons of Hamidy club, "but everyone was so carefree and fun chasing, that I couldn't get anyone to be serious enough to get anything started."[84]

Wally Jordan's vision of a peacetime national gay conference and a homosexual rights organization would have to wait. At times, even he seemed to be of two minds on the subject. Although he saw mainstream political organizing as one avenue by which gay men could achieve equality, he was also tempted by a protective withdrawal strategy. Upon learning of the wartime crackdowns where civilians' private parties "aren't even allowed to go unmolested," he reacted by claiming, "Someday I'm going to build a huge Fortress with walls 10 feet thick and 5 sets of steel gates. *Then* let anyone try to invade our party." Long after the war, Jordan would be taken by the idea of gays moving to a small, sparsely populated county in northern Wisconsin, where they could take over and, by dominating at the polls, elect their own public officials. A similar idea had been gaining momentum in Alpine County, California, slightly earlier. The California idea was criticized by gay activists as isolationist in that it did not encourage gays to engage in the broader political struggle. The Wisconsin concept remained just another daydream.[85]

Not Fighting Alone

More than 300,000 Wisconsinites served in the military during World
War II, and thousands of them were homosexuals. The stories that have
been recorded, though revealing, are but mere glimpses into the individuals' experiences. The existing materials demonstrate that many homosexuals were greatly reappraising their status, even if society at large was
not. America sent gay men from Wisconsin and elsewhere to do their bit
in fighting the war, but they in turn were compelled to fight homophobia,
which labeled them as unmanly and therefore unfit for the military. While
the army tried to weed them out, discharge them, and classify them as sick,
many gay men were making friends and contacts who exposed them to
new experiences and reinforced their own sense of self-worth.

After the war, returning veterans would fuel an outbreak of visible homosexuality at
UW–Madison. This 1945 watercolor by Lois Ireland features two sailors walking along
Observatory Hill on campus.

The writings of Keith McCutcheon, the memoirs of Robert Peters, the letters of Wally Jordan, and the stories of those apprehended at Truax Army Air Field all show how the war enhanced homosexuals' sense of identity and enabled them to see that there were many others like them. They were at times lonely, but the war also showed them they were not alone.

Most importantly, they seized the opportunity to tell their own stories. In the case of the Truax soldiers who participated in the UW medical study, their oral histories had real scientific impact. In *Departing from Deviance: A History of Homosexual Rights and Emancipatory Science in America*, Henry L. Minton looked at similar studies conducted in the 1930s and 1940s, including another urine study, and concluded that gay men and lesbians used their participation in research to get their voices affirmed. Their stories show, he wrote, "the multiple ways in which the gay men came to terms with their sexuality." By positing their own identities, the subjects educated the researchers. Their stories, even though filtered by the scholars when they were published, contradicted the prevailing narratives about homosexuality.[86]

Though homosexuals were criminalized, declared sick, and put in psych wards during World War II, they themselves did not accept such characterizations of their lives. In forming gay friendships, circles of correspondence, and social clubs, they built networks and communities. They found and exchanged tools, signals, slang, and comradeship, which inspired many to believe that the postwar world might be different.

6

WHO NEEDS A DOCTOR?

*Make it possible to commit the overt homosexual to a special institu-
tion, not for a term but until cured.*
—EDITORIAL IN THE *MILWAUKEE JOURNAL* IN 1946[1]

Only one of the selected twelve has made significant improvement.
—DR. BENJAMIN GLOVER, OF UW STUDENT HEALTH,
ON PSYCHIATRIC TREATMENT OF GAYS[2]

World War II and the military's treatment of gays shifted the discussion about homosexuality in America to a newer medical model
that saw homosexuals as sick. This presumption was made apparent in the
Truax study conducted late in the war, as discussed in the preceding chapter. Allan Bérubé documented wartime psychiatrists' arguments about
who was a true homosexual and whether psychiatrists could really detect
them. Medical screenings, which often included a three-minute interview,
failed to detect many gays. Nevertheless, author of *Gay New York*, George
Chauncey, records that psychiatrists' "prestige had grown enormously
during World War II because of the crucial role they had played in screening and managing the millions of people mobilized for military service."
Historians have shown that military medical professionals treated "cases"
of homosexuality differently: some attempted to treat or "cure" homosexuals, while others merely got rid of them as quickly as possible by rec-
ommending that they be dishonorably discharged. The postwar era would
see issues from this debate on the medicalization of homosexuality play
out in Wisconsin.[3]

Postwar America, seeking a restoration to normalcy, was shocked by the 1948 publication of *Sexual Behavior in the Human Male*, authored by Alfred Kinsey, Wardell Pomeroy, and Clyde Martin. Generally known as the Kinsey Report, the eight-hundred-page book was based on the study of twelve thousand individuals and contained the largest compilation and most explicit descriptions of male sexual practices that had ever been published. Though Kinsey's background was in biology, his study relied on anonymized data from interviewees who were encouraged to describe their experiences thoughtfully, an approach that eventually helped found the field of sexology in America. The report helped bring homosexuality into the realm of scientific inquiry rather than keeping it strictly in the realms of criminality or religious morality. Wisconsin academics added to this scientific literature in the postwar period. John Gillin's sociological work with Waupun prisoners, though based on research of the 1930s, was published in 1946. The Truax wartime study by Severinghaus and Chornyak, republished in 1947, added to the scientific literature promoting fact-based analysis. And other Wisconsin scholars would follow.[4]

In *The Modernization of Sex: Havelock Ellis, Alfred Kinsey, William Masters and Virginia Johnson*, author Paul Robinson correctly described Kinsey's report as one that sought to broaden the range of normative sexual behavior. The research data would also be used in the medical world. Former Wisconsinite Glenway Wescott, the writer who was living in New Jersey and New York at the time, helped recruit subjects for Kinsey, then a professor at Indiana University. In describing his methods, Kinsey introduces a map showing origins by state of his twelve thousand male subjects. The largest percentage of sources came from the Midwest (with Indiana contributing the most of all the states), followed by the East Coast. Approximately 250 are from Wisconsin, more than Texas or Florida. Kinsey cited the Truax study by Severinghaus and Chornyak in his bibliography.[5]

Kinsey's patron at his university, as shown in James H. Jones's biography entitled *Alfred C. Kinsey: A Public/Private Life*, was Herman B Wells, president of Indiana University. Wells had been in the doctoral program in business at the University of Wisconsin in the early 1930s. He used the Madison campus as a model in his drive to build "a greater and more progressive University" for the state of Indiana: a large, "publicly supported, multifaceted research-oriented institution staffed by distinguished

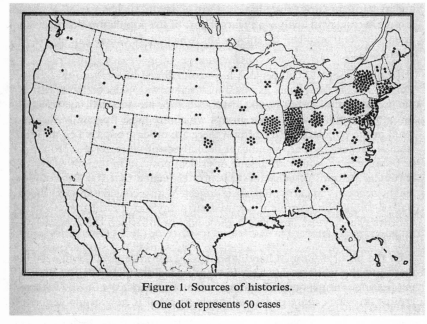

Figure 1. Sources of histories.
One dot represents 50 cases

This map from Alfred Kinsey's 1948 report on the sexual activities of males shows that he drew heavily from the histories of subjects from Midwestern states, including Wisconsin. *SEXUAL BEHAVIOR IN THE HUMAN MALE*

professors who were not only strong undergraduate teachers but publishing scholars and demanding graduate mentors." Kinsey fit Wells's model of the new university he was building.[6]

One of the discoveries in Kinsey's report that shocked the public was that homosexual play was as common as heterosexual play in preadolescent males. Kinsey noted, "About half of the older males (48%) recall homosexual activity in their preadolescent years." This would later lead some Wisconsin doctors to view homosexuality as puerile or as a youthful indiscretion. If the psychiatric diagnosis was essentially immaturity, these doctors reasoned, then perhaps homosexual tendencies could be cured as an individual matured.[7]

In the chapter on marital status, Kinsey notes that American sex law was based on the "reproductive interpretation of sex," and thus, "homosexual and solitary sources of outlet, since they are completely without reproductive possibilities, are penalized or frowned upon by public opinion and by the processes of the law. Concepts of perversion depend in part on this same reproductive interpretation of sex."[8]

The data showed over a third of the unmarried males in the study "having some homosexual experience." Among single males, Kinsey found, "Homosexual relations occur . . . least often in the group that goes to college." He also showed that higher occupational class, often including college graduates, corresponded with lower homosexual levels. But this variation did not mean that homosexual relations did not often occur among college graduates, they just occurred less frequently than among those who had only graduated from high school.[9]

Kinsey discoursed on the categorization of men who engaged in homosexual acts. One of the book's lasting conceptualizations was the heterosexual-homosexual balance, the famous scale from 0 to 6, with 6 being "exclusively homosexual." Today some gays still refer to themselves as "perfect sixes." Kinsey claimed that many doctors already acknowledged the fluidity of homosexual identity; for example, he said, "Mutual masturbation between two males may be dismissed, even by some clinicians, as not homosexual." Thus, he proposed that some men were more homosexual than others and encouraged the use of new terms to describe sexuality. Kinsey felt inaccurate terms "are often unfortunate because they obscure the interpretations of the situation which the clinician is supposed to help by his analysis."[10]

Tim LaHaye, an evangelical writer who prophesied the rapture, raised the question "Can We Trust the Kinsey Reports?" in his 1978 book *The Unhappy Gays: What Every One Should Know about Homosexuality.* The book begins with a chapter on the "Homosexual Explosion." LaHaye, who died in 2016, asserted that Kinsey was biased because he was of "the sexually permissive bent (or 'anything goes' crowd)." Perhaps more incisively, he noted, "Volunteers for sex research are not typical." LaHaye's overall judgment was that "it did make great propaganda for anything-goes sexual permissiveness. And it has probably done more to herald the present homosexual epidemic than any other single event in the last fifty years."[11]

Kinsey also had ideas about Americans' varying levels of acceptance regarding homosexuals. He observed, "The acceptance of the homosexual in top educational and social levels is the product of a wider understanding of realities, some comprehension of the factors involved, and more concern over the mental qualities and social capacities of an individual than over any-thing in his sexual history." As we will see in this chapter, many UW officials and doctors fit this profile in the 1940s and 1950s. Yet, individuals at higher educational and class levels could be acutely aware of the consequences of discovery. Referring to the upper class, Kinsey noted, "There is no disgrace that is more feared than that which may result from sexual scandal."[12]

In 1953, Kinsey published his second report, on sexual behavior in fe-males, though he used a smaller sample set (eight thousand women). His research indicated that homosexual play among young women was less frequent than among men. Among females who made homosexual con-tacts, psychological arousal was mentioned as being twice as prevalent as orgasm. Kinsey also observed, "Homosexual contacts are highly effective in bringing the female to orgasm." Only among single women did the re-search show significant lesbian contacts beyond age twenty. Interestingly, Kinsey found more lesbianism among Catholics than Protestants or Jews, though this was less true of devout Catholics. Of the 142 females in his sam-ple with extensive lesbian experience, 71 percent expressed no regrets.[13]

How much currency Kinsey's ideas had in Wisconsin cannot be pre-cisely measured. But both of his books were extensively reviewed in peri-odicals, and the concepts were picked up in the popular press, including Wisconsin newspapers. Certainly, some members of the educated classes in Wisconsin would have had the chance to see a review even if they did not read the book. A spring 1948 student theatrical on the UW–Madison cam-pus explicitly referred to "what Kinsey knew" as a way to indicate abun-dant sex. The phrase appeared both in the program and in the associated publicity, which was picked up in the state's newspapers. Kinsey's study of sexuality and sex practices among American men recategorized sexual issues in the mind of the nation. Rather than criminalizing homosexuality, his report reinforced its medicalization. Wisconsin citizens would grap-ple with how to deal with Kinsey's medical framework for years after the report's publication.[14]

A GENTLE CURE IN THE WELSH HILLS

The medicalization of homosexuality to which Kinsey contributed would frame the later life of Edward Harris Heth. While still a student at the

University of Wisconsin in Madison (see chapter 3), Heth was published in the book *Wisconsin Writings—1931: An Anthology*. After graduation, Heth went off to use his writing skills in an advertising career in New York, though he continued to write fiction, publishing several novels in the late 1930s. A 1945 novel about boyhood in Milwaukee and the protagonist's gambling father, *Any Number Can Play*, was a critical success. In 1949 it proved a financial success as well when it was made into a movie starring Clark Gable and Alexis Smith. In those prudish times, the movie poster advertising "MGM's Virile Romantic Drama" also bore the notice, "Not Suitable for Children."[15]

In *My Life on Earth*, a semiautobiographical work published in 1953, Heth wrote nostalgically about his "full breathless New York years." But the city had taken its toll, and he was suffering from nerves, high blood pressure, and hypertension. The doctor he consulted, noting that Heth worked in advertising, called him a "Madman." He then told his patient, "Six months out of the city, some place quiet in the country, and you'll be yourself again." Heth chose not to seek the solace of the Connecticut countryside, as many New Yorkers did, but went back to rural Waukesha County, Wisconsin, where his grandparents had once farmed. After some time in the country, Heth explored the possibility of going back to New York in advertising, but because he would have received only half his previous salary, he decided against it.[16]

Heth wrote of this time in Wisconsin, "It was lonely, living there in the rooms that had been planned for laughing easygoing crowds of friends. It was only a summer house, with New York friends arriving to sun on its terraces, sit in its gardens, drink and talk at night in the big farm kitchen." His moroseness was reflected in the line, "I had begun to think I would never find adventure again."[17]

While recuperating in Wisconsin, he wrote as the narrator of *My Life on Earth*, "For a year I had tried to keep neighbors from bothering me. Until, in the second spring Bud Devere dropped by. He was young and burly, and grinned when I opened the door." Devere invited Heth's narrator to church supper that night. But, the narrator recalled, the "next evening, I started out again to travel alone over the long silent roads." He left the house to avoid Devere, who said he might drop by the next evening. But avoidance was not going to work.[18]

Edward Harris Heth retreated to the Welsh hills of Waukesha County for a rest cure after leaving the frenetic world of New York advertising. *MY LIFE ON EARTH*, 1960

"Bud Devere," Heth's narrator continues, "that second spring, persisted in being a friend. . . . He came up for evening sessions of talk—uninvited, mostly, which did not bother him, and often unwelcome, which also did not seem to trouble him." Devere was not a static rural type, and Heth's narrator was attracted to that aspect of his personality. Devere, the reader is told, knew "the last corners of the earth, and not only because the Army took him there but because when he was there he took the time to absorb what he saw—a trick he seemed to have appointed himself to teach me. Even at home again, he didn't have to go far to enjoy the full prickly excitement of travel."[19]

One day, when they were out driving on Willow Road, the narrator recounts, "Bud raced the car along a few hundred feet. Then stopped, jumped out, leaped down a bank to a creek and came back with a dripping handful of watercress, like a merman dragging wet seaweed." The narrator's romantic image of a "merman" switches the gender of the more commonly romanticized mermaid. "He shoved a fistful in my mouth," the narrator continues, "It was cool and damp and spicy and tasted fresh as spring itself." The narrator describes the romance resuming on another day:

> I was glad that Bud stopped the car and decided to swim in the lake. When he shut the motor the deathliness grew, even greater, and a nearly-ended fear returned. I began sweating. Bud looked at me, seeming to worry. . . . "Come on!" Bud yelled harshly— he sounded annoyed, and afraid too. "For Christ sake, get into the water."[20]

After some persuading, the narrator finds his redemption:

> And once we were splashing in the water the frightening lapse of life filled in—you could feel the heart start to beat again. The cold water, too, made the nerves stop throbbing. Afterwards we stretched out on the lake's gravelly edge. . . . Bud was stretched out flat on his back, his arms flung apart. I knew he was thinking the same thing, feeling the same way.

The scene concludes with the narrator explaining: "Bud had reached over to tap me on the shoulder. 'You're all right. Nice to have you in the neighborhood.'" Here, in the McCarthy era, Heth used *My Life on Earth* to argue that the cure for the supposed "sickness" of homosexuality was not psychiatric treatment, but rather two males finding friendship and love.[21]

That the narrator could find such companionship in Wisconsin was significant: "You knew up ahead was all you ever wanted or needed—home, safety, comfort, someone who loved you more than anything else in the world. All your life you keep looking for this road again."[22]

The narrator's single status drew comments over the years. When one female neighbor commented, "Thought you might be lonely . . . being a bachelor and all," the narrator did not answer, especially since the neighbor was also unmarried. Heth's narrator also remembered when the contractor who built his house in the Welsh Hills asked, "Why did I need a kitchen the size of an old farmhouse kitchen, with a fireplace in it? Good humoredly, but with an admixture of wonder, he kept asking what a wife (I didn't have one, I reminded him. 'Ought to,' he answered.) would say to a kitchen where you had to walk a mile each day, traveling from the cupboards to the stove and back again." The narrator recalled other neighbors also "said I must be going to get married or why'd I have a sink and stove and so many cupboards and everything put in."[23]

Heth was not the only one in the vicinity who had escaped New York to live a rural life in Wisconsin. Quite nearby in the Welsh Hills was Ten Chimneys, the rural retreat of theater greats Alfred Lunt and Lynn Fontanne. Lunt, who was from Wisconsin, had polished his culinary skills at the Cordon Bleu in Paris. In fact, Heth, who published the cookbook *The Wonderful World of Cooking* in 1956, admitted to trading recipes with Lunt. Many visitors from the world of theater stayed at Ten Chimneys over the years, including gay playwright Noel Coward and his life partner, Graham Payn. According to local lore, Coward delighted in swimming naked in the pool. And some have never been too sure about Lunt's sexual orientation.[24]

My Life on Earth is most often referred to as semiautobiographical. Edward Harris Heth did build a house in the Welsh Hills, but he lived in it with his male partner, a well-known ceramist named William Chancey. The neighbors, including Heth's electrical contractor, generally knew the two were gay and seemed to accept them. Since this was the 1950s, a time of witch hunts against radicals and gays, Heth could not write openly about a domesticated gay couple in the country, so he wrote a late-appearing fiancée into the last part of his book for the narrator to marry. This plot echoes that of Heth's 1931 story about a phantom marriage that never took place. In Heth's 1951 *Almanac: A Handbook of Pleasure*, he acknowledged that "Mr. Chancey shares the House on the Hill." The small, self-published twenty-six-page document was basically a monthly calendar stuffed with local rural lore.

The unusual feature was artwork from, as Heth put it, "Wisconsin's noted young art group," including a picture of a pottery piece by Chancey. Several of the artists would later appear in other gay social circles.[25]

Perhaps in *My Life on Earth*, Heth had made a literary reference with the name Bud Devere. Certainly Heth knew of Herman Melville's novels. Was he using Billy Budd, Melville's iconic sailor character from the eponymous novel, as the naming source for his own supposedly fictional character? In *Billy Budd, Sailor*, the bachelor Captain Vere, who feels strongly attached to Budd, tragically must condemn the young sailor to death. Are the two literary characters Budd and Vere linked to make Bud Devere? Additionally, sailor Budd's first name is Billy, the diminutive form of William, the name of Heth's real-life partner.

In his later years, Heth, though still creating literary works, was known more for his folksy country cooking. Naturalist Euell Gibbons wrote an introduction for the second edition of his cookbook. Heth also had a show on Wisconsin Public Radio telling tales of the Wisconsin countryside. The home where he lived with Chancey, known as the House on the Hill, burned down in 1960 while the two were out of town. Though the house was rebuilt, Chancey committed suicide in 1961, and Heth sold the home they had shared. He moved into an apartment in Milwaukee and died on April 26, 1963. In a period when his own gay life could not be openly chronicled, Edward Harris Heth provided glimpses of how gay men searched for love and intimacy and, in his writings, guardedly continued to express that search.

SEX CRIMES AND SICKNESS

J. Edgar, the 2011 biopic of longtime FBI director J. Edgar Hoover, focused attention on his decades-long presumed same-sex relationship with a top deputy, Clyde Tolson. The questions about Hoover's sexuality, however, date back to the 1930s and 1940s. Much of the questioning was phrased in coded language, as people noted his "mincing step" and that he dressed "fastidiously." Charles E. Morris III, in a 2009 article in the *Quarterly Journal of Speech* titled "Pink Herring and the Fourth Person: J. Edgar Hoover's Sex Crime Panic," argued that Hoover's attack on sex crimes was meant to distract attention from his own homosexuality—by his obvious disapproval of sex deviates, it would be clear to all that he was not one.[26]

Hoover's first attack on sex criminals occurred in 1937 in a feature article published in the *New York Herald Tribune* magazine section with the screaming headline, "War on the Sex Criminal." The article, which described the enemy against whom the war was being waged as "the sex fiend," also described this foe as "the most loathsome member of the vast crime army." Hoover called for a study to determine "to what extent the recently widespread use of marijuana, or American hashish, has been responsible for the sex crime." He urged "a high state of public vigilance and indignation." Yet, Hoover avoided the suggestion that homosexuals were part of this vast crime army; rather, the FBI director expressed concern mainly in terms of "a sinister threat to the safety of American childhood and womanhood." For the most part, Americans dealing with the aftermath of the Depression and looming war clouds in Europe did not take up Hoover's proposed war on sex crimes at this time.[27]

In July 1947, however, Hoover relaunched his war on sex crimes with an article in *American Magazine*. "How Safe Is Your Daughter?" focused attention on the heterosexual sex criminal, using inflammatory terms like "sex maniacs," "sex fiend," "degenerates run wild," and "depraved human beings, more savage than beasts" to describe the wrongdoers. His opening line was, "The most rapidly increasing type of crime is that perpetrated by degenerate sex offenders."[28]

Later the same year, Hoover started to use the language of the medical profession to describe sex criminals, noting that some have "crystallized psychopathic traits." He discussed withholding parole from sex offenders "until the members of a board of competent medical authorities are willing to certify that the wrongdoer had been under successful medical observation and treatment." He also indicated that "no judge should ever agree to letting [sex offenders] come to trial without first being subjected to medical and psychiatric examination." In another example, a contemporary Michigan commission's psychiatrists "urged the public to support the expansion of existing psychiatric institutions and the development of new ones," all "in the name of protecting women and children from sex deviates.[29]

The national effort to engage in a war on sex crimes was greatly furthered by an article by journalist David G. Wittels with the cover lead "What Can We Do about Sex Crimes?" in the *Saturday Evening Post* of December 11, 1948. Again, the sex criminal was described as having a "psychopathic

personality, sometimes known as constitutional psychopathic inferior."
Wittels estimated that "tens of thousands" of "these creatures" were loose
in the country, and, like Hoover, he focused on women and children at
risk to build an argument for "the scientific isolation of such people." He
quoted a staff psychiatrist for the Municipal Court of Philadelphia: "When
they are detected—and this usually can be done early in life—we should
put them away for their own good and the good of society." Noting that
some jurisdictions had new laws dealing with "so called 'sexual psychopaths,'" Wittels faulted existing laws for not allowing the commitment of
these sexual types before they "committed overt crimes."[30]

While Hoover might have focused on sex deviates to deflect homosexual speculation about himself, once the ball was rolling there was no
telling where it would go. David K. Johnson, in his 2006 book *The Lavender
Scare: The Cold War Persecution of Gays and Lesbians in the Federal Government*, noted, "'Sexual psychopath' was an ambiguous term, but one
that frequently was conflated with 'homosexual,' since most observers
assumed that homosexuals were sick, could not control themselves, and
needed to recruit new members to their ranks."[31]

Estelle Freedman, in her 1987 article "'Uncontrolled Desires': The Response to the Sexual Psychopath, 1920–1960," showed that the postwar
climate was "conducive to the reemergence of the male sexual psychopath
as a target of social concern." She wrote, "Postwar psychiatric and social
welfare literature stressed the adjustment problems of returning servicemen, some of whom, it was feared, might 'snap' into psychopathic states."
Freedman also mentioned the general public's urge to recreate prewar
gender relations in the discussion of sexual normalcy. In addition, she
pointed out the overlapping use of the "terms *sex criminal, pervert, psychopath* and *homosexual*." As a result of this "heightened public consciousness
of homosexuality," she argued, the general public did not develop a supportive view of sexually nonconforming individuals.[32]

Most Wisconsinites shared the views Freedman described, and
Hoover's call for a war on sex crimes was widely covered by the Wiscon-
sin press. In 1947, the *Wisconsin State Journal* ran the headline, "Hoover
Asks Sex Crime War," the *Oshkosh Daily Northwestern* ran, "Drive on Sex
Crimes," and the *Sheboygan Press* printed a letter from state senator Gus
Buchen discussing "the recent wave of so-called 'sex crimes' in Wisconsin

and elsewhere." That same year the *Milwaukee Journal* editorialized, "Sex crimes seem to be increasing in Wisconsin." A 1968 *Wall Street Journal* story on enforcement of ancient sex statutes implied that Sheboygan, Wisconsin, had a higher rate of sex crime than New York City. Sheboygan's police chief, Oakley A. Frank, was quoted as saying, "This is a rather strait-laced community. We have high-principled people who find this kind of conduct abhorrent." Thus, the sense that waves of sex crimes occurred, even in Wisconsin, persisted for decades.[33]

An earlier incident in the state had stoked the fires of sex crime panic. On September 23, 1946, the *Milwaukee Sentinel* published a story with the headline, "Amnesty for Sex Convict Stirs Wrath of Law Here." The Milwaukee sheriff and the acting Milwaukee police chief were outspoken in their disapproval of an action taken by Governor Walter Goodland. A fifty-year-old man had been convicted in the municipal court on two counts of taking indecent liberties with a minor and one count of sodomy. However, contrary testimony threw doubt on one of the charges, and Goodland reduced the man's sentence from twenty-five years to ten. In the story in the *Sentinel*, the sheriff opined that the governor's action would "give encouragement to other sex criminals." The acting police chief emphasized "that sex crimes frequently account for a third of the total crime listed in the department's daily report." The article ended with the sheriff's claim that the Milwaukee Metropolitan Commission on Crime Prevention was preparing a bill for the next legislature for segregating sex criminals.[34]

Bernhard Gettelman, a Republican state senator from Milwaukee, plunged ahead and introduced a Wisconsin Sexual Psychopath Law to the legislature on April 3, 1947. Senate Bill 486 was referred to the Committee on Education and Public Welfare. *Wisconsin Sheriff Magazine*, in reporting on the law, noted the sponsorship of the legislation by the Milwaukee Metropolitan Commission on Crime Prevention. The state senate, composed of twenty-two Republicans, six Democrats, and five Progressives, passed its version on May 13 with no nay votes recorded; the Assembly passed a revised version on June 19, and after some more tinkering the bill was signed on July 30 by Governor Goodland. The bill, published on August 1, defined a sexual psychopath not by acts but by mental state, as one "suffering from condition of emotional instability or impulsiveness of behavior . . . as to render a person irresponsible for his conduct with respect to sexual matters and thereby dangerous to himself and to other persons."[35]

Under the Wisconsin law, a person did not have to commit any sexual crime—that is, an overt act—to fall under its purview. When accusations about a possible sexual psychopath were presented to a district attorney, the prosecutor could petition a court for a hearing. Two doctors were to examine the accused, and the accused could have defense counsel. At the end of the hearing, the court would determine whether the accused was a sexual psychopath. If found to be so, he would be committed to an institution designated by the Milwaukee County Board of Supervisors. The legislature had been told during the consideration of the law that a Milwaukee institution could cure such persons, though it would later be proven that no existing institution could.[36]

A news story in the *Capital Times* of February 7, 1945, about a similar bill proposed by Senator Gettelman in the previous legislative session sheds light on his intent to target homosexuals with a statewide bill. The article, "Offer Bill Aimed at Homosexuals," noted that although the bill mentioned only psychopathic personalities, "Gettlemann said it was aimed at homosexuals who he claimed were prevalent in Milwaukee and other cities." The intent behind the renewed push for a sexual psychopath bill in 1947 was similar. In support of the 1947 bill, Captain H. J. Erlach of the Milwaukee Police Department appeared before the state senate committee, saying, as paraphrased by the paper, "sexual psychopathic persons should be treated as bearers of highly contagious diseases and not disorderly conduct."[37]

Gay and lesbian historians and some academics would later assert that confinement as a sex criminal without having committed a sex crime but merely because one was determined by doctors to be a sexual psychopath raised constitutional issues. George Chauncey reported that in most states, police and many judges "argued that the gravity of the danger posed by 'sex deviates' justified the abrogation of traditional constitutional safeguards." But apparently Senator Gettelman did not consider constitutional issues to be of paramount importance. Completely disregarding the provision in the Constitution against cruel and unusual punishment, Senator Gettelman, in 1947, proposed the creation of state whipping posts for certain crimes, including sex crimes.[38]

In 1947, the *Milwaukee Journal* was a strong advocate for the sexual psychopath law. In fact, over a period of several years, starting as early as 1944, the paper had published dozens of editorials about the proposed law and its implementation. The phrases "slaves of lust" and "menace of sex perverts" appeared throughout its pages. Chauncey has posited, "The conflation of all forms of sexual nonconformity in press accounts of sex crime had particularly significant consequences for the public image of gay men." The argument in support of punishing homosexuals as psychopaths, as Chauncey recorded it, could be summarized as follows:

> Men who engaged in homosexual behavior had demonstrated the refusal to accommodate to social conventions that was the hallmark of the psychopath—and he could easily degenerate further. "Once a man assumes the role of homosexual, he often throws off all moral restraints," claimed *Coronet* magazine in the fall of 1950. "Some male sex deviants do not stop with infecting their often-innocent partners: they descend through perversions to other forms of depravity, such as drug addiction, burglary, sadism, and even murder."[39]

The *Milwaukee Journal* repeatedly used language demonstrating that the editors considered homosexuals to be part of the city's crime problems. In 1946, the *Journal* editorialized about "Sex Crimes in Milwaukee," citing police chief John Polcyn on "the growing menace of the rapist and the sex pervert in the community." The editorial praised the efforts of the Milwaukee Metropolitan Commission on Crime Prevention for its proposal, "which would make it possible to commit the overt homosexual to a special institution, not for a term but until cured." In an editorial on March 1947 supporting the bill introduced by Senator Gettelman, the paper described the bill as "the only hope for ending the vicious attacks on girls and young women and the corruption of boys and young men which are becoming an increasing problem." Again in March, the paper supported institutionalizing the sexual psychopath, even if "the commitment might mean for life." And in June, the paper illustrated the need for the law by citing the distress of a mother whose son had been molested by a thirty-nine-year-old man still at large.[40]

After the law was passed in August 1947, the *Milwaukee Journal* hoped that homosexuals would be caught and permanently isolated. In a February 20, 1949, editorial on "Wisconsin and 'Big Bill' Tilden," the paper noted the unsatisfactory outcome of short sentences for sex crimes. Tilden, a famous tennis player of the 1920s, had been sentenced in 1949 to one year on a road gang for molesting a sixteen-year-old boy at a time when he was on parole for a similar morals offense from 1946. Since Tilden had committed another offense before his 1949 sentence had been completed, the paper believed their call for permanent isolation was a more satisfactory solution.[41]

UW–Madison psychiatrist Dr. Benjamin Glover, writing in the journal *Federal Probation*, noted that the 1947 law as passed incorporated "many features elemental . . . in its medical management and combined medical and legal control." However, "the law never became operative, since no provisions were made to guard the constitutional rights of citizens by appeal or re-examination and no funds or facilities were designated for the diagnostic study or the treatment of those convicted of deviation." The legislature, four years later, replaced the unworkable law with a new sex deviate statute that required actual commission of a sexual crime prior to psychiatric confinement.[42]

One Wisconsin critic who challenged the fallacies of the 1940s sex panic was UW sociologist John Gillin. Writing in the *International Journal of Sexology* in 1954, he debunks the idea that "the number of homicidal sex deviates is very large." Gillin criticized early sex crime laws like Wisconsin's for curtailing civil liberties, since they purported to be civil laws rather than criminal laws, yet they restrained an individual's liberty for an indefinite term upon the claim of insanity or sickness. Gillin saw this as setting "dangerous precedents," abrogating due process. He asked, "Were those promoting the new laws interested in all who violated the moral code of sex relations of the Judeo-Christian culture, or even of any of the laws governing sex relations in the legal code?" His answer was a resounding "No." He noted that "the first such laws were quite indefinite," focused "much more closely on those deviates whose conduct had excited the greatest public reaction." Gillin supported the revised 1951 Wisconsin law with its new legal safeguards, though he still argued for "the importance of applying the new knowledge" in the prevention of crime.[43]

"Educative" Sex Discipline

Following the war, University of Wisconsin leaders from the president down through the deans were also confronted with the dilemma of how to handle homosexuality, and they chose a medical model based on psychiatry that seemed to fit their self-image as a progressive campus. This use of a newer medical science was thought to be a more benign approach than the one advocated by the promoters of sexual psychopathology. The campus sought to be an educational institution that used the most current techniques for managing student behavior. Of course, not all bad behavior required students to see a shrink. For instance, this era experienced an eruption of panty raids—male students assaulting the women's dormitories seeking to possess female undergarments. These episodes resulted in many students being put on disciplinary probation, but none were recommended for psychiatric treatment.

My review of many hundreds of University of Wisconsin files on student discipline from the 1930s revealed only one case concerning homosexuality. However, in the decade and a half after World War II, nearly fifty recorded cases are in some way related to homosexuality. Thus, the university faced a significant new problem and needed to fashion a response. In early 1948, before many cases of homosexuality had been uncovered, an associate dean, C. R. Reudisili, transmitted a paper to Professor Howard Jackson, head of the Student Conduct Committee. Ghoulishly titled "Knitting at the Guillotine: An Approach to the Therapeutic Handling of Discipline," the paper had been presented at the American College Personnel Association by Dean Robert J. Miner from Miami University of Ohio. Wisconsin's Reudisili considered it "a very worthwhile approach."[44]

In the paper Miner argued, "The modern concept of college discipline is predicated on the student personnel philosophy that discipline is an educative process, corrective not punitive." Addressing homosexuality more specifically, he wrote, "Sexual misdemeanors periodically occur. It seems impossible to eliminate window peeping, genital exposure, pregnancies, homosexual and heterosexual irregularities, many of them adolescent, some of them pathological." He continued by observing that getting into trouble and getting out of it are part of the learning process which train young people how to live and work in greater harmony and peace with each other. Careful therapeutic discipline can help the individual effect this reorganization of his behavior attitudes without damaging the morale of his contemporaries.

The likelihood of educative success was more probable, thought Miner, in a large university with a good health service, because "the mental hygiene clinic can diagnose whether the individual may be neurotic or psychopathic, and can furnish specialized psychiatric treatment if it is indicated by the diagnosis."[45]

In fact, the University of Wisconsin–Madison had already been heading in this direction. The one 1937 case with a summary sheet labeled "Perversion" noted that the campus action was to refer the student to a psychiatrist. The ensuing psychiatric report, written by a Dr. Bleckman, confirms that the student had been involved with mutual masturbation since high school but "shows no other homosexual tendencies." However, the doctor was cautious: "As you know, it is quite impossible for anyone to prophesy such a course for one who continued beyond adolescence with these rather puerile sexual reactions." As in other prewar examples, the medical establishment believed homosexual tendencies were linked to adolescence.[46]

One of the most experienced members of the campus psychiatry staff was Dr. Annette Washburne, who was appointed an assistant professor of neuropsychiatry in 1935 after completing her medical education at De Paul University and the University of Illinois. Her great-uncle Cadwallader Washburn had been a governor of Wisconsin, and her grandfather was secretary of state for President Ulysses S. Grant. In 1942, Washburne served as president of the Midwestern College Psychiatrists and Clinical Psychologists. From 1937 until 1953, she was senior consultant in the neuropsychiatry service, which she had organized on the Madison campus in the Department of Student Health. She was the only woman to hold a full professorship in the medical school in the late 1940s. A university news service release of March 1948 praised Dr. Washburne's leadership as head of the neuropsychiatry division and described her as having a

Dr. Annette Washburne treated homosexuals in the Student Health Clinic at the University of Wisconsin–Madison in the 1940s. UNIVERSITY OF WISCONSIN–MADISON ARCHIVES IMAGE S07324

"new attitude toward psychiatry." She was quoted in the UW news service release as saying, "This kind of medicine is very slow. Often weekly visits for several semesters are necessary." During her tenure, she established a policy of conducting psychiatric examinations on students in the School of Education who were candidates for teachers' certificates. The March 1948 release praised her work: "She radiates reassurance: each patient feels that here is an understanding that will encompass any revelation."[47]

One Student Health member who frequently served on the Student Conduct Committee was Dr. Benjamin Glover, also a psychiatrist. After the committee confronted multiple student discipline incidents involving gay men in 1948, the minutes of the September 1949 meeting described a unanimously adopted policy:

> [A] brief summary dealing with homosexuality which had been given
> by Dr. Washburne of the Student Health Clinic . . . was read to the

committee and a motion was made and carried unanimously that it be adopted as a guide to the committee in dealing with such cases. A motion was then made and approved unanimously that in all cases involving homosexuality of students, the conduct committee will consider for re-admission only those students who have taken treatment through the Student Health Clinic and recommended for re-admission thereby.[48]

As opposed to the state legislature's dramatic approach to dealing with homosexuality, the university's postwar policy simply developed out of earlier policies arrived at before such approaches were called "therapeutic discipline." During the war, in 1943, a number of opposite-sex couples used Observatory Hill for late-night romance, especially after the taverns closed. Many, if not most, of these couples were city residents, not college students. However, some university officials felt that these "morals cases" on campus grounds impinged on the good name of the university. Horace Fries, then head of the Student Conduct Committee, wrote District Attorney Norris Maloney about the effort "to prevent the occurrence of immorality on the Grounds." If there were students involved, Fries notes, "Judge Proctor has kindly consented to direct each student to report to Dr. Washburne, not for further penalization, but for guidance and advice." Fries, in a letter to A. F. Gallistel, the superintendent of buildings and grounds, further notes, "It is of considerable importance in the guidance work of Dr. Washburne there be a continuous minimizing of the attitude, which is still too prevalent, that consultation with a psychiatrist implies a mental disorder or abnormality."[49]

A letter from Gallistel to Fries in May 1943 indicated "that it is general practice in the 'Big Ten' institutions to have morals cases placed in the hands of faculty committees rather than the courts." Other documents from 1943 suggest that in the case of arrests made by city police and not campus police, the university wanted cases to go to the city court, rather than the circuit court, where there was less "chance for publicity." The university had a friend in Judge Roy Proctor of the Superior Court, who often reduced morals charges against students to disorderly conduct with a mere fine rather than conviction on more serious offenses.[50]

In 1948, Dr. Washburne initiated a discussion on the handling of student conduct cases outside the classroom. The campus philosophy was outlined in eleven points, the first being, "Punitive discipline is a narrow concept." The second established discipline as an educative process. The third explicitly supported "therapeutic discipline." Another point highlighted the importance of the university's health staff:

> Clinical psychologists and professional counselors must be available in making proper diagnosis and in carrying out appropriate remedial programs, particularly in cases involving severely disturbed or psychopathic individuals and in cases of subtly hidden causes of difficulty.[51]

An attached discipline report covering the period from January 1947 to April 1948 listed "Sex Misdemeanor" as the largest category of offenses, with most perpetrators referred to Dr. Washburne, though no breakdown as to type of sex case was provided. Window peeping and exhibitionism were also frequent offenses. Another report showed that eleven cases had been referred to Student Health prior to May 1948 for the academic year 1947–1948. These eleven cases, while a small percentage of the total 825 patients seen during the academic year for psychiatric difficulties, received a lot of attention. Of the eleven, only two were listed under the category of homosexuality, while indecent exposure led the list with seven. With little hope for a recommended cure, one of the two offenders was sent by the courts to Waupun for one to five years, the usual sentence for sodomy offenses.[52]

Of the two men listed as homosexuals, one, a forty-two-year-old Extension teacher, was returned to court custody by Student Health after a week of observation. The doctors, noting the long duration of his homosexuality, stated that no improvement should be anticipated. A campus doctor said that if Wisconsin in fact had a hospital for the confinement of sexual psychopaths as proposed by Senator Gettelman, such confinement would have been the most effective result for the case. At the time of the report, the other homosexual offender was in the student infirmary under observation, with outpatient treatment recommended for the rest of the semester and then withdrawal, perhaps to a smaller school. The two cases show the range of consequences that could befall homosexuals arrested in Wisconsin in the 1940s; both are punitive, but one resulted in prison confinement and the other in psychiatric treatment.[53]

Postwar Outbreak of Homosexuality

In June 1948, the City of Madison was treated to a sensational exposé. The *Wisconsin State Journal* headline of June 9, trumpeted, "Raid Reveals Obscene Reading; Two Men Arrested on Morals Count." The article reported that the raid concerned "unnatural sexual activities and campus and city police were questioning four additional men." The next day, the paper ran the follow-up: "12 More Face Morals Counts." The arrestees, some of whom were charged with sodomy, included at least four university students, a foreman in the UW Union's upholstery shop, an Oscar Mayer factory worker, a beauty school student, and a Central High student. Attorneys for some offenders asked for leniency, claiming their clients were not "vicious criminals." One defense attorney pleaded to Judge Roy Proctor of the Superior Court, "I realize it is a crime which cannot be condoned, and has effects and repercussions so terrific it has the whole city talking." In the end, most charges were pleaded down to disorderly conduct or possession of obscene literature. By June 21, the paper reported, "Morals Offenses Bring Probation; Proctor in Warning to Ex-Students." Four students were sentenced to one year's probation by the university for "participating in abnormal sexual activities."[54]

The sensational raid had targeted the Adams Street home of Arnold Meier, forty-seven, and Carl Boyd, twenty-six, which had been used as a "den" for lewd activities. According to the paper, the home was "lavishly decorated in an Oriental motif and contained expensive-appearing incense burners and perfume atomizers." The search warrant was issued after a John Doe hearing during which a nineteen-year-old beauty school student had implicated the pair in homosexual activities. The campus police started the investigation when they found two of the student suspects making out on campus in a car that contained an invitation to the house on Adams Street. Meier and Boyd, after release on $1,000 cash bail, were convicted on a charge of obscene literature and fined $300 each.[55]

One defense attorney spoke of his client as having had only two or three isolated instances of such behavior and said that the suspect "has not been involved in the proceedings which have been going on at the university for some time." One of the isolated occasions was "during a drinking party after a Haresfoot production theatrical rehearsal." Because boys were

Raid Reveals Obscene Reading;
Two Men Arrested on Morals Counts

Two Madison men were arrested Tuesday night on morals charges after police raided their home and discovered a huge supply of obscene literature and other evidence indicating unnatural sexual activities.

And while plans were being made to take the two men into court today, city and University of Wisconsin police continued to question four other men who are believed also to be involved in the licentious activities.

Plead Not Guilty

Those arrested were Arnold Meier, 47, manager of Mueller Heating Co., and Carl Boyd, 26, both of 1514 Adams st.

They pleaded not guilty in superior court this morning to charges of sodomy and possessing obscene literature and pictures.

They each posted $1,000 bail and trial was set for 10:30 a. m. June 18. Atty Carl Flom represented the two men.

There is a probability that further investigation will reveal more men who are involved in the "ring," Asst. Dist. Atty. Glenn Henry predicted.

Their lavishly furnished small home at 1514 Adams st., is believed by police to have been used as a "den" for lewd activities by men, Detective Capt. Milsted said.

A search warrant was issued for the premises late Tuesday by Superior Judge Roy H. Proctor, after one of the other four men under suspicion, a 19-year-old beauty school student, testified in a John Doe hearing held before Judge Proctor.

The student produced a letter which invited him to attend a "party" Tuesday night at the home.

Capt. Milsted, University Officer Joe Hammersley, and Detectives William J. Taylor, John Harrington, and Ralph Horbeck conducted the raid.

Find Evidence

They found a library of obscene books and literature, innumerable pictures and drawings, a large box of letters written between the two men, and other evidence.

One room of the home where police found much of the sensual evidence, was lavishly decorated in an Oriental motif, and contained expensive-appearing incense burners and perfume atomizers.

The investigation was started after Officer Hammersley and his university policemen found two of the suspects in a car during the weekend.

A headline announcing the raid on the Adams Street house where a homosexual ring was discovered. *WISCONSIN STATE JOURNAL*, JUNE 9, 1948

cross-dressing as women for that campus theatrical company, the attorney argued, perhaps his client was confused. Assistant District Attorney Glenn Henry, who directed the morals investigation, told the court, "The activities were by mutual consent and no force was used in any of the cases." For the students in the court proceedings, the university "dropped," or in effect expelled, the students in addition to any court fine or probation.[56]

Judge Proctor commented, "Some would have us believe that abnormal sexual behavior is natural and normal biologically but until our law making bodies see fit to change the statutes, such behavior is unlawful and violators must be punished." The judge, while seeming to embrace or at least acknowledge the existence of new views about homosexuality based on academic science and the Kinsey report, went on to scold the offenders: "Each of you should feel deeply ashamed. You have embarrassed your friends and relatives, none of whom I am sure had the slightest idea you ever could or would become involved as you have."[57]

The University of Wisconsin was not alone in having to deal with issues like these. Correspondence between Paul Trump, a UW official whose title was adviser of men, and the dean of students at the University of Illinois at Champaign-Urbana revealed a problem there, too. The Illinois dean, Fred Turner, wrote, "We have been having what amounts to a mild epidemic of this sort of thing but it seems to be centered chiefly among graduate students. The cases are always messy and we use our psychiatrist whenever we can but to date his reports have not indicated much hope toward helping the individuals." The use of therapeutic or educative discipline by university psychiatrists in Wisconsin and elsewhere for "curing" homosexuality reflected the belief that modern medicine could treat the "sickness" of gay sexuality. [58]

A GEOGRAPHY OF GAY WISCONSIN

Over the next decade or so, the approximately fifty cases in the student conduct files show that students engaging in homosexual activities came from all over the state and beyond. Of course, the bigger cities like Milwaukee, Madison, Racine, Green Bay, and Janesville were represented. But the students came from smaller Wisconsin cities like Slinger, Kewaskum, Hartland, Eagle River, Waukesha, and Wauwatosa, too. The out-of-state students came from Detroit, Michigan; Oakland, California; Danville, Illinois; St. Petersburg, Florida; and Sleepy Eye, Minnesota. One student may have known Edward Harris Heth from the Welsh Hills, as the younger man's artwork had been selected to appear in Heth's almanac. [59]

Students admitted to having sex in locations that included private spaces like homes, apartments, dorm rooms, and fraternity houses. One student wrote, "I shall not enter into detail on the wide-spread reputation for homosexual practices which the Madison Chapter of Mr. L——'s fraternity has." One student referenced the "so-called mattress room" at Wisconsin General Hospital, and others mentioned a backstage space at the Union Theater and the projection room of the Play Circle. A subset used, and were sometimes arrested in, the men's washrooms of Bascom Hall, Science Hall, the University Library/Historical Society, and North Hall. Other buildings mentioned included City Hall, the Madison Free Library, and the University Club. The Capitol Square was still a cruising area for pickups, as it had been during the war. Other leafy areas included Olin Terrace, the Arboretum, Vilas Park, University Drive (presumably

Willow Drive on campus, leading to Picnic Point), and Edgewood Park. The students also met people in the city's hotels, including the Loraine, as well as three theaters: the Majestic, Orpheum, and Strand. Popular bars mentioned were the Three Bells, Coronas, Wagon Wheel, and Palladium.[60]

The students ranged in age from their late teens to twenties and mid-thirties, though one summer session student, a high school teacher, was sixty. Right after the war, some of the students were older than average, as veterans were enrolling or reenrolling on the GI Bill. Overall, freshmen, sophomores, seniors, grad students, and even one high school student were caught. One averred, "I did a lot of reading about those things[,] sort of a hobby[,] and how to tell one about ten feet away."[61]

Details are available for eight of the fourteen students with homosexual charges during the academic year 1948, when the homosexual crisis on campus really set in. Not all were part of the so-called ring centered on Adams Street. Several got to know one another by their work at Wisconsin General Hospital on campus. Some admitted to the psychiatrist that they were homosexual, one having been arrested in 1944. This student, who had been undergoing psychiatric treatment since the 1944 arrest, claimed he hadn't had "any abnormal desires" but admitted that his story did not sound good, since he was arrested again in 1948 for receiving oral sex from a man. Others claimed an occurrence was a one and only offense, and Student Health concluded such a person was not "necessarily a 'true' homosexual," or a six on the Kinsey scale. Another student who was associated with Adams Street had been implicated in similar behavior in 1941, before his war service. He performed in Haresfoot in 1942 and 1948 and did entertainment shows in the army. The newspapers reported that at least three students from the ring had Haresfoot associations, and the police or the district attorney's office asked questions about several others in the theatrical troupe.[62]

Student enrollment at the university had blossomed from 11,900 before the war to 18,500 in the late 1940s, owing to a peak of returning veterans, with 4,100 veterans already registered in 1946. Wisconsin had made extensive plans to reintegrate veterans. The 1946 Wisconsin *Blue Book*, in writing about the Rehabilitation Program for Servicemen, notes, "To help veterans make the difficult transition from the rigors of war to the peace for which they fought, the University of Wisconsin has thoroughly oiled the gears of its educational machinery." The basic university response to the gay incidents of 1948, which involved many veterans, was to either place individuals on disciplinary probation or end their present student status. The decision on status was often contingent on a recommendation for psychiatric treatment, usually for at least a year.[63]

From the almost fifty cases, some twenty-five files contain either the period police reports from campus or city cops, or the district attorney's interrogatories. They reveal a fair amount about the law enforcement attitudes of those who were handling these presumed perversion cases. It should be acknowledged that the offenders caught up in these cases were often atypical of the many homosexuals on campus in that they had sex in semipublic places like washrooms or engaged with younger males in their teens. Considering Kinsey's data and modern statistics, many hundreds if not thousands of gay men who likely lived on campus at this time are not represented in the sample. Nevertheless, the cases of those who were caught in homosexual acts provide glimpses into some gay lives of the period.

A question frequently asked of those arrested, especially by campus police, was whether they had committed "the homosexual act." At times this question was posed even after the man in question admitted to participating in mutual masturbation. The phrase, as used in these questionings, implied a focus on oral-genital contact. Sodomy could be charged only if the penis of one party had contact with the mouth or rectum of another. Therefore in these cases from 1948 to 1961, officers tried to establish confessional evidence or include their own observations of such physical contact in their reports. One student, when asked, "Did you go down on him or did he go down on you at that time?" included in his response, "Don't they have a better word for it?" This idea of a "homosexual act" was tied to the image associated with the term *cocksucker* used to describe a homosexual. One question that certainly went beyond the information needed to make a sodomy charge was, did "both of you have ejaculations when your penis[es] were in each others mouths."[64]

Even more troubling than asking for details about specific acts, authorities also asked about sexual histories—such as when the individual began engaging in the "homosexual act." In one case, an officer asked, "You know what I mean about homo-sexual act?" The student answered, "Yes, sir." Often the police asked, "How many times did you commit this act?" One interrogation revealed that a student had begun when he was thirteen with a counselor at Boy Scout camp. In the exchange, the student also explained that he first heard about homosexuality after reading "an article in the paper [or] in a magazine. I imagine I was about twelve or thirteen years old." "Have you ever had relations with a woman?" and "Do you go with girls?" were other common questions. Perhaps this was an attempt to place the offenders on the Kinsey scale.[65]

Some sexual histories revealed that the men had begun homosexual experimentation at early ages, such as thirteen or sixteen. A few indicated having started during military service, sometimes in places as far away as India. One man who had served in the navy was asked if he had done it with both "officers and sailors." The answer was "both." Why an arrest in Madison should be linked to many of these questions seems legally quite dubious, inasmuch as Wisconsin police could not file charges for acts committed in military service overseas, on ships, or in India—though it was an old police presumption that status as a homosexual person corroborated a current arrest.[66]

Police sought names of the men's contacts and information on other homosexuals at the university and in the city. After being asked, "Can you give me the names of any other people?" one brave soul answered: "I do not care to give you the names of anyone." Others claimed not to remember, but the reports often noted the officers did not believe them. Police in one instance tried to link homosexual acts to Taliesin, presuming it was a place of non-normative behavior, by asking if the man had "ever been invited to Frank Lloyd Wright's home at Spring Green."[67]

Trying to get the accused to admit guilt, the police often asked multiple times, "Do you realize it is against the rules of Society and a violation of the law?" One respondent, not fully convinced, answered, "I suppose it is if you say so." Many offenders accepted the law's status, but pled, "This is the first (and I assure you the last) time that I will ever do anything illegal." Some, in their statements to the police upon questioning, refused the charge of homosexuality; one offender's file includes the line "denies he is a 'pervert.'" Another responded "that he has a 'lovely' wife and naturally not inclined to perversion." Indeed, the records state that many of those questioned were married. Some of the deniers claimed that alcohol had something to do with it, with one man mentioning having drunk four highballs and four martinis throughout the evening of the act in question. Others confessed; case files include notes like "admitted he was a homosexual," "admits being active in homosexual practices," and "had been a homosexual about 4 or 5 years."[68]

Even in those days, the ties between gay men could be strong. A number of men indicated that friends introduced them to other homosexuals. One boasted about belonging to a homosexual club known as "The Big Four." One, trying to shift the blame and guilt away from himself, complained about a "homosexual gang" that had a house used for "sex orgies." Another police report includes the statement, "I have tried to break away from these people which is very hard to do." In some instances, younger men, acknowledged by the police as juvenile delinquents, had demanded money for sex or alternatively offered up plans to "roll a queer" for his money. If younger criminals felt disinclined to respond to a sexual advance, the thought of overpowering and stealing money from a homosexual might be classified as "hitting an easy target" because of a victim's disinclination to involve police. An asking price of those truly hustling to homosexuals for sexual services was twenty dollars, though sometimes free beer seemed enough.[69]

In December 1950, responding to reports, the campus police made a concentrated enforcement effort around campus washrooms. Over a two-week period, twenty students were netted. One apprehended student had tipped the police off as to which buildings to visit, and, "Upon questioning by the police, further evidence was obtained of contacts or attempts at contacts for purposes of homosexual experiences." Throughout this sting operation, Paul Trump, who was then dean of men, wrote in 1950, "Consultations have been held . . . involving President [E. B.] Fred, the Deans of the Colleges or Schools whose students were involved." For fifteen out of the twenty apprehended students, Student Health determined they were not "psychotic, not homosexual," and they got lenient treatment—an example of doctors using Kinsey's 0–6 scale for homosexuality.[70]

One of the key officers involved in this flurry of homosexual arrests, after many years of patrolling restrooms, was Joseph Hammersley of the campus police. It was his initial arrest that started the 1948 ring scandal, and he continued through much of the next decade to arrest and question homosexuals on campus. Hammersley was involved in a public scandal in 1953 when going through a messy divorce from his second wife, who charged that "he drank too much," among other things. A local article, "Mud Is Thrown in Hammersley Case," covered his wife's charges of his associating with other women, including his former secretary, and parking in the Eagle Heights area with a woman. The trial, which the press referred to as a "mudfest," also revealed that Hammersley was moonlighting as a constable for the Village of McFarland and as a private detective. The charges ignited a feud within the university's police force, with other officers testifying against Hammersley in the divorce case.[71]

The *Daily Cardinal*, the campus newspaper, maintained that a feuding police force could not give efficient service and called for a housecleaning. The paper had questioned Officer Hammersley's attempt to search student dorm rooms during the Christmas vacation of 1949. In 1950, the *Cardinal* had argued that a campus police "should reflect the standards and influences of a progressive educational system" and that "the present department is unfit, by training or experience to occupy the position of trust, confidence, and great responsibility which it now holds." Volume 4 of the UW campus history stated that Hammersley's "no-nonsense and unforgiving attitude had infuriated generations of UW students." A budget cut in 1953 led to a reduction in his rank from special investigator to patrolman. In July 1959, Hammersley was arrested on drunk and disorderly charges; his blood alcohol content was .17 percent. Witnesses stated he shouted obscenities, and five city policemen testified he staggered and slurred his speech. But the judge dismissed the charges. Hammersley died in a car crash in September 1959. The *Wisconsin State Journal* noted that he had been "a controversial figure" on campus and had survived numerous attempts to oust him from the police force. A persecutor of homosexuals on campus for a decade, Hammersley was generally unpopular with students for his personal attitudes and policing methods, but the administration tried to find alternatives to some of his strong actions.[72]

THE TROUBLE WITH HARESFOOT

As the university's Student Conduct Committee dealt with numerous cases regarding homosexual behavior during the spring semester of the 1947–1948 academic year, many developed the perception that one organization was a particular locus for deviant behavior, perhaps providing encouragement to homosexual activities. The committee's minutes of July 6, 1948, closed with the following observation:

> In view of the fact that a number of the individuals involved in the cases above were members of the Haresfoot organization, the Committee discussed the desirability of requesting the Student Life and Interest Committee to investigate this organization. Due to the length of the session and the press of other matters, no formal action was taken.[73]

To follow up, Professor H. C. Jackson, chairman of the Student Conduct Committee, on July 8 conducted a memo poll of the committee members on the issue. He thought it "did not seem necessary to call another meeting" as he believed there was a consensus on the matter. Members marked and returned their copies, agreeing with the chairman that Haresfoot should be investigated. One professor cautioned that the inspection should be conducted "in such a way that no unreasonable accusations would be implied in any manner." With this approval, Jackson requested the investigation from Paul Trump, chairman of the Student Life and Interest Committee, on July 23.[74]

Though a complete record on the investigation does not appear in the archives, minutes from one two-hour meeting on Wednesday, October 6, at the University Club do exist. The list of individuals present includes a number of deans, several psychiatrists from Student Health, and the current and former student presidents of Haresfoot. The theatrical organization had always maintained strong ties with its alumni. Some were illustrious, like the actor Fredric March; Joseph Davies, FDR's ambassador to Soviet Russia; Philip Reed, board chairman at General Electric; and Herbert Stothart, chief musical director at MGM. Members who attended the October 6 meeting also included some Madison alums like Walter Frautschi of the Democrat Printing Company, who for many years had been an alumni associate and in 1923 had been the Keeper of the Haresfoot.[75]

On October 6, Dean Paul Trump, chairman of the gathering, opened by stating that the purpose of the meeting was "to discuss the problem of certain individuals in the Haresfoot organization and some of the public

A chorus line of Haresfoot members. UNIVERSITY OF WISCONSIN–MADISON ARCHIVES
IMAGE S01296

relations factors of Haresfoot tours." Professor Jackson "stated that Haresfoot as an organization was only incidental with their relationship to the
problem." Dr. Washburne, psychiatrist of Student Health, said that in
each of her eleven years of work at the university, she had "found some
[homosexual] cases who have been in Haresfoot," and that "dressing and
clothing of the opposite sex tends to accentuate the problem of homosexuality." One Haresfoot member asserted that the question of homosexuality had never come up until this year: "Just because fellows are
taking girl's parts, the show should not be condemned." The group's previous year's president, Bob Pierson, observed that the immediate postwar
group was not the same type as the prewar group. Prior to the war, he
said, Haresfoot appealed to outstanding campus leaders and athletes, but
right after the war, more men of homosexual tendencies were present.
However, Pierson claimed, they tried to weed out this type. Pierson also
believed it would help "if the officers [of Haresfoot] are conscious of the
homosexual problem." Dean Trump suggested perhaps Student Health
could help screen the students applying for Haresfoot, but Dr. Washburne
quashed this idea by pointing out that according to the medical codes,

"Information concerning homosexuality cannot be released unless the individual desires it."[76]

Another Haresfoot alum, W. H. Purnell, "strongly recommended censorship by the chairman of the Dramatics Committee." One member observed that when Purnell was president before the war, there had been no trouble with Haresfoot members. Frautschi affirmed that the group was "one of the university's fine traditions, and as the university gets larger, it should not lose its traditions."[77]

Another problem revolved around the past spring's Fond du Lac tour appearance for the 1948 show. The satire, an original campus work titled *Big as Life*, was a reimagining of the Paul Bunyan lumberjack tale. The year 1948 was Wisconsin's centennial of statehood, so the hero of the "rowdy" lumberjacks of the North Woods was a fitting theme for the time. The show's synopsis describes the female lead, Babe, who "just happens to know in 1830 what the Kinsey report will publish in 1947," implying that she engaged in plentiful, varied sex. In the Wisconsin Territory, Babe runs the Blue Ox Saloon and Dance Hall, and one scene is set in what is described as a "rooming house for girls" run by "one of the town's less reputable characters." The fact that all the female roles were played by men made the "rooming house," in effect, a male brothel. The troupe also performed a song titled "Timber," which certainly opens itself to double-entendres.[78]

At the Haresfoot investigation meeting, Dean Trump said the Fond du Lac Alumni Association reported that "a considerable portion of the audience left the Fond du Lac show." Further, the association told Haresfoot not to return the following year. Kenneth Little, director of Student Personnel Services, believed this was "a very important public relations" issue. Several Fond du Lac residents also wrote to university president E. B. Fred, with one noting that several people had walked out of the performance because they were so disgusted with its obscenity. This person "was scandalized at the theme, set around a brothel, for a University show." A Madison journalist reported other upstate theatergoers had also found the material too suggestive, including the song "Oversized and Undersexed." Kenneth Little responded to these letters at President Fred's request. Promising to look into the matter, he stated, "We all wish that nothing should occur to the discredit of the University." This was, of course, before the sex ring

The cover of the program for the 1948 Haresfoot production of *Big as Life*. UNIVERSITY OF WISCONSIN-MADISON ARCHIVES IMAGE 09042137

revelations became public in June 1948. One bit of fallout from the uproar over this performance was that E. B. Fred declined to send the letter from the university president that was usually included in the Haresfoot program for the subsequent year.[79]

A review of the Haresfoot student organization's minutes for the period reflects no mention or discussion of the "investigation." Indeed, from the reviews, the 1948 show *Big as Life* was a success. One Appleton reviewer wrote, "It's always the Haresfoot 'girls' who steal the show. They give themselves away a dozen times by pulling up their skirts as though they were trousers when they sit down; and by hobbling painfully on their high heels." A Madison reviewer stated, "Their hip-waving and prancing in skilled routines drew thunders of applause from the first nighters," though he also did note "all sorts of puns—including some 'blue' [i.e., off-color] ones."[80]

For the preceding 1947 show, which was part of the organization's rebirth after the war, Haresfoot put on Cole Porter's musical comedy *Anything Goes* with a company of sixty-five. The play had debuted on Broadway in 1934. Though married, Porter was a gay man who lived in the theater milieux of New York, London, and Hollywood. Following World War I, he lived in Paris and became part of the American expat scene that involved gay parties and cross-dressing. Charles Schwartz's 1977 book *Cole Porter, A Biography* details Porter's extensive homosexual life. It's quite possible that his homosexuality was known in campus theater circles. *Anything Goes*, which takes place on a luxury liner crossing the Atlantic, was described in Haresfoot promotional materials as having "a conglomeration of play boys, sailors, dancers, debutantes, Chinese converts, and numerous assorted characters." The show's hits include "I Get a Kick Out of You," "Blow, Gabriel, Blow," "Anything Goes," and "You're the Top." Even today, "Anything Goes" remains a favorite among gay men's choruses.[81]

Without a doubt, Haresfoot pushed societal boundaries, despite what the 1948 investigation may or may not have uncovered. In 1947, a newspaper account reported on a Madison fashion show in which, "instead of the usual glamorous girl models, 'Stan' Buckles, a university student who is a member of Haresfoot, the men's dramatic organization, modeled the clothes . . . to remind everyone that Haresfoot will soon be starting." In April 1948, as out-of-town Haresfoot alumni were returning to campus to celebrate the club's fiftieth anniversary, one paper reported, "We want to welcome those, who in their undergraduate days, pranced, romped and cavorted about daringly in female apparel." And the word *gay*, which started to adopt a new meaning after the war, was often used to describe Haresfoot shows, as in "a gay, enchanting modern musical" and "It's Big! It's Gay! It's a Riot of Fun." It is possible that Haresfoot may have attracted what today we would term transgendered persons.[82]

Haresfoot's troubles did not disappear after 1948. In October 1950, Theodore Zillman, the dean of men, filed a memo noting that two members of the Union staff had visited him. A doctor from Wisconsin General Hospital had warned the staff about two students, listed in the memo are T. W. and A. A., who "were seen together frequently" and "keeping dangerous company." Though the staff had no evidence of any overt activity by either student, they were alarmed "at the possible fact of H.S. [homosexual] activity in their theater group and wished to take whatever steps of a preventive nature possible." The Union staff "also reported hear-say evidence involving two other students connected with Theater and Haresfoot activity." Zillman's memo noted, "I thanked them and agreed that if it were possible, prevention rather than the cure would be the ideal solution." Dr. Washburne found in this instance that two of the four named students were already patients of Student Health's psychiatric doctors.[83]

Haresfoot's demise in 1962 was attributed to financial difficulties, but certainly the times had changed. Early women's movement views did not take kindly to stereotypes of women, especially those performed by spoofing men. A review of the 1961 show by John Patrick Hunter in the *Capital Times* carried the headlines "Haresfoot Show 'Not Very Good'" and "Days May Be Numbered." He opined, "It is time to raise the serious question about whether the University of Wisconsin ought to lend its name to this questionable female impersonation. Haresfoot, like potted palms, is out of date."

In closing, Hunter wrote, "Let's leave the lingerie to the women. This is where it does the most good." Yet, for decades, Haresfoot provided a place where artistic homosexuals, and possibly transgendered individuals, could and did find a sympathetic and supportive community.[84]

THROWN FROM THE CLOSET

"K—— tells me that his parents know nothing of the statement which he made to the police, nor anything whatsoever concerning the incident," a school official wrote in 1948. "I felt that it might be well to inform them of the facts." In fact, in this period, the UW's policy required officials to tell parents about their sons' homosexual behavior, effectively outing them without consent. One student asked "that the disgrace and shock to his mother" be taken into consideration. The official response noted in his file was that "It was agreed that C——'s parents should be notified." One student pleaded for mercy, writing, "The degree means so much to me and to my parents." Another student discipline record shows that a doctor met with both a student and his father, though at separate times.[85]

In one case the university did not need to inform the parents because the matter was covered in the newspaper. But some parents did correspond with Dean Zillman. One student's parents wrote, "It is our aim to place him under the care of a competent psychiatrist and also to arrange for a complete physical check-up at the Mayo Clinic. Our one purpose in life will be to get him back on the right path so he can take his proper place in society." The dean responded, "I feel certain that the understanding and assistance which D——'s situation is receiving from his parents can only lead to a happier life for him." This student was eventually let back into the university.[86]

For some, getting caught resulted in coming out, not only to their parents but also to clergy. One student, a member of the First Unitarian Society of Madison who worked with the church's youth group, felt the "situation necessitated" that he apprise the Reverend Max Gaebler. After the student offered to resign from the church's high school youth group, Reverend Gaebler was "so impressed with his complete frankness, his intelligent recognition of his difficulty and his eagerness to seek further psychiatric assistance" that Gaebler refused the resignation and wrote to Dean Zillman on the young man's behalf. The assistant director of the Union provided another character reference, and the student was permitted to continue at the university, though he was placed on disciplinary probation. In another case, a young man's attorney quietly withdrew from the record a pastor's letter written as a character reference—perhaps the clergyman got cold feet.[87]

One case put the university's policy to a real test. An official wrote, "I feel that this student would benefit by administrative handling and would recommend that his father, a physician, should be informed and cooperate in any therapeutic plan." However, the student expressed "the hope repeatedly that his parents learn nothing of the affair." Ultimately, the father was informed and called the dean to arrange a meeting for Wednesday of the following week. But on Monday, the family's pastor called to report the father had suffered a cerebral hemorrhage and passed away. The student told the school officials his father had died "with little or no insurance and while his mother insisted that he finish out the semester, he doubted that he could return to Wisconsin in the fall." The school official handling the matter concluded, "I do not think that there should be anything further done at this time."[88]

Before "coming out" and "outing" were part of the gay dialogue, the university already had a decided policy. Getting caught as a homosexual could mean a notation on a student's official transcript that the individual was "not entitled to honorable dismissal." This was similar to the military's dishonorable discharge. When former Wisconsin students sought to apply to other institutions, their homosexual pasts followed them, thanks to university officials. Regularly, UW staff sent out letters to officials at other universities, stating, for example, "Mr. D—— was unfortunately involved with a group of our students last spring who confessed to homosexual behavior," or that a student's "problem related to a sexual aberration." Some letters not only mentioned the incidents but also contained notes from students' medical records, such as, "He is a passive individual. He recognizes that he is easily disturbed and led by other more aggressive and dominant personalities." When a student withdrawing from Wisconsin asked if another college would hear about his case, the response was clear. One doctor wrote, "I pointed out to him that it was standard operating procedure for one university to inform another, in the case of a transfer student, not only of his academic work but of anything which might bear on his total personality picture."[89]

The man who sent most of these letters was Dean Theodore Zillman. Originally from Chicago, he had received his bachelor's degree in 1926 from Wisconsin, where "his special fields of study were administration, psychology and psychiatry." He attended law school and practiced law in Chicago, served in the army as a major, and became director of the UW Office of Veterans Affairs after the war. In May 1950, he became the university's dean of men, in charge of male student discipline. At this time, the university had a policy of acting in loco parentis to control student behavior in nonacademic matters. In a 1954 interview about students, Zillman explained: "I try to help them think through their behavior . . . to help them profit from their mistakes." However, he did have a reputation as a disciplinarian. In the same interview, he stated, "They must realize they have to follow laws not individual dictates."[90]

Students understood that university officials making others aware of their homosexual status could be harmful. One former student pleaded, "My position is particularly trying since without what is termed an 'honorable dismissal' from the University, no college however small will accept my application." One black student set to graduate was to have his degree withheld, but a mix-up sent it to him anyway. He wrote to Dean Zillman in

Madison while doing summer work in Tuskegee: "I believe that I can be of great service to my people if I am allowed to remain here. There is a great need among Southern Negroes for good teachers." Dean Zillman then corresponded with a psychiatrist in Tuskegee who was treating the young man: "We feel that the homosexual activity which he did exhibit on one occasion here demanded of us that any future employer of his be alerted to his difficulty." Zillman was concerned that the Tuskegee officials did not know about the young man's homosexuality and was hinting that the psychiatrist should tell them. "Have we played fair with Tuskegee Institute under these circumstances?" Zillman asked. The doctor did not want to reveal patient information, but the matter became moot as the student left Tuskegee after the summer.[91]

Wisconsin officials also cooperated with the military concerning former students. In one case, the military had the police record from a student's campus days and also knew the individual had visited the university psychiatrist. In this case, the navy commander of a Board of Officers wrote, "It is recognized that frequently psychiatric reports on a patient are unavailable but due to the importance of this matter, both to Mr. K—— and to the U.S. Navy, it is requested that either the report or a paraphrase of the report be made available to this Board." The university could not do so in this case because the doctor involved had left the university, taking his patient records with him.[92]

Psychiatrists treating students for homosexual problems often believed the students would "benefit rather well and rapidly from psychiatric help." "He is amenable to psychiatric treatment," wrote one. Another described a student who "proved to be a very cooperative patient and anxious to help himself and improve his situation." George Chauncey has noted that some American psychiatrists from this era believed society should not treat as sexual psychopaths the "relatively harmless nonconformist, such as people who engaged in premarital sex or homosexual relations, so long as they kept their behavior hidden." Not all cases could be dealt with so easily or quickly, however. Some students continued to be seen for incidents over a long period; one case covered "a considerable period of time during which period they have been in contact with Dr. Washburne's office."[93]

And not all students were thought of as suitable for a cure. One university psychiatrist wrote of a student he treated,

You may recall that we were by no means hopeful of what could be accomplished in the way of therapy. Our attitude was largely due to the belief that we were dealing with an essentially inadequate personality. . . . It is believed that this student will not substantially benefit by psychiatric therapy due to a lack of desire to effect a substantial change in his personality structure.

Another psychiatrist admitted "psychotherapy under compulsion is difficult." Even when a case was referred to a psychiatrist, the therapy was not always successful. A student caught "in flagrante delicto" in the UW Arboretum in the fall of 1953 had been seen "for the past two years and was making excellent progress with his problem" according to the record. Excess use of alcohol was blamed for his relapse in 1953.[94]

The Student Health Service put great store in applying "extensive objective psychological tests" to these students. The list of tests described as "psychometric" included the Bernreuter Personality Inventory, P-S Experience, Problem Checklist, Minnesota-Multiphasic, Wechsler-Bellevue, and Rorschach. One report on a student opined that the individual was "devoid of insight and exhibited marked emotional instability and immaturity during each conference, which apparently was associated with his former experimental incident of homosexuality in 1948." The Student Conduct Committee's view on disciplined students who might be permitted to continue or, if they had been suspended, seek readmission was expressed in the statement: "You were to receive psychiatric treatment indicating that you had been cured of your tendencies." Doctors did recognize that homosexual patients might experience realistic "anxiety concerning the recurrence of an investigation of events long past."[95]

Most students were quick to agree that they would be "happy to cooperate" in getting psychiatric treatment. One admitted, "I made a very foolish mistake which has done irreparable harm to my character and perhaps my future. . . . To attempt an explanation is impossible; such things cannot be explained." Another agreed he would "freely undergo any measures the psychiatrist may suggest to assure my proper adjustment in this matter." Another stated that his "homosexual contact had been quite frequent over the period of the last two years and that it was a matter of concern to him and he sincerely wanted to rid himself of the misbehavior pattern." Some truly believed the university was helping them by requiring psychiatry. One police officer noted, "Mr. L—— tells me that he should see a psychiatrist but has been afraid to go."[96]

Many students hoping for favorable consideration by the Student Conduct Committee declared that the treatment was working. One claimed that as a result of the psychiatric assistance, he had "abstained from any homosexual activities since that date." Another felt "certain that he has got his old difficulty well in hand and that we need have no fear on that count." Another claimed he had "everything under control," but the university official disagreed, writing, "I pointed out to him that this was patently not so, as evidenced by the record. He admitted the strength of that argument." One student made the statement that he had "not engaged in any homosexual activities at this time but that his desires to do so were sometimes

While this postcard image of students lounging on Bascom Hill presents the image of a tranquil campus, the University of Wisconsin–Madison's Student Conduct Committee dealt with many behavioral irregularities, including sexual ones, in the 1950s.

extremely high." This student felt that the doctor had "helped him some but does not believe the doctor has helped him to the extent that he can be sure of his actions." The Student Conduct officials firmly required a recommendation from Student Health based on a competent psychiatrist who was a member of the American Board of Psychiatrists before they would expunge a record or readmit a student to the university.[97]

Martin Duberman provided a good example of what may have been going through the minds of some homosexual students in his classic 1991 book *Cures: A Gay Man's Odyssey*, which describes his own college days at Princeton in the 1950s. "Many of us cursed our fate," he wrote, "longed to be straight. And some of us had actively been seeking the 'cure.'" He says he thought "about 'conversion' as my only hope for a happy life" and describes "fits of remorse over quitting therapy." Since Duberman went on to be an openly gay public man of letters and a professor of history at CUNY, he knew these earlier impulses to find a cure were misplaced. He later observed, "Orthodox psychiatry had based its negative conclusions about homosexuality on studies of people who had come to therapists for help or on captive populations in prisons and mental hospitals." Duberman's insights show the underside of therapeutic discipline as it was used on college campuses at this time, as well as the regret that could set in after cooperating in a "cure."[98]

On the other end of the spectrum, however, some students did not fully embrace the university policy or the therapy. A student from Milwaukee wrote, "I don't intend to submit myself to a court or committee to be smeared and muckraked by the local newspapers." Yet another expressed that to acknowledge the need for psychiatry would be "incriminating." One believed the proposed psychiatric treatment was of "a purely suggestive nature," although he also said, "I have succeeded in accomplishing the basic requisites for a normal adjustment." By 1960, another man had specifically challenged the Rorschach test, explaining the "validity of which . . . is most seriously doubted by many leading men in the field." The same student felt that since he "did not evince a hypocritical condemnation of homosexual relations as a whole while at the hearing," this hurt his case. He further asserted, "I have never had any interest in partaking of such a way of life."[99]

Others rejected the judgment that they needed help altogether. "I earnestly believe I am not in need of psychiatric treatment," said one student.

Another confirmed that he had not accepted a year of psychiatric help for two reasons: "Financial limitations have been of great importance, but there has also been a sincere question in my mind concerning the real need which I have of such help."[100]

The consequences of engaging in homosexual activity at the university and getting caught, although not as dire as the proposed treatment of sexual psychopaths, were still severe. Some students simply packed their bags and left. One such grad student sent a telegram to his professor indicating that he would not show up for his teaching assistant sections. In one instance, five students were referred to the Student Conduct Committee and two avoided official action by "voluntary withdrawal." One student who was dropped in 1953 took seasonal work, hoping to be readmitted. In 1956 he was granted probationary status as a student.[101]

For students who hoped to go into teaching professions, the repercussions could be dire. One student was informed that the School of Education had dropped him, denied him his teaching certificate, and withheld his course credits in education. Another who aspired to teach wrote, "I have been severely handicapped in seeking employment during the five-year period that has elapsed since I left Madison in June 1953." However, in some cases, officials believed the students accepted the university's actions. In one instance, an official noted that a student "agreed in our concern over the possibility of his engaging in the teaching profession and understood the University's desire that he refrain from entering the teaching profession, given his present difficulties."[102]

No matter the field of study, many students struggled in their searches for employment due to the university's actions. One student wrote, "Not knowing whether the degree will be granted is making it difficult to apply for positions, and even to complete writing of the thesis." This individual did eventually earn his degree because the psychiatrist reported that he had "made reasonable progress" and "has adjusted satisfactorily." Another student lamented, "Due to my not having my degree I have lost out on several job opportunities that would have been of great value." He also eventually got his degree. A student seeking employment with the Bank of America in California, however, learned that the university had sent a letter to the bank reporting that the young man "was involved with a group who confessed to homosexual behavior." And one student studying to be a doctor was told by the UW psychiatrist Benjamin Glover, "It is difficult to answer your question about entering medicine, but I believe that it would be extremely difficult for you to gain admission to a medical school under the circumstances of your past record."[103]

George Mosse, a gay faculty member who arrived at the university during this period, has described how he handled his homosexuality with his teaching colleagues in the history department. In *Confronting History: A Memoir*, originally published in 1999, he wrote, "The closet door had to be tightly closed, and was even so with the members of this group whom I knew to have had some gay adventures when younger." Members of the history department may have been even more paranoid than others because a few of the students who had been caught were history majors. In Mosse's published scholarship on masculinity, after he was more out, he wrote, "To a large extent the physician took over from the clergy as the keeper of normalcy." As he astutely observed, "The age of personal revelations was not yet upon us."[104]

WOMEN AND SEXUAL DISCIPLINE ON CAMPUS

Between the end of World War II and the early 1960s, while some fifty cases involving male homosexuality were being investigated by campus authorities at UW–Madison, a similar number of female students were being investigated by campus police, deans, and the Student Conduct Committee, but with one interesting difference. Of the forty-nine cases, every woman was being investigated for a heterosexual act.[105]

In twenty-eight cases, the reports indicate that the women were caught in flagrante delicto or that they confessed to cohabitating or to participation in sexual relationships. A number of cases involved adultery, such as female students having sex with married men. At least half were caught in parked cars; others were spotted out in the open. One report noted that the campus police officer observed for a while to make sure he understood what he was seeing. While some officers described exposed penises and women's clothing shed, one more delicately described "extreme intimacy." Finding privacy for sex on campus during these years was difficult, and women were most frequently apprehended at the Arboretum, Picnic Point, Willow Drive, and Observatory Hill.[106]

Another twenty-one women had stayed out late or slept over at hotels with men, but women who denied that any sexual activity had occurred were disciplined for violating the sign-out regulations of the women's residences or for underage drinking. In some heterosexual discipline cases, the files show that campus authorities notified the woman's parents but not the man's. Several couples attempted to justify their actions by pleading that they were engaged or about to be. Some couples practiced birth control by using condoms or performing mutual masturbation. Rarely was psychiatry suggested for these heterosexually active women, and only in cases of extreme immaturity. Most of the women under investigation were put on probation, and a number were dropped from the university. The men were also disciplined.[107]

It is fascinating that during the two decades that saw dozens of male students disciplined for homosexual activities, not a single case of lesbianism came to the attention of the campus authorities. That the total number of women under discipline for heterosexual activity nearly matched the number of men under discipline for homosexual activity shows the lopsided focus on gay men and a total ignorance or intentional avoidance of lesbianism.

PSYCHIATRIC SCIENCE

Dr. Benjamin Glover, a psychiatrist on the UW–Madison campus, published articles about the homosexuals he was trying to cure. Born in 1916 in Chicago, Glover did his academic study at Northwestern University, earning his medical degree in 1944. He served with the US Navy from 1944 to 1947 and for a while was an instructor at Allegheny College in Meadville, Pennsylvania. Though he had expected to be sent to the South Pacific, he served in naval hospitals on the East Coast, where he may have observed the military's medical treatment of homosexuals. He joined the UW staff in 1947 and was with Student Health for three years before joining the psychiatry department. During the late 1940s and 1950s he often served on or advised the Student Conduct Committee. When he retired from the university in 1981, his services were still in demand and he headed the Department of Psychiatry for the Veterans Administration hospital at Tomah for several years. He was active in civic life and served on the

Madison Commission on Alcoholism, the Dane County Child Guidance Center, the Special Review Board of Parole on Sexual Deviate Law, and the Wisconsin Welfare Association, in addition to speaking to alumni clubs around the state.[108]

In the early 1950s, Dr. Glover decided that the Wisconsin story on homosexuality and psychiatry, along with its lessons, should be published in a professional journal. At the time he was an assistant professor of neuropsychiatry in the UW Medical School. The article he published in May 1951 in the *Journal of Nervous and Mental Disease* was titled "Observations on Homosexuality among University Students." It was republished in 1954 in the book *The Homosexuals: As Seen by Themselves and Thirty Authorities*, edited by A. M. Kirch.[109]

In *The Homosexuals*, Glover remarked on "a noticeable increase in cases of homosexuality as well as other socially offending sex cases" on the UW campus since the war. Speaking from his experiences at Student Health, he said that a "great majority of the cases have been veterans." He also commented on the difficulty students had in discussing the "more active members of this group without implicating a large number of well-known homosexuals on the campus." Glover's comments show both that campus homosexuals apparently had an extensive network and that some campus homosexuals were recognized as such beyond medical offices.[110]

Glover selected twelve cases for his study, all white and single (though two mentioned that they regularly engaged in sexual relations with black students). He characterized all twelve patients "as true homosexuals—that is, overt performers of deviant sex practices with their own sex by reason of personal choice, without coercion, with enjoyment—who frequently sought the haunts and company and engaged in the activities of other homosexuals." From the case histories, Glover learned that his subjects "noticed they were different from others of their age group in childhood, and definitely in a different social category after puberty."[111]

Of the twelve cases, six were veterans of World War II and five of them had been active homosexuals during their time in the service. Glover was familiar with military psychiatry reports that indicated "most homosexuals are to be found in the secretarial branches, chaplain's aides, hospital assistants, photographers." None of the twelve cases had gone into combat and "none were introduced to homosexuality via the service."

One of the nonveterans had been a conscientious objector who spent three years in a prison camp.[112]

Glover stated that Student Health usually saw these individuals when they were in a "homosexual panic." This panic often resulted from an "intense fear of being caught, of being noticeably different, or the fear which slowly and deeply grows to depressing proportions, that of being unable to be like other people, to be happily married and to raise a family which will be their solace in later years." As a further sign of the 1950s' prevailing assumption about heterosexual couplehood as normative, Glover writes, "This fear of an old age loneliness was found in all individuals to be more important to them than was the immediate threat of ostracism at the present time should they be discovered." Yet, the twelve men were not currently lonely: "Each homosexual among the 12 felt that his present amour was a permanent one, different from the one before." The research showed most of the men had one sexual activity that they favored, "although all participants admitted they would tolerate another approach if they 'loved him enough.'" Glover noted, "Love is a commonplace word in conversation with homosexuals."[113]

The article also described how guarded homosexuals needed to be in this period: "Hearing of the nonjudicial psychiatric staff, these patients would make an appointment, and in interview would cautiously make inquiries as to the privacy of records and the connection of the staff to any administrative body." Psychiatrists accomplished little with homosexual patients during "the first two or three interviews except for inaccurate, frequently contradictory, records, which were corrected through several visits, changing 'no affairs' to 'a few childhood experiences' to 'innumerable nights of intimacy.'" Glover did observe, however, that as cases increased and news spread, new patients would "explode all at once in the first conference." He also noticed that these appearances "were often timed with publication of some local news item concerning exhibitionism or discovery of a group of consorting individuals in town."[114]

Glover described the twelve men as having attained "a fairly significant status." The group included one medical student, three advanced graduate students, two teachers, two dramatic arts undergraduates, two "mediocre" students, one professional symphony musician, and one radical politico. While under observation, they expressed interests in art, drama, ballet, music, and discussing human rights; not one mentioned organized sports. It was noted that in "frequenting musical and dramatic performances," the twelve men found occasions to make acquaintances. Musical favorites included works by Debussy and Tchaikovsky. And Glover noted that, as a whole, the group favored the terms "gay, queer, queen, and fan."[115]

Glover observed that his homosexual subjects often told each other "their own past histories" upon meeting, and many claimed to take the passive part in the initiation of homosexual activity, though admitting they later adopted "more aggressive and daring approaches." Glover found that "taverns and bars were most often centers of congregation. Glances and smiles are exchanged and through several hours aggressors move toward or away from various passives until in time a selection of a mate is made." This description of homosexual flirting in bars is notably similar to heterosexual bar flirting.[116]

Although Glover claimed that his Student Health department was "nonjudicial," he nevertheless used language and expressed views that portrayed homosexuals in a less than positive light. For example, he wrote, "These people represent a parody and a paradox in emotions; in a sense they burlesque love as a heterosexual knows it and yet they are a continual tragedy of failure to find either sex gratification or a person through whom they may enjoy continuously that measure of sex gratification they attain." Further, he claimed that homosexuals have "a narcissistic selfishness" and "no nationalistic or patriotic feeling," a serious charge to make in the 1950s, though how Glover squared this with the many gay veterans under his care is hard to understand. Drawing on common assumptions about the sickness of

Dr. Benjamin Glover, professor of psychiatry at the University of Wisconsin–Madison, wrote about treating homosexual students. UNIVERSITY OF WISCONSIN–MADISON ARCHIVES IMAGE S04382

homosexuals, Glover stated, "Their fantasies and investiture of simple events with markedly exaggerated interpretation, their paranoid trends, emotional immaturity and well-known instability and suicidal ideas indicate a large schizoid element in their personality."[117]

In his paper, Glover also weighed in on the issue of whether homosexuality is an inherent characteristic or a behavioral choice. While noting that the last century's trend was toward seeing homosexuality as an acquired characteristic, he claimed the "present attitude is toward the congenital anomaly or inherited tendencies in this group." He cited academic authorities who had a strong belief that homosexuality is genetic in origin, and he cited evidence of the "basic medical differences between homosexuals and normal individuals" from four authors, including his Wisconsin colleague Dr. Elmer L. Severinghaus. Glover's bias can be seen in his juxtaposition of homosexuals with "normal individuals." When talking about "homosexual idiosyncrasies" he said the studies show "practically no environmental influence to produce [a] personality molding toward such an aberration." Glover's use of phrases like "deviant sex practices" and "paranoid trends" in descriptions of his patients shows his overall negative views of homosexuality.[118]

Glover noted many ways in which doctors had failed in their attempts to change or "cure" (the quotation marks are his) homosexual behavior, such as the endocrine method, disciplinary measures, hypnotherapy, and narcosuggestion. He added that some doctors had claimed success with shock therapy, but he concluded that they were not substantiated. Without admitting the failure of psychotherapy, his chosen profession, Glover noted the resistance among homosexuals to having their "condition" referred to as a sickness. Many of the patients who cooperated with a doctor's attempts to "cure" them likely had made efforts to please authorities for the sake of returning to the university's good graces.[119]

Nevertheless, Glover believed that Student Health offered successful treatment through direct psychotherapy. There is, he said, "a possibility of reshaping [a homosexual's] life by reconditioning and reeducation." He thought reeducation also provided a "good opportunity to explain the logical development of restrictions of society on deviant sex practices," as well as "the accepted monogamous and purely heterosexual practices of the present mores of civilized man." Again, Glover's bias is revealed by the contrast of homosexuals with "civilized" men. In Glover's therapy, "great effort [was] devoted to encouraging a competitive sense, beginning with sports or games with the intent of diverting a usually large amount of unbalanced paranoid feeling to the control seen in competitive fair play." He also encouraged homosexual men to engage in public speaking but, perhaps with Haresfoot in mind, he never suggested drama.[120]

In the end, Glover reported "poor psychotherapeutic results" from his treatments. He lamented that "the stigma of [the homosexuals'] pattern follows them in time and their socialization is a most difficult thing in even the relatively enlightened atmosphere of a university." Although pleased that there were "no scholastic or psychiatric casualties in this group," he concluded that "only one of the selected 12 has made significant improvement" during treatment. Glover's observations of the large number of homosexuals on the Wisconsin campus and their active sex lives confirms what Gillin found with his sample of prisoners and what Severinghaus found with his servicemen: gay Wisconsinites were quite sexually active, had networks, and were reluctant to accept the strictures of society. Glover, like his academic predecessors in Wisconsin, placed the discussion about homosexuality in a rational and scientific, if still judgmental, context.[121]

Some years later, in 1976, the sixty-year-old Glover lectured about "sex among the elderly." While noting that "sexual taboos have loosened," he still thought people over sixty-five were "denying their sexuality." He debunked stereotypes of the "dirty old man" and "lewd old lady." He believed, according to a university science writer, that "normal is whatever is comfortable and satisfying for the people involved." Possibly, his views developed over the years.[122]

PATTERNS OLD AND NEW

Following World War II, people in Wisconsin responded to homosexuality in many different ways. And most responses reflected or were informed by the ongoing medicalization of homosexuality.

Seeking to cure his nerves, Edward Harris Heth followed a model demonstrated in Cooksville, Mineral Point, and New Glarus by establishing a gay life in a safe small town in the state. Indeed, after their service at Truax Field, Bob Neal and Edgar Hellum returned and reopened Pendarvis and reengaged in their gentlemanly hospitality. Though their lives might not be described as fully open in the modern sense, neither were they hidden.

The postwar visibility of homosexuals in Wisconsin, as shown in reports prepared by the Milwaukee Metropolitan Commission on Crime Prevention and by statements of various public officials from the cities of Milwaukee and Madison, required a response from the state. These indications of an increase in homosexuals were magnified nationally by the revelations of the Kinsey Report and press stories about sex deviates committing crimes across the nation. Things were changing, and Wisconsin responded in two major ways.

Seeking to crack down, the legislature, dominated by the Stalwart Republicans, undertook to deal harshly with "sodomists" as sexual psychopaths. The *Milwaukee Journal*, the state's largest and most prestigious newspaper, encouraged a constant hue and cry against homosexuals. Despite the lone voice of citizen lobbyist Gladys Walsh, the constitutional issues of locking up someone before he had committed a crime were ignored in the legislative rush to judgment. The belief of some law enforcement personnel and some psychiatrists that doctors could identify sex deviates before they committed overt acts drew on the faith in the efficacy of the military doctors' practice of screening for homosexuals at induction. Today, we know such screening failed more often than not.

Seeking a sounder scientific model, the University of Wisconsin, still one of the bastions of progressivism in the state, used a somewhat milder approach but one that still relied on doctors. Police and campus records show that some veterans returned to campus having had gay experiences and continued this behavior, while other younger college students also yielded to homosexual impulses. Whether self-admitting or self-denying, all young men apprehended for homosexual behavior faced the apparatus of the Student Conduct Committee's review.

Some of the self-admitting gays on campus, when confronted with student discipline and corrective psychotherapy, withdrew from the university. As a result, they were forced to imagine and create new lives without the formal education they had hoped to attain. For example, Madison's well-known personality "Blanche," who affected a cape and could often be seen dining in the Admiralty Room of the Edgewater Hotel, made a life not in the teaching profession for which his graduate studies in music had prepared him, but in music education, assisting students who came into the record stores on lower State Street by serving them as an extremely knowledgeable sales clerk.

Other gay students, mostly the self-denying or those hoping for a cure, submitted to the regime of the campus psychiatrists. Campus officials struggled to find the right response through educative discipline. Insofar as the Kinsey data had shown, homosexuality was more predominant in adolescents, and some authorities believed such tendencies in the young could be cured. Doctors happily reported progress in treatment and adjustment, though perhaps without such certainty as they might have wished. Nevertheless, the university used disciplinary tools to direct homosexuals away from vocations in education and medicine that were deemed inappropriate for them. And a wary eye was kept on Haresfoot, the campus theatrical group that permitted cross-dressing. Finally, officials deemed it necessary to tell parents and potential employers about students' sexual waywardness. While these punishments might seem milder than the lockup desired by the legislature for sexual psychopaths, they still cost many students their degrees, careers, and familial relationships.

While the UW psychiatrists were generally confident of their ability to cure homosexuals, not all homosexuals as reported by Dr. Benjamin Glover accepted the diagnosis of sickness and many others declined treatment. Some Wisconsin gays, having discovered their true identities, refused or at least questioned the depiction of homosexuality as either a crime or a disease. For them, as Glover recorded, "Love is a commonplace word."

7

WITCH HUNTS AND THE FAIRY DEAL

It is a curious fact in this connection that many rural politicians have reported there is more rank and file interest and concern about the revelation about homosexuality in government circles than about the more explosive issue about Communist sympathizers.
—JOHN WYNGAARD, GREEN BAY PRESS-GAZETTE, APRIL 26, 1950[1]

The University, in exercise of its disciplinary authority, should not be concerned with the homosexual orientation of a student, per se, any more than it is concerned with another student's heterosexual orientation. Instead it is activity, be it heterosexual or homosexual, which properly might subject a student to disciplinary act.
—MINUTES OF UW CONDUCT AND APPEALS COMMITTEE, 1962[2]

In an attack on the Truman administration on April 25, 1950, US Senator Kenneth Wherry (R-NE, 1943–1951) criticized what he called the "New Deal and Fair Deal and fairy deal" by linking two Democratic administrations and charging them with harboring subversives and moral perverts. The frequency with which gays were attacked in government in the 1950s has generally been lost to collective memory, though writers of gay history have tried to keep awareness alive. Allan Bérubé in the February/March 1983 issue of *Mother Jones* placed the roots of the postwar witch hunts in the periodic army and navy sweeps against gays and lesbians during World War II. He refers to this trend as a homosexual "postwar panic" that was fed by "reactionary political winds." John D'Emilio in *Sexual Politics, Sexual Communities: The Making of a Homosexual Minority in the United*

States, 1940–1970, published in 1983, further describes the oppression and hostility aimed at the menace of sexual perversion during the 1950s.[3]

The biggest step to correct this collective amnesia was taken by David K. Johnson in his 2004 publication of *The Lavender Scare: The Cold War Persecution of Gays and Lesbians in the Federal Government*, which gave this phenomenon a name to match and balance the familiar "red scare" that occurred in the US at the same time. Johnson shows that far more gays than Reds lost their jobs in DC during these witch hunts. However, the full ramifications of Senator Joe McCarthy's participation in the gay dimensions of this witch hunt and what it meant to Wisconsin are particularly unknown and unexplored. The junior senator from Appleton, Wisconsin, loudly denounced "egg sucking phony liberals" and anyone who "would hold sacrosanct those Communists and queers," with a particular focus on "the prancing mimics of the Moscow party line in the State Department."[4]

Recalling McCarthy's role in the lavender scare, former US senator Alan Simpson (R-WY, 1979–1997) wrote a foreword to Rodger McDaniel's book *Dying for Joe McCarthy's Sins: The Suicide of Wyoming Senator Lester Hunt*, published in 2013. Simpson affirmed, "A lesser-known element of that history and one that harmed far more people was the witch hunt McCarthy and others conducted against homosexuals." While noting that McCarthy was not alone, Simpson also charged: "Senators Joe McCarthy, Styles Bridges, and Herman Welker poisoned people to believe that homosexuals were not only 'sexual perverts' but that they were dangerous security risks." McDaniel, a former Wyoming state legislator for the decade of the 1970s and an ordained Presbyterian minister, presumably knows something of the structure of social and political sins.[5]

Senator Lester Hunt's son Buddy, a seminary student, was arrested on June 9, 1953, by an undercover DC police officer and charged with "soliciting for a lewd and immoral purpose." Initially the charge was withdrawn, but conservative Republican senators exerted pressure on the District police to refile it. The young man was then tried and convicted. The Senate of 1954 was split down the middle entering the midterm elections, requiring Vice President Richard Nixon to break ties. Senator Hunt, a Wyoming Democrat, had already been weighing whether he would run for reelection that year, but Republicans now threatened that if he did not resign, they would expose his son. The arrest had been a local police matter, but Hunt's

GOP colleagues threatened to make it a national scandal. Wyoming's Republican governor, once Hunt resigned, would appoint a successor, putting his party in the clear majority.[6]

In the end, tragically, Senator Hunt took his own life. At the time, journalist Drew Pearson, in a syndicated column, blamed McCarthy's Republican associates for Hunt's death, and columnist Marquis Childs of the *Washington Post* blamed "the McCarthy-Welker faction of the party." McDaniel's book found Joe McCarthy complicit in the death of Hunt, even suggesting that McCarthy's aide Roy Cohn may have been a party to the pressures put on Hunt. After Hunt's death, the Wyoming governor did appoint a Republican, who lost that 1954 election to Joseph O'Mahoney, a Democrat. The Hunt episode, however, was just one example of the gay attacks that were part of McCarthy's witch hunt.[7]

Lesbians, too, were targets for McCarthy and his supporters during this period. In *Odd Girls and Twilight Lovers: A History of Lesbian Life in Twentieth Century America*, Lillian Faderman discusses a remark attributed to some of the queer-baiters in *Washington Confidential*, the 1951 gossipy exposé of the nation's capital: "There are at least twice as many Sapphic lovers as fairies." As an example, Faderman told of a lesbian caught in a security check because she had discussed lesbianism with a psychotherapist in the 1940s. Faderman further emphasized, "Lesbians believed . . . that whatever opprobrium was expressed for gay males would apply to them." She argued, "The concern about homosexuals in government was not primarily that they constituted a security risk," but rather that they represented "discomfort with whatever was different." As an example of low security risks, Faderman cited male caretakers who were dismissed from the US Botanical Garden.[8]

Joseph McCarthy rose to prominence in early 1950 with a famous speech given at a Lincoln Day event in Wheeling, West Virginia, in which he claimed to possess a list of communists in the State Department. In the ensuing days the number of people McCarthy claimed to have on his supposed list fluctuated from more than 200 to 57 to 81, and the characterization of those on the list fluctuated from actual card-carrying Communist Party members to mere security or policy risks. This vague language permitted McCarthy to include homosexuals on his list, on the theory they were prime subjects for blackmail. In a six-hour performance in the Senate on February 20, 1950, where his remarks enjoyed congressional immunity, McCarthy went through a list and identified individual cases. In two of these cases, No. 14 and No. 62, he admitted the matter was primarily a "morals case," a not-so-veiled reference to homosexuality. He charged one man (Case No. 14), a translator in the State Department, with having "a bad background" and claimed that a security report "advised the subject should be dismissed as a bad security risk because he was flagrantly homosexual." Further, McCarthy claimed that this person "had extremely close connections with other individuals with the same tendencies, and who were active members of Communist front organizations, including the Young Communist League." The senator had no qualms about conflating homosexuality with subversion. He argued that Case No. 62 "was important because it sheds light on some rather unusual mental aberrations of certain individuals in the [State] Department." Though McCarthy admitted that this particular case was not about "communistic activities," he informed the Senate that "the new security officer has recommended that [the government] get rid of all that type of individuals regardless of whether they are shown to have any communistic connection or not."[9]

The climate of the time was represented by a March 25, 1950, headline in the *Capital Times*: "119 Ousted by the State Department in Morals Purge." The focus here was not on Communism, but morals, and most of the 119 cases involved homosexuals. The article notes that US Representative John Rooney (D-NY, 1944–1974) charged that some gays remained in the Commerce Department, though more than fifty had already been fired, and the weeding was continuing in earnest. Thus, the lavender scare was a national bipartisan attack on homosexuals.[10]

"Patrioteering Politicians" Gone Crazy

In the extensive national press coverage on the witch hunts of the McCarthy era, a long article in the *Saturday Evening Post* of July 29, 1950, stands out. Authored by noted journalists and known anticommunists Joseph and Stewart Alsop, it was titled "Why Has Washington Gone Crazy?" The Alsop brothers, who were related to Theodore Roosevelt, described themselves as "Republicans by inheritance and registration, and . . . conservatives by political conviction." However, in an argument against McCarthy's scare tactics, the brothers contended that America needed unity in the face of the Soviet threat: "The contribution of many conservative Republicans to American unity had been to spread the lunatic notion that the American government is honeycombed with perversion and treachery."[11]

As evidence, the Alsops pointed to a speech by George Kennan, who they described as the "brilliant chief planner for the State Department," the author of America's containment policy, and later a foreign policy professor at the Institute for Advanced Study. "It requires considerable courage to work for the Department of State these days," Kennan said in the speech. "This is so particularly since the revelation that ninety-one employees—out of 20,000—have been discharged as sexual perverts." The Alsops also quoted from a speech Kennan made earlier that year to an audience in his hometown of Milwaukee: "I must tell you that the atmosphere of public life in Washington does not have to deteriorate much further to produce a situation in which very few of our more quiet and sensitive and gifted people will be able to continue in the Government."[12]

The Alsop brothers were critical of these "patrioteering politicians" in a decade following one in which "war profiteering" had been a very dirty phrase. "It is not only the ham-handed Senator McCarthy, who has done this," they wrote, placing a collective blame on the patrioteers for the situation, "although McCarthy's outrageous performance has done harm enough." And, again, the issue of homosexuality was brought to the fore: "We have been treated to the spectacle of the Minority Leader of the Senate, Kenneth Wherry, attempting to elevate the subject of homosexuality to the level of a serious political issue, on the ground that sexual perversion presents a clear and present danger to the security of the United States. Examples of this sort of vulgar folly could be extended *ad nauseam*."[13]

In response to the Alsops, McCarthy wrote to the magazine's editor, Ben Hibbs, and read the letter aloud on the floor of the Senate so that it would appear in the *Congressional Record*. The *Record* heading for the August 8, 1950, item was, "REMOVAL OF SEXUAL PERVERTS FROM GOVERNMENT EMPLOYMENT." In the letter, McCarthy posited "that once the people of a Nation become complacent about moral degeneracy in its leadership, then that nation has not long to live," citing the decline and fall of the Roman Empire as an example. He continued, "I am sure you also realize that a moral pervert in a sensitive governmental position is dangerous to the security of the Nation because of his susceptibility to blackmail." Decrying the characterization of the effort to root out Reds and gays as "vulgar" and "nauseating," McCarthy wrote a sentence suggesting that he may have known that Joe Alsop, though married, was a closeted homosexual: "I can understand, of course, why it would be considered 'vulgar' and 'nauseating' by Joe Alsop." Hibbs drafted a reply to McCarthy, pointing out that the senator's charges did not make the brothers or the magazine unpatriotic: "The Alsops and the *Saturday Evening Post* are against the employment of 'traitors and perverts' in government, just as you are." Thus, Hibbs confirmed the impression that later generations have gained—that McCarthy's attack was widely known at the time to be against both Reds and gays.[14]

As the Alsops predicted, the witch-hunt charges were generally accepted by the American public, and the brothers were correct in additionally noting that the charges would have a special regional appeal. The Alsops believed some of the general political craziness was due to the threat of nuclear war, but beyond that they gave credit to the "other notion, equally loudly proclaimed in Chicago and points West, that government is now in the hands of perverts and traitors." "It is impossible to understand your publishing the sarcastic reference to people in Chicago and points West," McCarthy responded in his letter to the editor, "because they object to perverts and traitors in our Government."[15]

The Alsops were correct in their assumption that "Chicago and points West" were partly to blame for the red and lavender scares, as proven in a memo sent by Tom Coleman, the longtime boss of the Republican Party in Wisconsin, who then chaired the state party's Finance Committee. An industrialist and the head of Madison Kipp Corporation, he raised money from his fellow business leaders to fund Republican candidates. He had strongly supported McCarthy in the 1946 primary against Bob La Follette Jr. and had fought the La Follettes and progressives many times. The revealing election-year memo, dated April 20, 1950, was titled "Report to the Strategy Committee," referring to the national Republican Strategy Committee of which Coleman was a member. He was writing on behalf of party leader Art Summerfield of Michigan, who was recovering from a bout of pneumonia. Summerfield, who owned a major car dealership, was also active in party fund-raising, having devised a scheme whereby all Michigan car dealers would contribute to Republican coffers one dollar for each car sold. Summerfield would become chairman of the National Republican Committee in 1952, a reward for having delivered the votes of the Michigan delegation to Eisenhower at the party's national nominating convention.[16]

The Coleman memo urged support for Senator McCarthy's efforts, arguing that "bad security risks and unfit personnel in government departments has been established as a leading issue in the campaigns." As Coleman put it, "The New Dealers have been outmaneuvered, we believe, in their attempt to whitewash the State Department and to crawl out of a bad spot." Coleman described how he and Summerfield had been to Washington and "set up financial assistance for investigators, special counsel and publicity aides" to fuel the early witch hunts. They worked with the senatorial and congressional Republican committees. As members of the minority, the attacking Republican senators felt the need to expand their efforts beyond the resources available from government funds. Joe McCarthy, in his 1952 book, *McCarthyism: The Fight for America*, complained that the efforts of the Senate committee set up to investigate his disloyalty charges

Wisconsin Republican Tom Coleman, a supporter of and fundraiser for Senator Joe McCarthy, urged national Republicans to jump on the anti-homosexual band-wagon with McCarthy.
WHI IMAGE ID 34486

in early 1950 had initially been hampered because its Republican members had not been given a counsel. The bipartisan committee was chaired by Millard Tydings (D-MD, 1927–1951), who repeatedly demanded substantiation for McCarthy's allegations. Coleman and Summerfield were just the fund-raisers the Republicans needed to help in their battle. Some historians have noted Coleman's favorable reaction to McCarthy's efforts, but few have emphasized his provision of private resources at this key initial stage. McCarthy would continue to use his own agents outside official channels for years, while complaining, "I have a very limited staff of investigators."[17]

Coleman's strategy memo of April 1950 listed eleven important elements; number 7 was as follows: "The American people know from no less an authority than the Undersecretary of State and from the Washington Police Department that nearly 4000 homosexuals are employed in government departments." Coleman's final point made the strategy's intentions clear: "And best of all, we may get rid of many communist sympathizers and queers who now control policy." The memo reported that the Republican chairmen and vice chairwomen of nineteen Midwestern and Mountain states approved of the plan.[18]

Wisconsin's Coleman may have been adding to an already established myth about queers controlling foreign policy; the year 1950 saw Everett Dirksen of Illinois, for whom McCarthy campaigned, attacking the "Lavender Lads" in the State Department. However, David K. Johnson's recent academic work has shown that most of those actually discharged for homosexuality in the 1950s witch hunts were low-level clerks. There is, however, a possibility that Coleman may have known of rumors that the 1943 resignation of Sumner Welles, the undersecretary of state for Franklin Roosevelt, was due to Welles's homosexuality. Certain Republican senators associated with McCarthy were aware of the rumors about Welles, and the matter may have circulated more broadly in Republican circles before it was disclosed in the tabloid *Washington Confidential* in March 1956. In April 1950 McCarthy, as part of decrying those American diplomats who he believed were responsible for losing China to the communists (and Poland, too, for his Wisconsin voters), attacked the Institute of Pacific Relations, of which Welles was a member.[19]

Another McCarthy associate from Wisconsin was Urban Van Susteren, a personal friend and devoted supporter who later became an Outagamie

County judge. The two had met at Marquette Law School, and Joe McCarthy was best man at Van Susteren's wedding. Van Susteren helped manage McCarthy's 1946 Senate campaign. Later, in recalling the 1946 election, Van Susteren criticized Bob La Follette Jr. as "not cognizant of anything at all that's going on in the State Department." He continued, "There were a lot of homosexuals in the State Department, you know, for example that Sumner Wells [sic] was a very active homosexual." Van Susteren also observed, "A girlfriend for homosexuals is a boyfriend," implying that he did not consider gay men to be "real men." And he argued that gays recruited other homosexuals as fellow employees, commenting, "We had colonizing as it's called where they got all through the Department." Van Susteren knew personally of McCarthy's strong aversion to homosexuality. In a 1965 oral history interview, Van Susteren recalled having asked the senator, "What do you care if a man sucks someone else's cock?" McCarthy's response was a growl. Van Susteren would also later recall that "Joe really woke them up." He repeated the 1950s witch-hunt doctrine: "If you want to have the privilege of working for the government then conform to certain high standards, if you have a background that is undesirable you can't work for the government."[20]

Michael O'Brien, in his 1980 book *McCarthy and McCarthyism in Wisconsin*, asserted that state Republican leaders "seemed more concerned about McCarthy's charges that 'sex perverts' were employed in important government agencies than they were about Communists in the State Department." Noted Wisconsin political reporter and columnist John Wyngaard published his views on the McCarthy charges in the *Green Bay Press-Gazette* on April 26, 1950: "It is a curious fact in this connection that many rural politicians have reported there is more rank and file interest and concern about the revelation about homosexuality in government circles than about the more explosive issue about Communist sympathizers." The press reported about the mail McCarthy received after he made his initial charges: "Only a quarter of the twenty-five thousand writers expressed concern about 'red infiltration.'" The other three-quarters, the newspaper reported, "are expressing their shocked indignation at the evidence of sex depravity."[21]

A fellow Wisconsin Republican, Congressman Lawrence Smith of the First District in Racine, gave McCarthy credit in 1950 for action undertaken

by the Truman administration in regard to the State Department, saying, "Already his actions have flushed out homosexuals in that Department." Senator Styles Bridges (R-NH, 1937–1961), while critical of some
of McCarthy's methods, told a Wisconsin audience, "A man doesn't have
to be a spy or Communist to be a bad security risk. He can be a drunkard
or a criminal or a homosexual." One Wisconsin admirer of McCarthy's
witch hunts was John Chapple of the *Ashland Daily Press*, who had tried
unsuccessfully to expose Reds and gays in Wisconsin in the 1930s. Chapple
believed historians would remember McCarthy as "the most courageous
American."[22]

Arthur Herman, in something of a modern apologia, wrote the 2000
book *Joseph McCarthy: Reexamining the Life and Legacy of America's Most
Hated Senator*. He suggested that the reader should decide whether material now disclosed from the Soviet archives on actual Russian spying in
America might provide "vindication for McCarthy" on communists' presence in the US government in the 1950s. Even Herman, however, seemed
to be reluctant to fully endorse McCarthy's implication that Secretary of
State Dean Acheson had his own reason for shielding homosexuals and
other "perverts" in the State Department. "People . . . were horrified by
this assault," Herman pointed out, "just as today we can be horrified by
his and Kenneth Wherry's efforts to drive homosexuals out of sensitive
government jobs." Thus, even a more contemporary, McCarthy-friendly
voice has given belated acknowledgment to the reality that gays were on
McCarthy's target list.[23]

In His Own Words

While McCarthy's aim was primarily at communists and liberal sympathizers, especially the "China hands," who he claimed had lost China to
the Reds, he also targeted gays over an extended time. In advance of his
1952 election campaign, McCarthy authored *McCarthyism: The Fight for
America*, posing and answering questions about his crusade.

In response to the question, "How many sex deviates have been removed from the State Department?" McCarthy answered: ninety-one
prior to 1950 and fifty-four since that time. Yet, he elaborated by quoting
from the report of the Tydings Committee (his emphasis):

In most of those cases these known homosexuals were allowed to resign for 'personal reasons,' and no information was placed in the regular personnel files of the State Department indicating the real reason for resignation nor was the Civil Service Commission informed of the true reason for the resignation. . . . *Due to the manner in which these cases were mishandled, 23 of those 91 State Department employees found their way into other departments of government.*[24]

The next question he posed to himself was, "Do you claim that sex deviates removed from the State Department were all disloyal?" The answer: "No, but all are considered security risks. One reason why sex deviates are considered by all intelligence agencies of the government to be security risks is that they are subject to blackmail. It is a known fact that espionage agents often have been successful in extorting information from them by threatening to expose their abnormal habits." McCarthy continued (his emphasis), "*In addition to the security question, it should be noted that individuals who are morally weak and perverted and who are representing the State Department in foreign countries certainly detract from the prestige of this nation.*"[25]

Still addressing the question about disloyalty, McCarthy wrote:

The Special Senate Investigating Committee had this to say about the high percentages of sex deviates in government. [The homosexual has a] tendency to gather other perverts about him. Eminent psychiatrists have informed the subcommittee that the homosexual is likely to seek his own kind because the pressures of society are such that he feels uncomfortable unless he is with his own kind. Due to this situation the homosexual tends to surround himself with other homosexuals, not only in his social but in his business life. Under these circumstances, if a homosexual attains a position in government where he can influence the hiring of personnel, it is almost inevitable that he will attempt to place other homosexuals in government jobs.[26]

By publishing these Senate report passages, McCarthy circulated his charges to a much larger audience than were ever likely to read the report itself. Clearly, for the junior senator from Wisconsin, gays did not belong in government jobs. And he firmly believed that too many were already so employed.

Exploring the dimensions of McCarthy and his attitude toward homosexuals offers some strange twists. When he first arrived in Washington, he hired a young UW graduate to handle veterans' affairs. After the former student was arrested as a homosexual, McCarthy fired him. Yet, he later kept Roy Cohn, a closeted homosexual, as an aide. McCarthy even vigorously defended Cohn's work after some public hints emerged about his homosexuality.[27]

Ironically, when assisting the senator during his investigating the US Army, Cohn accused the army of providing "a map and offering up Air Force and Navy installations where homosexual officers could be found in order to steer suspicion away from the Army." In the formal hearings, John Adams, counsel for the army, denied Cohn's charge that the army had offered to trade "bigger bait" for the special treatment for Private David Schine, a McCarthy staffer. Many have supposed that Cohn was smitten with Schine. Adams insisted the army was not trying to deflect the suspicions about the army by offering homosexuals for investigation. Rather, he said, the army itself was investigating "some very serious allegations with reference to homosexual behavior on the part of a group of Army officers at a large base in the South." The army's hearings revealed the ways that McCarthy's encouragement of attacks on gays could affect even his own staff in the witch hunts.[28]

McCarthy's book contained repeated attacks on "perverts" as security risks; ultimately, however, he was all too willing to employ homosexuals when it served his purposes.

FORGETTING THE LAVENDER SCARE

The McCarthy-era witch hunt against gays is generally lost not only to national memory but also to Wisconsin memory, where McCarthy's presence is otherwise strongly remembered by both foes and friends. In 2009, Mike Miller of the *Capital Times* staff wrote a lengthy feature piece that appeared in the September 16–22 issue, "Bringing Down a Demagogue: The Cap Times Never Wavered in Its Fight against Joe McCarthy." Miller extolled the role of William T. Evjue, the paper's editor, but was completely quiet about homosexuals as victims of the witch hunts. William F. Thompson, in the sixth volume of *The History of Wisconsin: Continuity and Change, 1940–1965*, published in 1988, extensively covered the attacks on Reds and Tom Coleman's general involvement with McCarthy. But there is never a mention of gays as victims or the attacks on sexual perversion. Thompson was a personal friend of mine, and he even contacted me about whether gay rights advocates were active in the state by 1970, the book's informal cutoff date, because he wanted to include something on the gay struggle. But the McCarthy memory for him and so many others, myself included at the time, was that only the Reds and seeming liberal political sympathizers, often referred to as "fellow travelers," were attacked.[29]

As late as 2011, Jeremi Suri, the noted historian who was then E. Gordon Fox Professor at the University of Wisconsin–Madison, wrote a blog post titled "The New McCarthyism?" Suri drew a parallel between Joe McCarthy and Scott Walker, Wisconsin's governor since 2011. Yet, he failed to mention homosexuals and the role they played in McCarthyism. Contextualizing McCarthy as someone with Midwestern roots, Suri wrote, "He attacked the most vulnerable figures who had the weakest connections to small town politics: Jews, Hollywood celebrities, intellectuals, and government civil servants. . . . The outlaws, for McCarthy, were the national and international organizations that small town Americans distrusted most of all: the unions, the university professors, and of course, the communists." Thus, though he listed seven categories of victims attacked by the witch-hunting Wisconsin senator, even this distinguished historian failed to include gays.[30]

THE PROGRESSIVE: A CASE STUDY

When McCarthy began his witch hunt in 1950, *The Progressive* magazine, published in Madison, began immediately to cover the spectacle. Hardly an issue over the next five years did not mention the senator, McCarthyism, or those who were standing up to McCarthyism. Editorials referred to the senator as a demagogue, a bully, and a character assassin, and to his methods as totalitarian techniques and a game of smear. A July 1950 editorial opined, "The Progressive has nothing but contempt for McCarthy's motive and methods, and the broadside smear he employs."[31]

The magazine was the successor to *La Follette's Weekly*, which had been renamed *The Progressive* in 1929. The La Follettes' decision to stop publishing in 1948 raised a hue and cry, and staff under the former editor, Morris Rubin, reorganized the publication as a nonprofit. Rubin continued his editorship throughout this period. Though pitched to a national audience, *The Progressive* maintained a special relationship with Wisconsin and Madison, and with the founder and crusading editor of the *Capital Times* newspaper, William T. Evjue, a La Follette ally, who had preceded Rubin as *Progressive* editor. In April 1950, as editor and publisher of the *Capital Times*, Evjue went to the White House to discuss McCarthy with President Truman. The Wisconsinite reportedly told the president that McCarthy was "not a man to be setting a pattern of Americanism and patriotism for anybody." While in Washington, Evjue also met with progressive Wisconsin congressman Andrew Biemiller of Milwaukee, who is discussed later in this section.[32]

The Progressive first covered McCarthy's 1950 charges as a political news story. In the June 1950 issue, W. Neil Lowry wrote an influential article titled "Hit and Run—How It Works." At the time, Lowry, a former associate editor of the *Dayton Daily News*, was chief Washington correspondent for the four Cox newspapers—the two major Atlanta papers and the two major Dayton papers. His article reviewed McCarthy's February speech in Wheeling, West Virginia, during which the senator waved a paper purportedly listing 205 members of the Communist Party who worked in the State Department, noting that he later lowered the number to 57 and changed the descriptions of those on the list from card-carrying Communist Party members to security risks. Lowry also reminded readers that although McCarthy had promised to share his list with the Tydings Committee, he never did so. Rather, the journalist reported, on March 14, McCarthy gave Tydings a list of twenty-five federal employees said to be "poor security risks." On the same day, he also submitted one name in private, "allegedly the name of a man formerly in the State Department and the Central Intelligence Agency who had a 'police record' for 'homosexuality.'"[33]

Lowry emphasized the fact that homosexuality was involved in the witch hunt charges. He mentioned an April 1950 *Meet the Press* broadcast and also another related gay item. Lowry wrote:

McCarthy took part in a debate started by Sen. William E. Jenner, Indiana Republican, in which Jenner took up a subject whispered in Washington for two months previously and already out in the open in the House—the subject of alleged homosexuality in Government service. Jenner proposed that Tydings "tell the Senator from Wisconsin [McCarthy] where the homos are, if the Senator from Wisconsin will tell the Senator from Maryland about the 57 card carrying Communists."[34]

Lowry's story shows the interplay between the witch hunts and homosexuality and how *The Progressive* portrayed this interaction in early coverage: "'I know there is a great desire to shift from Communists to homos,' Tydings replied. And as if to confirm the statement at once, Sen. McCarthy informed the Senate that the name he had given in secret to the Tydings Committee—presumably the one on Mar. 14—was a 'homosexual' with a police record, formerly in the State Department, and in the Central Intelligence Agency." "The debate ended," Lowry continued, "with Republican Minority Leader Kenneth Wherry of Nebraska, who had been making himself an authority on homosexuals for the past months, triumphantly informing the Senate that an agency head had just called to report the man named by McCarthy had 'finally resigned.'" Thus, in the beginning of *The Progressive*'s coverage of McCarthy's witch hunts, reporters made clear that the senator saw both Reds and gays as security risks to be eliminated from government.[35]

Not quite a year later, *The Progressive* ran an article titled "My Confessions to McCarthy" by Stringfellow Barr, a professor of classics and former president of St. John's College in Annapolis, Maryland, who in 1959 would join Eleanor Roosevelt and others in signing a petition to abolish the House Un-American Activities Committee. Barr started by sarcastically admitting, "I was myself a Creeping Socialist and . . . this ugly truth about myself had in fact been creeping over me for some months." Continuing in the sarcastic vein, he wrote: "And things are moving fast. Who would have believed a few short months ago that Secretary [of State Dean] Acheson and former Sen. Tydings were fellow travelers? Or that our State Department, and possibly our whole national life, were ultimately dominated by sex offenders?" Though the statement is not explicitly about homosexuals, Barr seemed to be using "sex offenders" as a synonym for homosexuals, since they were the only sex offenders really talked about in the security discussions.[36]

Barr tried to demonstrate the ridiculousness of McCarthy's anti-subversive witch hunts aimed at gays. He wrote, "So far as I could remember, I was not a sex offender; but, then, probably the sex offenders whom Sen. McCarthy found teeming in the State Department thought they were innocent too. If so, let 'em read Freud, and then ask themselves candidly how they know they are innocent. There must be droves of sex offenders, I decided, all in contact, all linked with Moscow, or at least with Tito." Here, Barr was poking fun at the concept of "pinko fags," sex perverts who supposedly served the communist cause. Some years later, the 1965 Jonathan Winters movie *The Loved One* would use the phrase "pinko pervert influence" to explain a character's avoidance of government programs. The award-winning movie, cowritten by the gay writer Christopher Isherwood, also features Wisconsin's Liberace as a fey casket salesman.[37]

After the Barr article, the mentions of homosexuals as targets of McCarthy's witch hunts disappear from the pages of *The Progressive*. Michael O'Brien believes this is because liberal and Democratic strategists decided not to meet McCarthy head-on about the witch hunts. McCarthy also acknowledged this in his 1952 book: "One of the safest and most popular sports engaged in today by every politician and office seeker is to 'agree with McCarthy's aim of getting rid of Communists in government,' but at the same time to 'condemn his irresponsible charges and shotgun technique.'" Not everyone was willing to kowtow. A Madison group dedicated to condemning McCarthy's tactics formed in 1951. *McCarthy and McCarthyism* author Michael O'Brien described the organization's work:

In February 1951, Miles McMillin and Morris Rubin, editor of *The Progressive* magazine (Madison), spearheaded the drive to establish The Wisconsin Citizens' Committee on McCarthy's Record. A small group, consisting mostly of former La Follette Progressives and liberal newspapermen, held research and editorial sessions throughout the year and began compiling a comprehensive and critical booklet on McCarthy's career. Rubin, the editor, insisted on "impeccable accuracy and factual reporting."

Yet the citizens' committee's efforts to expose the truth in order to influence Wisconsin's 1952 election campaign did not work. Aldric Revell, a socialist and columnist for the *Capital Times*, where McMillin also worked, felt the committee "has been a flop because it sought to fight emotionalism with rationalism." Revell felt many people had been so misled as to believe McCarthy was on the ballot running against Joe Stalin.[38]

The Progressive's editors had hoped Wisconsin voters would not reelect McCarthy in 1952. It was briefly rumored that Governor Walter Kohler Jr. might challenge him in a Republican primary, but this did not happen, and McCarthy buried Thomas Fairchild, the Democratic challenger, that year. In the lead-up to the election, the magazine had also begun publishing about more anticommunist hysterics, including other American loyalty fanatics, such as US senator Pat McCarran (D-NV, 1933–1954). Editorials even criticized the Truman administration for not effectively dealing with the loyalty issue, despite Truman's 1950 statement: "The greatest asset that the Kremlin has is Senator McCarthy." Though the anti-McCarthy effort failed to prevent McCarthy's reelection, the 1952 votes for the witch-hunting senator in Wisconsin ran well behind Dwight Eisenhower's percentage and also that of the popular Kohler, who won reelection as governor.[39]

Senator McCarran had been a chief proponent of the Internal Security Act of September 1950, which required communist organizations and their members to register with the US Attorney General. Individuals in these groups could be barred from government employment and subjected to travel restrictions, including the cancellation of passports. *The Progressive* viewed the act as an infringement of civil liberties. Writing to Congress, UW law professor William G. Rice observed, "Decisions as to employment should always be on the basis of individual character and ability—like decisions as to innocence or guilt of crime." He also attacked the vague standards of the bill, which could be abused by a senator like McCarthy, calling him out by name. In the March 1950 Senate debate, Wisconsin's other senator, Republican Alexander Wiley, spoke in favor of McCarran's bill. Opponents argued that the measures were similar to the discredited Alien and Sedition Acts of the eighteenth century.[40]

One vigorous opponent of the bill in the House was Wisconsin congressman Andrew Biemiller of Milwaukee. Biemiller had been the editor of

During the witch hunts of the 1950s, Senator Alexander Wiley (left) supported the Internal Security Act requiring communist party members to register with the US government, while Congressman Andrew Biemiller (right) opposed it.
WHI IMAGE ID 141106, WHI IMAGE ID 141105

the *Milwaukee Leader*, the socialist paper, from 1934 to 1936 and had been elected to the state legislature in 1936 as a Progressive. In the late 1940s he had served two nonconsecutive terms in Congress as a Democrat. Although he stated he was not opposed to measures to "check the growth of communism and curb communist conspiracy," Biemiller thought McCarran's bill "could be used for a bad form of thought control, an un-American practice in itself." Nevertheless, in 1950 the bill passed both houses by wide margins. President Truman vetoed the measure in September of that year, asserting that it "would seriously damage the [federal government's] security and intelligence operations." (Later, in an oral history, Truman would recall, "There was a lot of hysteria at the time, why that is all the more reason the President has to speak out for what is right.") However, the veto was overridden, with Biemiller casting the only Wisconsin vote against both the original passage and in support of Truman's veto.[41]

Essentially, *The Progressive* waged a campaign against McCarthyism for four years, charging that its excesses were best countered by a vigorous "Americanism." The editors defended civil liberties and the right to a free political society, safe from witch hunts. But the magazine did not defend the supposed Communists or homosexuals who were the targets of McCarthy's charges. After all, in 1948, the magazine had refused to support the Progressive Party's presidential candidate, Henry Wallace, in part because of his Communist backers. Defending homosexuals who were technically seen as criminals in all fifty states also did not appear to be a promising strategy for the magazine.

After Stringfellow Barr's March 1951 article, the attacks on homosexuals disappeared from the pages of *The Progressive* for the rest of the McCarthy period. By focusing its energy on criticizing the attackers, the publication challenged McCarthy's methods, but not his goals. In the February 1954 article "McCarthyism under the Microscope," Stuart Chase laid out seven major questions, none of which address the rights of those attacked by McCarthy. Chase also tied the Wisconsin senator to Stalin and to Torquemada of the Spanish Inquisition. But he said nothing about the other earlier scapegoats, the homosexuals.[42]

In April 1954, *The Progressive* dedicated its forty-fifth-anniversary issue to "the people of the United States of America who share our determination to make the principles of democracy prevail over communism and McCarthyism." The issue, entitled "McCarthy: A Documented Record," was the longest the magazine had ever printed; in addition, thousands of extra copies were run off to allow broad distribution, beyond the subscribers. The issue repeated the story that Communist-influenced CIO unions in Milwaukee supported McCarthy and voted for him in the 1946 Wisconsin primary, while also highlighting the senator's questionable financial dealings. The anniversary issue did mention some of McCarthy's victims—more established figures he had attacked recently, such as General Douglas MacArthur, Secretary of State George C. Marshall, and various members of the mainline Protestant clergy—but it did not mention gays. Later in May 1954, the Most Reverend Bernard J. Sheil, auxiliary bishop of Chicago, wrote an article on "The Immorality of McCarthyism" that focused on supporting democratic American traditions such as the presumption of innocence until proven guilty. This was another example of the magazine supporting Americanism against McCarthy's tactics, but not defending those attacked.[43]

Also in 1954, while McCarthyism still seemed ascendant, the Wisconsin Democratic platform took an anticommunist tack, though one quite

In attempting to take down Senator Joe McCarthy, *The Progressive* created a special issue that was widely circulated. WHI IMAGE ID 48076

different from McCarthy's: "We are proud that the Democratic Party has struck at the roots of Communism with constructive economic and social policies. . . . Today in the name of anti-communism, political opportunists seek to impose a sterile conformity of thought and action upon traditionally free men." Such tactics could only have bad results, they argued. "With the principle of 'Guilt by association' and the method of 'Character assassination,'" the Democrats continued, "[these political opportunists] seriously threaten the liberty of thought, of expression and of assembly that has made America strong." Again, in this strategy, the political nature of the witch hunts was attacked, but the victims were ignored.[44]

In November 1954, with a Senate proposal to censure McCarthy pending, an editorial in *The Progressive* raised the question, "Is This the End of McCarthy?" The piece argued that "the decisive factor in the shaping of public opinion was McCarthy's own conduct." The editorial also included phrases from the Senate's own committee report on McCarthy's conduct, calling it "inexcusable," "contumacious," "reprehensible," "vulgar," and "insulting." Thus, the strategy of criticizing McCarthy's methods worked for *The Progressive* in that the magazine made a major contribution to the general attack on McCarthyism, but the forgotten homosexuals who were attacked during the witch hunt would find that cold comfort.[45]

MORE ANTI-HOMOSEXUALISM

Senator McCarthy was not Wisconsin's only legislator to attack homosexuals during this period. Alexander Wiley of Chippewa Falls, the state's senior US senator, did so as well. At the same time that the Eisenhower administration was preparing to take power in January 1953, *ONE*, the first widely distributed national publication for homosexuals, began printing on the West Coast. Rodger Streitmatter, in *Unspeakable: The Rise of the Gay and Lesbian Press in America*, describes *ONE* as a public communication for favorable ideas on homosexuals, which gave a voice to the incipient social movement. The job of trying to shut it down would fall to the US Post Office and Eisenhower's postmaster general, Art Summerfield, the old friend of Tom Coleman. *ONE* magazine characterized Summerfield as "that intrepid, filth-hunting crusader from the GOPork-barrel."[46]

The Los Angeles postal authorities "vetted each issue [of *ONE*] before deciding whether it was legal to ship under the Post Office's stringent anti-obscenity standards." The circulation of the August 1953 issue, with a cover feature on homosexual marriage, was held up while Washington was consulted but was finally released. Senator Wiley jumped on the antigay effort with a letter to Postmaster General Summerfield in 1954. Wiley, who had somehow acquired a copy of *ONE*, registered a "vigorous protest against the use of the United States mails to transmit a so-called 'magazine' devoted to the advancement of sexual perversions." Permitting the magazine to use the mails, Wiley wrote, "(a) runs utterly contrary to every moral principle, (b) runs utterly contrary to our intentions to safeguard our nation's youngsters, (c) likewise, it is the very opposite of the entire purpose of our governmental security program." Streitmatter called Wiley "the first member of Congress—many would follow him in future decades—to attack the lesbian and gay press."[47]

Wiley Plans to Bolster Anti-Pornography Laws

WASHINGTON ⑭ — Sen. Wiley (R-Wis) said today present anti-pornography laws are "shockingly inadequate" and that he plans to introduce legislation in the next Congress to tighten them.

"Present statutes barring lewd material from the mails are grossly inadequate to protect our youngsters," he said.

As an illustration, Wiley cited to a reporter a recent letter he received from the post ofice department stating it did not have a legal basis to bar a magazine published at Los Angeles devoted to homosexuals.

WILEY EARLIER IN THE year had written Postmaster General Summerfield protesting use of the mails to transmit the magazine.

In that letter Wiley said that for anyone to use government fa-cilities for transmittal of "this type of material runs utterly contrary to every moral principle."

In the recent reply to Wiley's letter. Abe M. Goff. solicitor of the Post Office department. said the postmaster at Los Angeles had sent in specimen copies of the magazine that were not sent as sealed first class mail.

"THE SEVERAL ISSUES IN-volved have been carefully studied to determine the nature of their contents and whether or not they are such as to render them non-mailable under the provisions of the postal obscenity laws." Goff said.

Goff said the issues were devoted to the legal and social position of homosexuals and added:

"They have not contained matter of an obscene. lewd. lascivious or filthy character within the meaning of the said section of the law as those terms have been defined by the courts.

WAUKESHA DAILY FREEMAN, OCTOBER 11, 1954

In 1954, a US Post Office solicitor ruled that the magazine was primarily devoted to legal and social issues of homosexuals and thus not barred by existing law: "They have not contained matter of an obscene, lewd, lascivious or filthy character within the meaning of the said section of the law as those terms have been defined by the courts." However, in his responding AP news story, Wiley was indignant, concluding that the present laws against pornography were "shockingly inadequate" and stating his "plans to introduce legislation in the next Congress to tighten them." Several years later, in 1960, Dal McIntire wrote an article in *ONE* characterizing McCarthy's moral censors as "Vigilantes of the Dirty Mind," with their "hysterical moralizing [that] almost rivals the lunatic vigor of the late Jr. Senator from Wisconsin, now departed to happier witch-hunting grounds."[48]

In 1954, the US Post Office, perhaps encouraged by the congressional pressure to be vigilant, seized the October 1954 issue of *ONE* on the grounds of obscenity. Lesbian historian Lillian Faderman reported that the issue included "a short story about a woman choosing to become a lesbian, 'Sappho Remembered.'" The magazine took the matter to court but lost in federal district court and in the Ninth Circuit Court of Appeals. Yet, in the 1958 case of *One, Inc. v. Olesen* (Otto Olesen was the Los Angeles postmaster), the US Supreme Court reversed the lower court rulings without oral arguments, thus setting aside the postal authorities' censorship action. Senator Wiley's efforts to enlist the Post Office to suppress the national gay press failed and *ONE* continued its publication until 1967. Wiley would lose the 1962 election to popular Democratic governor Gaylord Nelson.[49]

DUCK AND COVER

What could Wisconsin gay folks do in the atmosphere of the 1950s? Some took the bomb-preparedness advice given to citizens in the atomic age: "Duck and cover." One reason for seeking cover was illustrated in journalist David Halberstam's book *The Fifties*. He quoted a crack made by McCarthy at an impromptu press conference: "If you want to be against McCarthy, boys, you've got to be a Communist or a cocksucker." Gay Wisconsinites do not appear to have drawn McCarthy's fire, but almost none were openly gay during this period. McCarthy's remark is interesting because it implies that he might see gays as more than just perverts or potential security risks, but actual opponents. Although McCarthy probably did not fear gays, he may have been labeling his opponents as homosexuals to try to discredit them.[50]

Nationally, those involved in the early homophile movement reacted to the period with what historian John D'Emilio calls the "retreat to respectability." One group that followed this model was the Mattachine Society, the first postwar gay organization. Founded in Los Angeles and later expanding to several chapters around the country, it grew out of a local effort to organize "Bachelors for Wallace," supporters of the 1948 leftist presidential candidate. The group might have seemed doubly suspect to McCarthy adherents, for both its leftist slant and the proclaimed nonnormative unmarried status in the organization's name. In 1953, during the McCarthy period, the Mattachine organization replaced many of its earliest leaders who had communist ties. It emphasized the contributions homosexuals had made and sought tolerance from the larger society.[51]

Another group whose actions during the period could be characterized as a "retreat to respectablility" was based in Madison. A Wisconsin feature article published on May 17, 1950, mentioned the regular Madison east side gathering Ted Pierce had termed a "salon." The article described "a group of friends that are conducting a noble experiment in living." After mentioning a wide range of topics discussed and foreign languages used among the participants, the author established the bona fides of the age: "Regardless of the language their [sic] are two subject[s] on which you will find complete accord; the rabble rousing communist must be eliminated from American society, and the deplorable state of contemporary living." Thus, the writer, a member of the group from a neighboring small town, used the cloak of correct political attitudes toward communism to affirm that the members of this group, though gay, were not subversives.[52]

Later, in the 1970s, Wally Jordan of Rhinelander and Milwaukee started writing again to his old friend Jim Kepner out in Los Angeles. Even in those years, he affected an instinctive anticommunist stance that most Wisconsin gays would have assumed throughout the McCarthy period. In a letter dated January 18, 1970, he asked Kepner whether the "Gay Lib Fronts are commie controlled, supported or infiltrated." He elucidated, "The reason I ask about commies is that I don't want to have anything to do with them, they could ruin everything, including the American Republic, and there would be no profit in contacting any gay groups who are connected with the commie idealism." Ironically, and apparently without Jordan's knowledge, Kepner had once joined the Communist Party.[53]

Milt Sherman, who had been a student at the University of Wisconsin in the late 1930s and had written about "homosexualism" in the *Daily Cardinal* (see chapter 4), had moved to Chicago by the 1950s. Sherman had a labor background and as part of his radical past had sided with the students who went on strike against the *Daily Cardinal* over campus politics. Now, in the McCarthy period, he "burned the midnight oil discussing what he was doing, and being scared." He claimed the McCarthy attacks caused anguish with both his "gay friends and Jewish friends."[54]

George Mosse, a liberal UW faculty member who had campaigned for Henry Wallace for president while at the University of Iowa, and who

As a young faculty member at the University of Wisconsin–Madison, George Mosse did not reveal his homosexuality.
UNIVERSITY OF WISCONSIN–MADISON ARCHIVES IMAGE S04576

opposed McCarthy, nevertheless was circumspect when it came to his private life. He wrote about inclusion and exclusion in his scholarly work, though he acknowledged the omission of homosexuals from his early publications. His discreet sex life was conducted in Europe and Israel during the McCarthy period and would remain so until the American sexual revolution of the late 1960s. Thus, this "retreat to respectability" was a tactic, not of denial but of stepping back.[55]

A FEARLESS LESBIAN

One woman who attended the University of Wisconsin refused to bow to fears of the McCarthy period. Though Lorraine Hansberry's lesbianism has only recently become well known, she contributed to the lesbian publication *The Ladder*, published by the early lesbian organization the Daughters of Bilitis. Hansberry came to UW–Madison as a student in 1948 and stayed until 1950. The campus influenced her in many ways. Since she registered late, no dorm housing was available. Luckily she found a spot in off-campus women's housing. Langdon Manor, at 140 Langdon Street, was run by housemother Ann Miller, and Hansberry was the first African American to live there, the only one among the thirty other women that year. Another off-campus women's housing option, Groves Coop, was actually noted for its integrated living at the time. Janet Tripp in *The Importance of Lorraine Hansberry* suggests Hansberry was isolated and overwhelmed by the large, predominantly white college.[56]

Hansberry was in the journalism and theater programs and involved with the Wisconsin Players. For their production of *Awake and Sing!* by the leftist playwright Clifford Odets, she was listed as part of the scenery technical crew. Years later, she recollected that a university theater production of *Juno and the Paycock* by Irish playwright Sean O'Casey inspired her to portray oppressed people and use their own language in dialogue. Defiant female characters were popular in Ibsen's plays, which were part of the campus theatrical culture. In 1959, less than ten years after Hansberry left Madison, her play *A Raisin in the Sun* opened on Broadway. This work, marked by the techniques the playwright had learned in Wisconsin, was an immediate success. On March 29, 1959, the *Wisconsin State Journal* ran a New York review that hailed Hansberry as "the toast of the town."[57]

Lorraine Hansberry (third row from bottom, second from right), pictured here with her housemates in 1948, was the first African American woman to live in Langdon Manor, an off-campus residence at the University of Wisconsin–Madison. UNIVERSITY OF WISCONSIN–MADISON ARCHIVES 2018S00096

While at Madison, Hansberry's involvement in leftist politics grew. On September 30, 1948, the Young Progressives of America registered a campus chapter with Hansberry as president. The group listed itself as political, social, and cultural with meetings held every other Thursday. Its prime focus was to elect former vice president Henry Wallace as president of the United States. It is possible associations with homosexuals existed. Across the country in California, a Bachelors for Wallace group of gay male supporters would become the nexus of the nation's first real homophile organization. And on campus, she may have known some gay men through the Wisconsin Players. While at the UW, Hansberry wrote a letter to the *Daily Cardinal* protesting racial discrimination. It would become an entry in her FBI file. After leaving Wisconsin, Hansberry moved to New York, met African American singer and leftist activist Paul Robeson, and worked on his *Freedom* newspaper. While in New York, she was associated with the Communist Party and married then separated from Robert Nemiroff, who had produced *Raisin*.[58]

Examining recent material in the "restricted box" of Hansberry's archive, scholar Kevin Mumford discovered a list of her favorite things, composed during her college years. She wrote that she liked "to look at a well dressed woman" and "deeply intelligent women." After separating from her husband, Hansberry began to be associated with the Daughters of Bilitis and New York lesbian circles. It is reputed that on a later visit to Madison she connected with campus lesbian figures.[59]

Elements of *A Raisin in the Sun* also suggest Hansberry's interest in lesbianism. For example, the character of the younger sister, Beneatha, who plans to be a doctor, says, "if I ever get married." The possibility that a woman might not marry a man stuns the family. At one point, Beneatha is urged to "go be a nurse like other women—or just get married and be quiet." Clearly, though, Hansberry did not envision this future for the high-spirited young woman. Additionally, the play drew its title from a poem by Langston Hughes, who is thought to have been gay.[60]

During the McCarthy years, Hansberry proudly campaigned for an inclusive future for the country. Shaped in part by her Wisconsin years, she did not duck and cover during the McCarthy era but continued to fight for progressive causes.

IKE AND JOE

Once Eisenhower was elected president in 1952 and Republicans gained a Senate majority, some Democrats viewed McCarthy as a problem for the Republicans to handle. McCarthy was not placed in charge of the powerful Internal Security Subcommittee; rather, he became the chairman of the Committee on Government Operations, presumed unimportant by most senators and congressional leaders. However, McCarthy found his power base when he appointed himself chairman of the Senate Permanent Subcommittee on Investigations. With a decorated Republican in the White House in 1953, some thought McCarthy might not attack the government's executive branch, but Fighting Joe did not stop his crusade. Before the new Congress was a month old, McCarthy was creating turmoil again in the State Department. He found two file clerks who testified that "department records had been rifled of damning evidence of communism and homosexuality." Though softening a bit, McCarthy in November 1953 praised the Eisenhower cabinet for removing "1,456 Truman holdovers who were . . . gotten rid of because of Communist connections and activities or perversion."[61]

The disastrous Army–McCarthy hearings in early 1954 marked the turning point in McCarthy's fortunes. Censured by a Senate vote of 67 to 22 on December 2, 1954, Joe McCarthy's political force was spent; he had in effect been condemned. Afterward, President Eisenhower purportedly quipped to his cabinet that McCarthyism now had become "McCarthywasm." The witch-hunting senator's legacy, however, was not so quickly buried.[62]

One result of the change in administrations was that Eisenhower issued Executive Order 10450 to replace Truman's loyalty program, which had also been established by executive order. The Truman order, which sought "unswerving loyalty" to America, had been clearly aimed at "disloyal or subversive" persons in the federal government. Truman's standards were focused on rooting out those involved in sabotage, sedition, advocacy of revolution, disclosure of documents, serving the interests of another government, or membership in fascist or communist groups.[63]

The Eisenhower order, coming after McCarthy's two-pronged attack on commies and queers, broadened these categories considerably. Eisenhower's order defined a government employee as "unloyal" based on "any criminal, infamous, dishonest, immoral, or notoriously disgraceful conduct, habitual use of intoxicants to excess, drug addiction, or sexual perversion." This phrasing implicated not just those who got caught in a criminal sexual act, but also those with status as sexual perverts. The Eisenhower order aimed to establish that "persons privileged to be employed in the departments and agencies of Government, shall be reliable, trustworthy, of good conduct and character, and of complete and unswerving loyalty to the United States." Although the Truman order had applied only to the State Department and a few military agencies, the Eisenhower order applied to all federal employees. As David Halberstam noted in *The Fifties*, even as key players like Eisenhower prided themselves on being opposed to McCarthy, "they were still making significant accommodations to the norms he had established; a certain ugliness had entered America's bloodstream." After the witch hunts, a person's loyalty to America would no longer be as important as whether he or she was deemed suitable for employment by the heterosexual norms of the day.[64]

A Fear That Lingered

Joseph McCarthy died on May 2, 1957, and was buried in St. Mary's Cemetery in Appleton. His grave became a shrine to his most devoted followers. The loyalty scares, however, reverberated in state politics as late as September 1960. At that time, fifty-year-old Lieutenant Governor Philleo Nash, a Democratic cranberry grower from the Wisconsin Rapids area, was forced to defend himself against a smear campaign printed on pink handbills and based on old charges. The campaign had been started by a Wisconsin group called the National Action Movement, newly formed to fight "Communism, atheism, and agnosticism." In 1952, Senator McCarthy had listed Nash, then an aide to President Truman, in the *Congressional Record* materials as a former communist. The old, baseless charge resurfaced in 1960 as Nash sought reelection.[65]

To strike back, Nash released a letter signed by Donald Hansen in 1952. Hansen, then acting chairman of the White House loyalty board, gave Nash a complete security clearance, one of six such clearances Nash had received over the years. During his campaign, Nash also released a recent letter from former president Truman stating that he was "very sorry that gutter politics are making an appearance in Wisconsin." Truman wrote, "Your work for civil rights, for displaced persons, for the Point Four program, for American Indian affairs and for greater self-government in our territories and possessions was more effective in preventing the spread of communism than all of Joe McCarthy's wild accusations." Nash's narrow election victory in 1958, by 6,148 votes, had been part of a large Democratic sweep of all state offices, with Nash defeating then lieutenant governor Warren Knowles. Even though Democratic governor Gaylord Nelson and attorney general John Reynolds were reelected in 1960, Warren Knowles, who had served in the post from 1954 to 1958, won back the lieutenant governorship and later went on to serve three terms as Wisconsin governor. Communist accusations could still sway an election, even in 1960.[66]

The Naming of Names

During the McCarthy period, one of the most instructive critiques of witch hunts was Arthur Miller's 1953 play *The Crucible*. The play is ostensibly about the witch trials in seventeenth-century Salem, in the Massachusetts Bay Colony, yet the narrator references the twentieth century in Act I: "While there were no witches then, there are Communists and capitalists now, and in each camp there is certain proof that spies of each side are at work undermining the other." In the play, the witch hunters urge those being investigated to "name the names" of others who practice witchcraft. The chief character, John Proctor, refuses to do so, saying, "I like not to spoil their names." Similarly, in 1956 when playwright Miller was questioned by congressional investigators, he refused to name names and was cited for contempt. In the play, Miller's narrator also notes, "Our opposites are always robed in sexual sin, and it is from this unconscious conviction that demonology gains both its attractive sensuality and its capacity to infuriate and frighten." Although McCarthy himself never articulated such an illuminating connection between his charges and their sexual undertones, he clearly understood the tactic. This naming of names during the witch hunts unfortunately was used in one of the ugliest legacies of the McCarthy period in Wisconsin.[67]

The University of Wisconsin–Madison was largely spared from McCarthy's attacks, but some there seemingly learned the investigatory style of the witch hunts. The attitude of some at the UW toward the senator became apparent on May 13, 1951, when Joe McCarthy spoke to an audience made up primarily of students at the Madison campus. The *Capital Times* headline was "Local Audience Jeers at McCarthy 'Proofs,'" and the *Milwaukee Journal* headline read "UW Students Boo McCarthy." His speech, sponsored by the campus Young Republicans, drew only seven hundred to the Union Theater, which seated thirteen hundred. John Patrick Hunter in the *Capital Times* also reported that several hours after the senator's speech, a thousand people turned out in the same space to hear New York columnist Max Lerner "flay McCarthy." Lerner described the 1950s as "the age of the snoop." Lerner's speech was sponsored by the student-based Union Forum Committee after a faculty committee denied funding, concerned because Lerner had been named on a list as a communist. The columnist flatly denied the charge, claiming to be only a liberal. He received a standing ovation at the end of his talk.[68]

McCarthy, for his part, had provoked his audience to laughter by equating the great generalship of Douglas MacArthur with that of Genghis

Khan. When he called the *Capital Times* the "Madison edition of the *Daily Worker*," the audience booed. During the question-and-answer period, the senator denied having called President Truman "a drunken sot" but did remark that Truman "makes so many decisions late at night after one or two cocktails." There was no love lost between the president and the senator. Truman thought McCarthy a "ballyhoo artist." In a later reminiscence, the former president called him "a no-good son of a bitch" and a "coward." "A man like that—it's like a sickness," he stated. The question and answer period for McCarthy's Union speech was cut short after several sharp barbs when the senator claimed he had to catch a plane, provoking more audience laughter.[69]

Also revealing was an incident in which the university administration refused to bow to McCarthyism. James Wechsler, who was then the Washington correspondent for *The Progressive* magazine, reported on the incident in the June 1953 issue. Wechsler had had his own experience of a seventy-minute grilling in the witness chair by Senator McCarthy. Regarding the University of Wisconsin, Wechsler wrote, "To its everlasting credit it generated little of the hysteria that swept other campuses when McCarthy was riding high." For proof, he cited a letter from G. E. Sipple, commander of the Wisconsin Department of the American Legion, to E. B. Fred several months earlier, urging the UW president to ban the Labor Youth League as well as any speakers with a record of communist support, and suggesting that the campus check publications to see if they had been denied entry to the country. Fred's response was a defense of academic freedom:

> Because students must be convinced that they have the freedom
> and responsibility equal to citizens outside the university, we do not
> enact, and would oppose, restrictions on discussion and inquiry other
> than those applicable to all citizens in the state. . . . The University
> of Wisconsin supports the principles of American democracy by
> demonstrating faith in them. "Faith in freedom, not fear of freedom,
> is the American heritage."[70]

Yet as late as 1962, the witch-hunt atmosphere would crumble the shield of civil liberties for gays at the university. Journalist and early gay activist Ron McCrea did some of the first work uncovering what became known as the "Gay Purge." The purge, which McCrea characterized as "a full scale inquisition," ran from late 1961 to early 1962 and was led by the Department of Protection and Security as well as the dean of men. In a 1977 article for a local gay publication, McCrea stated that UW officials interviewing a gay man during the purge had "asked him for the names and other pertinent information about all the gay men that this man knew." Then they called in the other named individuals and asked if they would provide "further information such as other people you know in the community who are gay." By the end, the compiled list of names was thought to number "at least a couple of hundred," and there were indications the total was perhaps as high as six hundred. These efforts were explicitly described by those who survived the purge as "McCarthyistic tactics, snooping around and hearsay."[71]

The man whose story McCrea related for the *Renaissance Newsletter* of the Madison Gay Center had been a sophomore when university officials interviewed him. Gay editor George Stambolian, a writer and French scholar who was a graduate student at the time, also described his experiences years later. The police reports from the Gay Purge that survive are different from earlier police reports dealing with homosexuals. In those earlier years, the campus police usually caught gay individuals in compromising situations, or someone brought specific homosexual allegations about a student to officials' attention. In the 1961–1962 school year, the police reports show that campus police called in individuals for interviews, presumably identifying suspects from the lists of names. The reports state that many of the men being interviewed "conceded being implicated" or "readily admitted homosexual relations with several of the principals." In one particular case a student supposedly admitted that he "just took up with the 'Gay Circle' for a lark." Thus, the police knew they had a homosexual network to sweep up. Another student discipline report stated, "As near as can be determined Mr. W—— has always been discreet and careful in his conduct." So, mere homosexual status, not flagrant conduct, now clearly appeared to be a basis for disciplinary action.[72]

Some gay men brought in because their names were on the list would deny their homosexuality. According to one of the purge survivors, the sentiment was, "You had to lie your way out of it. . . . You couldn't talk to your parents because you were in the closet as far as they were concerned. . . . We were even afraid of each other for a while. There was a feeling of paranoia." One man changed his hair to make it short and neat because, as he said, "I didn't want to look like a fairy."[73]

A 2013 senior research paper by Madison undergraduate Gina Slesar linked UW's Gay Purge to McCarthyism, calling it "the hidden scar of a liberal institution." She noted "its lack of mention in published histories" of the university. Slesar also reported that the office of the dean of students was split by gender at that time, with a dean of men, Theodore Zillman, and a dean of women, Martha Peterson. Yet, the purge was conducted only on the male side. Martha Peterson, who went on to be the distinguished president of Beloit College, would later be known as a lesbian and lived with her longtime partner. She had no interest in the purge or Zillman's authoritarian style. Within four years of the purge, Peterson was commenting in the press, "It was inevitable that the university should move away from close supervision of a student's private life." Officer Peter Rordam of campus police led the investigations of the men's cases. It was the campus police force that also had ignited the 1948 scandal about homosexual students.[74]

Zillman recalled saying, "We can't allow admitted homosexuals on this campus." After the purge, in a letter to his secretary, Ruth Doyle, Dean Zillman summarized his views of both his and the university's roles in students' lives. He saw it as his responsibility to (emphasis by Zillman) "make [each student] *a moral, intelligent and well-informed citizen with a deep sense of his obligation to the community.*" He continued, "We are in the business of training good members of society. . . . The socially conscious man observes the law. . . . This is the lesson which I think the University has a compelling obligation to impart." Embracing the enforcement of Wisconsin law regarding homosexual acts did not necessarily make Zillman a McCarthyite. In fact, in the year of the purge, Zillman wrote to the dean of students, LeRoy Luberg, with some advice about the Socialist Club sponsoring a proposed speech by US Communist Party leader Gus Hall. Zillman's advice was, "Let the rascal speak."[75]

Slesar's research and a review of minutes of the Student Conduct Committee show that the 1962 purge was not a complete aberration from the norm. Disciplinary actions against gays had continued throughout the

Theodore Zillman, the UW–Madison dean of men, in 1954. WHI IMAGE ID 89358

1950s. In one 1959 incident, Madison city police arrested a first-year student for hugging and kissing another man in Vilas Park. The police advised him to seek medical attention and released him but also notified officials on campus. The student was suspended and not allowed to register for future semesters because he refused to seek psychiatric treatment. The overall 1959 student conduct report noted that "cases of sexual offenses and gross immorality" represented the second-most common reason that the university dropped a student from the university.[76]

The Gay Purge of 1962 represented a more systemic approach than had been previously attempted. At the time, the office of the dean of men kept a file labeled "H.S. [Homosexual] Problem File." The purge was hidden from view because administrators did not want the public or state government to know that a large number of homosexuals attended the university. When campus police called students in and told them they had been charged with homosexuality, they also told the students they would receive lighter punishment if they offered up names of some other homosexual students. The campus police were able to make these offers pursuant to an agreement with Dane County district attorney William D. Byrne.

This was explained by Mr. A. D. Hamman, head of protection and security, and Officer Rordam at the April 17 meeting of the Student Conduct Committee.[77]

Rordam explained to those accused of being homosexual that the district attorney was willing to permit the university to handle their cases to the extent that the student cooperated; but he said he could promise no such immunity to any student who refused to provide assistance. The campus also had an agreement in place starting in the fall of 1961 that routed "city police reports involving students through the Department of Protection and Security."[78]

Some students provided names when they were asked. George Stambolian recalled, "What is frightening in all of this is I have another friend who was told [']you have slept with these five people[']—and he was given the names of the five people who had signed statements saying they had sexual relations with him. Now, this man had sexual relations with a great many people, but not those five, as it turned out." Apparently, because Stambolian's friend was a well-known gay person, others felt they could name him rather than perhaps others who were lesser known. Stambolian was forced to leave campus, went on to study at the Sorbonne, and later wrote for gay magazines and taught as a professor of French. In the introduction to his book *Male Fantasies/Gay Realities*, Stambolian noted, "The calendar of historical events does not always coincide, of course, with the calendar of personal events, and it is the latter that receive the greatest attention." For him, the McCarthy era of the 1950s had affected his personal calendar all the way up to 1962.[79]

As a result of the Gay Purge, many UW students were expelled. One suicide attempt by wrist slashing was reported and investigated by Madison police. One individual was forced to resign from the University Hospital under threat of firing. Others were stripped of academic funding such as fellowships and withdrawn from teaching assistantships. Since the earlier days of 1948, an administrative section of the committee had decided most disciplinary matters. Now, the administrative section regularly recommended "to the appropriate departments that the University not offer . . . a subsidy in the form of appointments such as teaching assistant, etc." This indirectly forced many graduate students from school as a result of financial pressure. Of course, it meant that more people on campus knew of their difficulties, as well. Some were told not to bother finishing their degrees. A cloud descended over the network of gay individuals at the university.[80]

Many feared that things were getting out of hand and that perhaps gay faculty might also be named. The minutes of the Student Conduct Committee of February 21, 1962, reveal that Dean Zillman placed matters on the agenda that he "felt deserved full committee attention," rather than allowing these to be chosen by the administrative section. The topics on this particular meeting's list included a "committee review of its attitude toward the homosexual student, the window peeper, the exhibitionist, etc." It is notable that two items on this list involve explicit acts—peeping and exhibitionism—while homosexuals came under scrutiny of the committee simply based on an element of their identity.[81]

On April 3, 1962, the committee heard the case of an accused homosexual student who was awaiting his doctorate. In his appeal, the student claimed that the administrative section had "erred in its finding of fact that his past homosexual activity was indicative of a continuing emotional problem." He said the experience with the administrative section had "done him no good," and "the anxiety, guilt, loss of productive effort, etc. that it had produced were certainly of no benefit to him as he saw it." A statement by Dr. Jerome Szymanski, a resident in the Department of Psychiatry of Student Health, assisted the Student Conduct Committee deliberations. Szymanski suggested to the committee "that deviant or homosexual behavior, per se, is not necessarily evidence of homosexuality." One result was that the committee agreed "to discuss the general policy questions presented by the case here appealed."[82]

Dr. Herman Gladstone of Student Health, who headed the Psychiatric Division, played a key role in eventually shutting down the purge. In comments to the Student Conduct Committee, he criticized the "unethical way" that homosexual students were brought to the university's attention. One student who had ignored requests for a Rordam interview complained he was "dragged out" of work at the campus hospital. The minutes of April 12, 1962, record, "Dr. Gladstone refused to remain a party to normal committee-department procedure apparently because of objections to the investigation and his staff's conviction that effective evaluation under stress circumstances was not possible."[83]

Things came to a head at this April 12 committee meeting, chaired by Frank Remington of the law school. Other faculty members were present, whereas faculty were not part of the administrative section procedures. Minutes show that Dean Zillman recounted the history of the committee's handling of cases involving homosexual or deviant behavior. He felt the involvement of Student Health was "an evaluative aid." However, he acknowledged a "recent breakdown in this procedure culminating in that department's refusal to present the committee with evaluations in several cases now being considered." Since the inauguration of the campus procedure of therapeutic discipline, students suspected of homosexual orientation were sent to Student Health for an evaluation and treatment, and doctors at Student Health had been sending back many opinions that individuals were not really homosexuals or were susceptible to a cure. In these cases, the students could safely remain on campus and continue their education.[84]

Dean Zillman's file labeled "H.S. Problem," his code for "homosexual problem," contained a document with a handwritten list of seventeen names and several columns. One column shows four names as "determined by" Dr. Gladstone. Another column shows most of the names "determined by TZ"—that is, by Zillman himself, who had no medical qualifications for undertaking such a task. Another list in the H.S. Problem file lists thirteen individuals with all but one marked as "confessed."[85]

At the April 12 meeting, Dean Zillman and Dean of Students LeRoy Luberg presented the matter of the H.S. problem. They "reviewed the background of the present investigation—its beginnings, development, and cessation." After "considerable discussion," the minutes stated,

> The committee seemed to reach general agreement that the University, in exercise of its disciplinary authority, should not be concerned with the homosexual orientation of a student, per se, any more than it is concerned with another student's heterosexual orientation. Instead it is activity, be it heterosexual or homosexual, which properly might subject a student to disciplinary action.[86]

This was an important step forward in the equal treatment of gays on campus, but caveats remained. Despite having decided that homosexual orientation alone should not warrant disciplinary action, the "committee seemed to agree also that the fact of a student's homosexual orientation might well be of concern to the school or college granting him a degree and thereby certifying to his good character." A handwritten note in the H.S. Problem file specified the university's particular concern with students training to be teachers. Additionally, the committee seemed to come to "a general consensus that the 'recruiting' aspect of homosexual behavior was a matter of particular concern to the institution and ought to be met directly." Of course, the use of the word *recruiting* reflects the committee's fundamental misunderstanding of homosexuality.[87]

At the next meeting, on April 17, the committee sought to establish a consistent policy with the Department of Protection and Security. The head of security, Mr. Hamman, appeared conflicted by dual responsibilities to the university and the district attorney because of the existing agreement between the Dane County district attorney, William D. Byrne, and the campus police. Officer Rordam "explained that he had pursued the investigation of suspects only when they had been named by two or more interviewees. Further, he had asked interviewees for the names of others with whom they had personal involvement as well as those whom they thought or believed to be homosexuals." A faculty member "questioned the desirability of actively seeking hearsay information; Officer Rordam suggested the real need for such testimony in order to permit continued investigation."[88]

Dean Zillman reported "that he, as an agent of the committee, had requested and received only the names of those students who had confessed to homosexual activity." Dean Luberg reported that he, "acting as agent of the president, had received the entire list of names and had carefully referred them to appropriate University officers." The minutes note, "There appeared also to be some question over the appropriateness of preparing a list of names compiled from hearsay or unverified evidence." Some in the room likely felt the echoes of Senator McCarthy's witch hunts and his waving of lists.[89]

Ultimately, the committee did come to a sort of conclusion. The secretary recorded:

> After considerable discussion, it appeared that possible disagreement
> existed over the extent to which enforcement in these cases should be

pressed—over the aggressiveness which the University should display in uncovering homosexuality. Several committee members seem agreed that, with the exceptions of the professional homosexual, the assaultive student, the "recruiter" and the activity producing public display or embarrassment, the university investigative role here need properly be no more intensive or vigorous than is the case with enforcement directed toward illicit heterosexual activity.[90]

After the committee's April deliberations, homosexual cases continued to be reported at the university, yet they were handled differently. Many accused students were granted permission to reenter the university after submitting character recommendations from their pastors. Dr. Seymour Halleck, who became head of the Department of Psychiatry at Student Health in the fall of 1962, regularly provided a statement regarding gay students stating, "it does not appear that he is a danger either to himself or to the University Community." Halleck would later be part of the change in the wider psychiatric profession working to remove homosexuality as a mental disorder in the early 1970s. By the time the American Psychiatric Association dropped homosexuality as a mental disease in 1973, many students viewed as sick had been forced to leave the university.[91]

RISING ABOVE MCCARTHYISM

As noted earlier, Martha Peterson did not contribute to the Gay Purge on the UW campus. She considered Dean Zillman rigid and authoritarian and later recalled doing battle with him, often voting in opposition to him at disciplinary committee meetings. Peterson did not agree with the university acting in loco parentis, as she took a more mature view of students as young adults. In her oral history, Peterson recalls using professors to influence and soften the authoritarian judgments of Zillman. She was also proud of her good relations with psychiatry in Student Health.[92]

While reporting on Peterson's appointment as president of Barnard College in 1967, Lisa Witt of the *Chicago American* described Peterson as "Midwestern as a wheat field." Peterson had graduated from the University of Kansas in 1937 with degrees in math and German and taught high school math and girls' physical education out of college. Later, she returned to the University of Kansas to teach math and help in the office of the dean of women. She was then appointed dean of women at Kansas and did graduate work in counseling and educational psychology. Upon the retirement of Louise Troxell, longtime dean of women at UW–Madison, university president E. B. Fred recruited Peterson for that position. He may have wanted her at Wisconsin because of her civil rights record: in 1950s Kansas, while the US Supreme Court was pondering *Brown v. Board of Education of Topeka*, Peterson desegregated the University of Kansas sororities.[93]

The chancellor of the University of Kansas, who had been one of Peterson's classmates, warned Fred in 1956, "She is a strong feminist." Interview notes taken during her visit to the Madison campus revealed that Zillman, already dean of men, preferred another candidate. Another member of the interview team "raised the question about the chances for getting a married woman with a family for this position." But with strong support from the women interviewers, including Helen Connor Laird, a member of the Board of Regents, President Fred was pleased to recommend Peterson's appointment to the full Board of Regents in March 1956.[94]

One matter that caused Peterson to hesitate before taking the position at the UW was the reputation of Wisconsin senator Joe McCarthy, even though she was herself a Republican. But she accepted the deanship and completed her doctoral degree in educational psychology and counseling at Kansas. In 1963, Peterson was named a special assistant to the new UW president, Fred Harvey Harrington, and was later promoted to dean of student affairs. She left Madison in 1967 to become president of Barnard College, the sister school to Columbia University in New York City. Later, she returned to Wisconsin as president of Beloit College in 1975, and served on the boards of directors for many national corporations.[95]

From the beginning of her tenure in Madison, Peterson was a strong advocate for women. The UW news service highlighted a 1956 article she penned for the American Legion Auxiliary magazine in which she urged women, whom she referred to as the "potent majority," to be good citizens, including even "running for Congress." In 1957, the Wisconsin press covered her settling into her position as dean of women and noted her comment, "There are not too many doors closed to women today." She promoted the concept of equal pay for equal work and advocated for women to use their professional abilities, even if "to use these talents, they see that they will have

Martha Peterson, ca. 1965, during her tenure as Dean of Student Affairs at UW–Madison.
UNIVERSITY OF WISCONSIN–MADISON ARCHIVES IMAGE S07985

to give up other things—a husband and family." In the 1956 article for the American Legion Auxilary magazine, she recognized that some Americans were not ready to accept women as equal to men:

> Women who work for unpolluted water supplies, adequate juven-
> ile codes, self-respecting old age security or lasting world peace,
> are more likely to be called impractical idealists than great
> humanitarians. A woman who rises up in wrath and protests
> an injustice runs the risks of being accused of hysterics rather
> than righteous indignation.

Peterson was energetic about getting her messages out. She spoke to women's clubs and university groups around the state in the late 1950s. She told them, "We need more women in the fields of science and mathematics," and she deplored that these subjects were considered "a man's field." She reportedly said, "I haven't much patience with the idea that women cannot understand science."[96]

In the early 1960s, Peterson became more directly involved with empowering women in Wisconsin. A Dean's Office survey of the opinions of educated Wisconsin women about professional opportunities and civic issues led to a 1962 conference on continuing education for women. This initiative brought Peterson into contact with other woman activists, such as Madison's Kathryn Clarenbach, a feminist and later the first chairperson of the National Organization for Women. Peterson spoke at Governor John Reynolds's Governor's Conference on the Changing Status of Women in 1963.[97]

Peterson developed an important relationship with Dr. Maxine Bennett at the UW Medical School. When Peterson was being hired as the UW dean of women in 1956, President Fred told Bennett, his colleague, that she should get to know Peterson. Fred encouraged the two to meet because, as Bennett remembered, he said, "I think you should get to know her because Kansas and Nebraska are neighbors."[98]

Maxine Bennett was born in 1916 and grew up a tomboy in western Nebraska. After graduating in 1936 from Hastings College, a Nebraska Presbyterian school, she taught high school. However, unlike many women in her day, Bennett taught algebra, geometry, and biology, plus women's physical education thrown in for good measure. She would later observe that most of her high school classmates went on to be farm wives or housewives. After two years of teaching she went to medical school, though she said she had grown up "never having known a woman physician." At the University of Nebraska Medical School she was one of three women in her class. While there, she formed a close friendship with Dr. Margaret "Jo" Prouty, her first longtime partner.[99]

When Bennett graduated in 1942, the army did not have female doctors, though she could have become a nurse in the military. Instead, she took a seven-year internship at Madison, specializing in ear, nose, and throat medicine. By 1953 she was working full time at the UW Medical School in the Department of Surgery, where she was the only woman in the department. She later observed about women in medical schools, "Those that succeeded needed an exterior toughness to be accepted by many of their male peers." After retiring early in 1978, Bennett was given emerita status and recognized by the Wisconsin Medical Society as a fifty-year member. Meanwhile, Jo Prouty joined the Department of Pediatrics at Madison's Jackson Clinic, where she was the only female doctor. Together the two built and shared a house on Lake Waubesa, south of the city.[100]

Bennett's nickname, "Matterhorn," came from her many mountain-climbing experiences. While in medical college, she and Prouty worked as summer mountaineering counselors at a camp in Colorado. The pair climbed mountains together for years, including Mount Rainier and the Grand Tetons. In 1949, the two ascended the Matterhorn in Switzerland with crampons and ice axes. Bennett later recalled getting up at two o'clock in the morning to climb before the sun hit the glaciers and reaching the top by eleven a.m. Their joint activities also included membership in the Altrusa Club, a women's civic organization in Madison.[101]

The relationship that formed and blossomed in the late 1950s between Bennett and Martha Peterson did not go unnoticed in these pre-Stonewall days. A UW news release featuring staff traveling during the summer of 1959 informed folks that "Dean of Women Martha Peterson and Dr. Maxine Bennett, [are] touring Scandinavia." The Madison society magazine

Dr. Maxine Bennett on Matterhorn in 1953. She returned to the mountain decades later with her partner Martha Peterson. UNIVERSITY OF WISCONSIN–MADISON ARCHIVES IMAGE 2017S00548

Select published a 1964 feature on the "Halfway House," jointly owned by Peterson and Bennett. The article noted, "It all began three years ago when 'Max' and Martha purchased . . . a 200-foot frontage on the Lake Michigan side of Door County's 'thumb,' two miles from Jacksonport." Noting that "both hold responsible positions in Madison," the article commented that Bennett and Peterson's house was furnished with antiques, many of which they had refinished on their own workbench. A picture showed them in matching University of Wisconsin sweatshirts restoring antiques. Later the two would open an antique shop in Door County. When Peterson went to Barnard in New York in 1967, Bennett took a sabbatical year during which she also lived in New York and worked at Columbia Presbyterian Hospital.[102] After a few years, Peterson returned to Wisconsin as president at Beloit College.

Upon Bennett's retirement in the summer of 1978, a surprise dinner party was held at the Madison Club for fifty friends. "Among them," the paper noted, "was Miss Martha Peterson, New York City, president of Barnard College." When Peterson was serving on the board of directors for Exxon, she noted about other members, "It was awfully hard when they came with their wives" to board meetings and trips, because it was often presumed she had no partner to bring. When Peterson was told she could bring somebody, Bennett accompanied her, and together they witnessed the launching of an Exxon tanker in Japan.[103]

In 2006, Peterson's obituary in the *New York Times* observed that she was "survived by her companion Dr. Maxine Bennett." The Madison obituary referred to "her longtime friend and partner, Maxine Bennett, MD," and noted that they "shared many friends [and] world travels and experienced life to its fullest." Appropriately, the notice stated, "She was a wonderful role model for young women."[104]

MCCARTHY'S LEGACY

Senator Joe McCarthy's crusade against Communists in government occurred simultaneously with his and others' crusade against homosexuals in government. Particularly in Wisconsin, his home state, McCarthy found support for his antihomosexual efforts and resources to support his overall witch hunting. Although it was acknowledged at the time that

McCarthy was in fact targeting gays, this prolonged episode has largely been forgotten in recent years, both nationally and in Wisconsin. In part, this collective amnesia is due to the strategy of McCarthy's enemies of the day, including *The Progressive* magazine, which determined that the best way to attack the junior senator was to refrain from defending his victims and, instead, to attack his methods and background—the "record," as they referred to it. Still, some of the most progressive forces in the state, such as congressman Andrew Biemiller of Milwaukee; journalists at *The Progressive*, the *Capital Times*, and the *Milwaukee Journal*; and the University of Wisconsin did resist the witch-hunt hysteria. Although progressive forces in the McCarthy period met with little electoral success, they fought the senator's witch-hunting crusade in their own way.

These anticommunist liberals believed that the antidote to McCarthyism was Americanism. Yet although the fight for Americanism was an honorable strategy, it did not aim to protect homosexuals, and indeed it did not protect them. Gays in Wisconsin sought protective cover by proclaiming their own anticommunist views, thereby proving their Americanism. The Wisconsin legacy of McCarthy's witch hunts unfortunately reverberated throughout the state for at least a decade. Most tragically, it influenced the 1962 Gay Purge at the University of Wisconsin–Madison, where the McCarthyesque naming of names was used to seek out and "discipline" homosexuals on campus. As McCarthy and his followers sought to rid the government of card-carrying communists and fellow travelers who had taken no actions against America, so university officials sought to purge the campus of homosexuals who confessed to being gay but had not committed ostensible homosexual acts on campus.

Ultimately, the University of Wisconsin's strong tradition of faculty governance was one factor that helped to shut down the Gay Purge. The Student Health professionals realized that their participation in disciplinary procedures to seek a "cure" for these homosexuals was not benefiting the students but did impinge on their own professionalism. The campus psychiatrists forced a change in attitudes. While the campus was not yet welcoming by modern standards, it had moved beyond the punitive witch hunts that were commonplace in the late McCarthy period.

8

FINDING OURSELVES

Goodness sakes, I should have had a little education about this.
—BOB LOCKHART, RECALLING HIS
1950S DISCOVERY OF HOMOSEXUALITY[1]

How can this man ever hope that the world will ever accept the Gay crowd when even individuals among them refuse to accept others of their own kind?
—A WISCONSIN WRITER TO *ONE:
THE HOMOSEXUAL MAGAZINE*, 1958[2]

I n 1959, J. D. Mercer published *They Walk in Shadow*, a study of bisexuals and homosexuals, though mainly with an emphasis on the latter. Identifying himself as an "ambisexual" who had "struck a happy balance between his own nature and the world at large," he stated, "We who walk in shadow usually stand outside the law and are therefore in constant danger." Since all fifty states at the time outlawed homosexual behavior, the description of homosexuals as outlaws was accurate. In fact, J. D. Mercer was the author's pseudonym. Like Donald Webster Cory, the author of the 1951 tome *The Homosexual in America*, who also published under a pseudonym, many authors of books about homosexuality still did not feel comfortable using their real names during this era. Mercer's use of the word *shadow* harkens back to many similar earlier references—McCutcheon's "twilight verses" and even "the love that dare not speak its name" in the Oscar Wilde trial.[3]

During the 1960s, while things were starting to change both nationally and in Wisconsin, *Life* magazine in July 1964 published a feature article on

"Homosexuality in America." The teaser on the cover read, "The Secret World of THE HOMOSEXUAL Gets Bolder and Broader," and the article opened with the claim that as the gay world comes to light, "Society is forced to look at it—and try to understand it." Though the article perpetuated stereotypes about "brawny young men in their leather caps," it noted that "for every obvious homosexual, there are probably nine nearly impossible to detect." *Time* magazine followed in January 1966 with an article entitled "The Homosexual in America." "Beset by inner conflicts," this piece stated, "the homosexual is unsure of his position in society, ambivalent about his attitudes and identity—but he gains a certain amount of security through the fact that society is equally ambivalent about him." The *Time* article included some pseudoscience, such as the idea that homosexuality "is caused psychically, through a disabling fear of the opposite sex" and that it is "curable." But both articles accurately observed that homosexual visibility and identity were developing, and this proved true in Wisconsin.[4]

In the years between World War II and the Stonewall riots of 1969, gay people in Wisconsin had to endure charges of both sickness and subversion, but they were also creating and developing community. In the shadowy world before Stonewall, gay people endeavored not only to find their own identity, but also to find each other. Gay men and lesbians in Wisconsin had been doing this before the war in limited ways, sometimes solely for purposes of sex. Nevertheless, Wisconsin in the decades after the war saw more gay people affirming their sexual identities and forming early community social organizations well before the gay rights and gay liberation movements achieved any true status. The loose fairy network of the 1930s, the gay club mentioned by the servicemen of Truax at the end of the war, Wally Jordan's Sons of Hamidy in the North Woods, and the groups of homosexuals uncovered on the UW campus in the 1950s and 1960s are examples of early social organizations. This chapter explores how Wisconsin gay men accelerated this work to build identity and community in the decades prior to Stonewall.

MADISON'S GAY "SALON"

Though Madison police raided the Adams Street house on Madison's west side in 1948 and broke up the homosexual "ring" centered there, they missed the east side's gay circle, which revolved around the Jenifer Street home of writer Keith McCutcheon and his partner, Joe Koberstein. Ted Pierce, who was appointed messenger in the Executive Office by Governor Phil La Follette in the 1930s (see chapter 4), referred to his gay group on Madison's east side as a salon of the French order. In later writings, Pierce called it "a magic Group centered on the 700 block of Jenifer Street" that was "lively and highly witty." He even gave me a book in the 1980s called *The Salon* about the French social institution to make sure I understood the elevated social nature of the circle.[5]

Pierce used his connections from Jenifer Street to advocate for civil rights. The African American stage and screen actor Canada Lee, who was a Pierce correspondent, stayed with Pierce when he came to town in 1945. A newspaper photo of an NAACP reception for Lee shows McCutcheon among the guests (see page 142).[6]

Among Pierce's scrapbook souvenirs is a 1950 clipping from a local weekly that provides an enlightening glimpse into the activities of the salon, though without explicitly naming any names. The column's un-named author, a member from Rock County, described the group as "deeply concerned over the apparent inability of modern man to live a gracious, refined, and hospitable way of life in the press of unstable times." He further noted that "these young men are attempting in a modest way to recreate a friendly leisurely manner of living." In the 1950s, a boom time of growing factories and tract houses in suburbia, the lifestyle being pursued by these "young men" was notable and unusual.[7]

Among the group, he noted, one "will find representatives in the field of the theater, ballet, art, music, politics, literature, horticulture, and agri-culture," who may converse in French or Spanish "to increase the fluency of their acquired tongues." They were described as enjoying "Café Diablo," a sweetened coffee with flaming brandy and whipped cream—not exactly an ordinary drink in mid-America. Even though all the participants were men of very modest income, their homes displayed "refined and impeccable taste." Some men preferred modern décor (reflective of their residing in the land of Frank Lloyd Wright), some arranged their homes as showplaces of antiques, and some "bolder spirits . . . combined period pieces with the ability of interior decorators." The group's members are identified with the non-normative art of creating domestic environments, like the bachelor men of the 1930s in Cooksville, Mineral Point, and New Glarus.[8]

"On the subject of friendship they are equally adamant," the author

Joe Koberstein, Keith McCutcheon's partner pictured here gardening at 739 Jenifer
Street in the 1950s, was one of the men who provided hospitality for the gay circle on
the east side of Madison. FROM THE AUTHOR'S COLLECTION, COURTESY OF TED PIERCE

wrote. Some had "at home" gatherings on Sundays when friends dropped
in, took off their shoes, raided the icebox, discussed aesthetics, and had
enlightened conversation. "Whenever a light is burning in any of these
homes," the author writes, "it is like a beacon of hospitality, for owners
have endeavored to make their firesides a haven for unexpected guests."
Photographs from Ted Pierce indicate that this circle invited young men
from the traveling rodeos to drop by their firesides. These Sunday "at
homes" provide a counterpoint to the family Sunday dinners of the straight
world at the time, showing the fullness of the gay social life that flourished

even in the 1950s. The journalist, who clearly admired this alternative community, concluded his article with a hope for a brighter future: "They have dedicated their lives to better living in beautiful surroundings with emphasis on hospitality, friendliness, informality, and comfort. A remarkable experiment that is finding more and more adherents each year."[9]

One Madison couple with connections to the Jenifer Street scene, Bob Lockhart and Clarence Cameron, were introduced by a mutual friend in 1960 when Cameron worked in a funeral home and Lockhart was apprenticing in architecture in Spring Green. The two bonded quickly because, as Lockhart noted, "Part of the spontaneity was because you didn't know when the police were going to come." Neither man had figured out he was gay until his twenties; as Lockhart observed, "Goodness sakes, I should have had a little education about this." Lockhart served in the military in

Handsome cowboys at Keith McCutcheon and Joe Koberstein's house on Jenifer Street in Madison. FROM THE AUTHOR'S COLLECTION, COURTESY OF TED PIERCE

postwar Germany, but Cameron, in an act of self-affirmation, wrote on his induction form, "I'm an active homosexual," which prevented his military induction. The men recalled, "Even in liberal Madison, police at the time trapped gay men in restrooms and pressured them to confess the names of gay friends, who then often lost their jobs." Lockhart quietly recalled fifty years later, "We were all closeted." In their own lives and stories, Lockhart and Cameron exemplified much of the period's gay history by living partly in the shadows, but also affirming their identity and building social networks.[10]

LESBIANS IN THE DRIFTLESS

One Wisconsin lesbian couple in the pre-Stonewall era was linked to the Dane County village of Mount Horeb. Betty Sebenthall, born in Eau Claire in 1917, lived most of her life on Thompson Street in Mount Horeb. Sebenthall met her life partner, Mary Locke, in New York in 1940, and Locke relocated to Mount Horeb. During World War II, the two women worked in munitions plants. In the early 1940s, Sebenthall began publishing the first of her fifteen novels, many of them mysteries or novels of suspense, using male pseudonyms like Harry Davis and Paul Krueger. Her most serious novel, *The Desperate Wall*, which she published under the name Roberta Hill, was about hypocrisy in a small town—a theme that hit a bit too close to home for some folks in Mount Horeb. One New York reviewer, however, hailed Sebenthall as "a new writer who would be compared to Sherwood Anderson."[11]

In the 1960s, Sebenthall turned to poetry. Her volume *Acquainted with a Chance of Bobcats* came out in 1969. Felix Pollak, a University of Wisconsin–Madison librarian and a poet, described her as "underrated and unrecognized." One of her views on normative sex was expressed in the poem "Lady in a Big Old House." It described getting the chores done and then, "last things at night she dusted off sex, that white / elephant of a wedding gift / she never quite dared take to the attic." Sebenthall's poem "The Dance of the Seven Veils" drew on themes of masks and hiding, dating from the postwar Mattachine period. It opens, "The sane wear veils and never doubt / the veils are there: / the mad have cast pretensions out /

An author photo of Betty Seben-thall from the late 1960s. *ACQUAINTED WITH A CHANCE OF BOBCATS*, 1969

and they go bare." A set of three poems in *Acquainted* are described as "A Brooklyn Bouquet," perhaps written as a present to her partner from New York. One of these poems describes a day visiting the Botanical Gardens in the Bronx: A couple arrives early and packs a lunch that isn't allowed. The poem closes with the line, "All evening looked at each other from eyes still kindly with stones and grass, still gentle with sky." Sebenthall died in January 1979 at age sixty-two. Within months, Locke died, apparently of natural causes, but it was rumored that she had left a note saying she could not live without Sebenthall. The two women are buried next to each other and share a common headstone in Mount Horeb Union Cemetery.[12]

The Two-Spirited

While gay and lesbian life in south central Wisconsin was developing, another Wisconsinite in the 1950s reported on a disappearing alternative identity in the state. Nancy Oestreich Lurie, born in Milwaukee in 1924, earned her bachelor's degree from the University of Wisconsin in 1945, her master's from the University of Chicago in 1947, and her doctorate from Northwestern in 1952. After serving as a research associate in North American Indian Studies at Harvard University's Peabody Museum, she became a professor at the University of Wisconsin–Milwaukee in 1963. In 1972, she became curator and section head of anthropology at the Milwaukee Public Museum, a research institution, while remaining an adjunct professor at the university.[13]

In addition to these positions, Lurie also served as an expert witness for tribal petitioners in legal cases before federal courts, serving on review committees for the National Endowment for the Humanities and

Nancy Lurie wrote about the two-spirited tradition among the Ho-Chunk for her doctoral degree in anthropology. She later became the chief anthropologist for the Milwaukee Public Museum, pictured here.

the National Endowment for the Arts. Her knowledge of American Indian affairs was extensive: she was on the editorial board of the *Handbook of North American Indians* and, in 1987, she authored the book *Wisconsin Indians*. That she was an academic heavyweight showed in her service from 1983 to 1985 as president of the American Anthropological Association.[14]

Lurie published an article in the December 1953 issue of *American Anthropologist* based on her doctoral field research on the "Winnebago Berdache," conducted between 1945 and 1947. Today, the Winnebago tribe is known as the Ho-Chunk in Wisconsin. Lurie had a number of tribal contacts whom she interviewed about her subject matter.[15]

Berdache was a term used by anthropologists in the mid-twentieth century for an American Indian male who took on a female role. In French, the word *berdache* refers to the passive partner in sodomy, a catamite or a boy prostitute, with earlier connotations from Persian and Arabic as a captive or slave. The French traders who had early interactions with the tribes of the Western Great Lakes and the Plains in the seventeenth and eighteenth centuries used this word, which they thought fit a phenomenon that was not exactly European. George Catlin, in his 1830s sketches of American Indians, artistically recorded a "berdache dance" among the Sauk-Fox (today known as Mesquakie), another tribe with Wisconsin associations. (The best-known member of this tribe was Chief Black Hawk, a Sauk leader who resisted white settlement in Wisconsin during what was known as the Black Hawk War.) The Winnebago language had its own native word for the phenomenon, *siange*, which Lurie often used in her article in addition to *berdache*. Today the term "two-spirit" or "two-spirited" is preferred for individuals who blend gender roles in American Indian cultures.[16]

While Lurie's article did not discuss homosexuality as it was known in European-based cultures, she reported that the berdaches "sometimes married other men." One was described as a bachelor who had acted as a "foster mother" to several children belonging to his sister or half-sister. Lurie first encountered the concept in 1946 when a tribal contact mentioned that her mother had referred to "men who dressed as women." Readers at the time easily could have conflated the berdache concept with homosexuality. After all, the French had made a similar error in the seventeenth and eighteenth centuries. In more modern terms, some of these individuals might be called transgendered.[17]

George Catlin's painting *Dance to the Berdash*, dated 1835–1837, features a two-spirited individual (standing on the right) from the Sauk-Fox tribe. SMITHSONIAN AMERICAN ART MUSEUM

In the Ho-Chunk tradition, during the spirit quest all two-spirited individuals were directed by the moon, recognized as a female spirit. Lurie reported that the "berdache dressed as a woman, performed women's tasks better than any normal woman could perform them, and had the ability to foretell future events." Blessed by the moon, the berdache, being among the tribe's prophets, was a "highly honored and respected person."[18]

Through association with Europeans during the seventeenth century, the Winnebago "had become ashamed of the custom because the white people thought it was amusing or evil." When Lurie asked about the berdaches, one female Winnebago replied, "That is something we want to forget and not talk about." Other interviewees told Lurie the Winnebago term *siange* should be translated as "no good" or "a eunuch," or "an unmanly man." According to Lurie's research, the word *siange* "was still in common use in Wisconsin in 1947, but was used among young men as an insult or teasing epithet. These young men claimed to know nothing more about the word except that it carried connotations of weakness and effeminacy."[19]

Lurie reported that the concept was also known in other tribes, including the Omaha, the Ponca, and the Oglala. Her work was cited frequently by Walter L. Williams in his 1986 book *The Spirit and the Flesh: Sexual Diversity in American Indian Culture*, who noted that Lurie's findings paralleled those of other, more recent researchers. In the 1940s, when Lurie encountered tales of the last-known berdache among the Winnebago, she was told that "his brothers threatened to kill him if he 'put on the skirt.'" It was reported to her that this individual "then affected a combination of male and female clothing, fearing that he would die if he did not at least attempt to follow the directions given him in his vision of the moon." She reported in 1953, "The last berdache died somewhat over fifty years ago."[20]

Today, history has caught up with 1950s research. Kohl Miner, a Ho-Chunk who resides in Minneapolis and has extensive experience in theater, has expressed his two-spirit nature in various artistic works. Miner is executive director of the First Nations Composer Initiative. His work *The Semi-Conscious Memoirs of a Negligent Native* has been described as a series of monologues portraying a modern-day two-spirit as he maneuvers through life and men. In 2012, Miner read Lurie's 1953 article about the Winnebago berdache and contacted her. It turned out that he had an old tribal photo that showed the very person Lurie had been told was the last of the two-spirited people: Blue Lake Woman. Nancy Lurie's original research showed that alternative sexualities in Wisconsin had not been confined to European-based cultures. Her latter-day encounter with a modern two-spirit person demonstrates that alternative traditions continue to overcome suppression.[21]

A TALIESIN TRIAL

Frank Lloyd Wright's architectural school associated with his home at Taliesin in Spring Green, Wisconsin, brought many young men together in an intellectually challenging environment. In the 1930s, Keith McCutcheon had gone to Taliesin and written poems about Wright and his buildings. An unpublished poem, "Taliesin," includes the following stanza:

> But now, once more, the Shining Brow is Crowned:
> Upon a rounded crest of sun warmed hill,
> Not far from the Wisconsin's riffles gleam,
> Reclines, in cat-like stealth, a house—a dream

Crouching along the ridge as if to fill
Itself among the rocks 'tis made of: spill
Itself un-noticed midst the trees, and seem
More as a part of Nature's own that scheme
Of cunning mind and power of man's will.

McCutcheon, as noted previously, had grown up in Arena, a river town upstream from Taliesin, and was associated with Wright for a year, perhaps as his secretary. Bob Lockhart also studied at Wright's school of architecture at Taliesin.[22]

In *The Fellowship: The Untold Story of Frank Lloyd Wright and the Taliesin Fellowship*, authors Roger Friedland and Harold Zellman write about two sex clubs that existed at Taliesin: one gay and one straight. The administration at the Taliesin school in the late 1940s did not want its architectural students, or apprentices as they were called, searching for "relaxation" with local girls, getting them pregnant, and creating bad feelings between the school and the town. According to Friedland and Zellman, Frank's wife, Olgivanna Wright, arrived at the idea that the men should "seek each other out rather than creating all this problem in Spring Green." At a secret meeting, she arranged some of the single male apprentices into "two lines facing one another" and "paired the incredulous young men" so they could provide mutual sexual relief.[23]

Friedland and Zellman reported that "while Olgivanna's 'solution' may have served to contain some amount of sexual activity within the Fellowship, for many it was also redundant. For gay men had been thriving at Taliesin, at least discreetly, from the very beginning." They also noted that many of the men "were profoundly grateful for this safe haven" and that "gay men were central to this community." Noted gay architect Philip Johnson visited Taliesin at Wright's invitation in the early 1930s. Apparently Johnson's sexual orientation was known at the time, as Wright once referred to "Johnson's architecture department at [New York's Museum of Modern Art] as the 'Pansy Patch of the Museum of Foreign Art,' once even presenting Johnson with printed stationery bearing that letterhead."[24]

Nevertheless, the balance at Taliesin was upset when Jack Howe, Wright's chief draftsman, became aggressive in pursuing newer apprentices and began causing rumors. Howe had also attracted Johnson's eye during visits. In 1949, while the Fellowship was at winter quarters at Taliesin West in Arizona, the apprentices were called to a meeting that became known as "the trial." Wright, who sought to end the rumors, reportedly said, "We should not be recognized as this kind of place." Despite some calls for Howe's expulsion, he was retained but made to apologize individually to members of the Fellowship. After Howe told some Fellowship members that he was bisexual, later efforts were made to find him a wife.[25]

Friedland and Zellman also noted that in April 1949, shortly after the "trial," Wright went public with his views on "intersexuality" at the Western Round Table on Modern Art in San Francisco. Wright insulted fellow panelist Marcel Duchamp by describing the Frenchman's famous painting *Nude Descending a Staircase* as degenerate. Incredulous, the composer Darius Milhaud, another panelist, reminded the audience that the Nazis had also labeled art degenerate. Wright purportedly asked Duchamp, "You would say that this movement which we call modern art and painting has been greatly in debt to homosexualism?" Duchamp responded: "The homosexual world has more interest or more curiosity, are more interested in a new movement like modern art." Evaluating Wright's response and attitude, the authors concluded, "Homosexuality, in Wright's view, was a forbidden and dangerous refreshment, a degenerative snack that could be fatal to one's manhood." But the gay apprentices remained, and Taliesin continued to be a place for homosexual men to assemble well into the twentieth century.[26]

GAY CONSUMERS AND PHYSICAL CULTURE

In an article published in the July 2010 *Journal of Social History*, David K. Johnson argues that gay identity was formed in the American consumer culture of the mid-twentieth century. Among his arguments, he posits that physique, or physical culture, magazines provided an early entrée into gay life for many men. And the national gay commercial market for these magazines helped create a consumer network and gay identity well before Stonewall. Indeed, the *Time* story of 1966 had noted that "newsstands make room for 'beefcake' magazines of male nudes."[27]

Citing historian John D'Emilio, Johnson noted that while membership of the political Mattachine Society in the 1950s numbered fewer than a thousand, physique magazines sold in the hundreds of thousands during this era. Though some gay historians have dismissed physical culture publications as a serious research topic because they border on eroticism or pornography, gay consumers in the mid-twentieth century were certainly buying these materials.[28]

ONE magazine had little doubt of physique magazines' role in gay culture. In December 1957, ONE's "Tangents" section noted some snide fighting among the newer muscle magazines. *Physique Pictorial*, a publication that was clearly pitched to gay buyers, had jokingly called *Strength & Health* "its sister magazine." Then *VIM*, another of the newer model-type publications, chimed in to say that the remarks praising *Strength & Health* should have been called "Tribute to an Old Aunt." This demonstrates the precedence of the older muscle magazines, which presented male nudes while still hoping to be considered prim and proper.[29]

The nearly nude photos in physical culture magazines from the beginning of the twentieth century often showed strongmen holding swords or spears suggestive of erections. Because the German immigrant tradition strongly supported participation in the Turners movement, known for the encouragement of both physical exercise and male comradeship at gymnastic clubs, physical culture had appeal in Wisconsin, which had received many German immigrants in the nineteenth century. In the 1920s, a Madison man, Julius Vogel, created his own scrapbook on physical culture that included correspondence with national physical culture experts. He kept items and writings in his scrapbook that might suggest that he was a homosexual—for example, a questionnaire on which he had acknowledged having bad dreams and a complaint about "weak wrists." Also included in the scrapbook were several pamphlets for barbells, with the usual strongmen in nude and seminude poses. A sampling of some later physical culture magazines available to Wisconsinites shows that Wisconsin men participated in this proto-gay consumer market.[30]

In the early and mid-twentieth century, physical culture periodicals could provide mixed signals for homosexuals. An example is found in the September 1939 issue of the magazine *Strength & Health*, devoted to "the culture of mind and body." On the third page of this issue is a full-page advertisement for a book titled *Your Sex Life*, written by the magazine's

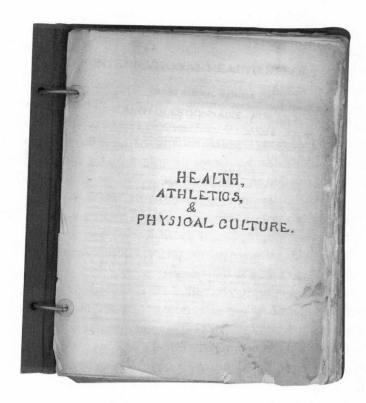

HEALTH,
ATHLETICS,
&
PHYSICAL CULTURE.

Some gay men amassed physical culture collections like this one from the author's collection. Purchased at an estate sale in Madison, it includes sources going back to the 1920s.

editor, Bob Hoffman. A detailed table of contents shows one of the topics: "Homosexuality, such a common condition in modern life that it is discussed at length." However, while acknowledging same-sex activity as a "common condition," the overall tone of the contents clearly presents and upholds the traditional view of sexual abstinence outside of marriage, which Hoffman called "a goal that every ambitious young unmarried man should strive to attain."[31]

During this period, *Strength & Health* (*S&H*) included a recurring feature called the S&H Leaguers Page with letters from readers. The December 1957 issue of *ONE* noted that the *S&H* Leaguers had "allowed 'lonely bodybuilders and others' to form 'fruitful friendships'" over the years. Several readers, for example, wrote in seeking a vacation companion. Others, such as one Wisconsin *S&H* Leaguer, Paul E. Scheele of Sheboygan, noted he "would like to exchange physique photos with other leaguers." One 1939 issue of *S&H* also published a physique photo from Vernon Schenke, described as a "husky newcomer" at 153 pounds and listed as a Milwaukee City middleweight champ who pressed 196 pounds.[32]

In the issue's back pages are the usual ads for posed photos of strongmen. These include an ad for Tony Sansone's "Nudleaf" photos. While the mention of "Nudleaf" presumes some discreetly placed genital coverage, Sansone is featured in other magazines in full frontal nude photos, as noted in David Chapman's *Adonis: The Male Physique Pin Up 1870–1940*. The same *S&H* issue included an article on Eugene Sandow, in which the strongman, dubbed "the handsomest Man in the World," declines a Shakespearean role offered to him by a "dapper, dandified" producer because he would have to "throw" a fight. Clearly publishers of physical culture magazines knew they had a homosexual market for male physique images and catered directly, if discreetly, to that market.[33]

As World War II was ending, *S&H* continued to run discreetly worded ads for posing photos in the back pages. It also started a section titled "Especially for S&H Boys," which ran photos of younger men that surely appealed to some gay readers. *Your Physique*, another magazine published in Montreal during this period, had a similar section titled "Our Boys Department" with discreetly posed nude young men and ads for posing photos. Yet, the formal front of heterosexuality was carefully upheld, so pictures of women weight lifters were included, as well. In the case of the *S&H* photos, for example, Robert R. Kordes appears in the boys' section and is described as having "already built this wonderful body by the time he was 16," but any implication of homosexuality was undercut by the added note that the photo was sent by a woman, one "Miss Violet Tomczyk of 709 So. 6th St. Milwaukee, Wis. who signs herself 'an ardent S&H fan.'"[34]

Indeed, *S&H*'s efforts to eschew the stigma of being a homosexual publication while selling to the gay market drew a rebuke in June 1953 from *ONE*. A three-page editorial deplored the sexual ignorance of *S&H*'s editor and argued that magazines of this type "take a crack at the 'weak, the perverted, the cowardly pansies, the unmanly.' Yet almost the whole of their circulation depends upon those who dote upon the undraped male figure." *ONE* reprinted a letter from a sixteen-year-old boy who sent in a question to the *S&H* Ask the Doctor column: "What causes homosexualism and how can it be cured?" In his letter, the boy wrote, "The attraction

of other fellows is as strong as any normal boy could have toward a girl."
For *ONE* editors, "The heart-wrenching touch is not in what he writes
but in the answer." *S&H* advised the young correspondent, "This is an
unfortunate condition as homosexualism is an inborn trait brought about
by maladjustment of glands. Sometimes an adjustment comes about naturally and sometimes an operation is successfully resorted to; however, we
have on hand reports of heavy physical exercise giving the subject more
masculine tendencies." *ONE* deplored this frustrating, sexually confused,
and consumeristic response.[35]

The cover of the
February 1963
issue of *Physique
Pictorial.*

The traditional weight-lifting physical culture magazines with their ambiguous approaches were challenged after World War II by newer physique magazines that made little pretense that they were into body images, and not really the muscles of physical culture. Now, new gay entrepreneurs were appealing directly to a gay consumer market. The Athletic Model Guild (AMG), founded in 1945 by Bob Mizer and others, was originally a referral service for models. When Mizer founded the magazine *Physique Pictorial* in 1951, it became one of the popular magazines that featured male models posing with no weight-lifting equipment whatsoever in view. Other, similar magazines followed in the mid-1950s, including *The Male Figure*, founded by Bruce of Los Angeles, which was the pseudonym of photographer Bruce Bellas.[36]

A February 1963 issue of *Physique Pictorial* ran a photo spread on "New Model Candidates" for the magazine and its products. The caption read, "On these two pages we bring you a number of new AMG models recently photographed who haven't yet been cataloged by AMG, but we are very eager to get your comments and appraisals so we will know which fellows to feature the most strongly, which to call back for more work (where possible) etc." Among the eighteen new models is John Baradin, age twenty, five feet eight inches tall, 166 pounds, of Slinger, Wisconsin, described as active in all sports including gymnastics and boxing. It is noted that he trained to be a printer but wants to be a cop. He is touted as an up-and-coming AMG film star. Bob Mizer's own pseudo-neoastrological system can be seen in symbols superimposed over the photographs of the models, which are supposed to indicate some of their interests. The codes indicate that Baradin was gay and proud, with a pleasant personality, and that he was a good moneymaker. The boom in gay consumer culture, as shown in physique magazines, spread across the nation—a business that could even reach a young man in the small town of Slinger, Wisconsin.[37]

Another gay Wisconsinite seems to have had access to the world of physique photo production. Olin Wood, who had a master's degree from the University of Wisconsin and was a teacher of French at the UW Extension, lived in Madison in the 1970s. Around that time, Wood took photos in California of the young actor Richard Thomas lying over a large chunk of driftwood on a sandy Pacific beach, clad in only a posing strap, as well as a portrait photo of the young actor dated November 1971. The beach

John Baradin from
Slinger, Wisconsin,
featured in the Feb-
ruary 1963 issues of
Physique Pictorial.

photo, with an overlay of the words "RICHARD THOMAS by Olin Wood,"
was reproduced and used as an inclusion in Wood's Christmas card for
1971, which was sent to a number of friends in Madison. Another Madison-
ian, a member of the Jenifer Street circle, recalled being in the Play Circle
at the Memorial Union with "Lynn" (probably Olin) Wood and Richard
Thomas. Wood had invited the actor to the city to consider studying theater. This would have been right before Thomas began his breakout role as
television's John-Boy Walton in late December of the same year. [38]

While some straight men of the mid-twentieth century searched for
photo spreads showing women's bare breasts in *National Geographic*, some
gay men searched for nude or nearly nude men in the physical culture
magazines, especially of the 1950s and 1960s. Well before Stonewall, Wisconsin men found access to the emerging gay consumer market via the
networks of subscriptions and pen pal exchanges, as well as the photos of
male models featured in physical culture publications.

Homosexual Panics

On September 7, 1960, the *Waukesha Daily Freeman* blared the headlines, "Arrest 10 Men for Illicit Sex Activities in City Area" and "City as Center of Illicit Sex Ring." The story, which had been developing since mid-August, had been withheld by the *Freeman* and the Milwaukee papers at the request of the district attorney and the police chief to permit an undercover investigation to proceed without premature release. Up to six undercover police detectives per night had staked out the restroom in Waukesha's Frame Park after learning it was being used as a gay meeting place for illicit sex. For the whole month of September, the *Freeman* ran multiple front-page stories on the scandal's developments, and other papers in the state such as the *Capital Times* and *Wisconsin State Journal* joined in on the reporting. One of the most colorful headlines was printed in the *Milwaukee Sentinel* on September 8: "Arrests Break Deviate Ring in Waukesha."[39]

In addition to the ten arrested men who were directly associated with activity at the park, police indicated that a dozen other suspects would be questioned in the next week. On September 12, two more men appeared in court on morals charges citing homosexual activity in their own home. Two other men who met each other in the park but did not engage in any sexual acts were trailed by the police to a parked car, where they were arrested. And later, another man was charged with taking indecent liberties with a fifteen-year-old boy in the park. Later in the month, on September 22, another man who had engaged in "sex perversion" with a different fifteen-year-old boy was committed to the state mental institution instead of being sent to prison.[40]

The newspaper stories noted that the phrase "Go to Frame Park, Waukesha" was passed around among homosexuals in the Midwest. The suggestion "Have you tried Frame Park, Waukesha, Wis." was reportedly written on restroom walls in Milwaukee, Chicago, and Detroit. From comments made by those arrested, the park had had this reputation for several years. Yet, the reports given by the arrestees demonstrated that all came from the Milwaukee metropolitan area or had ties to it. Clearly, the gay men in Milwaukee had established an effective communications network.[41]

When the "sex ring" was discovered, panic set in among many in Waukesha, which had a population of thirty thousand. Before widespread

Postcard view of Frame Park, Waukesha, where gay men were known to meet.

suburbanization, the relatively small Wisconsin city was largely industrial; in 1960 it was still a county seat of independent political and social identity. This type of notoriety and the resultant panic about homosexuals seemed to alarm local officials.

The dimensions of the panic were several. Local gay folks worried they would be denounced and arrested, as so many already had been. Gay men also worried about an area-wide crackdown in Milwaukee's parks, where sexual activity in Juneau Park was even more notorious. Waukesha's moral guardians were in a panic because they no longer had a "clean town." Public officials worried about the community's good name and about prominent individuals being the subjects of rumors. Community institutions like schools fired teachers or forced them to resign. The Waukesha Medical Society worked quickly to expel the two doctors arrested for homosexuality.[42]

On September 8, the day after the story broke, some local officials tried to calm the waters and end the sensationalism. Waukesha police o GPO : 1976 - 220-462

MASTER
1-4 (Rev. .5-9-72)

MASTER

12-8-87

UNITED STATES DEPARTMENT OF JUSTICE
FEDERAL BUREAU OF INVESTIGATION
IDENTIFICATION DIVISION
WASHINGTON, D.C. 20537

The following FBI record, NUMBER   778 841 E   , is furnished FOR OFFICIAL USE ONLY.
Information shown on this Identification Record represents data furnished FBI by fingerprint contributors.
WHERE DISPOSITION IS NOT SHOWN OR FURTHER EXPLANATION OF CHARGE OR DISPOSITION IS
DESIRED, COMMUNICATE WITH AGENCY CONTRIBUTING THOSE FINGERPRINTS.

CONTRIBUTOR OF FINGERPRINTS	NAME AND NUMBER	ARRESTED OR RECEIVED	CHARGE	DISPOSITION
PD Milwaukee WI	Eldon Eugene Murray 78225	7-20-57	dis (sex)	$25
PD Milwaukee WI	Eldon Eugene Murray 78225	8-26-64	disorderly (sex)	sent susp
PD Milwaukee WI	Eldon Eugene Murray 78225	3-12-66	disorderly (sex)	$100 & C

FINGERPRINT SECTION

RECEIVED

JAN 0 2 1988

Dissemination Criteria

KAE CD 3666

Eldon Murray, a Milwaukee businessman, was arrested several times for homosexual
activity in the 1950s and 1960s. Later, as a gay activist, he proudly secured a copy of
his record. UNIVERSITY OF WISCONSIN–MILWAUKEE ARCHIVES

chief Walter Moody was quoted as saying he did "not believe Waukesha is a 'center' of homosexual activity." As if to defuse the situation, the district attorney, George Lawler, noted that although there had been increasing complaints about homosexual activity in recent months, they had come from all areas of the county, not just Waukesha. The Waukesha police chief stated, "This is not a haven for homosexuals."[43]

Nearly two weeks later, on September 21, District Attorney Lawler urged a "crackdown" on rumors naming Waukeshans as homosexuals: "Because of these vicious rumors I have asked Police Chief Moody to conduct an investigation into the sources of the rumors and who is spreading them." Lawler said he would prosecute rumormongers, noting that the penalty for defamation was $1,000 and a year in jail. Countering Joe McCarthy's earlier views, Lawler said, "Talking about others just on hearsay is ridiculous and criminal."[44]

As time passed, more prominent people were drawn into the scandal. Perhaps the most well-known was the dean of men at Waukesha's Carroll University. In addition to the dean, arrestees included an elementary school teacher in Waukesha; a former Carroll athlete by then teaching in Grosse Point, Michigan; and a Roman Catholic priest attached to the church of Saints Peter and Paul in Milwaukee. These arrests caused concern that homosexuals might be influencing the young in Waukesha. Also caught in the net were the vice president of a local oil company, an accountant, a dentist, and three physicians.[45]

The youngest man arrested was twenty-two and the oldest was fifty-eight. Most accounts showed that the activity in question had been consensual sex between adults, though, as mentioned previously, two charges involved fifteen-year-old boys. All the arrested men were subjected to the criminal justice system; most were jailed and then had to post bail. Trials and hearings occurred over the course of the month. Most were convicted, though some pled guilty to lesser charges. Their names and actions were mentioned in the press, linked in stories and headlines proclaiming "morals charges," "sex perversion," "indecent liberties," "sex deviates," and "disorderly conduct" (in the most morally ambiguous circumstances). The nature of the press response to such cases had not changed much in Wisconsin since the time of the Oscar Wilde trials.[46]

Readers of the *Waukesha Daily Freeman* who wrote letters to the editor had various takes on the sex scandal. One deplored the publishing of the stories, particularly citing the pain caused to family members. Another reader, whose letter was signed "a Waukesha Parent," praised the paper and police for their actions, rather than handling the issue with kid gloves or sweeping the whole thing under the rug. That letter ended, "The citizens of Waukesha want a clean town." Another writer noted the frequency of such incidents: "This affair has happened in other cities of this size throughout the nation before, and with our society's laxness on sexual mores will happen (however unfortunate) again in cities this size." One reader specifically criticized the actions of the prominent arrestees: "There is something wrong with our standard of values when we allow men who are prominent and well educated such as most of these men were, to go unpunished. They should be setting standards for our youth." Another viewed the issue from a medical standpoint, writing, "Most of these people had good educations, good families but are sick and need help badly."[47]

Some arrestees were sentenced to state mental institutions based on the perception that they were sick. One was incarcerated at Waupun for an indeterminate sentence under the revised sex deviate law of 1951, under which psychiatric confinement was not justified unless the person had committed a prior sexual crime. Others were whisked to a local sanatorium for psychiatric evaluations. At least one, the Catholic priest, had his psychiatrist testify at the trial on his need for mental help. The economic ruin of those involved was noted in press accounts as the Carroll University dean and the elementary teacher both resigned from their jobs. The Waukesha Medical Society took steps to expel the two doctors who had been arrested, even though one had his charges dismissed because the state failed to prove a crime. The basis for the Medical Society's action was "a principle of medical ethics requiring that the medical profession safeguard the public and itself against physicians deficient in moral character or professional competence." In an indirectly related story, the *Waukesha Daily Freeman* noted that a Milwaukee teacher, a bachelor, had been "ousted" from his job for discussing prostitution, premarital relations, and homosexuality in his classroom.[48]

Nevertheless, there was no denying that gay people existed in Waukesha and were finding ways to connect. Of course, when the scandal hit the small Wisconsin city, the authorities used the same methods to deal with the crisis that officials had been using in Wisconsin for decades: shame the gays in public, declare them sick, lock them up, and destroy their liveli-hoods. This would not be the last such incident that made homosexuality visible and led to panic in Wisconsin.

Homosexual "rings" did not exist just in the southern part of Wis-consin. On April 14, 1966, the *Ladysmith News* broke the story of "a male homosexual 'club' operating in Ladysmith which involved adults and juveniles." The club was "raided at 7 p.m. Wednesday of last week, re-sulting in the eventual arrest of six adults and questioning of 'five or six' juveniles." The Milwaukee papers also carried the story, quoting the Rusk County district attorney's statement that the club had been operating for several years. [49]

Ladysmith had a population of 3,500 at the time, in a county of 15,000; it is located between Eau Claire and Superior. The police were tipped off that a weight-lifting room in a hotel-type structure "was the center of homosexual activities," which included the showing of indecent movies and the sharing of obscene literature. Apparently, gay consumer culture had penetrated even small-town Wisconsin by the mid-1960s. The build-ing owner entered a guilty plea to nine morals charges, while six other counts were dismissed. A number of the arrested men were charged with sexual perversion or lewd and lascivious behavior. Several pleaded "no contest" to morals charges. Most of the arrestees were from Ladysmith, though one was a teacher from Milwaukee. [50]

Later reporting would indicate that while people had initially been concerned about the possible corruption of youth, the group of youths from the high school who used the weight-lifting room "had no connec-tion with the group charged in court." The homosexual activities took place in rooms other than the gym. After this information was revealed, the local sensational headlines disappeared and the charges appeared only under the "Court News" section of the paper. Perhaps to calm speculation in the community, the newspaper ran an editorial clarifying that "in the United States until the jury or judge decides on the evidence placed before them that a man is guilty, that man in all minds should be considered in-nocent." The city followed up by strengthening its ordinances on "Public Nuisances Offending Morals and Decency." The Ladysmith sex panic again showed how the uncovering of a homosexual network could shock a small

Wisconsin community both by exposing the mere presence of gay men and revealing that they had found a way of networking and importing gay sexual materials into the community.[51]

HOOKING UP AT THE BARS

The most enduring local homosexual cultural institution in the pre-Stonewall time was the gay bar. Will Fellows's 2010 book *Gay Bar: The Fabulous True Story of a Daring Woman and Her Boys in the 1950s* describes early gay bar culture in Los Angeles. Fellows reprinted Helen Branson's autobiographical narrative, originally published in 1957, of running a California gay bar. He describes the original book as "a homespun memoir by a woman who enjoyed the company of homosexual men and deplored their plight." The dust jacket for the 1950s edition asks readers to "make no mistake about it. The people who are Helen Branson's customers are not the depraved and sinister characters so often presented as typical of the homosexual. Instead they are responsible, well-behaved human beings no different from anyone else except in the direction of their loves." In a 1958 *ONE* magazine article entitled "The Gay Bar," Robert Gregory wrote, "This article is not the place for detailed descriptions of the Gay Bar . . . as the job has already been done excellently by others." He went on to include Branson's book among those so praised. The California Supreme Court had weighed in on the side of gay bars during the 1950s to permit their existence, and the 1960s saw a rapid increase in gay bars around the country.[52]

There was even early scholarly recognition of the significance of gay bars during this general era. Joseph Harry published an article on "Urbanization and the Gay Life" in the *Journal of Sex Research* in 1974. He notes that "the gay bar is one of the central institutions of the gay world, serving both as a sexual marketplace and as a meeting place for friends." Harry's article points out the limits of gay research up to the early 1970s, in which, according to his view, the data had focused only on specialized samples of either the largest urban places or on the small populations of members of the early homophile organizations. His study of 1,980 American gay bars—based on data collected from the *Guild Guide* (1972), census data of 1970, and gay bars and places of interest—was proclaimed to "constitute the only national data on gay institutions to date."[53]

As Martin Meeker argues in his 2005 book *Contacts Desired*, early guild guides were important examples "of how changing networks of communication helped to bring a social group into being, how the narrative of a communications shift is tantamount to the history of a homosexual identity forming into a collective sense of itself." The guides were publications that listed by state gay-friendly bars, though occasionally parks, beaches, and hotels were also listed as cruising sites. Lesbian bars were also sometimes included. The Harry study noted that 426 cities were listed in the 1972 guide, and many cities had multiple bars, though some were of mixed clientele. He mentioned that there were several such guides and "they greatly facilitate the social life of a newcomer to a strange city." He also observed, "Bartenders serve as excellent informants in the gay community because of their communicational centrality." Harry concluded his article with this important note: "For various reasons of personality, social exclusion, or labeling, gays create a segregated set of institutions."[54]

Joseph Harry chose the 1972 *Guild Guide* from among several different published guides of gay bars because he believed it to be the most accurate. Some of the guides charged others with borrowing from one another for information. The *Guild Guide* tried to make its publication participatory. In a personal message to users, the editors stated, "We need your help if this Guide is to grow in both usefulness and availability." Yet, it cautioned, "If you go into the dullest bar in the world and meet the nicest person in the world, this is not sufficient to ask that this bar be listed. On the other hand, if you go into a place filled with lonely young men and just cannot make friends, this is no reason not to let us have the listing!" In the 1966 *Guild Guide*'s introductory essay, the editors noted, "We are always anxious for listings and corrections anywhere in the world, but resort areas, college towns and areas with military installations are of particular interest to vacationers." The significance of college towns will reemerge in the next volume of our Wisconsin story.[55]

Some gay Wisconsinites found others through the listings, and in doing so, found out more about themselves. The *Lavender Baedeker Guide*'s first issue, published in San Francisco in 1963 by Guy Strait, listed five Wisconsin cities with gay spots, one each in Fond du Lac, Green Bay, and Marinette, six in Madison, and twelve in Milwaukee. In Green Bay, the Mayfair Lounge on Adams Street made the early listings and was joined in later issues by the Astor Hotel Bar and the Spanish View Grill. At one point, Green Bay listings also included Point Beach State Forest, noted as seven miles north of Two Rivers. The Colony, a bar in Fond du Lac, continued to appear in the listings for many years. Other places, like the Raulf Hotel Bar in Oshkosh, also appeared in the *Lavender Baedeker Guide* for a few years.[56]

The Madison listings included the Belmont Hotel Bar (now the YWCA), the Fireside on Regent Street, the Kollege Klub on lower State Street, Marty's on Wilson Street, the 602 Bar on University Avenue, and the Uptown Restaurant on mid–State Street. All listed establishments were either

In the 1950s and 1960s, Madison's Belmont Hotel Bar served as a gay gathering place on the weekends.

near campus or downtown. In 1964, the same Madison spots were listed in the *Directory 43* guide published in Minneapolis, but this guide included an additional Appleton bar and another bar in Green Bay. In 1963, Milwaukee had twenty-one listings, including many cruising places. The 1964 *Guild Guide* published in Washington, DC, added Lombardo's Piano Lounge on East Main Street and the Three Bells on University Avenue to the other Madison listings.[57]

For Milwaukee, that old favorite from World War II, the Royal Hotel Bar, appeared in the first guides. The Mint Bar on Milwaukee's State Street, which opened in 1949 and was also known as Tony's, was included, though it was described as "plain." When its area of State Street was targeted as the building site for the Bradley Center in 1986, the bar moved to the South Side. The intriguingly named bar The Fox on Plankinton also made it into the first guides.[58]

Sometimes the guides were very specific. For instance, in one guide the Antlers Hotel Bar in Milwaukee, which had appeared in the first guides, was recommended as a place to go on Saturday night, and rooms on the tenth or eleventh floor were mentioned for homosexual activity. But business at the hotel must have been good, because a later guide specifies the seventh to eleventh floors. If a sailor was your desired partner in Wisconsin's big city on the lake, then you could try the Seaway Inn (presumably named after the St. Lawrence Seaway), the Castaways, the River Queen on Walter Street, or, for a brief period, the Pirates Den. The Castaways guide entry, which showed an early ad depicting two sailors with arms around each other on a blanket, and where dancing was not only permitted but "almost encouraged," noted: "Caution: Has been raided." Nite Beat, which opened in the mid-1960s, was listed as a "Girls Bar" or "Where Women Meet." Its early ad showed two mermaids with arms around each other under the slogan "the Gayest Spot in Town." Your Place, though it did not appear in the first guides, became a regular listing. Unsurprisingly, Juneau Park was listed for the Cream City, though by 1971, its listing came with the warning, "Bad scene: muggings, beatings, vice-squad." The 1966 *Male World Guide* noted one Milwaukee bar, Godfrey's 1800 Club, as "mainly colored." Other mainstream places that showed up in the guides include the Columns at the Pfister (coat and tie recommended), Gimbels, the Milwaukee Library, and the YMCA.[59]

The Castaways was a popular gay tavern in Milwaukee. The name could refer to those ostracized from society or those escaping the restrictions of society. WISCONSIN LGBTQ HISTORY PROJECT

Nite Beat in Milwaukee was the state's sole lesbian bar when the early gay bar guides came out in the 1960s. WISCONSIN LGBTQ HISTORY PROJECT

The 1969 *International Guild Guide*, published on the eve of Stonewall, expanded the Wisconsin listings to include a bar in Wisconsin Dells and one in Kenosha. In this guide, codes were used to make the listing more informative. The Madison bar with the most codes was the Clinique, 110 North Hamilton, which is still fondly remembered by older gays. The listing characterized the bar as "lively every night" and as having "many collegians." Other codes applied to it were "G," "YC," and "WE-especially," which meant gay, young crowd, and weekends, respectively. The Velvet Swing at 317 Gorham had the code "M," which meant mixed or "appears straight but sufficiently active to make it worthwhile." The guide also noted the Velvet Swing had go-go girls, so there were sexual overtones to the place. The Three Bells on University Avenue also earned an "M," with a further note, "Popular with construction workers." Unlike the Kenosha entry, none of the Madison entries had the code "AYOR," which stood for "at your own risk" or "Designates an entry where you might like the people there, but it is highly questionable that they will like you." The codes helped homosexuals evaluate risks and find partners for friendship or sex.[60]

In 1970, presumably based on 1969 data, both nationally popular gay guides—the longstanding *Guild Guide* and the newer *Bob Damron's Address Guide*—reduced the listings in Madison to only three or four in each guide. But one newcomer was the Pirate Ship on North Fairchild Street, the first gay bar in Madison into which I stepped, in the early 1970s. Behind the Pirate Ship, people held infamous parking lot parties. Folks would buy six-packs and party on after the bars closed until four o'clock in the morning. One 1970 guide also noted that outside cruising occurred in Burrows Park from 11 a.m. until dark. As documented in earlier studies, other early gay cruising occurred around the Capitol Square, which had the nickname "Bull Ring." The piano bar at the Edgewater Hotel, although not an official gay bar or in any listings, was popular with gays who wanted to sing show tunes. Sometimes a popular Republican state senator with the queer nickname "Dolly" could be seen on the premises.[61]

Of course, gay bars persisted and multiplied after Stonewall. The Wisconsin gay history website maintained in Milwaukee has attempted to list all the gay and lesbian bars in Wisconsin from 1969 to 2010 as a tribute to the important role they played, and continue to play, in gay community building, noting that "Milwaukee especially has always hosted a large

The interior of the Pirate Ship in Madison. In the tradition of pirates, swashbuckling gay men gathered here in the evenings.

number of gay bars at any point in time; an unusually large quantity of bars compared to other American cities of comparable or even larger size." This may well reflect the traditions of a brewery town. Since my own family hails from German-influenced Ohio—three of my great-grandfathers worked in the brewery business and one great-grandmother was a dealer in "wet goods"—I am familiar with the older brewery business structure. Each brewery sponsored bars around the town to make it easy for customers to buy their product, so German-settled areas like Milwaukee often had many, many taverns. As *Today's Guide to Milwaukee Taverns*, a 1984 booklet, put it, "There is no doubt about it. Milwaukee is a tavern town." Among the gay bars featured in this primarily straight guide, Your Place was said to have patrons that "appear to be having a gay old time at this comfortable little bar." The tavern guide also includes important information on drinking games like Bizz Buzz, Indian, Thumper, and Blow Pong.[62]

One truly post-Stonewall note is that *Bob Damron's Address Guide '76* included an entry for Rodney Scheel's Back Door Bar on North Park Street in Madison: "No sign—just 4 blinking lights—use rear entrance to one of the friendliest bars anywhere." When the publishers of *GLB*, a Milwaukee newsletter, took a road trip to Madison bars that year, they wrote, "Go to the Back Door, go there just to see the mural of a young Judy Garland captioned, 'I don't think we're in Kansas anymore, Toto.'" Rodney Scheel would go on to transform the Hotel Washington complex, including the basement bar, Rod's, into the Capital City's premier gay entertainment venue. The *GLB* publishers also commented, "Madison seems to be more open than most cities in Wisconsin. Perhaps the University has an effect on the gay scene, but the people in Madison seem to take being gay more seriously, and the straight population seems to have a better understanding of the word tolerance."[63]

Many gay folks have found important parts of our identity, friendships, and community in gay bars. Before Stonewall, few other places existed where gay people could be open and public about their sexuality. Many still find comfort and community in such establishments, but today, thanks to the post-Stonewall blooming of gay culture, homosexuals are openly accepted in many other places.

Brotherhood Makes All Men One

As gay bars were established and began to represent an important social institution for homosexuals starting in the 1950s, the political organizing of a gay movement also began in the 1950s. While there was no formally organized gay community in Wisconsin until after Stonewall, there is ample evidence of the state's gay residents joining forces with the early homophile movement and forging attitudes and bonds that would support later activism. The earliest national public efforts of gay activism after World War II started in southern California. *ONE*, the first truly national gay publication, was launched in 1952. The name derived from a quote by the Scottish historian and essayist Thomas Carlyle: "A mystic bond of brotherhood makes all men one." The magazine provides glimpses of the good, the bad, and the ugly that comprised gay life in Wisconsin in the 1950s and early 1960s.[64]

In *Unspeakable: The Rise of the Gay and Lesbian Press in America*, Rodger Streitmatter notes that most of *ONE*'s five thousand monthly copies were sold on newsstands in large cities, including Milwaukee. *ONE* also had about a thousand subscribers. In 1954 it was so bold as to publish the number of subscribers by state (though it did not publish people's names), and twenty-six were from Wisconsin. Wisconsin ranked eleventh in terms of subscribers—a little better than its population rank of fourteenth. The largest number of subscribers, 276, lived in California. But it's worth noting that there were Wisconsin folks in the 1950s who boldly subscribed to a journal that proudly proclaimed itself "The Homosexual Magazine" on its front cover. Henry Eichhorn, an early Wisconsin subscriber who was active with the gay community into the twenty-first century, recalled having no reservations about his subscription, especially since the magazine came in a plain brown wrapper. Reading the monthly issues helped many men overcome the isolation of the period, as well as a sense of being the only person dealing with homosexuality.[65]

ONE followed the general tradition of "little magazines" and included literary work, both fiction and poetry, and there were reviews of books with gay subject matter. Serious policy discussions and polemics on the topic of homosexuality appeared regularly. Some writers were nationally known (such as Norman Mailer) and others were of more limited renown. Staff writers like Jim Kepner often penned pieces under multiple pseudonyms to make it seem like there was a plethora of contributors. Editorials spoke to issues and conditions. A recurring feature called "Tangents" contained homosexual news tidbits. These often came from clippings sent in by subscribers, since the staff proclaimed they could not afford a clipping service. Thus many of the Wisconsin news bits probably originated from Wisconsin readers of the publication.[66]

Additionally, ONE printed letters from subscribers and other correspondents. A dozen brave Wisconsin folks appear in the letters over the years, though generally identified by initials only, demonstrating that many felt they still needed to hide or disguise their gay identity. A present-day reader might wonder, for instance, whether Mr. R. from Madison is the same person as the Mr. R. from Milwaukee who makes an appearance a few years later. However, some letter writers were not afraid to have their personal information published. A Mr. H. from Watertown informed the editors in August/September 1956, "You may include my name and address as a homosexual. In fact, please do include it." Most Wisconsin letters came from Milwaukee, but Kenosha, Racine, Green Bay, Madison, Delavan, Watertown, and two unidentified small towns were also represented.[67]

The poignancy of these letters from across the country is quite stirring, especially since *ONE* was likely one of the only outlets for self-expression available to gay people at that time. The magazine featured on the cover of its January 1960 issue a drawing of a young man with pen in hand under a superimposed line of type, "I Just Had to Write." The writers of the Wisconsin letters mostly expressed positive feelings about their homosexual lives. Mr. B. from Milwaukee, who described himself as being in his fifties, wrote in 1959, "I have for many years considered myself fairly well adjusted." Doctor K. noted, "It may be of interest to you that though everyone in this small town is convinced that I am 'queer,' I have a huge practice. I never date girls; I have many boys who come to visit; my lover comes up often enough to be recognized and greeted on the streets and no one seems to mind. Quite tolerant I feel." In addition to a quiet acceptance from his neighbors, the doctor experienced a successful professional life, a social circle of gay friends, and a domestic partner—all in 1962.[68]

Some letters convey how important the magazine was to its Wisconsin readers. Mr. R of Madison was eager to receive his monthly copy because he believed *ONE* was "certainly to be congratulated upon its wonderful work in the field of advancement of the homosexual's lot." In June/July 1957, Miss K., of Racine, wrote as a new subscriber to congratulate the staff "on the fine work they are doing." In August 1955, Dr. P. from Kenosha sent a check in response to a request for funds for more efficiency in publishing. Another person identified as "a grateful friend" from Wisconsin sent twenty-five dollars in December 1964 to "facilitate investigation and self discovery. Those afraid and alone need such an organization as *ONE* to guide their self understanding." Going even further, Dr. K. from Wisconsin informed the editors in November 1965 that to contribute to their work he was sending "my complete Gay library," which he said consisted of quite a few boxes. He also sent one hundred dollars, because he wrote, "I glory in your work."[69]

Many of the Wisconsin letters reveal the authors' awareness of events relating to gay life happening outside the boundaries of the state, especially in nearby Illinois. Mr. B. of Milwaukee in April 1963 reported on a newly revised law that decriminalized homosexuality statewide in Illinois. After discussing this development with his friends from that state, he noted that "one couple who lived together were a little relieved or had less inward guilty feeling or tenseness about their condition." The following year, in

ONE encouraged readers to write and send letters to the magazine. USC DIGITAL LIBRARY.
ONE NATIONAL GAY AND LESBIAN ARCHIVES

July of 1964, Mr. H. B. of Milwaukee (could it have been the same person?) wrote about bar raids in Chicago that culminated in the publication of the names and addresses of all persons caught, resulting in "an awful lot of people looking for new jobs." His letters show that gay folk from Wisconsin were in communication with other nearby gay communities and had networks for sharing information and evaluating public policy changes.[70]

Letter writers from other states sometimes commented about Wisconsin politics and politicians, as well. A writer from California in early 1955 complained: "Ever since the Grand Inquisitor from Wisconsin got under way I have strongly resented the implication that because of what I am, I am also a traitor to my country, if not an avowed communist. The distance between non-conformity and treason is infinite, and frankly I can't see any homosexual with a degree of intelligence embracing communism."[71]

Some letters offer proof that gay people in Wisconsin collected scrapbook items and accumulated articles about homosexuality, even in the decades before Stonewall. Mr. B. H. of Milwaukee, who included himself in the category of "old people," reports that even though he had had difficulties with the post office, he had nevertheless succeeded in getting additions to his "picture collection in other ways," asserting that these pictures, obtained presumably for erotica purposes, were a "nice amusement." In his letter, this man also mentioned an article in the September 1963 issue of SEXOLOGY, which noted same-sex behavior among male dolphins. Mr. B. H. concluded, "So who says it's unnatural?" Thus, he had access to multiple sources for reinforcing his positive views on his homosexual identity.[72]

Mr. R. of Madison wrote in to comment on a story of November 1958 titled "Homosexuals without Masks." In the story, Tom, a homosexual, complained about a slim young man who "minced" past him. This internal homophobia, even on the part of gay men who intellectually seemed to accept stereotypes about themselves as valid, showed in Tom's further comments about "disgusting queens," "flaming faggots," and "shorthaired, stomping dykes." Mr. R. wrote, "If the attitude of many homosexual men is such as that, then we may as well give up the ship. How can this man ever hope that the world will ever accept the Gay crowd when even individuals among them refuse to accept others of their own kind?" Here

Mr. R. revealed that even in 1959, he knew that there were a lot of gays, or at least enough to make a crowd, and that the fight against internal homophobia and for an inclusive community was serious work. Mr. R. concluded with a patriotic flourish by using a quote attributed to Ben Franklin: "We must all hang together or most assuredly we shall all hang separately."[73]

Other writers also used their letters to express sentiments about the importance of role models and support networks among self-identifying gays, as well as the effort to gain wider societal acceptance. Mr. B., in his letter of June 1959, took to task another writer who felt that at age thirty-seven he no longer needed the magazine: "I do agree wholeheartedly with him that it must be a great help to younger men—so what's wrong with continuing to support it, hoping it will reach more of the younger men and help them get on the right track? *ONE* can't do that without help from some of us adjusted ones." In one of his earliest letters, from March 1958, Mr. B. congratulated *ONE* on winning its postal case (see chapter 7). He went on to say, "It must make all you people feel as though your work is not in vain. It will take a long, long time, but I hope that just as in this case, one by one, your aims will be accomplished." One cannot know what Mr. B. considered a long time. But his and other similar expressions of hope in the 1950s formed the base upon which Wisconsin gays achieved future gains beyond the dreams of the "homophile" community.[74]

Mr. B. from Green Bay, being a new reader, claimed in January 1965 that the magazine had influenced "my perspective to homosexual life." Noting a comment about gays in his town, he reported that Green Bay has "some discreet, and some otherwise." He also praised interracial relationships. His experience traveling to larger cities for sex provoked him to take a swipe at bigger-city homosexuals: "[some] gays think I am a dumb ugly farmer."[75]

Mr. C. of Delavan, in March 1965, claimed to be a student doing research for a term paper to explain why he was writing. He said he was seeking "material on the homosexual movement, its history, effect on society, why people become homosexual and other aspects." Yet his questions conveyed his knowledge that a movement was afoot. He also asked for information on "any other homosexual organizations that I may contact."[76]

In his book *Letters to ONE: Gay and Lesbian Voices from the 1950s and*

1960s, the scholar Craig Loftin described the importance of the magazine's correspondence:

> The letters vividly capture the fears, anxieties, and disasters that befell gay people during these years of McCarthyite repression and institutionalized homophobia, but they also demonstrate a countervailing trend: the significant growth of gay and lesbian communities after World War II. . . . The letters represent an unprecedented national dialogue about the status of gay people in the United States.

And Wisconsinites were part of that dialogue.[77]

ONE magazine also published news from Wisconsin that it communicated to the rest of the nation. These items usually appeared in the "Tangents" section, though some complained that too often "Tangents" depicted the negative aspects of gay life. In October 1959, an editorial defended the section, explaining that "less than one third of the space has been given to arrests, trials, murders, police action and such unsavories—though we receive far more such stories than 'Tangents' retells." Ultimately, the editors wrote, "What we think is needed, which has never before been available, and what ONE is attempting to supply, is the frank and full truth about homosexuals, both the good and the bad."[78]

The news items ranged in content from celebrity lawsuits to medical research. In September 1958, the magazine reported that Wisconsin native Liberace had received a $40,000 settlement from Confidential magazine for "their snide article about him." Another story in August 1959 reported the "flamboyant pianist" won a libel case in a British court by denying that he was a homosexual. In February 1959, ONE reported on University of Wisconsin–Madison researcher Harry Harlow and his controversial study of macaque monkeys. By monitoring how baby rhesus macaques responded to "mother macaques" made of wire covered with terrycloth versus "mothers" made of bare wire but able to give milk, Harlow found that contact and affectional comfort were more important to the babies than nursing. The news items reprinted in ONE quoted the study in their conclusion: "It is cheering to realize . . . that as more and more women go to work, 'the American male is physically endowed with all essential equipment' for serving in the maternal capacity."[79]

In January 1960, ONE reported on a Chicago socialite who died in Genoa City, Wisconsin, a town on the Mississippi River. She left a fortune to a young co-ed "whom she'd lavishly sponsored in school" and with whom she had exchanged letters "expressing deep affection." The socialite also left a large sum of money to another longtime woman friend.[80]

ONE in 1960 carried the news that "the head of Wisconsin's Motor Vehicles Dept. asked for and the legislators introduced a bill to revoke driving licenses of all convicted sex deviates." The administrator wanted the bill to go further, such as banning all known deviates from driving. In the same issue, another article reported on acting Milwaukee County Board chairman John Doyne's "proposed plan for the county to hold all suspected deviates in jail till they could be examined by private psychologists (at $150 per patient) bypassing the state hospital for mental diseases." Supervisor Doyne was seeking ways "to keep sex deviates off the streets" in 1960, because owing to "lack of staff, [the] county hosp[ital] for mental diseases had stopped screening suspected sex deviates arrested on misdemeanors."[81]

In February 1965, ONE picked up an item reporting that in Milwaukee the public health service was "concentrating on male homosexuals" because of new cases of infectious syphilis. The article recognized the public officials' difficulty of reaching and trying to get the cooperation of a population whose sexual activity was illegal. ONE editors commented, "The homosexual grapevine, we predict, would in time produce gratifying grapes in the form of sensational statistics for the US Public Health Service." Yet the implication was that the Milwaukee gay community was certainly sexually active. Such public health indices about homosexuals as this suggest an increasing level of sexual activity within the gay community, a likely sign of growing confidence that gay men could lead homosexual lives in these times.[82]

Wisconsin's Frame Park fracas also caught the attention of ONE. In October 1960, the magazine ran a letter from a Mr. B. in Milwaukee on the Waukesha arrests, noting that he imagined the incident would "lead to demands for a general crackdown on all parks by 'righteously outraged' citizens." In November, a follow-up news item in ONE reported on the charges of sex perversion with possible prison sentences that had resulted and the prominence of some of those arrested. It concluded that after the initial busts, "several other arrests [were] made in following weeks, with police showing little regard for proper arrest methods." *ONE* frequently preached about the fact that homosexuals did not get equal justice at the hands of the police.[83]

Waukesha was not the only Wisconsin city to appear in the pages of *ONE* for homosexual arrests. In November 1960, *ONE* also reported on Elroy Schulz, a brewery worker with a previous sodomy conviction, who had been picked up by vice cop Thomas Thelen after Schulz supposedly made indecent proposals in Milwaukee's Juneau Park. At the jail, "Schulz had to be treated for injuries to his eye, mouth, dentures and side." After being bailed out by a friend, the magazine story continued, "he died of severe internal injuries, fractured ribs and brain hemorrhage an hour later. And who here was the criminal?" A follow-up story covered Milwaukee County judge Christ T. Seraphim's call for a "war on perversion" in Juneau Park owing to the "abnormal" sex acts taking place there. The problem persisted into 1963, as *ONE* reported that "Milwaukee police say their Juneau Park has 'a national reputation as a meeting place for deviates' and they're really out to clean it up."[84]

Earlier that year, in July, *ONE* reported that some Milwaukee gay bar owners had been arrested for "inadequate lighting," a development the magazine characterized as a "typical harassment action where authorities have no legitimate complaint." Also mentioned was a Milwaukee pastor of the Church of the Open Door, who was arrested for persistently phoning youths to suggest indecent acts. In another story covered by *ONE*, "a South Milwaukee alderman was robbed and beaten by a man he met in a tavern and accompanied home for a drink." A 1961 item mentioned a man who committed suicide after being arrested for a morals offense with an eighteen-year-old youth. These news items presented both Milwaukee's gay scene and its tensions with the police to the nation in these pre-Stonewall days.[85]

These examples demonstrate that a substantial number of gay Wisconsinites used the national platform of *ONE* to communicate. For the most part, they discussed their attitudes and their lives in positive terms. The articles about gay issues and life in the state showed the rest of the nation that, while visible gay activity and institutions like bars could be targeted, Wisconsin had an active gay community that would not be suppressed.

POWERFUL SISTERHOOD

The Ladder, published monthly from 1956 until 1972, was the first nationally distributed lesbian publication in the United States. It provided Wisconsin lesbians with a place to communicate and trade information, as *ONE* did for Wisconsin's gay men. The magazine was sponsored by the Daughters of Bilitis (DOB), a lesbian organization founded in San Francisco by Phyllis Lyon and Del Martin, who had experience in journalism. When the magazine began printing, in the McCarthy period, Lyon and Martin used pseudonyms, but they soon switched to their real names in an effort to encourage their readers not to hide. Lesbian historian Lillian Faderman, in *Odd Girls and Twilight Lovers*, is a bit critical of the DOB for the group's narrow appeal to middle-class lesbians. For example, the organization had in the 1950s advocated a "mode of behavior and dress acceptable to society."[86]

Early issues of *The Ladder* were duplicated by mimeograph and hand stapled. Subscribers were assured that the names on the mailing list were kept secret and protected. Circulation was limited to 400 brave subscribers in 1957, but had climbed to 3,800 by 1970. The lesbian magazine maintained friendly relations with *ONE* magazine, the primary gay male publication out of Los Angeles. *The Ladder* also was connected with Frank Kameny of the Washington, DC, Mattachine Society, as he contributed articles. Feature articles focused on famous lesbians from history such as English author Radclyffe Hall and Christina, Queen of Sweden. The journal also published both fiction and poetry. *The Ladder* ran stories on "The Homosexual Vote," "The Homosexual Minority in America," and "The History of S.F. Homophile Groups"; in addition, it featured several articles on homosexuals picketing for gay rights in the nation's capital—the cover of the October 1965 issue showed a photo of the picket line.[87]

The Ladder was delighted to report to its readers in December 1963 that Felix Pollak, curator of rare books for the UW–Madison Memorial Library, had recognized the DOB publication as a valid "little magazine," a category on which he was the national expert. Pollak wrote an article in the September 1960 issue of the *Library Journal* that publishing a journal like *The Ladder* would have been unthinkable thirty or even twenty years earlier. He wrote, "We are today witnessing the emergence of publications like *ONE*, *Mattachine Review*, and *The Ladder*, presenting with candor and fortitude the position of male and female homosexuals in our society." He felt these journals were "a variant manifestation of the time-honored little magazine concern with the outsiders of society, the outcasts, the deviators from majority-sanctioned 'norms' with minority rights, problems, and aspirations. . . . Even though the minorities in this case have to be their own spokemen and defenders."[88]

Barbara Grier contributed a great deal of material to *The Ladder* over the years, under several names including her own, especially as a book reviewer; she took over as editor in 1968. The magazine aimed to make its readers aware of "lesbiana" or material published with lesbian content, and Grier later became the publisher for Naiad Press, which put out many lesbian volumes. In 1975, when a reissue of *The Ladder* was published, she wrote of the original, "[the editors] believed that they were moving the world with their labors, and I believe that they were right."[89]

Another contributor to *The Ladder* was Jeannette Howard Foster, whose 1956 book *Sex Variant Women in Literature: A Historical and Quantitative Survey* was one of the earliest comprehensive works of lesbian scholarship. While this self-published pioneer work in lesbian studies was never widely read, Diana Press and Naiad Press reissued editions in 1975 and 1985, respectively. The black playwright Lorraine Hansberry, author of *A Raisin in the Sun*, contributed two letters to the *Ladder* editor.[90]

While *The Ladder* did not print many news items, some occasionally appeared scattered among its pages. In the August/September 1970 issue, it was reported that Dr. George Albee, from the faculty of Case Western Reserve University, who was then president of the American Psychological Association, had spoken to the Wisconsin Psychiatric Association on June 17 of that year. He branded "repressive forces" as "patrists" and criticized people with exaggerated masculine values and a thirst for cutthroat competition. About these patrists, he asserted, "Women are accorded in this group low status: men use them rather than accept them as equals. At the same time the importance of chastity is stressed and strict controls are imposed on the freedom of women." Presumably, Albee felt his Wisconsin audience would be receptive to such a critique.[91]

The magazine, which had printed articles on homosexual marriage in previous years, was probably delighted to present to its readers the 1971 news item, "Two Black Women Seek Marriage License" in Milwaukee. The brief notice told the story of Donna Burkett, age twenty-five, and Manonia Evans, twenty-one, who filed a suit in federal district court after having been denied a marriage license by county officials. The couple said they were "being deprived of marital benefits such as inheritance rights and the filing of a joint income tax return." They would go on to lose their court case, but were married in a church ceremony.[92]

Lesbians from Wisconsin connected to *The Ladder*. In November 1958, J. W. D. from Mauston wrote that she was pleased with her recent subscription and commended the editors "most highly." She was moved to send along a small donation. From her small city of 3,200 in Juneau County, she proclaimed herself "isolated here" and said it was refreshing "to read about those that I have things in common." J. W. D. was "greatly interested in the books listed on page 15, Lesbiana." She hoped she might be able to order them through the magazine's office. Sure enough, in May 1960, the magazine, after "many requests from friends and readers," announced the establishment of the DOB Book Service, which offered a small selection of lesbian titles for sale and struggled to maintain the subscription service over the years. *The Ladder* never did have many correspondents. In fact, the editors noted in July 1959, "Letters from our readers commenting on articles and stories appearing in *The Ladder* are becoming fewer and fewer."[93]

In its June/July 1971 edition, the magazine published a letter from Donna Martin of Milwaukee, a pseudonym sometimes used by Donna Utke. Just a year earlier, in 1970, Utke had been one of five brave people to sign her real name as one of the founding members of Milwaukee's Gay Peoples Union. Utke had attended UW–Madison as a graduate student in English. There she befriended fellow student and later Madison activist Barbara Lightner in the 1960s. Both women were closeted at the time. A librarian with the Milwaukee Public Library, Utke was also an active member of Grapevine, a feminist writers' guild, and helped found the Lesbian Alliance of Metro Milwaukee in 1989.[94]

To *The Ladder*, Utke wrote that she had been an eager reader for some months. She praised the publication's focus on women's liberation, since she also proclaimed herself a member of NOW. Utke said that she found "camaraderie and relaxation" with her sisters at the local gay bar, but intellectual excitement among her sisters at NOW. She claimed that Milwaukee had "the only Lesbian bar in the state" at the time. In her letter, she advanced a theory of "sexual timidity" about lesbians, observing that lesbian bars were "everywhere far outnumbered by male gay bars." She believed this led to a false theory there were fewer lesbians than male homosexuals. She also believed "suppressed" women were told to accept second best and not develop their vocational potential, which led to women being "discouraged from developing [their] sexual potentialities." Utke deplored the idea that unmarried women over age thirty should accept "the bleak joys of celibacy" after presumably losing their sexual desire. "In short," she wrote, "in our society, women, like the spring ephemerals, seem doomed to a brief and fragile flowering."[95]

Utke argued that women with "deviant proclivities" were subject to the same mechanisms that oppressed women in general. "The chances that the latent Lesbian will break out of her cocoon," she reasoned, "are, it seems to me much less than that the male homosexual will come to see himself as such." At the time of her writing in 1971, she claimed to be an unwilling celibate, not finding attractive and interesting women at the bar scene. She would later, however, find a life partner of many years.[96]

Over the years, the volunteers who published *The Ladder* wrote about their growing pains and noted that the issues were often shaped by "funds available and labor willing." When the magazine ceased publication with the August/September 1972 issue, Barbara Grier (writing as Gene Damon) said, "Many women reading this will be upset, many will be sorry. None of you will be as sorry as we are to have to take this step." Surely many lesbians in Wisconsin in the 1950s and 1960s felt that their lives were changed by *The Ladder*, as many gay men's lives were changed by ONE.[97]

MATTACHINE ORGANIZING IN WISCONSIN

While some Wisconsinites participated in the nascent national dialogue about homosexuals in the pages of *ONE*, a few souls sought to politically organize gays in Wisconsin during the 1950s. A number of letters from Badgers show up in the California archives of the Mattachine Society, the first national homophile organization in America.

Apparently the first Wisconsinite to write to the California-based Mattachine Society was Sig Piotrowski of Milwaukee in 1953, asking for "full

information on conducting discussion and organizing chapters in my city."
The respondent asked Piotrowski's permission "to put you in contact with
others in your area who have expressed an interest in the Society and its
organization there." Enclosed with the response letter was the latest bro-
chure with details on the group's aims and principles. Also in 1953, Gilbert
Frohe of Milwaukee wrote to the society after seeing an ad in *ONE*. In his letter, he wonders whether "Chicago may not already have a chapter in which
one can meet congenial individuals." In 1954 Steve Van Kirk from Little
Chute received a response similar to the one Piotrwoski received explaining,
"We do not have a chapter in your area as yet. However, we would welcome
the formation of such a chapter." By 1955, when Carl Kroll of Milwaukee
wrote for information on the Mattachine Society, he was referred to the
"Area Council in Chicago, the nearest branch to Milwaukee."[98]

In 1956, the Mattachine Society received an interesting letter from
Glenn Bacon, MD, a psychiatrist in Racine. He presented his Wisconsin
city as "fairly rigid," saying, "There is a great deal of sexual repression
and a tendency to take a dim view of any sexual practices other than those
condoned by the community." Further, he explained, "From the court
system here, everyone arrested for sodomy or even on suspicion of homosexuality is referred to my office for 'treatment.'" He noted that the
twenty-five gays in his caseload "present the common symptom of not
wanting 'treatment.'" He realizes they nevertheless come to see him versus the alternative of being "sent to Waupun Prison Hospital under the
Wisconsin Sexual Deviate Act."[99]

Dr. Bacon concluded "that the only form of therapy available for these
patients would be group psychotherapy of some sort." In the model Bacon
used for his therapy, "no attempt is made to 'cure' these individuals, but
deals merely with the social problems arising from their status in society."
This idea came from a seminar Bacon had attended at the Moreno Institute
in New York. After working with his gay patients for two months, he found
they were "quite interested in forming some sort of protective alliance so
that they would have a means of dealing with the law when apprehended."
Since Dr. Bacon found the judge sympathetic, he had decided to write *ONE*
"in an attempt to find out whether you have any branches in the middle
western portion of the United States."[100]

The response to Dr. Bacon came from D. C. Olson, secretary of the soci-

After a Racine judge referred homosexuals appearing before his court to medical counseling, Dr. Glenn Bacon sought to connect them to an early homophile organization.

ety's board of directors. On behalf of the Mattachine Society, he wrote, "We are very much enthused by your fine letter and applaud your interest and activity on behalf of the homosexual. It is not often that one finds someone who is so willing to help." Unfortunately, Olson added, the nearest society branch was in Chicago, but it is "not a very active one."[101]

Olson also wrote, "We would be most interested in hearing more about the local situation in Racine as regards homosexuality. . . . It is gratifying to hear of the apparent interest shown by the Judge in Racine. This kind of interest and understanding is the only thing [that] can lead to a better life for the homosexual." About Mattachine, he said, "It is not the intention of the Society to form an organization for homosexuals only, exclusive of heterosexuals. We believe in the need for integration of the homosexual into his surroundings." In the letter, Olson went on to describe an attempt to connect Dr. Bacon with Dr. Evelyn Hooker, who would soon release research on gays at a Chicago symposium. Olson expressed the view that the homosexual "needs the understanding and help that can lead to his acceptance as another human being. When this is accomplished, he can be a productive person and a valuable person to the community in which he lives." While the men from Wisconsin who hoped to become involved in the Mattachine Society did not find great success because of the organization's limited national presence, their efforts do demonstrate the need for political organizing and advocacy in the days before Stonewall.[102]

There was an additional Wisconsin intersection with the Mattachine Society. In 1962 the Washington, DC, Mattachine Society was given non-profit status as a registered organization for charitable purposes. Since the government of the federal district was subject to congressional control, a bill was introduced to deny them charitable status. The bill's sponsor, Representative John Dowdy (D-TX, 1952–1973), said the purpose was to "refuse government sanction of any kind to organizations whose activities are not deserving of such recognition and encouragement." Dowdy specifically mentioned "the Mattachine Society of Washington, an organization formed allegedly to protect homosexuals from discrimination." Dowdy was offended that "the District of Columbia was placing its brand of approval on this organization by issuing them a permit to solicit charitable contributions." The record made clear that this group was "operating in various parts of this country and abroad" and had a sinister purpose, which Dowdy attempted to demonstrate by quoting the DC branch's co-founder, Frank Kameny: "Our primary effort, thus far, has been an attempt, by lawful means, to alter present discriminatory policy against the homosexual minority—a minority perhaps almost as large as the Negro minority."[103]

This was an early congressional vote on a bill that clearly aimed to suppress the emerging homophile rights movement. Opposing Dowdy in debate were congressmen William Ryan (D-NY, 1961–1972) and James Roosevelt (D-CA, 1955–1965). Roosevelt in debate appeared familiar enough with the Mattachine efforts to state they had never raised $1,500, the required threshold for mandatory registration for nonprofit status. Three of the ten Wisconsin congressmen voted against the bill—Representatives Robert Kastenmeier (D-Watertown, 1959–1991), Alvin O'Konski (R-Mercer, 1943–1973), and Henry Reuss (D-Milwaukee, 1955–1983). O'Konski had earlier in his career been a Progressive member of the state legislature. This 30 percent Wisconsin vote for the Mattachine was higher than the overall House vote of only 19 percent against. Although this congressional action likely had minimal effect on the Washington chapter's very limited finances, it reveals the nation's continued animus directed toward any homosexual organizing efforts at the time, despite some favorable votes from Wisconsin.[104]

"Homocrats" Stir Up Wisconsin

One indicator that political winds toward homosexuals might be chang-ing came in 1966 from Wisconsin, which probably surprised homophile activists on the coasts. The first serious gay rights demonstrations are generally said to have taken place on July 4, 1965, in front of Independence Hall, Philadelphia, and later that year in front of the White House—four years before Stonewall. Homosexuals were claiming that they too were citizens and therefore entitled to equality under the law promised by the Declaration of Independence. That this novel idea was to find public ex-pression in Wisconsin less than a year later might not have been predicted by many. After all, as recently as 1962 there had been the Gay Purge at the UW–Madison, one of the state's most progressive institutions.

Perhaps as a reaction to that blatant attack, in 1966 the UW–Madison campus chapter of the Young Democrats of America adopted a resolu-tion to be forwarded for consideration at the organization's March state convention on homosexuality, in Manitowoc. The proposed platform plank—so-called presumably because party candidates could stand on the planks in the platform as they campaigned for office—said, "We favor the abolishment of laws directed toward preventing those persons who are homosexually inclined from freedom of action." Interviews with sev-eral of the surviving UW participants of 1966 did not uncover any known gay participation in the effort; rather, the plank was part of the Young Democrats' broad progressive agenda for equal rights. Another proposal from the Madison Young Democrats called for the repeal of laws against unnatural sex acts between males and females. The two proposals were combined with one from UW–Milwaukee at the state convention into an overall call for the abolition of all laws restricting sexual relations between consenting adults that do not violate the rights of others. The measure after heated debate was adopted on a vote of 76 to 55.[105]

Statewide media quickly dubbed this "the sex plank," and it caused a furor of comment and condemnation. Most of the press had believed the big news of the convention would be the organization's stance on the Vietnam War, with the Young Democrats likely to be mildly or harshly critical of the Johnson administration. Pro-administration and antiwar floor demonstrations took place on the first night, with national speakers

The Young Democrats of Wisconsin adopted a sex plank calling for decriminaliz-ing homosexual acts at the organization's 1966 convention, which took place at the Manitowoc Hotel.

addressing the war issue. But the stance on Vietnam was quickly over-shadowed in the state press by the sex plank adopted on the last day of the gathering. One critic described the platform with the popular slogan, "Make Love, Not War."[106]

This controversial provision was just one of a number of issues the Young Democrats had opinions on in 1966. Others included a uniform state drinking age of eighteen, voting at age eighteen, four-year terms for governors, rent subsidies for the poor, a repeal of the Taft–Hartley provisions that permitted "right to work" laws, a study of a proposal aimed at a guaranteed annual minimum wage, a proposal against adding the militant black organization called the W. E. B. DuBois Club to the attorney general's list of subversive organizations, and the elimination of the state's ban on colored oleomargarine. Only in Wisconsin could a pre-Stonewall debate on gay rights be paired with a debate about the right to buy yellow margarine.[107]

The *Milwaukee Journal* made a prediction on Monday, March 28, claiming that during the debate, "opponents of the original plank said specific mention of homosexuals was an enlightened point of view but would merely provide campaign fodder for Republicans." On Tuesday evening, the same paper reported that their prediction had come true, as John Hazelwood, chairman of the Greater Milwaukee Republican League, denounced the Young Democrats' platform because it "clearly indicates that that organization has been captured by radicals." Hazelwood charged that the platform "blatantly encourages the legal acceptance of homosexuality and adultery" and would encourage "free love." Not long after, the Republican Party newsletter said the plank was "encouraging homosexuality." When the Young Republicans met a month later, despite the fact that the "sex plank was one of the main topics of conversation" among delegates, their leaders headed off any action. Though their executive committee had previously criticized the sex plank, their convention was, reported the *Milwaukee Journal*, "conspicuous" in its official silence on the subject. One young GOP member said, "We sort of left the sex field to them,"—that is, the Democrats.[108]

But Hazelwood had lots of company in opposing the platform, as the *Milwaukee Journal* and other papers continued to report over the next several weeks. The Third State Senatorial District Democrats in Milwaukee

Sex Plank Debate Rages

'Decent' Dems Should Quit Y-Dems, Sen. Benson Says

By JOHN PATRICK HUNTER
(Of The Capital Times Staff)

Sex, not Saigon, continued to be the main political issue in Wisconsin today.

It all began last Sunday when the Young Democratic Clubs of Wisconsin adopted a convention platform that included a p l a n k which calls for abolition of all laws restricting sexual relations between consenting adults.

Thursday, some, but by no means all, Republican politiocs lashed out at the offending juniors.

* * *

Today, a well known Democrat joined their ranks. Sen. Taylor Benson (D-Franksville) called on "decent" Democrats to quit the Y-Dems. The sex plank was inspired, Benson charged, by the "beatniks and kooks from the University of Wisconsin."

"Members of the Young Democrats who believe in the principles of decency, moral integrity and sanctity of the family should quit the present party and start fresh," said Benson.

Gov. Knowles shied away from the controversy. He said he did not want to discuss the issue.

Conrad G o o d kind, M a dison, state Y-Dem chairman, said he was disappointed to hear that Benson had "overlooked the important positions taken by t h e Young Democrats on issues like Viet Nam, the structure of state government, oleomargarine, highway safety and higher education."

* * *

Goodkind said most of the University of Wisconsin delegation had left the convention in Manitowoc by the time the sex plank was discussed, making Benson's reference to UW "beatniks and kooks" unfair.

Republican glee over the action of the Y-Dems could be short-lived.

The Young Republican convention starts in Oshkosh April 29. Last year the Y-GOP caused a hassle that raged for six months when the membership chairman resigned charging the YGOP favored "reactionary causes."

Read The WANT-ADS for Profit!

The sex plank of the Young Democrats was featured for over a month in the state's press and even made the *New York Times*. CAPITAL TIMES, APRIL 1, 1966 on the night of Tuesday, March 29, adopted a motion made by Democratic state senator Casimir Kendziorski disapproving of the sex plank stand. Chairman Ronald Hintzke told delegates that "if they remained silent they would be approving the stand." Democratic state senator Taylor Benson of Franksville, in Racine County, called the platform "an example of filth" and went further, saying, "Every Young Democrat who believes in the principles of decency, moral integrity and the sanctity of the family" should quit the organization and start a new one. Benson attributed the sex plank to beatniks and radicals from UW–Madison. By April 5, thirty-six Young Democrats from southeastern Wisconsin had signed a statement that they "supported the solidarity of the family" and were opposed to "adultery, homosexuality and prostitution." The signers stated that sex had no place in a political platform.[109]

As proclaimed in a headline of the *Milwaukee Sentinel* on April 5, the state's highest official, Republican governor Warren Knowles, joined the chorus of "No Place for Sex in Party Platform." The governor noted a tendency on the part of both Young Democrats and Young Republicans to become involved with philosophical issues, which are not a part of government. Knowles said, "It is unfortunate that the question was raised in any respect." The governor deplored party splits and noted, "The homocrats against the Democrats is going a little too far." Knowles's comments sounded quite similar to earlier comments made by Ody J. Fish, state GOP chairman, who said, "I doubt if the people of Wisconsin favor sex as a statewide political issue." Wainwright Churchill, in his 1967 book *Homosexual Behavior among Males: A Cross Cultural Species Investigation*, comments on the reaction to the Wisconsin Young Democrats' action. He observed that it was an "illogical assertion since those who made this criticism must certainly believe that sex has a very definite place in the penal code."[110]

Conrad Goodkind from Madison, state chairman of the Young Democrats, responded to the criticism of the sex plank, noting, "If Democrats are for it and Republicans are against it, that might account for the fact that there are more Democrats." Goodkind thought the Democratic Party "should be able to embrace divergent views." One Young Democrat, Jim Miller, chairman of the Fifth Congressional District Young Democrat Clubs (Milwaukee), though opposed to the sex plank, complained that the newspaper articles were tinged with sensationalism. Eugene Burns of the Marquette University Young Democrats, who authored the substitute language, noted in an April 8 letter to the editor of the *Milwaukee Sentinel* that all press accounts left out the first part of the plank that affirmed, "We recognize the government has no right to legislate personal sexual ethics, therefore we favor the abolition of all restrictions on sexual relations involving consenting adults which do not violate the rights of others." Another letter to the editor in a later issue complained that Burns used a quote from *Playboy* magazine to make his case, instead of using the Bible as an authority.[111]

The *New York Times* joined the fray on April 10 and noted the related context of British action on the Wolfenden report, a policy document from the British government, on decriminalizing homosexuality. The House of Lords had adopted the recommendations in 1965, and they were pending in the House of Commons at the time. The British Labour Government of Harold Wilson would see them pass in 1967. Regarding Wisconsin, the *New York Times* remarked, "An advocate said this was the first time the issue had become an American political party plank." Wainwright Churchill mentioned the groundbreaking action in calling for US reform in his 1967 book *Homosexual Behavior among Males*.[112]

In late April, John Huettner, chairman of the Young Democrats' platform committee and a senior in political science at UW–Milwaukee, debated the sex plank on campus with the president of the Methodist Wesley Foundation, the campus Methodist center. Huettner noted that since the Wisconsin Young Democrats had pioneered the sex plank, similar measures had been approved by Young Democrats in Minnesota and the District of Columbia, and by the College Young Democrats of America. This pioneering action, however, did not make it into one history of the Democratic Party covering the years 1949–1989. Just two years earlier, in October 1964, A. E. Smith had published an article in *ONE* titled "The Myth of the Homosexual Vote." Smith claimed there was no such thing, given that "We can't vote 'for' homosexuality. No party holds out anything to us." The Wisconsin Young Democrats and the sex plank brought a bit of hope to that bleak future vision.[113]

Senior Democrats were none too happy with the sex plank in 1966. Building the modern Democratic Party had been the work of the Democratic Organizing Committee after World War II, when some Progressives, Socialists, and old-line Democrats joined to build a new movement. Wisconsin's Democratic lieutenant governor Patrick Lucey, who as state chairman had been part of building the modern party, dismissed the sex plank incident as "a flash in the pan." *Wisconsin State Journal* columnist John Wyngaard wrote on April 11 that the outspoken youngsters were embarrassing the party:

> The sexual freedom platform demand of the Young Democrats is especially awkward and distorted when the ethnic and religious composition of the Wisconsin Democratic party as a voting group is considered. Indeed it would be difficult to devise another declaration that would be quite as offensive, or astounding, to large blocs of voters without whom the Democrats of Wisconsin cannot hope to prosper.[114]

In its coverage, the *New York Times* suggested that "the regular Democrats were furious that the issue was raised, although publicly they expressed chagrinned amusement." Yet, by the bicentennial year, many would eventually change their tune. In 1976, the state Democratic Party platform, with much spirited debate, as I personally recall, included the following language: "We support the extension of full civil rights to people of variant sexual inclinations, and the abolition of criminal sanctions on the private sexual activity of consenting adults." Ten years earlier the Young Democrats of 1966 had set the stage for Wisconsin's most significant response to Stonewall, when the senior party finally supported "full civil rights." The next volume of this book will show how this pioneering 1966 action was fought for and implemented by Democrats in the 1970s and 1980s.[115]

THE HOMOSEXUAL COMMUNITY

"The subjection of homosexuals to legal punishments and social condemnation has produced a complex structure of concealed social relations which merit sociological investigation," wrote Maurice Leznoff and William Westley in "The Homosexual Community," a chapter in the 1963 book *The Problem of Homosexuality in Modern Society*. While their outsiders' view was still judgmental, the book provided an insightful glimpse into the dynamics of the pre-Stonewall gay community in America. These authors wrote:

> Since the homosexual group provides the only social context in which homosexuality is normal, deviant practices moral, and homosexual responses rewarded, the homosexual develops a deep emotional involvement with his group, tending toward a ready acceptance of its norms and dictates, and subjection to its behavior patterns. The regularity with which he seeks the company of his group is a clear expression of his dependency.

They went on to describe overt and secret groups among homosexuals with "a number of common interests and common moral norms." Leznoff and Westley believed the homosexual community of a city was "linked with other homosexual communities in Canada and the United States, chiefly by the geographical mobility of its members."[116]

A somewhat more sympathetic view of the new world emerging from the shadows was portrayed in *The Gay World: Male Homosexuality and the Social Creation of Evil* by Martin Hoffman, a retired psychiatrist who had taught at the University of California–Berkeley. In the book, published in 1968, he observed that the gay bar "is the central public place around which gay life revolves and is to be found in all large and medium-sized cities across the country," because "homosexuals have really no place else where they can congregate without disclosing to the straight world that they are homosexual." In his epilogue, "What Is to Be Done?" he wrote, "I suggest that we view homosexuals as a minority group, and begin to seriously consider giving them the full legal rights and social privileges that we have finally given to some minority groups (e.g., Roman Catholics) and that we talk about giving to others." As Hoffman saw it, the result would be "the end of the gay world as a hidden, deviant subculture lurking in the unhappy interstices of the larger society."[117]

A few years later, as America continued changing, Del Martin and Phyllis Lyon wrote a chapter on "The New Sexuality and the Homosexual" in *The New Sexuality*, published in 1971. Both women had been sponsors of *The*

Ladder, the first lesbian publication in the United States, and founders of the Daughters of Bilitis, the first lesbian organization to be founded in the period of the Mattachine Society for men. In their chapter, they made the distinction that "whereas homosexual denotes sex with same, homophile connotes love of the same. Too often people think of homosexuality solely in terms of specific sexual acts and do not regard the homosexual's behavior in context, as a single facet or characteristic of the whole person."[118]

Martin and Lyon observed:

> The knowledge that "I am not alone" had a terrific impact on ho-
> mosexuals across the country. They began to seek each other out to
> organize for mutual protection and to promote public education and
> research. . . . With support of their peers they have learned to accept
> themselves and have gained a sense of identity and dignity as human
> beings. Through the security of the group, they have attained a sense
> of community in which they can deal with and overcome society-
> imposed guilt and fear.[119]

Throughout the twentieth-century decades before Stonewall, we see gay men and lesbians in Wisconsin affirming their own identities, as Clarence Cameron did in responding to the draft, or like the men who wrote letters to *ONE* magazine and the women who wrote to *The Ladder*. We see them building the social networks of community like the Jenifer Street salon and even the "rings" of deviates in Waukesha and Ladysmith that had operated for years before being smashed.

The seeds of community were growing around the state, fed by long-standing traditions and energized by new ways of expression. Taliesin overcame its moment of trial and continued to be a gathering space for many gays in the Wisconsin tradition of friendly nonurban enclaves. The Winnebago two-spirited tradition survived its repression. Gay communication happened locally and via national networks such as physical culture magazines and bar guides, and with the emerging homophile organizing efforts. The Young Democrats of Wisconsin in 1966 took a bold and progressive stance on homosexual equality, acting well before any other organized political party group in America.

The congressional vote on the Washington, DC, Mattachine issue showed how the increasing visibility of homosexuals and the homosexual community could elicit a reaction from actors in mainstream political life. It also showed three members of the Wisconsin delegation, two Democrats and one Republican, refusing to side with the fearmongers, a foretaste of Wisconsin's bipartisan support for gay rights in the 1970s and 1980s. The growing interactions between the mainstream political forces and the emerging Wisconsin gay and lesbian communities will be the story told in the next volume, *Coming Out, Moving Forward*, on Wisconsin's LGBT history from Stonewall to the present.

EPILOGUE
EMERGING FROM THE SHADOWS

*W*e've *Been Here All Along* reveals how the forces of law and order in Wisconsin have punished and patrolled non-normative sexual and gender behavior since the state's territorial days. Before the arrival of European Americans who established the state we now know as Wisconsin, the American Indians living in this area honored and respected non-conforming gender expression, as some continue to do today. By uncovering the vestiges of homosexual life in the state, beginning with press reactions to the Oscar Wilde trials in the late nineteenth century, we can see that the suppression of homosexuality in Wisconsin stretches back many decades.

Pushing back against the labels of criminality and sickness, gay men, lesbians, and other gender nonconforming individuals struggled to define their own identities. They also contemplated ways to present themselves to society and built networks to reinforce their sense of community. Many collected photographs, news items, and bits of ephemera in scrapbooks to strengthen their senses of identity and, in some cases, to verify their existence to later generations. In some instances, they constructed safe spaces or enclaves where "artistic" lives could be led. Trans individuals, too, were included in this larger category of "others," even if nobody had a word for them.

During and around the time of World War II, Wisconsin's LGBT people began expressing aspirations to live more fully authentic lives out of the shadows. They increased their networking and organizing. By participating in various academic studies, they placed their own voices on the record. These brave souls rejected the efforts to suppress their personhood and their lifestyles, rejected the derogatory labels attributed to them, and expressed that they, like most people, simply wanted to love and be loved.

As a national gay social and political culture emerged in the decades prior to 1969's Stonewall Riots, Wisconsinites found ways to participate in and contribute to this national movement. They wrote to national magazines like *ONE* and *The Ladder*. They connected through physical culture publications. They even sought out nascent homophile organizations. In short, they began the journey to their own liberation. Whether society would more openly accept liberated LGBT Wisconsinites and change its attitudes, laws, and institutions is the story of *Coming Out, Moving Forward: Wisconsin's Recent Gay History*.

Gay men found community at the 602 Club in Madison in the mid-1960s.
PHOTO BY JOHN RIGGS, CIRCA 1965

Acknowledgments

A work of this scope is possible only with the assistance and encouragement of many others. I wish to thank them from the deep places of my heart. However, in mentioning some who have helped with this volume, I'm sure I have forgotten others. I beg readers' indulgence for any oversights here, as well as for any errors that may appear in this book.

Nadine Zimmerli provided translations of the Wisconsin German-language newspapers; thanks to John Tortorice of the George L. Mosse Program in History for steering me to her. And thanks to John for several lunches at the University Club and for roping others into our discussions, like Professor Jim Steakley, who provided many good ideas and hints for sources. Will Fellows has been invaluable in breaking some of this ground in his books and in providing me with concepts and sources. Larry Reed, keeper of the Cooksville Archives, provided valuable access to materials and cheery companionship. Thanks also to Kyle Morgan, who sent copies of the Kepner and Jordan letters at the *ONE* archives.

The patience and knowledge of archivists at the UW–Madison Archives, especially David Null and Troy Reeves, were most helpful. And thanks to my fellow workers on the community committee for furthering that archive's LGBT special collection: Scott Seyforth, Michele Besant, Pat Calchina, Kalleen Mortensen, and Katherine Charek Briggs. The UW–Milwaukee Archives with its LGBT collection was also invaluable, and its originator and caretaker Michael Doylen encouraged my early efforts by displaying its rich resources. The archivists at the Wisconsin Historical Society assisted with many boxes. The staff of the Legislative Reference Library proved extremely helpful, as did the library staff at the Wisconsin Veterans Museum. The Wisconsin Law Library staff aided me, a non-lawyer, in finding rich documents. The staff of the Mineral Point Library also made wonderful materials available.

LGBT community members made this work possible with their memories and collections. My many chats with Ted Pierce, some over dinner, always proved delightful. I was very moved by his decision to share his rich trove of images of the Jenifer Street circle with me. Bob Davis shared some of Ted's papers. Joe Koberstein's niece recalled many stories about her uncle, his partner Keith McCutcheon, and the Jenifer Street circle. I am sure the spirits of Joe and Keith have hovered over me as I wrote this book in the historic Sauthoff House, the dwelling they and other gay men shared for many decades.

Several times, the late David Adamany drew on his memory to share his history of coming out to Governor Patrick Lucey. Elena Sherman told tales of her father, Milt Sherman, and shared wonderful pictures from the late 1930s. Ron McCrea, an engaging storyteller and a longtime friend,

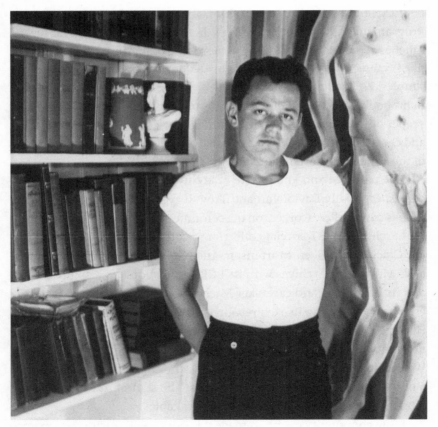

Ted Pierce was very generous in sharing images of the Jenifer Street circle, including this one of Lil' Wayne posing before some nude adult male art in Pierce's house. FROM THE AUTHOR'S COLLECTION, COURTESY OF TED PIERCE

was among the first to record the stories of gay men in Wisconsin. My old friends Henry and Susan Eichhorn shared Henry's original collection of *ONE* magazines. Brian Bigler's early research and ongoing clues helped with my work on this book. Patrick Farabaugh at *Our Lives* magazine encouraged me to write stories of our history and proved to me that an audience exists.

Then there was my Patrick, who took me to places where materials could be found and inspired me with his enthusiasm for Haresfoot history. Thanks to everyone who read a chapter or two. Another support has been my faith community, which believes the Holy One holds all in mercy. Most of all, my great friend and book coach Mark Webster, who has walked this journey with me, deserves unending appreciation for his guidance and encouragement.

For the production of this book and its companion volume, my heartfelt appreciation goes to the donors who made it possible, and especially the plotters—Kathy Borkowski, Paula Bonner, Ann Schaffer, Mark Webster, and Mary Strickland—who reaped the harvest. The Wisconsin Historical Society staff has opened itself to LGBT history as part of the Wisconsin story, and thanks for that are due to Kathy Borkowski, Brian Thompson, and others. At the Press, Kate Thompson has been there from the beginning, as has Elizabeth Wyckoff, a very dedicated editor who has made this volume so much better. I am honored to contribute to the ongoing documentation of gay history in Wisconsin.

NOTES

Introduction

1. David Carter, *Stonewall: The Riots That Sparked the Gay Revolution* (New York: St. Martin's Griffin, 2004), 1; see also "Post Stonewall: 1969–1970," in Martin Duberman, *Stonewall* (New York: Dutton, 1993).
2. Will Fellows, *Farm Boys: Lives of Gay Men from the Rural Midwest* (Madison: University of Wisconsin Press, 1969); Will Fellows, *A Passion to Preserve: Gay Men as Keepers of Culture* (Madison: University of Wisconsin Press, 2004); Michail Takach, *LGBT Milwaukee* (Charleston, SC: Arcadia, 2016).

Chapter 1

1. "Wilde's Disgrace," *Superior Evening Telegram*, April 4, 1895.
2. Editorial, *Wisconsin State Journal*, April 8, 1895.
3. Jonathan Katz, *Gay American History: Lesbians and Gay Men in the U.S.A.* (New York: Thomas Y. Crowell, 1976).
4. For good discussions of earlier male same-sex activity that was not linked to an emerging homosexual identity, see Graham Robb, *Strangers: Homosexual Love in the Nineteenth Century* (New York: Norton, 2004) and George Chauncey, *Gay New York: Gender Urban Culture and the Making of the Gay Male World 1890–1940* (New York: Basic Books, HarperCollins, 1994). The comprehensive Wilde biography is Richard Ellmann, *Oscar Wilde* (New York: Knopf, 1988). A more colorful treatment is Frank Harris, *Oscar Wilde* (New York: Dorset Press, 1989).
5. Lloyd Lewis and Henry Justin Smith, *Oscar Wilde Discovers America, 1882* (New York: Benjamin Bloom, 1936); Matthew Hofer and Gary Scharnhorst, eds., *Oscar Wilde in America: The Interviews* (Urbana: University of Illinois Press, 2010), 96, shows a Chicago reporter who characterized the Milwaukee audience as philistines.
6. Neil Miller, *Out of the Past: Gay and Lesbian History from 1869 to the Present* (New York: Vintage Books, Random House, 1995), see the chapter "Pioneers of Sexology," 13–28; Lillian Faderman, *Odd Girls and Twilight Lovers:*

A History of Lesbian Life in Twentieth-Century America (New York: Penguin, 1992), especially the chapter "A Worm in the Bud: The Early Sexologist and Love between Women," 37–61.

7. *Wisconsin Blue Book*, 1900.

8. The Wisconsin press in the 1890s, like most across the nation, was just sorting out what to think about what today we might call objective journalism. See Michael Schudson, *Discovering the News: A Social History of American Newspapers* (New York: Basic Books, 1978) on developing the concept of journalistic objectivity. The *Milwaukee Journal*, under the editorship of Lucius Nieman, was leading the English-speaking press in Wisconsin in the objectivity effort, according to the institution's histories. See Will C. Conrad, Kathleen F. Wilson, and Dale Wilson, *The Milwaukee Journal: The First Eighty Years* (Madison: University of Wisconsin Press, 1964) and Robert W. Wells, *The Milwaukee Journal: An Informal Chronicle of Its First 100 Years* (Milwaukee: Milwaukee Journal, 1981) for another insider's view. Of those not striving for objectivity, Nieman observed, "Headlines often made it obvious where the editor's sympathies lay" (quoted in Wells, *The Milwaukee Journal*, 12). Though less overtly biased than others, the *Milwaukee Journal* did not offer a positive view of Wilde. John Murphy of Superior was a more colorful journalist, with his visions of the growing Northland. See Bill and Richard S. Nickeson Beck, *Murphy: The Beginning of a Media Empire* (Superior, WI: Evening Telegram Company, 1996).

9. H. Montgomery Hyde, ed., *The Trials of Oscar Wilde: Regina (Wilde) v. Queensberry, Regina v. Wilde and Taylor*, 4th ed. (London: William Hodge, 1952).

10. Merlin Holland, *The Real Trial of Oscar Wilde: The First Uncensored Transcript of the Trial of Oscar Wilde vs. John Douglass (Marquess of Queensbury), 1895* (New York: Fourth Estate, HarperCollins, 2003).

11. Editorial, *Racine Times*, April, 5, 1985.

12. Editorial, *Green Bay Gazette*, April 9, 1895.

13. "Wilde's Disgrace," *Superior Evening Telegram*, April 4, 1895.

14. "Newspaper Press, German Language in the United States," in Thomas Adam, ed., *Germany and the Americas, Culture Politics, and History* (Santa Barbara, CA: ABC- Clio, 2005), 822–826. The German-language press is discussed in Trudy Knauss Paradis, *German Milwaukee: Its History—Its Recipes* (St. Louis, MO: G. Bradley, 2006). Though some papers were

associated with related religious publishing, they did not seem more or less moralistic than other papers. Dateline, *Milwaukee Herold*, April 5, 1895; Editorial, *Wisconsin Vorvärts* (Milwaukee), May 26, 1895. All translations from German newspapers are by Nadine Simmerli.

15. The author's review of major Wisconsin papers and two New York papers noted as being followed by Wisconsin editors is based on comments on other stories in the news.

16. "Der Process Wilde—Queensbury," *Abendpost*, April 5, 1895; "Shame for Oscar," *Wisconsin State Journal*, April 3, 1895.

17. "Oscar Wilde's Character," *Superior Evening Telegram*, April 3, 1895; "Wilde versus Queensbury," *Milwaukee Daily News*, April 4, 1895; "Says Wilde Will Be Acquitted, The Marquis of Queensbury Does Not Look for a Conviction," *Milwaukee Sentinel*, May 25, 1895; "Oscar Wilde's Suit," *Milwaukee Journal*, April 4, 1895.

18. "Wilde in Court," *Milwaukee Journal*, April 6, 1895; "Wilde Poses in Court," *Milwaukee Journal*, April 11, 1895; "The Poetry of Work," Oshkosh *Northwestern*, May 25, 1895.

19. "Oscar Wilde in a Cell," *Milwaukee Sentinel*, April 6, 1895; "Oscar Wilde in His Cell," *Milwaukee Sentinel*, April 8, 1895; "Wilde is Arrested," Oshkosh *Northwestern*, April 5, 1895; Editorial, *Superior Evening Telegram*, April 9, 1895.

20. "Held Without Bail," *Green Bay Gazette*, April 19, 1895; "Says 'Not Guilty,'" Eau Claire *Daily Leader*, April 27, 1895; "Wilde Is Convicted," Racine *Times*, May 25, 1895.

21. "The Last Act of the Trial of Oscar Wilde," *Milwaukee Sonntags-Post*, May 26, 1895; Editorial, *Appleton Post*, May 30, 1895.

22. "Wilde Must Work Now," *Milwaukee Daily News*, May 25, 1895; "Wilde Gets Two Years," *Wisconsin State Journal*, May 25, 1895; "The Poetry of Work," Oshkosh *Northwestern*, May 25, 1895.

23. "Against Oscar Wilde," *Madison Democrat*, May 28, 1895.

24. Editorial, *Superior Evening Telegram*, April 9, 1895.

25. "Shame for Oscar," *Wisconsin State Journal*, April 3; "Beastley Wilde's Case," *Wisconsin State Journal*, April 4; "Wilde in Disgrace," *Wisconsin State Journal*, April 5; "Wilde's Case Gets Worse," *Wisconsin State Journal*, April 6; "England's Shame," *Wisconsin State Journal*, April 7, 1895.

26. "Wilde versus Queensbury," *Milwaukee Daily News*, April 4, 1895; "Dis-

grace Complete," *Superior Evening Telegram*, April 5, 1895; "Great Britain," *Germania*, April 9, 1895.

27. "The Wilde Case," *Sonntags-Post*, April 21, 1895; "Oscar's Home Sold," *Wisconsin State Journal*, April 24, 1895.

28. "Oscar Wilde in Court," *Milwaukee Herold*, May 3, 1895.

29. "Wilde Is Arraigned," *Superior Evening Telegram*, April 11, 1895; Editorial, *Superior Evening Telegram*, May 22, 1895.

30. "Oscar Wilde in His Cell," *Milwaukee Sentinel*, April 8, 1895; "England's Shame," *Wisconsin State Journal*, April 8, 1895.

31. "Wilde Not Suicidal," *Milwaukee Herold*, April 9, 1895; "More Filth Coming," Oshkosh *Northwestern*, April 8, 1895; "Wilde Is Limp," *Superior Evening Telegram*, April 19, 1895; "Oscar Wilde Ill," *Der Sebote*, May 10, 1895.

32. Editorial, *Superior Evening Telegram*, April 6, 1895; "Wilde Is Held Without Bail," *Milwaukee Daily News*, April 6, 1895.

33. "Oscar Wilde's Collections at Auction," *Abendpost*, April 23, 1895; "Sheriff Sells Wilde's House," *Milwaukee Journal*, April 25, 1895; "Receiver for Wilde," *Milwaukee Journal*, May 3, 1895; "Receiver for Wilde," *Madison Democrat*, May 3, 1895; "Oscar Wilde Is Bankrupt," *Green Bay Gazette*, May 2, 1895.

34. "Oscar Wilde's Sun Has Set," *Green Bay Gazette*, April 5, 1895.

35. "Not Withdrawn Plays," *Milwaukee Sentinel*, April 9, 1895; "An Evil Trend," *Milwaukee Sentinel*, April 12, 1895; "Electrische Funken," *Abendpost*, April 12, 1895.

36. Editorial, "Banishing Wilde's Books," *Racine Times*, April 13, 1895.

37. "An Evil Tendency," Oshkosh *Northwestern*, April 13, 1895; "Second Oscar Wilde," Oshkosh *Northwestern*, April 22, 1895; "An Evil Trend," *Superior Evening Telegram*, April 12, 1895; Editorial, *Appleton Post*, May 30, 1895.

38. Editorial, *Madison Democrat*, April 6, 1895; Editorial, *Wisconsin State Journal*, April 8, 1895.

39. "Compositions in Prison," Oshkosh *Northwestern*, April 9, 1895; Editorial, Oshkosh *Northwestern*, May 27, 1895.

40. Editorial, Oshkosh *Northwestern*, April 10, 1895; Editorial, Oshkosh *Northwestern*, May 23, 1895; "Does Not Believe the Aesthete Guilty," "She Champions Oscar Wilde," Beloit *Free Press*, April 11, 1895.

41. "Banishing Wilde's Books," *Racine Times*, April 13; Editorial, *Racine Times*, April 22, 1895.

42. Editorial, *Wisconsin Vorvärts*, May 26, 1895.

43. Editorial, *Der arme Teufel*, June 1, 1895; parts excerpted in *Wisconsin Vorvärts*, June 9, 1895.

44. Editorial, *Der arme Teufel*, June 1, 1895.

45. Editorial, *Der arme Teufel*, June 1, 1895.

46. Editorial, *Der arme Teufel*, June 1, 1895.

47. "The Wilde Trial," *AbendPost*, April 30, 1895; "Wilde on Stand," *Milwaukee Journal*, April 30, 1895.

48. "Two Years for Wilde," *Milwaukee Journal*, May 25, 1895; "Wilde Found Guilty," *Milwaukee Sentinel*, May 26, 1895; "Oscar Wilde is Convicted," *Milwaukee Herold*, May 28, 1895; "He Dotes on Youth, Oscar Wilde's Significant Note While Awaiting His Fate," Oshkosh *Northwestern*, May 27, 1895; "Wilde is Guilty," *Superior Evening Telegram*, May 26, "Wilde Makes a Statement," *Wisconsin State Journal*, May 28, 1895.

49. Leslie Taylor, "'I Made Up My Mind to Get It': The American Trial of 'The Well of Loneliness' New York City, 1928–1929," *Journal of the History of Sexuality* 10, no. 2 (April 2001): 250–286.

50. Taylor, "The American Trial," 277.

51. Lutie E. Stearns, "Weed at Your Peril!," *Wisconsin Library Bulletin*, October 1929, 296ff; "New Broadway Plays," *Capital Times* (Madison), November 19, 1929; "Schoolman's Lecture on *The Well of Loneliness* Will Attract Crowd," *Wisconsin Jewish Chronicle*, October 7, 1932; "On Books Written by Women," *Wisconsin Jewish Chronicle*, September 30, 1932.

52. "Portraits Aids Miners," *Appleton Post-Crescent*, March 25, 1928; "Seen and Heard In New York," *Appleton Post-Crescent*, August 17, 1932; Eleanor Evans Wing, "Books and Bookman," *Appleton Post-Crescent*, October 17, 1931.

53. Wing, "Books and Bookman."

54. Wing, "Books and Bookman."

55. "The Moral of This Sensational Trial Is Plain to All," *Racine Times*, May 25, 1895.

Chapter 2

1. Case file of Leo M., John Lewis Gillin Papers, Wisconsin Historical Society Archives, Madison, Wisconsin.

2. John Lewis Gillin, *The Wisconsin Prisoner: Studies in Crimogenesis* (Madison: University of Wisconsin Press, 1946), 106.

3. Merle Curti and Vernon Carstenson, *The University of Wisconsin: A History 1848–1925*, vol. 1, 616, 643; see *Wisconsin Blue Books* for population data.

4. See Richard Zacks, "Parkhurst and the Sin Tour" in Richard Zachs, *Island of Vice: Theodore Roosevelt's Doomed Quest to Clean Up Sin-Loving New York* (New York: Doubleday, 2012), 7–24.

5. Karen Abbott, *Sin in the Second City: Madams, Ministers, Playboys and the Battle for America's Soul* (New York: Random House Trade, 2008), 15–16, 49.

6. Abbott, *Sin in the Second City*, 161–174; Milwaukee was included in the "homosexual capitals" by Xavier Mayne (Edward Irenaeus Prime-Stevenson), *The Intersexes: A History of Similisexualism as a Problem in Social Life*, (n.p.: privately printed, 1908), 640; quoted in John Lauritsen and David Thorstad, *The Early Homosexual Rights Movement (1864–1935)* (New York: Times Change Press, 1974), 36.

7. David J. Pivar, *Purity Crusade: Sexual Morality and Social Control, 1868–1900* (Westport, CT: Greenwood Press, 1973), 137ff, 157.

8. Ernest Bell, *Fighting the Traffic in Young Girls or War on the White Slave Trade*, (n.p.: L. H. Walter, 1911), 482.

9. Zacks, *Island of Vice*, 19.

10. Abbott, *Sin in the Second City*, 48; Addams's companion and relationship are described in Rodger Streitmatter, "Mary Rozet Smith and Jane Addams," chapter 4 in *Outlaw Marriages: The Hidden Histories of Fifteen Extraordinary Same-Sex Couples* (Boston: Beacon Press, 2012); John D. Buenker, *The History of Wisconsin, Volume IV: The Progressive Era, 1893–1914* (Madison: State Historical Society of Wisconsin, 1998).

11. "Took in the Town, Exploit of Two Imitators of Dr. Parkhurst," *Milwaukee Sentinel*, April 7, 1895; Scott Herring, *Queering the Underworld: Slumming, Literature, and the Undoing of Lesbian and Gay History* (Chicago: University of Chicago Press, 2007), 5.

12. Jessica R. Pliley, *Policing Sexuality: The Mann Act and the Making of the FBI* (Cambridge, MA: Harvard University Press, 2014), 3, 133.

13. *Statutes of the Territory of Wisconsin*, published by authority of the Legislative Assembly (Albany, NY: Packard, Van Benthuysen and Co., 1839).

14. See section on Wisconsin in George Painter, "The Sensibilities of Our Forefathers: The History of Sodomy Laws in the United States," https://glapn.org/sodomylaws/history/history.htm.

15. Alice E. Smith, *The History of Wisconsin*: vol. 1, *from Exploration to*

Statehood (Madison: State Historical Society of Wisconsin, 1973), 384–385, 400, 405; *Revised Statutes of the State of Wisconsin* (Southport: C. Latham Sholes, 1849).

16. Quoted in Judge Richard Posner in No. 14-2526, *Virginia Wolf, et al. v. Scott Walker, et al.* in the United States Court of Appeals for the Seventh Circuit, 28.

17. *Wisconsin Blue Book*, 1897, profile of Herbert J. Green; Legislative Journals of the Wisconsin Senate and Assembly, Jan–April 1897; *Milwaukee Journal* for the period of January to March reporting on legislative actions takes no particular notice of Green's SB 61 bill.

18. *Revised Statutes of the State of Wisconsin*, various editions (Chicago: W. B. Keen, 1858); David Taylor (Chicago: E. B. Meyers, 1871); Sanborn and Berryman (Chicago: Callaghan and Company, 1889); Sanborn and Berryman (Chicago: Callaghan and Company, 1898).

19. Brief of Plaintiff in Error; Brief of Defendant in Error; *Cases and Briefs*, vol. 796, *Means v. State*, 125 Wis. 650, Wisconsin Law Library.

20. Supreme Court of Wisconsin Decision, *Means v. State*, Wisconsin Reports, 125 Wis. 650.

21. *Abaly v. State*, 163 Wis. 609, January Term 1916.

22. *Abaly*, 163 Wis. 609.

23. *Abaly*, 163 Wis. 609.

24. *Abaly*, 163 Wis. 609.

25. *Abaly*, 163 Wis. 609.

26. *Abaly*, 163 Wis. 609.

27. *Garrad v. State*, Wisconsin Reports, 194 Wis. 391, August Term 1927.

28. *Garrad*, 194 Wis. 391.

29. *Verhaalen v. State*, Wisconsin Reports, 195 Wis. 345, January Term 1928.

30. Case-trial court record, Western District of Waukesha County; Appellant's Brief by Shannon & Cronin and Jacobson & Malone, Attorneys for the Defendant; Brief of Defendant in Error by Scott Lowry, District Attorney of Waukesha County and James E. Finnegan, Attorney General, and J. E. Messerschmidt, Attorneys for Defendant in Error; *Gutenkunst v. State*, 218 Wis. 53-126, January Term 1935.

31. *Gutenkunst*, 218 Wis. 53-126.

32. *Gutenkunst*, 218 Wis. 53-126.

33. *Gutenkunst*, 218 Wis. 53-126.

34. *Gutenkunst*, 218 Wis. 96.

35. *Gutenkunst*, 218 Wis. 96.

36. *The Social Evil in Chicago: A Study of Existing Conditions with Recommendations by the Vice Commission of Chicago* (Chicago: Gunthorp-Warren Printing Company, 1911). See also St. Sukie de la Croix, *Chicago Whispers: A History of LGBT Chicago Before Stonewall* (Madison: University of Wisconsin Press, 2012), section of the Vice Commission, 23ff.

37. *Social Evil in Chicago*, 3, 25–47.

38. "On Male Prostitutes," in *Social Evil in Chicago*, 290.

39. "On Sex Perversion," in *Social Evil in Chicago*, 295–298.

40. *Social Evil in Chicago*, 296f; Mack Friedman, *Strapped for Cash: A History of American Hustler Culture* (Los Angeles: Alyson Books, 2003), 37.

41. *Social Evil in Chicago*, 297.

42. *Social Evil in Chicago*, 298.

43. Pliley, *Policing* Sexuality; quoted in Paul Hass, "Sin in Wisconsin: The Teasdale Vice Committee of 1913," *Wisconsin Magazine of History* 49, no. 2 (Winter 1965–1966): 138ff; *Wisconsin Blue Book*, 1913, 138–151; letter from M. W. Perry to Howard Teasdale, October 6, 1913, in correspondence files, Teasdale Committee files, Wisconsin Historical Society Archives.

44. *Report and Recommendations of the Wisconsin Vice Committee* (Madison: Democrat Printing Company 1914), 8ff, hereafter, *WI Vice Report*; letters from Steadwell in committee correspondence files; Friedman, *Strapped for Cash*, 47, on the Philadelphia anti-vice Commission.

45. Hass, "Sin in Wisconsin"; *Wisconsin Blue Book*, 1913; the thirteen votes in the Assembly against the bill creating the committee were cast mainly by Democrats from eastern lakeshore counties.

46. Various notes in typed transcripts of committee investigators.

47. Hass, "Sin in Wisconsin." The *WI Vice Report* was submitted as "Report and Recommendations of the Wisconsin Legislative Committee to Investigate the White Slave Traffic and Kindred Subjects." *WI Vice Report*, 70.

48. *WI Vice Report*, 108–109, 115–116, 118.

49. *WI Vice Report*, 26, 39, 122.

50. "Statement of Hon. Howard Teasdale (Dictated April 4, 1914)," in typed transcripts of investigations, 307; investigator typed transcripts, 102; investigator typed transcripts, 19; "Statement of Hon. Howard Teasdale (Dictated May 21, 1914)," in typed transcripts, 332; all transcripts in Vice Committee papers; letter of Chairman Howard Teasdale November 4, 1913, to David Groh, Teasdale Committee files.

51. *WI Vice Report*, 91–92, 97–98; in the Vice Committee papers are various letters informing the committee of specific vice situations or offers to help.

52. *WI Vice Report*, 97–98, 147–151.

53. Recommendations, *WI Vice Report*, 174–179.

54. Typed statement with annotations, "Statement of Mr. Victor L. Berger before the Teasdale Committee of the Wisconsin Legislature," in Vice Committee papers; platform in *Wisconsin Blue Book*, 1913, 603.

55. Howard Teasdale to Mr. W. S. Wadleigh, October 6, 1913, Galesville, Wisconsin, Vice Committee papers.

56. M. W. Perry to Howard Teasdale, October 6, 1913.; G. D. Jones to Howard Teasdale, January 19, 1914; Flora M. Beselack to Hon. Vice Commission, July 18, 1914; Northwestern Detective Agency "Vice Sleuths Stir Eau Claire's Ire," January 28, 1914; all in Vice Committee files.

57. "Statement of E. A. Ross, Professor of Sociology at the University of Wisconsin," *WI Vice Report*, 185–194; Merle Curti and Vernon Carstensen, *The University of Wisconsin: A History 1848–1925*, vol. 2 (Madison: University of Wisconsin Press, 1949), 63–67, 143, 343.

58. Julius Weinberg, *Edward Alsworth Ross and the Sociology of Progressivism* (Madison: State Historical Society of Wisconsin, Madison, 1972), 123.

59. "Statement of E. A. Ross," *WI Vice Report*, 185ff.

60. E. A. Ross, *The Social Trend* (New York: The Century Co., 1922), 38, 40, 48.

61. Ross, *Social Trend*, 38, 40, 48.

62. Madison Police Department, *Annual Reports* (1899–1913, 1920–1921, 1923–1930, 1932, 1934–1937, 1939–1964, 1966–1969); Chief of Police of the City of Milwaukee, *Annual Reports* (1909–1920, 1927–1946).

63. Madison and Milwaukee, *Annual Reports*.

64. Madison and Milwaukee, *Annual Reports*.

65. Madison and Milwaukee, *Annual Reports*.

66. Matthew J. Prigge, "The 'Girl-Man' of Milwaukee," *Wisconsin Magazine of History* 96, no. 3 (Spring 2013): 14–27.

67. Madison and Milwaukee, *Annual Reports*.

68. Madison and Milwaukee, *Annual Reports*.

69. Madison and Milwaukee, *Annual Reports*.

70. Madison and Milwaukee, *Annual Reports*.

71. Madison and Milwaukee, *Annual Reports*.

72. Madison and Milwaukee, *Annual Reports*.

73. Gillin biographical file, University of Wisconsin–Madison Archives.

74. Gillin biographical file.

75. Gillin biographical file.

76. John Lewis Gillin, *The Wisconsin Prisoner: Studies in Crimogenesis* (Madison: University of Wisconsin Press, 1946).

77. Gillin, *Wisconsin Prisoner*, v–viii.

78. Gillin, *Wisconsin Prisoner*, 3, 4, 97–107, 203–258.

79. Gillin field material, WisMss VF MAD 4/26/S5-7, Wisconsin Historical Society Archives. Hereafter, Gillin research files.

80. Gillin, *Wisconsin Prisoner*, 6.

81. Gillin, "The Making of the Sex Offender," chapter 7, *Wisconsin Prisoner*, 88–131.

82. Gillin, *Wisconsin Prisoner*, 97–107.

83. Gillin, *Wisconsin Prisoner*.

84. Gillin, *Wisconsin Prisoner*.

85. Gillin, *Wisconsin Prisoner*.

86. Gillin, *Wisconsin Prisoner*.

87. Gillin, *Wisconsin Prisoner*; case files on sodomy offenders, Gillin research files.

88. Case files on sodomy offenders.

89. Case files on sodomy offenders.

90. Case files on sodomy offenders.

91. Case files on sodomy offenders.

92. Case files on sodomy offenders.

93. Andrew Jastroch, autobiographical statement, 23 pages, with one attached handwritten page presumably by the research assistant, Gillin research files.

94. Jastroch, autobiographical statement.

95. Jastroch, autobiographical statement.

96. Jastroch, autobiographical statement.

97. Jastroch, autobiographical statement.

98. Ibn LoBagola, autobiographical statement, 68 pages, Gillin research files; John Gillin to Dr. Beatrice Hinkle, New York, December 14, 1934; John Gillin to Helen Brown, Brotherhood House, New York, December 14, 1934; John Gillin to Dr. Frederick Houk Law, New York, December 14, 1934, all in Gillin research files. Houk and Hinkle had given blurbs used in praising LoBagola's book.

99. "African Bush Man Speaks to Students," *Madison Mirror*, May 18, 1933.

100. LoBagola, autobiographical statement.

101. "Dramatic Tale Is Related by Ibn LoBagola," *Kenosha Evening Times*, May 19, 1933.

102. "Dramatic Tale."

103. "Dramatic Tale."

104. "Civilization and Savagery, Both LoBagola's Lot," *Kenosha Evening Times*, June 3, 1933; *Lobagola: An African Savage's Own Story* (New York: Alfred A. Knopf, 1930); advertisement for "Return Engagement Lobagola," *Kenosha Evening Times*, June 6, 1933.

105. "Speak Tonight," *Kenosha Evening Times*, June 8, 1933; "Children Flock to LoBagola," *Kenosha Evening Times*, June 8, 1933.

106. "Jail LoBagola on Boy's Story of Misconduct, African Bushman Lecturer Arrested," *Kenosha Evening Times*, June 10, 1933; "LoBagola Still in County Jail," *Kenosha Evening Times*, June 12, 1933.

107. "LoBagola Still in County Jail."

108. "LoBagola Goes Back to Jail for Jury Trial," *Kenosha Evening Times*, June 15, 1933.

109. "LoBagola Goes Back to Jail."

110. "Unfortunate," *Kenosha Evening Times*, June 16, 1933.

111. "LoBagola Gets Year in Prison, Goes at Once," *Kenosha Evening Times*, April 9, 1934.

112. David Killingray and Willie Henderson, "Bata Kindai Amogoza Ibn LoBagola," in Bernth Lindfors, ed., *Africans on Stage: Studies in Ethnological Show Business* (Bloomington: Indiana University Press, 1999), 228–265.

113. Killingray and Henderson, "Beta Kindai Amogoza Ibn LoBagola."

114. LoBagola, autobiographical statement.

115. LoBagola, autobiographical statement.

116. Killingray and Henderson, "Beta Kindai Amogoza Ibn LoBagola," 256.

117. Killingray and Henderson, "Beta Kindai Amogoza Ibn LoBagola."

118. Gillin, *The Wisconsin Prisoner*, 90–96.

119. Gillin, *The Wisconsin Prisoner*.

120. Gillin, *The Wisconsin Prisoner*.

121. Gillin, *The Wisconsin Prisoner*.

122. Gillin, *The Wisconsin Prisoner*.

Chapter 3

1. Glenway Wescott, *Good-Bye Wisconsin* (New York: Signet, 1964), 11.

2. Will Gundry to Bob Neal, June 6, 1933, Mineral Point Room, Mineral Point Library.

3. "How Ya Gonna Keep 'em Down on the Farm?," music by Walter Donaldson, words by Joe Young and Sam M. Lewis, 1919.

4. Julian Mitchell, *Another Country* (Ambergate, Derbyshire: Amber Lane Press, 1982); Dan Savage and Terry Miller, eds., *It Gets Better: Coming Out, Overcoming Bullying, and Creating a Life Worth Living* (New York: Plume, 2012).

5. James Baldwin, *Another Country* (London: Corgi Books, 1965).

6. Allan Bérubé, foreword to *Barrack Buddies and Soldier Lovers: Dialogues with Gay Young Men in the U. S. Military* (New York: Harrington Park Press, 1993).

7. Jerry Rosco, *Glenway Wescott Personally: A Biography* (Madison: University of Wisconsin Press, 2002), 5, 29; Robert Phelps with Jerry Rosco, eds., *Continual Lessons: The Journals of Glenway Wescott, 1937–1955* (New York: Farrar, Straus and Giroux, 1990), entry for March 7, 1944, 121; see also Marc E. Vargo, *Noble Lives: Biographical Portraits of Three Remarkable Gay Men—Glenway Wescott, Aaron Copland, and Dag Hammarskjold* (New York: Harrington Park Press, 2005), 3–41.

8. Rosco, *Glenway Wescott Personally*, 7ff.

9. Rosco, *Glenway Wescott Personally*, 16ff.

10. Rosco, *Glenway Wescott Personally*, 29; Jerry Rosco, "Glenway Wescott: The Apple of the Eye," in Tom Cardamone, ed., *The Lost Library: Gay Fiction Rediscovered* (New York: Haiduk Press, 2010), 189–197; Francis Steegmuller, *Cocteau: A Biography* (Boston: Little, Brown, 1970).

11. Rosco, *Glenway Wescott Personally*, 38ff.

12. Wescott, *Good-Bye Wisconsin*, 9–11.

13. Wescott, *Good-Bye Wisconsin*, 18–19.

14. Wescott, *Good-Bye Wisconsin*, 11, 19.

15. Wescott, *Good-Bye Wisconsin*, 14, 21, 22.

16. Wescott, *Good-Bye Wisconsin*, 21, 26; Katherine Anne Porter, "Comments on Good-Bye Wisconsin," foreword to *Good-Bye Wisconsin* (New York: Signet, 1964).

17. Rosco, *Glenway Wescott Personally*, 44f, 218ff.

18. Frank Shay, W. Adolphe Roberts, Lloyd A. Collins, and Stuart Palmer, eds., *Wisconsin Writings—1931: An Anthology* (New York: Mohawk Press, 1931), vff.

19. Paul M. Fulcher, "What Chance Has the College Writer?," in Shay et al., eds., *Wisconsin Writings*, 3–15.

20. Edward Harris Heth, "A Party," in Shay et al., eds., *Wisconsin Writings*, 68, 72.

21. Edward Harris Heth, "A Party," 78, 81, 89.

22. Edward Harris Heth, "A Party," 99–100.

23. Edward Harris Heth, *Any Number Can Play* (New York: Harper & Brothers, 1945).

24. Edward Harris Heth, *My Life on Earth: The Story of a City Man Who Returned to the Country* (New York: Simon & Schuster, 1953), 1, 4, 13, 18.

25. Will Fellows, *A Passion to Preserve: Gay Men as Keepers of Culture* (Madison: University of Wisconsin Press, 2004), 161ff; unattributed biography of Ralph Warner, Ralph Warner papers, Cooksville Village Archives, in possession of Larry Reed.

26. Unattributed biography of Ralph Warner, Cooksville Village Archives.

27. Warner to Harold March, March 10, 1933, Ralph Warner papers; Ralph Warner travel diaries 1928–1929, Ralph Warner papers.

28. Undated clipping, though later than the 1923 *House Beautiful* story that it references; "House Next Door, Secluded Home of Naturalist and Collector," *Wisconsin State Journal*; clipping, "Antique Collector in 'House Next Door' Dislikes Modernism," probably the *Milwaukee Journal*, August 8, 1926; clippings from Ralph Warner papers; Fellows, *A Passion to Preserve*.

29. Ralph Warner travel diaries, November 2, 1928, November 6, 1928.

30. Ralph Warner travel diaries, January 12, 1929, January 18, 1929, January 23, 1929.

31. Ralph Warner travel diaries, February 25, 1929, March 2, 1929, March 5, 1929.

32. Ralph Warner travel diaries, December 2, 1928, December 4, 1928, December 7, 1928.

33. Ralph Warner travel diaries, December 4, 1928, December 12, 1928; Matt Houlbrook, *Queer London: Perils and Pleasures in the Sexual Metropolis, 1918–1957* (Chicago: University of Chicago Press, 2005), 46ff, 153ff.

34. Ralph Warner travel diaries, December 12, 1928.

35. Fanny Stage Stone, "Cloverly and the House Next Door," *House and Garden*, May 1914.

36. Adelaide Evan Harris, "The Man in the House Next Door: The Remarkable Owner of a Remarkable House," *House Beautiful*, January 1923.

37. Harris, "Remarkable House."

38. Harris, "Remarkable House"; George Chauncey, *Gay New York: Gender, Urban Culture, and the Making of the Gay Male World, 1890–1940* (New York: Harper's Basic Books, 1994), 17ff, 76ff; Randall Sell and Jonathan Katz, "'Millions of Queers,' A View from 1940," *International Gay and Lesbian Review* 21, no. 1 (January–February 2015): 23–26.

39. Mary L. Bauchle, "The Land of Long Ago," *Wisconsin Magazine*, September 1925.

40. "Antique Collector in 'House Next Door.'"

41. Betty Cass, Madison Day by Day, *Wisconsin State Journal*, undated clipping, Ralph Warner papers.

42. Eleanor Mercein, "Adventurous Cookery," *Ladies' Home Journal*, March 1933.

43. Mercein, "Adventurous Cookery."

44. Mercein, "Adventurous Cookery."

45. Mercein, "Adventurous Cookery."

46. Mercein, "Adventurous Cookery."

47. Ralph Warner travel diaries, November 27, 1928.

48. Handwritten entry in Ralph Warner scrapbook, Ralph Warner papers.

49. Harris, "The Man in the House Next Door"; Mercein, "Adventurous Cookery."

50. Handwritten entry in Ralph Warner scrapbook, Ralph Warner papers; at a garage sale on my own block, I picked up a scrapbook of physical culture from the 1920s from the estate of a man who collected magazines of seminude and nude men in wrestling and artistic poses.

51. Clipping, "Fairly Gifts" by A. H. Perkins, Ralph Warner scrapbook.

52. Clipping, "Is it Manly to Eat Salad?," Ralph Warner scrapbook.

53. "Antique Collector in 'House Next Door'"; Bauchle, "The Land of Long Ago"; "Maker of Pioneer Paradise, Now Critically Ill," *Capital Times* (Madison, WI), July 23, 1932.

54. Ralph Warner guest book, Cooksville Village Archives; Pendarvis guest books, Mineral Point Room, Mineral Point Library.

55. Joan Emerson Young, *Joseph Gundry, 1822–1899: Family Man and Entrepreneur* (Mineral Point, WI: Mineral Point Historical Society, 2005), 79ff, C-8; "Musical Soiree at the University," unidentified clipping in Will Gundry scrapbook, Mineral Point Room, Mineral Point Library.

56. Various items in Will Gundry scrapbook.

57. Various clippings in Will Gundry scrapbook; see also Will Gundry photo scrapbook.

58. "A Progressive Firm: The Gundry & Gray Store Enlarged and Greatly Improved," *Mineral Point Tribune*, October 14, 1897, in Will Gundry scrapbook; Young, *Joseph Gundry*, 86.

59. Will Gundry scrapbook.

60. Will Gundry scrapbook.

61. Fellows, *A Passion to Preserve*, 192.

62. Will Gundry to Bob Neal, June 6, 1933, Bob Neal papers, Mineral Point Room, Mineral Point Library, hereafter, Bob Neal papers.

63. Gundry to Neal, June 6, 1933; Houlbrook, *Queer London*.

64. Gundry to Neal, June 6, 1933.

65. Gundry to Neal, June 6, 1933.

66. Gundry to Neal, June 6, 1933; Will Gundry to Bob Neal, January 9, 1933; both in Bob Neal papers.

67. Bob Neal to Will Gundry, June 7, 1933, Bob Neal papers.

68. Bob Neal to Will Gundry, May 20 and 21, 1933, Bob Neal papers.

69. Bob Neal to Will Gundry May 27, 1933, Bob Neal papers.

70. Bob Neal to Will Gundry, May 27, 1933, June 7, 1933, June 17, 1933, Bob Neal papers.

71. Bob Neal to Will Gundry, June 17, 1933, and September 19, 1933, Bob Neal papers.

72. Bob Neal to Will Gundry, May 27, 1933, September 8, 1933, September 19, 1933, Bob Neal papers.

73. Bob Neal to Will Gundry, July 1, 1933, September. 8, 1933, September 19, 1933, Bob Neal papers.

74. "A Prodigal Returns: And Discovers His Native Land," by W. R. J., an undated and nonattributed clipping in Bob Neal papers.

75. "A Prodigal Returns."

76. "A Prodigal Returns."

77. Fellows, *A Passion to Preserve*, 191ff.

78. Betty Cass, "Madison Day by Day," clipping from spring 1939 in Bob Neal papers; "Cornish Mining Village Is Restored in Wisconsin," *Chicago Daily News*, November 27, 1939.

79. Betty Cass, "Madison Day by Day," *Wisconsin State Journal*, September 10, 1935.

80. Cass, "Madison Day by Day," September 10, 1935.

81. "Veal and Parsley Pie"; "Two Young Men and an Ideal."

82. Cass, "Madison Day by Day."

83. Inflation calculator based on the Consumer Price Index.

84. Fellows, *A Passion to Preserve*; McCann, "Remembering." As director of the Wisconsin American Revolution Bicentennial Commission, I had the pleasure of meeting Neal and Hellum and contributing to their recognition. As a sponsor of early Historic Preservation Week activities, the commission arranged for Neal and Hellum to be honored by Governor Patrick Lucey in May 1975. Would that I had known then their full story.

85. Cass, "Madison Day by Day."

86. "Two Young Men and an Ideal," *Janesville Daily Gazette*, May 11, 1939; "Pendarvis House," *Fennimore Times*, December 18, 1935.

87. William T. Evjue, "Good Afternoon Everybody," *Capital Times* (Madison, WI), June 28, 1937; "Veal and Parsley Pie, Delicious Ginger Cookies Cornish Favorites," *Milwaukee Journal*, October 27, 1939.

88. Will Fellows, interview of Edgar Hellum, December 17, 1997, transcript shared with author.

89. Fellows, *A Passion to Preserve*.

90. "UW Leaders to Record Cornish, Music School Project Wants Mineral Point Residents Cooperation Here Soon," unidentified clipping in Bob Neal papers.

91. Hellum, interview with Fellows.

92. Hellum, interview; Dennis McCann, "Remembering with the Bard of Pendarvis," *Wisconsin State Journal*, October 17, 1999.

93. "Pendarvis Founder Dies," *Wisconsin State Journal*, July 22, 1983; "Bob Neal—Equal to the Challenge," *Democrat Tribune* (Mineral Point), July 28, 1983; "Pendarvis Founder Bob Neal Remembered," *Dodgeville Chronicle*, July 28, 1983; Obituary for Edgar Gorby Hellum, *Dodgeville Chronicle*, March 23, 2000; "Historic Preservation Pioneer Dies at Age 94," *Democrat Tribune*, March 23, 2000.

94. Chester Holway, edited by Larry Reed, "A Visit to Mineral Point and Taliesin," *Wisconsin Magazine of History* 81, no. 2 (Winter 1997–1998): 109ff; a clipping in the Bob Neal papers has the same Holway section on Mineral Point headlined "Cornish Town Lies Serene in Wisconsin Hills."

95. C. P. Holway, *How to Profit from the Tourist Business* (Milwaukee: Jay Rathburn, 1949), n.p.

96. Holway, *How to Profit*, 35ff.

97. "Stricken at Ripon, Edwin P. Barlow, Benefactor, Dies," *Monroe Evening Times*, September 23, 1947; "Edwin P. Barlow," *Monroe Evening Times*, September 24, 1957; "New Glarus Chamber of Commerce and Tourist Information," New Glarus town website, swisstown.com.

98. "Der Kreis," Wikipedia; "LGBT Rights in Switzerland," Wikipedia; Heather Cassel, "Swiss Gay Pioneers Visit SF," *Bay Area Reporter*, February 2, 2015.

99. Leslie Cross, "Mr. Kubly Looks Homeward," *Milwaukee Journal*, n.d.

100. "Edwin P. Barlow," *Monroe Evening Times*, September 24, 1957.

101. Holway, *How to Profit*, 37.

102. Korinne Oberle, quoted in Chris Jones, "The Hidden Story of Mineral Point," *Chicago Tribune*, September 7, 2003.

Chapter 4

1. Keith McCutcheon, "Sonnets to Leon," unpublished chapbook, Keith McCutcheon papers, in possession of the author. All unpublished McCutcheon material from McCutcheon papers in possession of the author, destined for the LGBT collections, UW–Madison Archives, Madison, Wisconsin. Hereafter, McCutcheon papers.

2. Milt Sherman, "Feelthy Book," *Daily Cardinal* (UW–Madison student paper), December 9, 1937.

3. Martin Duberman, *Jews, Queers, Germans: A Novel/History* (New York: Seven Stories Press, 2017).

4. Pendarvis guest books, Mineral Point Room, Mineral Point Library; House Next Door guest book and Warner travel diary, Cooksville Village Archives, in possession of Larry Reed.

5. Aiken Welch, "The Happiest Man I Ever Knew," *American Magazine*, January 1949; "Betty Cass—Today," *Capital Times* (Madison, WI), January 4, 1949; "Frank M. Riley, Prominent Madison Architect and Builder, Dies at

73," *Wisconsin State Journal*, May 23, 1949; "Frank M. Riley," *Wisconsin State Journal*, May 24, 1949.

6. Welch, "The Happiest Man."

7. "Little Woodland God," included in letter to Riley from Gary Miller (November 30, 1942), Script Department Archives; copy with added typed title in Bob Neal papers, Mineral Point Room, Mineral Point Library.

8. Frank Riley obituary, May 23, 1949, *Wisconsin State Journal*.

9. Old Helena story from clippings in McCutcheon's clipping book, August 3, 1938, McCutcheon papers.

10. McCutcheon on Arena, McCutcheon papers.

11. McCutcheon mention in *Wisconsin Alumni Magazine*, November 1930.

12. McCutcheon, untitled, undergraduate essays, McCutcheon papers.

13. McCutcheon, "A Letter Sent and a Letter Received," undergraduate essays, McCutcheon papers.

14. McCutcheon, "Values," undergraduate essays, McCutcheon papers.

15. McCutcheon, "At the Gate," undergraduate essays, McCutcheon papers.

16. "Buckets of Blood," *Proletarian* 1, no. 2 (1924), possession of author.

17. McCutcheon unpublished poems, McCutcheon papers.

18. August Derleth, *The Wisconsin: River of a Thousand Isles* (New York: Rinehart, 1942); Dorothy M. Grobe Litersky, *Derleth: Hawk and Dove* (Aurora, CO: National Writers Press, 1997).

19. Derleth, *The Wisconsin*, 325.

20. McCutcheon, unpublished poems, McCutcheon papers.

21. McCutcheon, *Lyrics of the Night and Other Verses*, unpublished chapbook, McCutcheon papers.

22. McCutcheon, *Lyrics of the Night*.

23. McCutcheon, *Twilight Verses*, unpublished chapbook, McCutcheon papers.

24. McCutcheon, *Twilight Verses*.

25. McCutcheon, *Twilight Verses*.

26. McCutcheon, *Twilight Verses*.

27. McCutcheon, *Mountain Summer*, 27-page manuscript, McCutcheon papers.

28. McCutcheon, *Mountain Summer*.

29. McCutcheon, *Mountain Summer*.

30. Michael Bronski, ed., *Pulp Friction: Uncovering the Golden Age of Gay Male Pulps* (New York: St. Martin's Griffin, 2003), 79–124.

31. McCutcheon, *Lyrics of the Night* (Mazomanie, WI: Mazomanie Sickle, 1931), copy with inscription in Special Collections, Memorial Library, University of Wisconsin–Madison, Rare Books.

32. McCutcheon, *Lyrics of the Night.*

33. The McCutcheon clippings book has hundreds of items, which he published in the paper with penciled dates, McCutcheon papers.

34. McCutcheon, "A Group of Love Songs," *The Beacon* (Wales, WI), 1934, copy in McCutcheon papers; Cass in McCutcheon clippings book, McCutcheon papers; Keith McCutcheon, *Seven Sonnets: Sung Softly from the Soul* (WI: self-published, 1935), in Wisconsin Historical Society Library; Keith McCutcheon, *Japanese Prints: Seven Love Poems of Old Nippon Transcribed from the Ancient Book of Imagination* (WI: self-published, 1935), UW–Madison LGBT collections.

35. McCutcheon, *Two Pieces of Venetian Glass* (Rio, WI: Rio Journal Press, 1941), in collection of author, copy also in Special Collections, UW–Madison.

36. McCutcheon, *Two Pieces.*

37. McCutcheon clippings book.

38. McCutcheon clippings book.

39. McCutcheon clippings book.

40. McCutcheon clippings book.

41. McCutcheon clippings book.

42. McCutcheon clippings book.

43. McCutcheon clippings book.

44. McCutcheon clippings book.

45. McCutcheon clippings book.

46. For a good general discussion of the forced-labor camps, see Richard J. Evans, *The Third Reich in Power* (New York: Penguin Books, 2005), 81ff.

47. James D. Steakley, *The Homosexual Emancipation Movement in Germany* (Salem, NH: Ayer, 1982), see chapter 4, "The Final Solution," 103–119.

48. Richard Plant, *The Pink Triangle: The Nazi War against Homosexuals* (New York: Henry Holt, 1986), see chapter 4, "Persecution," 105–149; John Lauritsen and David Thorstad, *The Early Homosexual Rights Movement (1864–1935)* (New York: Times Change Press, 1974); Erik Jensen, "The Pink Triangle and Political Consciousness: Gays, Lesbians, and the Memory of Nazi Persecution," in Dagmar Herzog, ed., *Sexuality and German Fascism*

(New York: Berghahn Books, 2002), traces the development of postwar memory but does not indicate any prewar memory as demonstrated by McCutcheon.

49. McCutcheon clippings book.

50. "Theodore Pierce: Biographical Highlights," dated July 27, 1998, Theodore Pierce Papers, Wisconsin Historical Society Archives, Madison, Wisconsin, hereafter, Pierce papers; "Mrs. Hetty Pierce Dead; Reported 115 Years Old," *Capital Times*, June 13, 1944.

51. "Sam Pierce, Smiling Guardian of Six Governors, Dies at 66," *Wisconsin State Journal*, May 15, 1936; Betty Banks, "Remembering Those Who Paved the Way," *Umoja*, February 2015, 48–49; "Sam Pierce Draws High Praise at Funeral," undated clipping, Pierce papers.

52. "Governor's Messenger Says It Would Help Youth," undated clipping, Pierce papers; telegram from Phil LaFollette, May 15, 1936, in Pierce papers.

53. Rob Zaleski, "Lonely for Willy Street," *Capital Times*, August 1–2, 1998, Pierce papers.

54. "Pierce: Biographical Highlights."

55. Doug Moe, "Gay Social Scene Will Get a Boost," *Capital Times*, July 23, 1998; Ted Pierce, letter to author, June 1993; Ted Pierce obituary, *Capital Times*, January 3, 1999; other conversations with notes over the years, possession of author.

56. *The Tower* (East High School yearbook), 1924; photo including Pierce with handwritten attribution, "Elite of the younger set in Madison," album 3 in Pierce papers, PH MMS 934.7.

57. Notes on conversation with Ted Pierce, June 1993, in possession of author.

58. See extensive Pierce correspondence in Pierce papers.

59. Pierce correspondence.

60. Don Pryse Jones to Pierce, Pierce papers, box 1, folders 2 and 3.

61. Pierce, letter to author.

62. Various clippings on dance by David Zellmer writing for the *Daily Cardinal*; "Haresfoot at It Again," *The Badger* (UW–Madison yearbook), 1939; "Home from War Zellmer Resumes Career in Dance," *Capital Times*, 1945; "Graham Dancers Open Weeks Run," *New York Times*, February 25, 1947; "Martha Graham Dance Scene," *New York Times*, January 28, 1946; "Graham Dancers in 'Punch and Judy,'" *New York Times*, January 28, 1946,

"Graham Dance to Grant Zellmer a Homecoming," *Wisconsin State Journal*, November 3, 1946; Merce Cunningham to Pierce, Pierce papers.

63. Zellmer to Pierce, April 24 (undated but 1945 from context), Pierce papers, box 1, folder 5.

64. Zellmer to Pierce, December 26, 1945, Pierce papers, box 1, folder 5.

65. Postcards from Herbert Kubly to Pierce, November 9, 1953, November 17, 1953, Pierce papers, box 1, folder 6.

66. Harold Linedermann to Pierce, August 27, 1951, Pierce papers, box 1, folder 6.

67. Christmas card with Richard Thomas posing, photo credited to UW Professor Olin Wood, and several letters from Wood to Ted Pierce in the early 1970s, provided to author by Bob Davis, Pierce's executor.

68. Various clippings in Pierce supplemental material from Bob Davis, possession of the author.

69. "Canada Lee," Wikipedia; "Bigger, 'Native Son,' Threatens," *Wisconsin State Journal*, January 11, 1942; "Give Negro Soldiers Equal Rights, Canada Lee Pleads," *Milwaukee Journal*, January 22, 1942; clippings in Pierce papers, box 3, folder 5.

70. "Greet Noted Negro Actor," *Capital Times*, October 15, 1945; "Actor Canada Lee Visits State Capitol," *Wisconsin State Journal*, October 15, 1945; "Canada Lee, Noted Negro Actor, Dies," *Wisconsin State Journal*, May 10, 1952; clippings in Pierce papers, box 3, folder 5.

71. Doug Moe, "Books Find Way to Caring Hands," *Capital Times*, October 5, 2001, clipping from Bob Davis, Pierce's executor; Willard Motley, "The Education of a Writer," speech to UW Athenian Society, in *The New Idea: Magazine of Student Thought and Writing*, Winter 1960; "Identity," in Motley papers, Special Collections, Memorial Library, University of Wisconsin–Madison, hereafter Motley papers; Jerome Klinkowitz, James Giles, John T. O'Brien, "The Willard Motley Papers at the University of Wisconsin," *Resources for American Literary Study*, 2, no. 2 (1972): 218–273.

72. Motley to Pierce, November 23, 1954, April 10, 1958, November 12, 1938, November 4, 1953, all in Motley papers.

73. Motley to Pierce, August 26, 1946, October 25, 1949, December 21, 1954, September 14, 1948, October 7, 1947; Pierce to Motley, March 8, n.d.; Pierce to Motley, December 13, 1954; all in Motley papers.

74. Motley to Pierce, November 23, 1954, December 21, 1954, Motley papers.

75. "Willard Motley Dies in Mexico; Author of 'Knock on Any Door,'" *New York Times*, March 6, 1965; "Best Seller Author Tells 8 Years' Work," *Chicago Sun*, June 22, 1947.

76. James Levin, *The Gay Novel: The Male Homosexual Image in America* (New York: Irvington, 1983), 98; Alan Wald, "American Writers on the Left," in Claude Summers, ed., *The Gay and Lesbian Literary Heritage* (New York: Henry Folk, 1997), 56; St. Sukie de la Croix, *Chicago Whispers: A History of LGBT Chicago Before Stonewall* (Madison: University of Wisconsin Press, 2012), 211–213; Anthony Slide, *Lost Gay Novels: A Reference Guide to Fifty Works from the First Half of the Twentieth Century* (New York: Harrington Park Press, 2003), 135–136.

77. Motley to Elizabeth McKee, October 31, 1960, Motley papers.

78. Milt Sherman, BA in journalism, 1940, listed in Wisconsin Alumni Association database.

79. Elena Sherman, interview by author, November 16, 2009.

80. Sherman, interview.

81. Sherman, interview.

82. Photos shared and copied from Elena Sherman, 2009; *The Badger*, 1938, 1939; various *Daily Cardinal* news items, in possession of author.

83. *The Badger*, 1938, 1939.

84. E. David Cronon and John W. Jenkins, *The University of Wisconsin: A History*, vol. 3, *1925–1945* (Madison: University of Wisconsin Press, 1994), 634–640.

85. See staff listings in *The Badger*, 1938, 1939, 1940; various items in *Daily Cardinal* over the years; on the strike see also Cronon and Jenkins, *The University of Wisconsin*, 633.

86. Sex series covered in *Daily Cardinal*, March 17, 1938, and April 1, 6, and 15, 1938.

87. "Feelthy Book," *Daily Cardinal*, December 9, 1937.

88. "Feelthy Book"; Slide, *Lost Gay Novels*, 51–55.

89. Case of R. G., UW Student Discipline files, 1937, UW–Madison Archives.

90. Lillian Faderman, *Odd Girls and Twilight Lovers: A History of Lesbian Life in Twentieth-Century America* (New York: Penguin, 1992), 14.

91. Susie Habernicht, unpublished manuscript, interview notes, and biography, in Charlotte Russell Partridge and Miriam Frink Papers

1862–1980, box 15, folder 10, and box 16, folder 3, UW–Milwaukee Archives, Milwaukee, WI. Hereafter, Partridge/Frink papers.

92. Habernicht, unpublished manuscript; clipping in papers identified as *Milwaukee Sentinel*, June 14, 1919, box 12, folder 1, Partridge/Frink papers.

93. Habernicht, unpublished manuscript; Partridge interview by Dr. Harlan Phillips, June 12, 1965, in Partridge/Frink papers, box 12, folder 5.

94. Habernicht, unpublished manuscript; "Studio in Fox Point Is Built by Artists," *Milwaukee Journal*, September 14, 1930.

95. Habernicht, unpublished manuscript; and Habernicht, draft Partridge obituary, box 15, folder 7, Partridge/Frink papers.

96. Habernicht, unpublished manuscript; Miriam Frink to Holger Cahill, director, Federal Art Project, Partridge/Frink papers, box 14, folder 9; Habernicht biography; all in Partridge/Frink papers.

97. Miriam Frink, "Literature in an Art School," *Smith Alumnae Quarterly*, February 1925, 172–175, in Partridge/Frink papers, box 14, folder 8.

98. Miriam Frink interview by Susie Habernicht, taped May 1974, side 6B, in Researcher's Files, 1920–1976, box 15, folder 10, Partridge/Frink papers.

99. Frink interview by Habernicht, taped May 1974, box 15, folder 10, Partridge/Frink papers; "Richard Leopold," Wikipedia; Alex Sainsbury, "Ray Johnson Please Add to & Return," www.ravenrow.org/texts/14/; Wayne Snellen, "Recent Donations and Acquisitions," *The Archive: The Journal of the Leslie/Lohman Gay Art Foundation* 19 (Spring 2006); John Suiter, "Last Post," www.warholstars.org/andywarhol/articles/rayjohnson/ind.html; "Karl Priebe," Wikipedia; Anne Donlon, "Archival Practices at MLA," http://anndonlon.org/archival-pratices-at-mla/; "Carl Van Vechten," Wikipedia.

100. Various items on the Berger connection, box 14, folder 7, Partridge/Frink papers; Constance Daniel, "Time to Be Busy," *Milwaukee Journal*, September 1, 1965; "Layton School: Its Birth, Its Life and the Twilight," *Milwaukee Journal*, March 10, 1974; "Layton Long Served This Community Well," *Milwaukee Journal*, March 11, 1974; Habernicht, unpublished manuscript, Partridge/Frink papers; Faderman, *Odd Girls*, 23.

101. Robert Cohen has written on campus radicalism in the 1930s; see his *When the Old Left was Young* (New York: Oxford University Press, 1997)

and "Activist Impulses: Campus Radicalism in the 1930s," http://newdeal
.feri.org/students/essay01.htm.

102. Cronon and Jenkins, *University of Wisconsin*, 250ff.

103. Paul W. Glad, *The History of Wisconsin*, vol. 5, *War, a New Era, and Depression, 1914–1940* (Madison: State Historical Society of Wisconsin,
1990); Edward N. Doan, *The La Follettes and the Wisconsin Idea* (New
York: Rinehart, 1947); Donald Young, ed., *Adventure in Politics: The Memoirs of Philip La Follette* (New York: Holt, Rinehart and Winston, 1970).

104. Merle Curti, foreword to *Selig Perlman's Lectures on Capitalism and Socialism*, ed. A. L. Reisch Owen (Madison: University of Wisconsin Press,
1976); Owen, *Selig Pearlman's Lectures*, 3.

105. "Red Flags Fly in City," *Wisconsin News*, May 1, 1935; "Disloyalty," editorial, *Wisconsin News*, May 1, 1935; "Hit Normal School Here in Quiz,"
Wisconsin News, May 3, 1935; "Call Head of School, Probe WERA Play,"
Wisconsin News, April 25, 1935. On May 1, 1935, the *Capital Times* reported that Marvin Baxter, the Socialist mayor of West Allis, advocated
the abolition of capitalism from the steps of the UW Memorial Union.

106. "'Red' Inquiry Unjust; Will Hurt U.—Ross," *Milwaukee Leader*, April 18,
1935.

107. "Senator Quits in Red Probe," *Wisconsin News*, April 23, 1935.

108. *Wisconsin News*, April 23, 1935; "Snell Lays Ouster to Expose," *Wisconsin
News*, April 26, 1935.

109. *Wisconsin News*, April 26, 1935.

110. *Wisconsin News*, April 27, 1935.

111. *Milwaukee Leader*, April 26, 1935.

112. "Ousted Dean Tells Lurid Tale of 'Misconduct' in Milwaukee," *Capital
Times*, April 26, 1935.

113. "Investigation by Special Committee of the Board of Regents of the
University of Wisconsin as to Conditions in the University of Wisconsin
Extension Division Center at Milwaukee," bound transcript of testimony,
November 7, 1934, November 21, 1934, January 11, 1935, March 4, 1935,
and March 9, 1935, Board of Regents Papers, 1/6/3 box 1, UW–Madison
Archives.

114. "Snell Poses as Morals Martyr; Lays Blame for 'Mess' on Frank," *Capital
Times*, April 26, 1935.

115. "Hollywood Male Triangle Uncovered in Film Slaying," *Milwaukee Leader*, April 27, 1935.

116. "John B. Chapple," Wikipedia; William T. Evjue, *A Fighting Editor* (Madison: Wells Printing, 1968), 601ff.

117. *Wisconsin Bluebooks* for the 1930s.

118. "'Free Love' Charges Subpoenaed for Quiz," *Ashland Press*, April 15, 1935; "Sensation Charges in 'U' Quiz," *Ashland Press*, April 26, 1935; "Teachers Morals Are to Be Investigated," *Ashland Press*, May 2, 1935; "Communistic Tie-Up Revealed," *Ashland Press*, May 3, 1935.

119. "What about President Frank," *Ashland Press*, April 30, 1935.

120. "Improper Conduct of 'U' Faculty Member Charged," *Ashland Press*, May 11, 1935; other papers also carried this story.

121. John B. Chapple, foreword to *La Follette Road to Communism: Must We Go Further Along That Road?* (Ashland, WI: self-pub., 1936), 62–63.

122. Chapple, *LaFollette Road*, 63.

123. "Good Afternoon Everybody," *Capital Times*, April 26, 1935.

124. "Glenn Frank Turns 'Color' Says Chapple," *Capital Times*, April 28, 1935; Letter to *Capital Times*, May 2, 1935; "Told of Communist Bogey-Man," *Capital Times*, May 3, 1935; "Red Probe Fine Exhibit for Hitler, Groves Says," *Capital Times*," May 9, 1935; "Time to Stop These Legislative Rackets," *Capital Times*, May 9, 1935; "Professor Ross Urges Boycott for Hearst Newspapers," *Capital Times*, May 14, 1935.

125. "U.W. Paper Flays Solons and Papers for Maligning School," *Capital Times*, April 29, 1935; "Athletes Hit Slurs on U.W. in Red Probe," *Capital Times*, May 9, 1935; "U.W. Morals Are Better Than Average, Students Maintain," *Capital Times*, May 11, 1935.

126. "The Investigation," *Milwaukee Leader*, May 1, 1935.

127. "Re-affirm Liberalism at U.W.," *Capital Times*, May 18, 1935; Lawrence Larsen, in his biography of Frank, *The President Wore Spats* (Madison: State Historical Society of Wisconsin, 1955), spells Senator Brunette's name wrong (Burnette) and places him in the Republican Party.

128. "House Balks Fund for Senate Probe of U.W.," *Capital Times*, May 8, 1935; "Probe Is Denounced on Assembly Floor," *Milwaukee Leader*, May 9, 1935.

129. The vote tally and list of members appears in "House Balks Fund," *Capital Times*, May 8, 1935; the party identification analysis comes from crosscheck with the *Wisconsin Blue Books* of the 1930s.

130. "Teachers' Body Calls Red Probes, Disgrace; Out to Hit U.W. Budget," *Capital Times*, May 11, 1935.

131. "Ohl Adds to Protest against More Cash for 'U' Probe Body," *Milwaukee Leader*, May 15, 1935; "Officers' Report to the Forty-Fourth Annual Convention Wisconsin State Federation of Labor," printed by Co-Operative Printery, 1936.

132. Election results from *Wisconsin Blue Books*, 1930s.

133. "Red Menace at U Is Myth, Probers View," *Capital Times*, June 23, 1935.

134. "Frank and Doris Hursley," Wikipedia.

135. Cronon and Jenkins, *The University of Wisconsin*, 299–315.

136. Evjue, *A Fighting Editor*, 601ff.

137. "Ask Funds Immediately to Continue 'U' Radicalism Probe," *Ashland Press*, May 2, 1935.

Chapter 5

1. Wally Jordan to Jim Kepner, June 12, 1943, *ONE* National Gay & Lesbian Archives, University of Southern California Libraries, Los Angeles. Hereafter, ONE Archives.

2. E. L. Severinghaus and John Chornyak, "A Study of Homosexual Males," *Psychosomatic Medicine* 7 (September 1945): 302–305, reprinted in *Journal of Nervous & Mental Disease* 105, no. 5 (May 1947).

3. Allan Bérubé, *Coming Out Under Fire: The History of Gay Men and Women in World War II* (New York: Free Press, 1990); John D'Emilio and Estelle B. Freedman, foreword to Allan Bérubé, *Coming Out Under Fire: The History of Gay Men and Women in World War II* (Chapel Hill: University of North Carolina Press, 2010). Further citations come from the 1990 edition.

4. Clippings in Keith McCutcheon's clipping notebook of some published writings indicate that they are from the *Rio Journal*. The early war period clippings are not always dated, though the period is discernible. McCucheon's notebook is in possession of the author.

5. McCutcheon, clippings book.

6. McCutcheon, clippings book.

7. McCutcheon, clippings book.

8. McCutcheon, clippings book.

9. McCutcheon, clippings book.

10. Steve Estes, *Ask and Tell: Gay and Lesbian Veterans Speak Out* (Chapel Hill: University of North Carolina Press, 2007), 13–17, 197.

11. Bob Thomas, *Liberace: The True Story* (New York: St. Martin's Press, 1987), 29, 35.

12. Betty Cass, "Day by Day," *Wisconsin State Journal*, Sunday, February 14, 1943.

13. Materials on Truax Field, Wisconsin Veterans Museum Research Center, Madison, WI; includes several undated yearbook-type publications for Truax Army Air Field. Hereafter, Truax materials.

14. Betty Cass, "Day by Day," February 14, 1943.

15. Truax materials; "GI Drag: A Gay Refuge," in Bérubé, *Coming Out*, 114.

16. Truax materials.

17. Bérubé, *Coming Out*, 114; "Michelle's Club 546," *History of Gay and Lesbian Life in Milwaukee*, www.mkelgbthist.org/business/bars/club546.htm; "Royal Hotel's Reign Ends," *GPU (Gay Peoples Union) News*, September 23, 1973.

18. John W. Fitzmaurice, *The Shanty Boy or Life in a Lumber Camp* (Cheboygan, MI: Democrat Steam Print, 1889); "Shanty Boy on the Big Eau Claire," Harry B. Peters, ed., *Folk Songs Out of Wisconsin*, collected in 1923 from Mathilda Kjorstad-Myer by Frank Rickaby (Madison: State Historical Society of Wisconsin, 1977).

19. "Biographical History" from the Robert Peters Papers, University of California, San Diego, Geigel Library, Mandeville Special Collections.

20. Robert Peters, *Crunching Gravel: A Wisconsin Boyhood in the Thirties*, (Madison: University of Wisconsin Press, 1993), see "Gym," 113, and "Columbus Lake," 85–87.

21. Robert Peters, *For You, Lili Marlene: A Memoir of World War II* (Madison: University of Wisconsin Press, 1995), xiii, 7.

22. Peters, *For You*, 38–39; "Don Mark Interviews Robert Peters," in Winston Leyland, ed., *Gay Sunshine Interviews*, vol. 2 (San Francisco: Gay Sunshine Press, 1982), 123–141.

23. Peters, *For You*, 4, 94.

24. Peters, *For You*, 38.

25. Bérubé, *Coming Out*, 62–64; Peters, *For You*, 42; Peters's sister's recollection that before the war he thought about being a Lutheran pastor is in Nell

Peters with Robert Peters, *Nell's Story: A Woman from Eagle River* (Madison: University of Wisconsin Press, 1995), 65.

26. Peters, *For You*, 44.

27. Peters, *For You*, 88.

28. Peters, *For You*, 89, 94–95.

29. Peters, *For You*, 96.

30. Peters, *For You*, 105.

31. For published work by Kepner, see Jim Kepner, *Rough News, Daring Views: 1950's Pioneer Gay Press Journalism* (New York: Harrington Park Press, 1998); Wayne R. Dynes has an excellent foreword to *Rough News*, placing Kepner in his times.

32. Jordan to Kepner, February 28, 1943. For the following, the Wally Jordan and Jim Kepner letters are part of the Jim Kepner Papers in the ONE Archives.

33. Kepner to Jordan, March 4, 1943.

34. Jordan to Kepner, March 12, 1943.

35. Kepner to Jordan, March 16, 1943.

36. Jordan to Kepner, March 19, 1943.

37. Kepner to Jordan, March 22, 1943.

38. Kepner to Jordan, March 22, 1943.

39. Jordan to Kepner, March 19, 1943.

40. Jordan to Kepner, March 19, 1943.

41. Jordan to Kepner, March 36, 1943; Jordan to Kepner, April 6, 1943; Jordan to Kepner, May 14, 1943; Kepner to Jordan, April 10, 1943; Kepner to Jordan, April 21, 1943.

42. Jordan to Kepner, June 22, 1943; Jordan to Kepner, July 5, 1943.

43. Jordan to Kepner, March 26, 1943.

44. Jordan to Kepner, April 6, 1943; Donald Webster Cory (pseudonym of Edward Sagarin), *The Homosexual in America: A Subjective Approach* (New York: Greenberg, 1951); Jordan to Kepner, May 21, 1943.

45. Jordan to Kepner, March 26, 1943; Jordan to Kepner, June 12, 1943.

46. Jordan to Kepner, September. 8, 1943; Cory, *Homosexual in America*, 110.

47. Jordan to Kepner, March 28, 1944; Jordan to Kepner, February 6, 1944.

48. Jordan to Kepner, June 18, 1944.

49. Jordan to Kepner, September 8, 1944.

50. "Edgerton Man Hit by Flak on Munich Trip," *Capital Times* (Madison, WI),

July 14, 1944; "Former Haresfooter Entertains in Army," *Daily Cardinal* (UW–Madison student paper), December 18, 1942; "Haresfoot Secretary Draws $100 Fine," *Wisconsin State Journal*, June 17, 1948; Student Discipline Files, UW–Madison Archives, Madison, WI.

51. James Zeasman transcript (OH 384, 1995), Wisconsin Veterans Museum Research Center.

52. Sigurd Sivertson transcript (OH 190, 1995), Wisconsin Veterans Museum Research Center.

53. John L. Bach transcript (OH 40, 1994), Wisconsin Veterans Museum Research Center.

54. Frank Duesler transcript (OH 54, 2002), Wisconsin Veterans Museum Research Center.

55. Jordan to Kepner, May 21, 1943.

56. "Bill Aimed at Sodomists Is Given Airing," *Capital Times*, February 22, 1945.

57. "Bill Aimed at Sodomists."

58. "Bill Aimed at Sodomists."

59. Jordan to Kepner, April 6, 1943; Jordan to Kepner, May 21, 1944.

60. Kepner to Jordan, June 19, 1944; Jordan to Kepner, July 6, 1944.

61. "V-mail," Wikipedia.

62. Kepner to Jordan, August 20, 1944.

63. Jordan to Kepner, December 28, 1943.

64. David Margolick, *Dreadful: The Short Life and Gay Times of John Horne Burns* (New York: Other Press, 2013); David Margolick, "A Caveat or Two about the Greatest Generation," *New York Times Magazine*, June 16, 2013.

65. Ted Pierce oral interview by Brian Bigler, series of interviews on "Gay Madison: A History," 1996, Wisconsin Historical Society Archives.

66. Pierce, oral interview.

67. Severinghaus and Chornyak, "A Study of Homosexual Males."

68. Severinghaus and Chornyak, "A Study of Homosexual Males."

69. Information on Severinghaus from "Biographical Information for the Wisconsin Union's Faculty Portrait Collection," May 21, 1942, UW–Madison Archives; and undated draft press release by University of Wisconsin News Bureau, Severinghaus Faculty File, UW–Madison Archives.

70. "Biographical Information for the Wisconsin Union's Faculty Portrait

Collection"; undated draft press release by University of Wisconsin News Bureau, UW–Madison Archives.

71. Chornyak appears in "Society Transactions: Philadelphia Psychiatric Society, March 13, 1936," *Archives of Neurology and Psychiatry*, 193.

72. Alfred C. Kinsey, "Criteria for a Hormonal Explanation of the Homosexual," *The Journal of Clinical Endocrinology* 1, no. 5, (May 1941): 424–428; Severinghaus and Chornyak, "A Study of Homosexual Males."

73. Severinghaus and Chornyak, "A Study of Homosexual Males."

74. Severinghaus and Chornyak, "A Study of Homosexual Males."

75. Severinghaus and Chornyak, "A Study of Homosexual Males."

76. Severinghaus and Chornyak, "A Study of Homosexual Males."

77. Severinghaus and Chornyak, "A Study of Homosexual Males."

78. Severinghaus and Chornyak, "A Study of Homosexual Males."

79. Jordan to Kepner, March 26, 1943.

80. Jordan to Kepner, March 19, 1943.

81. Jordan to Kepner, March 26, 1943; R. E. L. Masters, *The Homosexual Revolution: A Challenging Expose of the Social and Political Directions of a Minority Group* (New York: Julian Press, 1962), 45–47.

82. James Sears, *Behind the Mask: The Hal Call Chronicles and the Early Movement for Homosexual Emancipation* (New York: Harrington Park Press, 2006), 107; Jordan to Kepner, August 8, 1959. For other treatments of Jordan's Sons of Hamidy and Kepner, see also Lillian Faderman and Stuart Timmons, *Gay L.A.: A History of Sexual Outlaws, Power Politics, and Lipstick Lesbians* (New York: Basic Books, 2006); and also C. Todd White, *Pre-Gay LA: A Social History of the Movement for Homosexual Rights* (Urbana: University of Illinois Press, 2009). Chris West has written on science fiction's later influence on the early gay movement: "Homophile Fictions: Fan Writing, Science Fiction, and the Birth of Gay Communities in Post-war America," *Left History* 9 (Spring/Summer 2004): 161–189.

83. Jordan to Kepner, September 8, 1943.

84. Jordan to Kepner, December 7, 1944.

85. Jordan to Kepner, May 21, 1943.

86. Henry L. Minton, *Departing from Deviance: A History of Homosexual Rights and Emancipatory Science in America* (Chicago: University of Chicago Press, 2002), 75.

Chapter 6

1. "Sex Crimes in Milwaukee," *Milwaukee Journal*, September 14, 1946.

2. Benjamin Glover, in A. M. Krich, ed., *The Homosexuals: As Seen by Themselves and Thirty Authorities* (New York: Citadel, 1954), 152.

3. Allan Bérubé, "Pioneer Experts Discover the Gay G.I.," *Coming Out Under Fire: The History of Gary Men and Women in World War II* (New York: Free Press, 1990); George Chauncey Jr., "The Postwar Sex Crime Panic," in William Graebner, ed., *True Stories from the American Past*, (New York: McGraw-Hill, 1993), 166.

4. Alfred C. Kinsey, Wardell B. Pomeroy, and Clyde E. Martin, *Sexual Behavior in the Human Male* (Philadelphia: W. B. Saunders, 1948).

5. Paul Robinson, *The Modernization of Sex: Havelock Ellis, Alfred Kinsey, William Masters and Virginia Johnson* (Ithaca, NY: Cornell University Press, 1989).

6. James H. Jones, *Alfred C. Kinsey: A Public/Private Life* (New York: Norton, 1997), 314ff.

7. Kinsey et al., *Sexual Behavior*, 168ff.

8. Kinsey et al., *Sexual Behavior*, 263.

9. Kinsey et al., *Sexual Behavior*, chapter 21, "Homosexual Outlet," 610–659.

10. Kinsey et al., *Sexual Behavior*, 636ff, 616.

11. Tim LaHaye, *The Unhappy Gays: What Everyone Should Know about Homosexuality* (Wheaton, IL: Tyndale House, 1978), 17ff.

12. Kinsey et al., *Sexual Behavior*, 384–385.

13. Alfred C. Kinsey, Wardell B. Pomeroy, Clyde E. Martin, Paul H. Gebhard, *Sexual Behavior in the Human Female* (Philadelphia: W.B. Saunders, 1953,112, 446 ff.

14. Periodical reviews of Kinsey and Wisconsin newspaper accounts.

15. Edward Harris Heth, *Any Number Can Play* (New York: Harper & Brothers, 1945).

16. Edward Harris Heth, *My Life on Earth: The Story of a City Man Who Returned to the Country* (New York: Simon & Schuster, 1953), 18, 31.

17. Heth, *My Life on Earth*, 2, 14.

18. Heth, *My Life on Earth*, 4–6.

19. Heth, *My Life on Earth*, 35, 37.

20. Heth, *My Life on Earth*, 43–46.

21. Heth, *My Life on Earth*.

22. Heth, *My Life on Earth*, 47, 58.

23. Heth, *My Life on Earth*, 106, 26, 77.

24. Edward Harris Heth, *The Wonderful World of Cooking: From Hearty to Epicurean All Told as the Seasons Pass in a House on a Country Hill* (New York: Simon & Schuster, 1956), later republished as *The Country Kitchen Cook Book* (New York: Simon & Schuster, 1968).

25. Edward Harris Heth, *The Edward Harris Heth 1951 Almanac: A Handbook of Pleasure* (Waukesha, WI: Gordon Neilson, 1950). Says the author writes "a popular newspaper column, from the House on the Hill." The artists contributing illustrations include Karl Priebe, John Wilde, Edward Grover, and William Chancey, the last mentioned thus: "A native of Alabama, Mr. Chancey shares the House on the Hill, teaches ceramics."

26. Charles E. Morris III, "Pink Herring and the Fourth Persona: J. Edgar Hoover's Sex Crime Panic," *Quarterly Journal of Speech* 88 (May 2002): 228–244.

27. J. Edgar Hoover, "War on the Sex Criminal!," *New York Herald Tribune*, September 26, 1937.

28. J. Edgar Hoover, "How Safe Is Your Daughter?," *American Magazine*, July 1947.

29. Quoted in George Chauncey Jr., "The Postwar Sex Crime Panic," in Graebner, ed., *True Stories from the American Past* (New York: McGraw Hill, 1993), 160–178.

30. David G. Wittels, "What Can We Do about Sex Crimes?," *Saturday Evening Post*, December 11, 1948, 30ff.

31. David K. Johnson, *The Lavender Scare: The Cold War Persecution of Gays and Lesbians in the Federal Government* (Chicago: University of Chicago Press, 2006), 31, 56–57.

32. Estelle B. Freedman, "'Uncontrolled Desires': The Response to the Sexual Psychopath, 1920–1960," *Journal of American History* 74 (June 1987): 83–106, 85ff.

33. "Hoover Asks Sex-Crime War," *Wisconsin State Journal*, August 13, 1947; "Drive on Sex Crimes," *Oshkosh Daily Northwestern*, August 13, 1947; "Sex and the Law: Some Officials Invoke Ancient Sex Statutes Selectively, Critics Say," *Wall Street Journal*, July 5, 1968.

34. "Amnesty for Sex Convict Stirs Wrath of Law Here," *Milwaukee Sentinel*, September 23, 1946; "The Predatory Sex Offender," *Milwaukee Journal*,

September 26, 1946; "Stricter Sex Offense Laws Asked by State Police Chiefs," *Sheboygan Press*, October 3, 1946.

35. "The Sexual Psychopath," *Wisconsin Sheriff Magazine*, January 1948; "Hospitals, Not Jails, for Sex Offenders," *Wisconsin Sheriff Magazine*, April 1948.

36. SB 486, Wisconsin statutes, Relating to sexual psychopaths and the treatment thereof, and providing penalties; signed by Governor Rennebohm, July 30, 1947.

37. "Bill Aimed at Sodomists Is Given Airing: Ask Perverts Be Placed in Institutions," *Capital Times* (Madison, WI), February 22, 1945; "Urge Sexual Psychopaths Be Treated As Ill," *Capital Times*, April 17, 1947.

38. Chauncey, "Postwar Sex Crime Panic," *Milwaukee Journal*, November 18, 1947; *Wisconsin State Journal*, November 19, 1947.

39. Chauncey, "Postwar Sex Crime Panic," in Graebner, ed., 171 n3.

40. The intensity of the *Milwaukee Journal*'s editorial effort can be seen in the following selection of examples: "A Neglected Social Problem," March 10, 1944; "The Problem of Sex Deviates," February 22, 1945; "Sex Crimes in Milwaukee," September 4, 1946; "Another Sex Crime," March 14, 1947; "To Control Sex Predators," May 3, 1947; "Segregate Sex Psychopaths," May 31, 1947; "Menace of the Sex Perverts," June 3, 1947; "Curbing Sex Marauders," June 7, 1947; "Citizens Your Vital Sex Psychopaths Bill Is Coming Up," June 11, 1947.

41. "Wisconsin and 'Big Bill' Tilden," *Milwaukee Journal*, February 20, 1949.

42. Benjamin Glover, "Control of the Sex Deviate," *Federal Probation*, September 1960.

43. John L. Gillin, "'Sex Deviate' Laws in the United States," *International Journal of Sexology* 8, no. 2 (November 1954): 59ff.

44. Robert J. Miner, "Knitting at the Guillotine: An Approach to the Therapeutic Handling of Discipline," attached to letter of April 19, 1948, from C. E. Reudisili, associate UW dean, to Professor Howard C. Jackson, in Student Conduct files, UW–Madison Archives, Madison, Wisconsin. The Student Conduct files contain correspondence by deans, minutes of various committees with their actions, and actual files on student misconduct that may contain police reports and correspondence with Student Health. The main sources are listed as Student Affairs Discipline Records, series 19/5/1 UW–Madison Archives. Student names are included only in the rare cases

of the person's name also appearing in the newspapers, hence part of a public record. Thus, named student files are not listed. Other items such as committee minutes/actions may appear in a labeled file mixed in with the conduct files. Files from the 1930s through the early 1960s, in several large boxes, were reviewed for this chapter. Hereafter, Student Conduct files.

45. Miner, "Knitting at the Guillotine."

46. Student Conduct files.

47. Annette Washburne, faculty file, UW–Madison Archives.

48. Student Conduct files.

49. Student Conduct files.

50. Student Conduct files.

51. Student Conduct files.

52. Student Conduct files.

53. Student Conduct files.

54. *Wisconsin State Journal*, June 9, 1948, June 10, 1948, and June 21, 1958; *Capital Times*, June 9, 1948, June 12, 1948, and June 18, 1948.

55. *Wisconsin State Journal*, June 9, 1948, June 10, 1948, and June 21, 1958; *Capital Times*, June 9, 1948, June 12, 1948, and June 18, 1948.

56. *Wisconsin State Journal*, June 9, 1948, June 10, 1948, and June 21, 1958; *Capital Times*, June 9, 1948, June 12, 1948, and June 18, 1948.

57. *Wisconsin State Journal*, June 9, 1948, June 10, 1948, and June 21, 1958; *Capital Times*, June 9, 1948, June 12, 1948, and June 18, 1948.

58. Student Conduct files.

59. Student Conduct files.

60. Student Conduct files.

61. Student Conduct files.

62. Student Conduct files.

63. *Wisconsin Blue Book*, 1946, 174. See also 75, 108 for pictures of counseling, probably by the Veterans Officer (later a dean) Theodore Zillman.

64. Student Conduct files.

65. Student Conduct files.

66. Student Conduct files.

67. Student Conduct files.

68. Student Conduct files.

69. Student Conduct files.

70. Student Conduct files.

71. "Mud is Thrown in Hammersley Case," *Capital Times*, July 7, 1953.

72. For Hammersley, see E. David Cronon and John W. Jenkins, *The University of Wisconsin, A History*, vol. 4, *1945–1971* (Madison: University of Wisconsin Press, 1999), 415ff.

73. Student Conduct files.

74. Student Conduct files.

75. Student Conduct files.

76. Student Conduct files.

77. Student Conduct files.

78. Student Conduct files; Haresfoot Program booklet for *Big as Life*, 1948, copy in possession of author.

79. Student Conduct Files; Haresfoot scrapbook, UW–Madison Archives.

80. Haresfoot scrapbook.

81. Haresfoot scrapbook; Charles Schwartz, *Cole Porter: A Biography* (New York: Dial Press, 1977); the popularity of the song "Anything Goes" shows up in an internet search, with numerous gay choruses linked to the Porter tune.

82. Haresfoot scrapbook.

83. Student Conduct files.

84. "Haresfoot Show 'Not Very Good,'" *Capital Times*, April 11, 1961.

85. Student Conduct files.

86. Student Conduct files.

87. Student Conduct files.

88. Student Conduct files.

89. Student Conduct files.

90. Student Conduct files.

91. Student Conduct files.

92. Student Conduct files.

93. Student Conduct files.

94. Student Conduct files.

95. Student Conduct files.

96. Student Conduct files.

97. Student Conduct files.

98. Martin Duberman, *Cures: A Gay Man's Odyssey* (New York: Dutton, 1991), 3, 9, 38.

99. Student Conduct files.

100. Student Conduct files.

101. Student Conduct files.

102. Student Conduct files.

103. Student Conduct files.

104. George L. Mosse, *Confronting History: A Memoir* (Madison: University of Wisconsin Press, 2000), 157, 161; George L. Mosse, *Nationalism and Sexuality: Middle-Class Morality and Sexual Norms in Modern Europe* (Madison: University of Wisconsin Press, 1985), 10; see also George L. Mosse, *The Image of Man: The Creation of Modern Masculinity* (New York: Oxford University Press, 1966).

105. Student Conduct files.

106. Student Conduct files.

107. Student Conduct files.

108. Various items in Benjamin Glover faculty file, UW–Madison Archives.

109. Glover in *The Homosexuals*.

110. Glover in *The Homosexuals*, 141–153.

111. Glover in *The Homosexuals*, 141–153.

112. Glover in *The Homosexuals*, 141–153.

113. Glover in *The Homosexuals*, 141–153.

114. Glover in *The Homosexuals*, 141–153.

115. Glover in *The Homosexuals*, 141–153.

116. Glover in *The Homosexuals*, 141–153.

117. Glover in *The Homosexuals*, 141–153.

118. Glover in *The Homosexuals*, 141–153.

119. Glover in *The Homosexuals*, 141–153.

120. Glover in *The Homosexuals*, 141–153.

121. Glover in *The Homosexuals*, 141–153.

122. Glover faculty file.

Chapter 7

1. *Green Bay Press-Gazette*, April 26, 1950.

2. Minutes, UW Conduct and Appeals Committee, April 12, 1962, UW–Madison Archives, Madison, WI.

3. Allan Bérubé, "Coming Out Under Fire," *Mother Jones*, February/March

1983, 23ff; John D'Emilio, *Sexual Politics, Sexual Communities: The Making of a Homosexual Minority in the United States, 1940–1970* (Chicago: University of Chicago Press, 1983).

4. David K. Johnson, *The Lavender Scare: The Cold War Persecution of Gays and Lesbians in the Federal Government* (Chicago: University of Chicago Press, 2004), 30; Robert Griffith, *The Politics of Fear: Joseph R. McCarthy and the Senate* (Lexington: University Press of Kentucky, 1970), 89; Neil Miller, *Out of the Past: Gay and Lesbian History from 1869 to the Present* (New York: Vintage Books, 1995), 258–279.

5. Alan Simpson, foreword, in Rodger McDaniel, *Dying for Joe McCarthy's Sins: The Suicide of Wyoming Senator Lester Hunt* (Cody, WY: Wordsworth, 2013), vii–xi.

6. McDaniel, *Dying*, 280ff.

7. McDaniel, *Dying*, 269ff.

8. Lillian Faderman, *Odd Girls and Twilight Lovers: A History of Lesbian Life in Twentieth Century America* (New York: Penguin, 1992), 142–145.

9. For a good review of McCarthy's overall trajectory see David M. Oshinsky, *A Conspiracy So Immense: The World of Joe McCarthy* (Oxford, UK: Oxford University Press, 2005); *Congressional Record*, February 20, 1950, page 1961 for case 14 and pages 1978 and 1979 for case 62.

10. *Capital Times* (Madison, WI), March 25, 1952.

11. Quoted in Joseph Alsop and Stewart Alsop, "Why Has Washington Gone Crazy?," *Saturday Evening Post*, July 29, 1950.

12. Alsop and Alsop, "Why Has Washington Gone Crazy?"

13. Alsop and Alsop, "Why Has Washington Gone Crazy?"

14. *Congressional Record*, August 8, 1950, 11979. On Hibbs's response, see Jack Anderson and Ronald W. May, *McCarthy: The Man, the Senator, the "Ism"* (Boston: Beacon Press, 1952).

15. Quoted in Alsop and Alsop, "Why Has Washington Gone Crazy?"; *Congressional Record*, August 8, 1950.

16. Thomas A. Coleman Papers, correspondence in Wisconsin Historical Society Archives, Madison, Wisconsin, hereafter, Coleman papers. The memo stationery reads "Republican Party of Wisconsin, State Finance Committee, 201 Waubesa Street, Madison 10, Wisconsin"—that being the address of Madison Kipp Corporation.

17. "Report to the Strategic Committee," April 20, 1950, Coleman papers; Joe

McCarthy, *McCarthyism: The Fight for America* (New York: Arno Press, 1977), 2, 10.

18. Coleman papers.

19. Coleman papers.

20. Urban Van Susteren, tape-recorded interview by Richard Cresswell, November 1965, partial transcript, Wisconsin Historical Society Archives; Arthur Herman, *Joseph McCarthy: Reexamining the Life and Legacy of America's Most Hated Senator* (New York: Free Press, 2000), 218.

21. Michael O'Brien, *McCarthy and McCarthyism in Wisconsin* (Columbia: University of Missouri Press, 1980), 101; John Wyngaard, "Government and Politics," *Green Bay Press-Gazette*, April 26, 1950, 14; Johnson, *Lavender Scare*, 19.

22. Johnson, *Lavender Scare*, 19, 23; Chapple, quoted in Thomas Reeves, *The Life and Times of Joe McCarthy: A Biography* (New York: Stein and Day, 1982), 326.

23. Herman, *Joseph McCarthy: Reexamining*, 3, 186.

24. McCarthy, *McCarthyism*, 14.

25. McCarthy, *McCarthyism*, 14–15.

26. McCarthy, *McCarthyism*, 15.

27. Reeves, *Life and Times*, 112.

28. Herman, *Joseph McCarthy: Reexamining*, 272; Emile de Antonio and Daniel Talbot, *Point of Order: A Documentary of the Army-McCarthy Hearings* (New York: Norton, 1964).

29. Mike Miller, "Bringing Down a Demagogue: The Cap Times Never Wavered in Its Fight against Joe McCarthy," *Capital Times*, September 16–22, 2009; William F. Thompson, *The History of Wisconsin, Vol. VI: Continuity and Change, 1940–1965* (Madison: State Historical Society, 1988), 528–611;

30. Jeremi Suri, "The New McCarthyism?," *Global Brief* (blog), March 23, 2011, http://jeremisuri.net/archives/804, originally appeared at http://globalbrief.ca.

31. "The President's Chance," *The Progressive*, July 1950, 3.

32. *Capital Times*, April 26, 1950.

33. W. McNeil Lowry, "Hit and Run—How It Works," *The Progressive*, June 1950, 7ff.

34. Lowry, "Hit and Run."

35. Lowry, "Hit and Run."

36. Stringfellow Barr, "My Confession to McCarthy," *The Progressive*, March 1951, 24ff; "Tangent," *ONE* (San Francisco), January 1960.

37. Barr, "My Confession."

38. O'Brien, *McCarthy and McCarthyism*, 114, 124.

39. "Mr. Truman Dallies with Evil," *The Progressive*, January 1952, 34; David McCullough, *Truman* (New York: Simon & Schuster, 1992), 768; election results in Wisconsin *Blue Book*, 1954.

40. *Congressional Record*, September 20, 1950, 15191 and 15218.

41. *Congressional Record*, August 29, 1950, 13759, and 13769–13770; "Andrew Biemiller," Wikipedia; *Wisconsin Blue Book*, 1950, 21; veto message, *Congressional Record*, September 22, 15629ff; Merle Miller, *Plain Speaking: An Oral Biography of Harry S. Truman* (New York: Putnam's, 1974), 415; *Congressional Record*, September 22, 1950, 15632–15633.

42. Stuart Chase, "McCarthyism under the Microscope," *The Progressive*, February 1954, 5ff.

43. "McCarthy: A Documented Record," *The Progressive*, April 1954; Bernard Sheil, "The Immorality of McCarthyism," *The Progressive*, May 1954, 10ff.

44. *Wisconsin Blue Book*, 1954.

45. "Is This the End of McCarthy?," *The Progressive*, November 1954, 3ff.

46. Rodger Streitmatter, *Unspeakable: The Rise of the Gay and Lesbian Press in America* (Boston: Faber and Faber, 1995), 18–20; Dal McIntire, "Tangents," *ONE*, January 1960, 18.

47. Jim Burroway, "Today in History: *ONE* Magazine versus the U.S. Post Office," January 13, 2008, Box Turtle Bulletin, www.boxturtlebulletin. com/2008/01/13/1273; Streitmatter, *Unspeakable*, 32–33.

48. "Lewd Material in Los Angeles Mail Charged," AP story reprinted in *ONE*, November 1954; McIntire, "Tangents," 18.

49. Faderman, *Odd Girls*, 146; Streitmatter, *Unspeakable*, 35; "*One, Inc. v. Olesen*," Wikipedia; McIntire, "Tangents," 18.

50. Quoted in David Halberstam, *The Fifties* (New York: Villard Books, 1993), 54; Glover, "Homosexuality among University Students," 146.

51. D'Emilio, *Sexual Politics*, chapter 5, "Retreat to Respectability," 75–91.

52. "Ramblin' Around," signed S.R.A., clipping dated May 17, 1950, possibly from a weekly newspaper in Edgerton or Evansville.

53. Wally Jordan to Jim Kepner, January 18, 1970, *ONE* National Gay &

Lesbian Archives, University of Southern California Libraries, Los Angeles, California.

54. Author's conversation with Elena Sherman, adopted daughter of Milt Sherman, June 20, 2014, Madison, Wisconsin.

55. Karel Plessini, *The Perils of Normalcy: George L. Mosse and the Remaking of Cultural History* (Madison: University of Wisconsin Press, 2014), 14, 24, 215 n35.

56. Patricia C. McKissack and Fredrick L. McKissack, *Young, Black, and Determined: A Biography of Lorraine Hansberry* (New York: Holiday House, 1998); Janet Tripp, *The Importance of Lorraine Hansberry* (San Diego: Lucent Books, 1998); picture of Langdon Manor residents in *Badger* 1949; "Race Had No Part of It," *Wisconsin State Journal*, March 1959.

57. *Awake and Sing!* program, Lorraine Hansberry file, UW–Madison Archives; "The Theater and Sean O'Casey," in Tripp, *The Importance*; "Ex-U.W. Co-ed Becomes 'The Toast of New York,'" *Wisconsin State Journal*, March 29, 1959.

58. Author cross-referenced student discipline files for homosexuals with the 1949 and 1950 *Badger* yearbook pages on the Wisconsin Player; Letter to *Daily Cardinal*, Hansberry file; Susan Sinnott, *Lorraine Hansberry: Award-Winning Playwright and Civil Rights Activist* (Berkeley: Conari Press, 1999).

59. Kevin Mumford, "Opening the Restricted Box: Lorraine Hansberry's Lesbian Writing," http://outhistory.org/exhibits/show/lorraine-hansberry/lesbian-writing; Trish Bendix, "Lorraine Hansberry's Secret Lesbian Herstory Touched upon in New Documentary," https://intomore.com/; Imani Perry, *Looking for Lorraine: The Radiant Radical Life of Lorraine Hansberry* (Boston: Beacon Press, 2018); author interview with Kathleeen Nichols, Madison, Wisconsin, April 29, 2018.

60. Lorraine Hansberry, *A Raisin in the Sun* (New York: Modern Library, Random House, 1995), 22, 34.

61. Quoted in Richard H. Rovere, *Senator Joe McCarthy* (New York: Harcourt, Brace, 1959), 189.

62. Richard M. Fried, *Nightmare in Red: The McCarthy Era in Perspective* (New York: Oxford University Press, 1990), 141.

63. Harry S. Truman, "Executive Order 9835," signed March 21, 1947, Harry S. Truman Library and Museum website, www.trumanlibrary.org/dbq/loyaltyprogram.php.

64. Dwight Eisenhower, "Executive Order 10450—Security Requirements for Government Employment," signed April 27, 1953, www.archives.gov/federal-register/codification/executive-order/10450.html.

65. "30 in State Group Which Attacks Nash," *Capital Times*, September 16, 1960; "Phileo Nash," *Congressional Record-Senate*, 1952, 581.

66. "Nash Discloses Letter of Loyalty Clearance," *Milwaukee Journal*, September 18, 1960; "Truman Helps Philleo Nash in Slash at Anti-Nash Campaign," *Milwaukee Sentinel*, September 19, 1960.

67. Arthur Miller, *The Crucible* (New York: Penguin Books, 1976), 33, 34, 130.

68. "UW Students Boo McCarthy," *Milwaukee Journal*, May 14, 1951; "Local Audience Jeers at McCarthy's 'Proofs': He Fails to Name 'Reds,'" *Capital Times*, May 14, 1951; "1,000 Turn Out to Hear Lerner Flay McCarthy," *Capital Times*, May 14, 1951.

69. "Local Audience Jeers"; McCullough, *Truman*, 768; Miller, *Plain Speaking*, 420.

70. James A. Wechsler, "McCarthy Close Up," *The Progressive*, June 1953, 9ff.

71. Ron McCrea, interview on "Madison Gay Purge," first appeared in *Renaissance Newsletter*, Madison Gay Center, reprinted in *Midwest Gay Academic Journal* 1, no. 3 (1978): 25–30.

72. The police reports from the purge are in the H.S. Problem file; LGBT Liaison Historical material, box 1, UW–Madison Archives; Student Conduct Files, Student Affairs Discipline Records 19/5/1, UW–Madison Archives.

73. McCrea, interview.

74. Gina Slesar, "'That Would Never Happen Here': The 1962 Gay Purge at the University of Wisconsin–Madison," undergraduate thesis, UW–Madison, May 12, 2013, copy in possession of author.

75. Quoted in Slesar, "'That Would Never'"; Matthew Levin, *Cold War University: Madison and the New Left in the Sixties* (Madison: University of Wisconsin Press, 2013), 70.

76. Slesar, "'That Would Never'"; "Campus Behavior Strictly Personal," *Milwaukee Sentinel*, April 4, 1966.

77. H.S. Problem file.

78. Minutes of Student Conduct Committee, April 17, 1962, Student Conduct files; *Wisconsin Blue Book*, 1962.

79. Slesar, "'That Would Never'"; George Stambolian, *Male Fantasies/Gay Realities: Interviews with Ten Men* (New York: Sea Horse Press, 1984), xii.

80. Student Conduct Files; H.S. Problem file; McCrea, interview.

81. Student Conduct files.

82. Student Conduct files.

83. Student Conduct files.

84. Student Conduct files.

85. Student Conduct files.

86. Student Conduct files.

87. Student Conduct files; H.S. Problem file.

88. Student Conduct files.

89. Student Conduct files.

90. Student Conduct files.

91. Student Conduct files.

92. Martha Peterson, 1962 oral history interview transcript, interview no. 264; Martha Peterson, "Those Were the Days, My Friends: A Collection of Recollections of Real Happenings in Fifty Years as a Teacher, Administrator, and Corporate Board Member, 1937 to 1987," summer 2002, manuscript autobiography; both in Martha Peterson Collection, LGBT Collections, UW–Madison Archives.

93. "Midwesterner to Head Barnard College," *Chicago American*, June 11, 1967, clipping in Martha Peterson faculty file, UW–Madison Archives.

94. Hiring materials in President E. B. Fred's files, boxes 268 and 269, UW–Madison Archives; UW news release, March 10, 1956, on Peterson appointment, in Peterson faculty file.

95. "New Women's Dean Is a Phi Beta Kappa," *Milwaukee Journal*, March 11, 1956, clipping in Peterson faculty file; "New Dean May Act to Abolish Race Bars in Co-ed Housing," *Capital Times*, March 12, 1956, clipping in Peterson faculty file; Peterson, oral history interview.

96. UW news release, December 4, 1956, and other clippings in Peterson faculty file.

97. "Women's Power Isn't Underestimated," *Wisconsin State Journal*, February 21, 1962, clipping in Peterson faculty file; UW news release, October 28, 1963, Peterson faculty file.

98. Maxine Bennett, "The First Eighty," July 9, 1996, manuscript autobiography in Martha Peterson Collection; Maxine Bennett, oral history interview no. 589, Maxine Bennett faculty file, UW–Madison Archives.

99. Maxine Bennett, oral history interview, May 13, 1977, History Project on

Women in Medicine, Archives of the Medical College of Pennsylvania, Philadelphia, Pennsylvania; Bennett, "First Eighty."

100. "Ear, Nose, and Throat Expert Bennett Retiring," UW–Madison News Service, press release, July 3, 1978, Maxine Bennett faculty file; Memorial Resolution of the Faculty of the UW–Madison on the Death of Professor Emerita Eleanor Maxine Bennett, Bennett faculty file.

101. Bennett, "First Eighty"; Bennett, oral history interview.

102. Various items, mainly news releases on faculty travels, Peterson faculty file; "Halfway House Is Half Way," *Select*, May 1964, copy in Peterson faculty file.

103. Louise Marston, "Dr. Maxine Bennett Honored," undated clipping from *Wisconsin State Journal*, Bennett faculty file.

104. "Martha Peterson, 90, Barnard President in Vietnam War Era, Dies," *New York Times*, July 20, 2006; Peterson obituary, July 25, 2006, www .madison.com/.

Chapter 8

1. Doug Erickson, "Love's Long Journey," *Wisconsin State Journal*, October 13, 2013.

2. Letter, from Mr. R., Madison, WI, *ONE* (San Francisco), March 1959, 29.

3. J. D. Mercer, *They Walk in Shadow: A Study of Sexual Variations with Emphasis on the Ambisexual and Homosexual Components and Our Contemporary Sex Laws* (New York: Comet Press Books, 1959), foreword, 7, 13. The book has both technical glossary and slang vocabulary appendixes.

4. "Homosexuality in America," *Life*, June 26, 1964, cover and 66–80; "The Homosexual in America," *Time*, January 21, 1966, 52ff.

5. Several variations of draft statements written by Ted Pierce "To the Committee of the MARQUETTE*WILLIAMSON Garden Tour," Ted Pierce Papers, box 2, folder 5, Wisconsin Historical Society Archives, Madison, Wisconsin, hereafter, Pierce papers; author's interactions with Pierce.

6. Photo in Ted Pierce papers shows nine guests at NAACP reception by Smith Wolin Studios, with a credit line of names including Ted Pierce, Keith McCutcheon, and several well-known early African American civil rights activists, Pierce papers, folder 2.

7. "Ramblin' Around," signed S.R.A., clipping dated May 17, 1950, possibly from a weekly newspaper in Edgerton or Evansville, given to author by Pierce.

8. "Ramblin' Around."

9. "Ramblin' Around."

10. Erickson, "Love's Long Journey."

11. "The Sebenthall Project," *Past Times*, Mount Horeb Area Historical Society, January 2013 and April 2013.

12. R. E. Sebenthall, *Acquainted with a Chance of Bobcats* (New Brunswick, New Jersey: Rutgers University Press, 1969), 18, 25–27, 30; Betty Stebenthall entry, www.findagrave.com/memorial/98045780/betty-sebenthall.

13. "Nancy Oestreich Lurie," Wikipedia; "Nancy O. Lurie," Wisconsin Academy of Sciences, Arts and Letters, www.wisconsinacademy.org/contributor/nancy-o-lurie.

14. "Nancy O. Lurie."

15. Nancy Oestreich Lurie, "Winnebago Berdache," *American Anthropologist*, 55, no. 5 (December 1953): 708–712.

16. "Two Spirit," Wikipedia; George Catlin, "Dance to the Berdash," *North American Indians. . . Written . . .1832–1839* (1903), Smithsonian American Art Museum, viewable at http://americanart.si.edu/collections/search/artwork/?id=4023.

17. Lurie, "Winnebago Berdache."

18. Lurie, "Winnebago Berdache."

19. Lurie, "Winnebago Berdache."

20. Lurie, "Winnebago Berdache"; Walter L. Williams, *The Spirit and The Flesh: Sexual Diversity in American Indian Culture* (Boston: Beacon Press, 1986).

21. "Kohl Miner New Director of First Nations Composer Forum," *The Circle: News from a Native American Perspective*, December 5, 2009, http://thecirclenews.org/; "Kohl Miner to Perform Piece about Two-Spirit People at Patrick's Cabaret," City Pages website, March 23, 2012, www.citypages.com.

22. Keith McCutcheon, "Taliesin," Keith McCutcheon papers, in possession of the author; Keith McCutcheon, "This and That," clipping book of *Rio Journal* columns, handwritten date September 14, 1933, in McCutcheon papers, possession of the author.

23. Roger Friedland, and Harold Zellman, *The Fellowship: The Untold Story of Frank Lloyd Wright and the Taliesin Fellowship* (New York: Harper Perennial, 2006), 99, 429ff.

24. Quoted in Friedland and Zellman, *The Fellowship*.

25. Friedland and Zellman, *The Fellowship*.

26. Friedland and Zellman, *The Fellowship*.

27. David K. Johnson, "Physique Pioneers: The Politics of 1960s Gay Consumer Culture," *Journal of Social History* 30 (July 2010): 867–892.

28. Johnson, "Physique Pioneers," citing John D'Emilio, *Sexual Politics, Sexual Communities: The Making of a Homosexual Minority in the United States* (Chicago: University of Chicago Press, 1983), 136; "The Homosexual in America," *Time*, January 21, 1966.

29. "Tangents," *ONE*, December 1957.

30. Annette Hoffman, "Turner Societies," in *Germany and the Americas, Culture, Politics, and History*, ed. Thomas Adam (Santa Barbara, CA: ABC CLIO, 2005); Julius Vogel, scrapbook on physical culture, in possession of the author.

31. *Strength & Health*, September 1939, 3.

32. *ONE*, December 1957, 22; *Strength & Health*, September 1939, 8, 17, 20, 45.

33. David Chapman, *Adonis: The Male Physique Pin Up 1870–1940* (Swaffham, UK: Editions Aubrey Walter, 1997), 56–57.

34. *Strength & Health*, March 1945, 16, 17, 38; *Strength & Health*, December 1945, 36.

35. *ONE*, June 1953, 5–8.

36. Timothy Lewis, intro. to Winston Leyland, ed., *Physique: A Pictorial History of the Athletic Model Guild*, photography by Bob Mizer (San Francisco: Gay Sunshine Press, 1982); Kevin Clarke, "Gay History: in Detail, in Color, and in the Flesh," intro. to Stephan Niederwiesser, ed., *Heavy Traffic* (Berlin: Bruno Gmünder, 2011).

37. *Physique Pictorial*, February 1963, 17; Lewis, intro.

38. Christmas card and photographs in possession of the author.

39. "Arrest 10 Men for Illicit Sex Activities in City Area," *Waukesha Daily Freeman*, September 7, 1960; "Charge 9 Men in Sex Case at Waukesha," *Capital Times* (Madison, WI), September 7, 1960; "Waukesha Sex Case Crackdown," *Wisconsin State Journal*, September 8, 1960; "Waukesha Police Arrest 10 in Parks," *Milwaukee Journal*, September 7, 1960.

40. "Elm Grove Residents Held in Morals Case," *Waukesha Daily Freeman*, September 12, 1960; "Physician Pleads Guilty to Reduced Count Here," *Waukesha Daily Freeman*, September 28, 1960.

41. "Arrest 10."

42. "Praises Police and Press in Difficult Situation," *Waukesha Freeman*, September 22, 1960.

43. "Soften Attitude about City as Center of Illicit Sex Ring," *Waukesha Daily Freeman*, September 8, 1960; *Wisconsin Blue Book*, 1962.

44. "Crackdown on Rumors Urged," *Waukesha Daily Freeman*, September 21, 1960.

45. "Arrest 10."

46. "Delay Verdict in Morals Case," *Waukesha Daily Freeman*, September 20, 1960; "Morals Case Is Dismissed Here," *Waukesha Daily Freeman*, September 26, 1960; "Gets Probation in Morals Case," *Waukesha Daily Freeman*, September 27, 1960; "Physician Pleads Guilty to Reduced Count Here," *Waukesha Daily Freeman*, September 28, 1960.

47. "Questions Necessity of Publishing Scandal," letter from Mrs. Bruce Meyer; "Praises Police and Press in Difficult Situation," letter from a Waukesha Parent; "Commends Police Department, Recommends a Clinic," letter from Harry Vredenbregt, Wales; "Says Prominence Is No Bar to Publicity," letter from a Reader; "Pens Praise for Work Done by Police Here," letter from a Waukesha Resident; "Queries Board on No Swim-Suit Rule," letter from a Concerned Parent, Waukesha; all printed in the *Waukesha Daily Freeman* during September 1960.

48. "Gets Probation."

49. "Officers Raid 'Club' at Wright-o-Tel Here," *Ladysmith (Wisconsin) News*, April 14, 1966; "Homosexual Club Broken in Rusk Co.," *Milwaukee Journal*, May 3, 1966.

50. "Officers Raid 'Club.'"

51. "Wright-o-Tel Gym Group Not Involved," *Ladysmith News*, April 21, 1966, 1; "Court News," April 21, 1966, 6; "Court News," April 28, 1966, 2; "Court News," May 12, 1966; "Court News," May 19, 1966; "Court News," June 13, 1966; "Court News," June 23, 1966, all in *Ladysmith News*; "The Courts Decide," *Ladysmith News*, June 30, 1966; "City Nuisance Ordinance Voted by Council Monday," *Ladysmith News*, June 1, 1966.

52. Will Fellows and Helen P. Branson, *Gay Bar: The Fabulous, True Story of a Daring Woman and Her Boys in the 1950s* (Madison: University of Wisconsin Press, 2010), ix, xv; Robert Gregory, "The Gay Bar," *ONE*, February 1958, 5.

53. Joseph Harry, "Urbanization and the Gay Life," *Journal of Sex Research* 10, no. 3 (August 1974): 238–247.

54. Martin Meeker, *Contacts Desired: Gay and Lesbian Communications and Community, 1940s–1970s* (Chicago: University of Chicago Press, 2006), 9.

55. Don Schwamb, "Chronology of Guides to Wisconsin Gay Venues," Milwaukee LGBT History, www.mkelgbthist.org/media/guide-chronology.htm. The early gay guides and their Wisconsin listings are on the website and acknowledgment is made to the Gerber-Hart Library in Chicago for early guides. Some of the individual Wisconsin bars also have their own page at this website.

56. "Chronology of Guides."

57. "Chronology of Guides."

58. "Chronology of Guides."

59. "Chronology of Guides."

60. "Chronology of Guides."

61. "Chronology of Guides"; Hank Bova, interview by author, August 11, 2007; Bill Deidrich, discussion with author, 2011.

62. "Chronology of Guides"; Lynn Soli and Barb McCaig, *Today's Guide to Milwaukee Taverns* (Cudahy, WI: Reminder Printing, 1984).

63. Lewis Bosworth, *RODS (A Tenth Anniversary Commemorative History Booklet)* (Madison: The Back Door, Ltd., 1989).

64. *ONE*, January 1963, cover.

65. Roger Streitmatter, *Unspeakable: The Rise of the Gay and Lesbian Press in America* (Boston: Faber and Faber, 1995), 28; Jim Kepner, *Rough News, Daring Views: 1950s' Pioneer Gay Press Journalism* (New York: Harrington Park Press, 1998), 12; Henry Eichhorn, interview by author, Madison, WI, September 18, 2009.

66. Foreword by Wayne R. Dynes in Kepner, *Rough News*, vii.

67. *ONE*, issues cited and one letter reprinted in Craig M. Loftin, ed., *Letters to ONE: Gay and Lesbian Voices from the 1950s and 1960s* (New York: SUNY Press, 2012); Mr. H., Watertown, letter to *ONE*, August/September 1956.

68. Dr. K., Wisconsin, letter to *ONE*, October 1962, 30; Mr. R., Madison, WI, letter to *ONE*, March 1959, 29; Mr. B., Milwaukee, letter to *ONE*, April 1963, 32; Mr. B. H., Milwaukee, letter to *ONE*, January 1964, 30; Mr. B, Milwaukee, letter to *ONE*, June 1959; Dr. K., Wisconsin, letter to *ONE*, October 1962.

69. Mr. R., Madison, letter to *ONE*, March 1959, 29; Miss K., Racine, letter to *ONE*, June/July 1957; Dr. P., Kenosha, letter to *ONE*, March 1959; Dr. K., letter to *ONE*, October 1962; Dr. K., Wisconsin, letter to *ONE*, November 1965; Alice Horvath, "Homosexuals without Masks," *ONE*, November 1958, 5–8.

70. Mr. B., Milwaukee, letter to *ONE*, June 1959, 31; Mr. B., letter to *ONE*, March 1958, 29; Mr. B., Milwaukee, letter to *ONE*, April 1963; Mr. H. B., Miluwakee, letter to *ONE*, July 1964.

71. George, suburb of San Francisco, letter to *ONE*, April 24, 1955, reprinted in Loftin, *Letters to ONE*, 36–38.

72. *ONE*, September 1963; Mr. B. H., Milwaukee, letter to *ONE*, January 1964.

73. *ONE*, November 1958; Mr. R., Madison, letter to *ONE*, March 1959; Horvath, "Homosexuals," 5–8.

74. Mr. B., Milwaukee, letter to *ONE*, June 1959; *ONE*, March 1958.

75. Mr. B., Green Bay, letter to *ONE*, January 1965.

76. Mr. C., Delavan, letter to *ONE*, March 1965.

77. Loftin, *Letters to ONE*, 3.

78. Streitmatter, *Unspeakable: The Rise*, 26–27; *ONE*, October 1959, 4–5.

79. "Oddments," *ONE*, September 1958, 19; "Oddments," *ONE*, August 1959, 13; "We Believe in Freedom BUT Department," *ONE*, February 1959, 15.

80. *ONE*, January 1960.

81. *ONE*, November 1960.

82. "One Hand Gives You 20 Years, the Other Gives Penicillin," *ONE*, February 1965, 15.

83. *ONE*, October 1960, November 1960.

84. *ONE*, November 1960, October 1963.

85. *ONE*, November 1960, 20.

86. Streitmatter, *Unspeakable*, 54–60; Lillian Faderman, *Odd Girls and Twilight Lovers: A History of Lesbian Life in Twentieth Century America* (New York: Penguin, 1992), 170–180.

87. "Editorial—Growing Pains," *The Ladder*, October 1959, 4; "The Ladder (magazine)," Wikipedia.

88. "Cross Currents," *The Ladder*, December 1963, 14.

89. Grier quoted in Streitmatter, *Unspeakable*, 153; "Barbara Grier," Wikipedia.

90. Joanne E. Passet, "Foster, Jeannette Howard," American National Biography Online, anb.org/articles/16/16-00328-article.html.

91. *The Ladder*, August/September 1970, 31.

92. "Cross Currents," *The Ladder*, February/March 1972.

93. "Readers Respond," *The Ladder*, November 1958, 22; "Beginning—DOB Book Service," *The Ladder*, May 1960, 9; "Editor's Note," *The Ladder*, July 1959, 26.

94. "Readers Respond," *The Ladder*, June/July 1971, 49–50.

95. "Readers Respond," *The Ladder*, June/July 1971, 49–50.

96. "Readers Respond," *The Ladder*, June/July 1971, 49–50.

97. "Editorial," *The Ladder*, August/September 1972.

98. Sig Piotrowski, letter to *ONE*, November 19, 1953; Gilbert Frohe, letter to *ONE*, December 3, 1953; Steve R. Van Kirk, letter to *ONE*, June 17, 1954; Carl Kroll, letter to *ONE*, January 27, 1955; Dale Olson, responses in *ONE*, April 8, 1954, April 26, 1954, February 10, 1955, and August 7, 1956, all from Mattachine files, *ONE* National Gay and Lesbian Archives, University of Southern California Libraries, Los Angeles, California.

99. Glenn A. Bacon, MD, to Mattachine Society, Los Angeles, July 19, 1956, Mattachine files.

100. Bacon to Mattachine Society.

101. D. C. Olson to Glenn A. Bacon, August 7, 1956, Mattachine files.

102. Olson to Glenn A. Bacon.

103. "Amending District of Columbia Charitable Solicitation Act," *Congressional Record-House*, August 11, 1964, 18943–18949.

104. "Amending District," 18943–18949.

105. "Sex Plank in Platform," *Milwaukee Sentinel*, March 28, 1966; "Young Democrats Ask End to Curbs on Sex," *Milwaukee Journal*, March 28, 1966; Conrad Goodkind, interview by author, July 6, 2009, Madison, Wisconsin; Peter Peshek, interview by author, June 29, 2009, Madison, Wisconsin; "Y-Dems Pass Weaker Viet War Resolution," *Daily Cardinal* (Madison), March 29, 1966.

106. "Humphrey Applauded but GOP Is Roasted," *Milwaukee Journal*, March 27, 1966, 26; "Urge Vietnam Truce: Young Democrats Platform," *Milwaukee Sentinel*, March 28, 1966; "Y-Dems Pass Weaker," *Daily Cardinal*; "'Grow Up,'" letter from Kenneth Joop, *Milwaukee Sentinel*, April 11, 1966, 12.

107. "Young Democrats Ask," *Milwaukee Journal*.

108. "Young Democrats Ask," *Milwaukee Journal*; "Y-Democrats Platform

Hit," *Milwaukee Sentinel*, March 29, 1966; "Foe Blasts Democrats' War Stand," *Milwaukee Journal*, March 29, 1966; "YGOP Eyes Sex, Spending, Saigon," *Wisconsin State Journal*, April 30, 1966; "YGOP Raps 'Hate' Paper, Its Distributor," *Wisconsin State Journal*, May 2, 1966; "YGOP Parley Mulls Democrats' Sex Stand," *Milwaukee Journal*, April 30, 1966; "Young Republicans Avoid Sex Plank," *Capital Times*, May 2, 1966.

109. "Democratic Group Raps Stand on Sex," *Milwaukee Journal*, March 30, 1966; "Oust 'Beatniks,' Democrats Told," *Milwaukee Journal*, April 1, 1966; "Because of 'Sex' Plank, New Young Democratic Group Urged," *Wisconsin State Journal*, April 1, 1966; "'Decent' Dems Should Quit Y-Dems, Sen. Benson Says: Sex Plank Debate Rages," *Capital Times*, April 1, 1966; "36 Young Dems Don't Approve of 'Sex Plank,'" *Capital Times*, April 6, 1966.

110. "No Place for Sex in Party Platform," *Milwaukee Sentinel*, April 5, 1966; "Freer Sex Plank Stirs Wisconsin: Young Democrats Termed 'Homocrats' by Governor," *New York Times*, April 10, 1966; Wainwright Churchill, *Homosexual Behavior among Males: A Cross Cultural and Cross Species Investigation* (New York: Hawthorn Books, 1967), 231; "Sex and the Single Party," *Milwaukee Sentinel*, April 1, 1966.

111. "Y-Dem Leader Hits GOP for Sex Plank Attack," *Capital Times*, April 8, 1966; "Sex Plank," letter from Jim Miller, *Milwaukee Sentinel*, April 6, 1966; "'Lesser Evil,'" letter from Eugene Burns, *Milwaukee Sentinel*, April 8, 1966; "Defends Y-Dems' Sex Law Stand," Susan Kime, *Capital Times*, April 6, 1966; "Sex and Morality," letter from R. K, *Milwaukee Sentinel*, April 25, 1966.

112. "Freer Sex Plank," *New York Times*; Churchill, *Homosexual Behavior*, 230–231.

113. "Complete Sex Freedom Is Debated Here," *Milwaukee Sentinel*, April 27, 1966; A. E. Smith, "The Myth of the Homosexual Vote," *ONE*, October 1964, 6–8.

114. John Wyngaard, "Outspoken Youngsters Embarrass Parties," column, *Wisconsin State Journal*, April 11, 1966.

115. "Freer Sex Plank," *New York Times*; Dem Platform in *Wisconsin Blue Book*.

116. Maurice Leznoff and William A. Westley, "The Homosexual Community," in Hendrik M. Ruitenbeek, ed., *The Problem of Homosexuality in Modern Society* (New York: Dutton, 1963), 162, 163, 169ff, 173.

117. Martin Hoffman, *The Gay World: Male Homosexuality and the Social Creation of Evil* (New York: Basic Books, 1968), 52, 200, 202.
118. Del Martin and Phyllis Lyon, "The New Sexuality and the Homosexual," chapter 14 in Herbert A. Otto, ed., *The New Sexuality* (Palo Alto, CA: Science and Behavior Books, 1971), 198.
119. Martin and Lyon, "New Sexuality," 199.

INDEX

Page numbers in *italic type* refer to illustrations.